Identity and Loyalty in the David Story

Hebrew Bible Monographs, 22

Identity and Loyalty in the David Story

A Postcolonial Reading

Uriah Y. Kim

Sheffield Phoenix Press

2008

Published by Sheffield Phoenix Press
Department of Biblical Studies, University of Sheffield
Sheffield S10 2TN

www.sheffieldphoenix.com

A CIP catalogue record for this book
is available from the British Library

Typeset by Forthcoming Publications
Printed by Lightning Source

ISBN 978-1-906055-58-5
ISSN 1747-9614

To
Crystal
Hope and Adam
with much *ḥesed/jeong*

CONTENTS

ACKNOWLEDGMENTS

This monograph is a continuation of a postcolonial reading of the Deuteronomistic History I began with my first book, *Decolonizing Josiah*. I hope to complete three more volumes in the future. The English Bible translations are those of the New Revised Standard Bible, unless indicated otherwise. I revised significantly my article, 'Uriah the Hittite: A Con/Text of Struggle for Identity' (*Semeia* 90/91 [2002], pp. 69-86), and used the material in Chapter 6 of this book; I wish to thank the Society of Biblical Literature for giving me the permission to use the article in the present work. In Chapter 1 I used the material from my article 'Postcolonial Criticism: Who Is the Other in the Book of Judges?', in Gale E. Yee (ed.), *Judges and Method* (Minneapolis: Fortress Press, 2nd edn, 2007), which is used here with the kind permission of Augsburg Fortress Publishers.

I wish to thank David Clines of Sheffield Phoenix Press for patiently accepting the many changes I made to my manuscript along the way. I would like to thank the Wabash Center for granting me a Summer Fellowship which allowed me to focus solely on my book during the summer of 2007. I also want to express my gratitude to the following people who have played a role in helping me to complete the book: Ian Markham, former dean of Hartford Seminary and current president and dean of Virginia Theological Seminary, and Efrain Agosto, current dean of Hartford Seminary, for their encouragement and friendship during the last three years it took to finish this book; Christy Lohr for taking over my duty as the editor of *Reviews in Religion and Theology* during the final days of completing my manuscript; M.T. and M.E. for letting me use their house to write during the Holy Week of 2008; and my students at Hartford Seminary who patiently listened to me talk about this book—some students having to endure this more than once—and gave me helpful feedback, especially Gwen Haley whose careful reading of my final draft saved me from making many errors. Finally, I want to thank and dedicate this book to my dear wife, Crystal, whose *ḥesed* I cherish and depend on, and our two wonderful kids who are God's *ḥesed* to us. Hope and Adam, we love you dearly!

August 2008

Abbreviations

AB	Anchor Bible
ABD	David Noel Freedman (ed.), *The Anchor Bible Dictionary* (New York: Doubleday, 1992)
BWANT	Beiträge zur Wissenschaft vom Alten und Neuen Testament
CBQ	*Catholic Biblical Quarterly*
DH	Deuteronomistic History
Dtr	Deuteronomist
ETL	*Ephemerides Theologicae Lovanienses*
HSM	Harvard Semitic Monographs
Int	*Interpretation*
JBL	*Journal of Biblical Literature*
JBQ	*Jewish Biblical Quarterly*
JSOT	*Journal for the Study of the Old Testament*
JSOTSup	*Journal for the Study of the Old Testament*, Supplement Series
LXX	Septuagint
MT	Masoretic Text
NRSV	New Revised Standard Version
RRT	*Reviews in Religion and Theology*
SOTSMS	Society for Old Testament Study Monograph Series
ST	*Studia theological*
VT	*Vetus Testamentum*

1

INTRODUCTION: TOWARD A POSTCOLONIAL READING OF DAVID

The Apologist's Image of David

The narrator of the David story, 1 Samuel 16 to 1 Kings 2, is certainly more of an apologist than an objective historian,[1] spinning stories with superb narrative skills in order to defend David's innocence of bloodguilt during his rise to power (1 Sam. 16–2 Sam. 5) and to depict him as a kind and meek father who is taken advantage of by his sons and servants during Absalom's revolt (2 Sam. 13–20) and Solomon's succession (1 Kgs 1–2).[2] This David invokes awe and adoration on the one hand and profound sympathy on the other. He is a hero of faith many of us strive to imitate, and, at the same time, he is an all-too-human character to whom we can relate and in whom we see our frailties. He is a complex figure, a multifaceted character who refuses to be reduced to a one-dimensional man, no matter how pious and theologically correct and useful that image may be, and who embodies paradoxes and tensions of being the political and military leader on the one

1. See P.K. McCarter, Jr, 'The Apology of David', *JBL* 99 (1980), pp. 489-504, for a succinct articulation of this position. McCarter summarizes it in this way: 'In short, the history of David's rise or the apology of David, as we are now entitled to call it, shows David's accession to the throne of all Israel, north as well as south, to have been entirely lawful and his kingship, therefore, free of guilt. All possible charges of wrongdoing are faced forthrightly, and each in its turn is gainsaid by the course of events as related by the narrator' (p. 502). See McCarter's commentary, *I Samuel: A New Translation with Introduction, Notes, and Commentary* (AB, 8; Garden City, NY: Doubleday, 1980), for a more detailed explication of this position.

2. The question of when the David story was written is a complicated one. There is much evidence to suggest that most of the narrative was composed during the time of David and Solomon, most likely in order to promote the founder of the dynasty and to support Solomon's succession. There is also evidence to support the view that the narrative was composed using varied sources, although they cannot be identified with comfortable certainty, and some editorial activity that surely can be attributed to the Deuteronomist(s). The objective of this study is not to examine and evaluate these matters.

hand and the charismatic and theological visionary on the other.[3] He seems transparent yet remains enigmatic; we think we know him but we are not quite sure who he *really* is. It is no wonder that this David has captured the imagination and the heart of so many people over the years.

Really, how can anyone not 'love' David? The narrator portrays him as God's favorite, a man 'after God's own heart' (1 Sam. 13.14). His story is inspirational: A shepherd boy who kills a giant Philistine with faith in one hand and a sling in the other becomes king of Israel and Judah with God on his side and surrounded by men and women who 'love' (*'hb*) him. We are reminded that the Hebrew word *'hb* ('to love') means more than emotional affection or attachment to another person; it has the meaning of loyalty or allegiance, especially in a political context.[4] Everyone seems to love him, even those who should hate him, like the members of the house of Saul. Saul loves him the first time he sees him (1 Sam. 16.21); at their first meeting Jonathan loves him as his own soul (1 Sam. 18.1, 3); and the narrator tells us, not once but twice, that Saul's daughter Michal loves him (1 Sam. 18.20, 28). Surely the Philistines, those hated enemies of Israel, the uncircumcised, would hate him? But at least three groups of Philistines—the Cherethites, the Pelethites, and the Gittites—become the backbone of David's army and remain most loyal to him throughout his career. No doubt the narrator wants us, the readers, to love David, arousing emotional attachment to him but also demanding that we give our allegiance to him as we read the story.

Not everyone, however, loved David. The fact that the narrator makes a great effort to exonerate David of all wrongdoings indicates that there must have been those who had a grudge against him and who accused him of

3. Keith Bodner (*David Observed: A King in the Eyes of his Court* [Hebrew Bible Monographs, 5; Sheffield: Sheffield Phoenix Press, 2005]) explores the complexity of David's personality by reading the David story through the eyes of David's supporting characters. Bodner argues that David's complexity is augmented by the tension between David as the political and military leader and the theological visionary.

4. W.L. Moran ('The Ancient Near Eastern Background of the Love of God in Deuteronomy', *CBQ* 25 [1963], pp. 78-79) compared ancient Near Eastern sources, particularly the Amarna letters and the Assyrian treaties, with the use of the verb 'love' in Deuteronomy and elsewhere in the Hebrew Bible, and concluded that the term was used to describe the loyalty and friendship joining independent kings, sovereign and vassal, king and subject. In commenting on the statement 'All Israel and Judah loved David' (1 Sam. 18.16), Moran stated that 'the writer implies that the people at the point were already giving David a *de facto* recognition and allegiance' (p. 81). J.A. Thompson ('The Significance of the Verb *Love* in the David–Jonathan Narratives in I Samuel', *VT* 24 [1974], pp. 34-38) summarized the use of the verb 'love' in the larger David narrative in this way: 'In the skillful unfolding of this complex political drama the ambiguous verb *'āhēḇ* is used at several critical points, all of which are pregnant with political significance' (p. 338). David is 'loved' especially in the so-called History of David's Rise, 1 Sam. 16 to 2 Sam. 5 (1 Sam. 16.21; 18.1, 3, 16, 20, 22, 28; 20.17; 2 Sam. 1.26).

peccancy, like Shimei, who calls David 'a man of blood' (2 Sam. 16.8). S.L. McKenzie lists in a convenient fashion ten accusations against which the narrative defends him: David sought to advance himself as king at Saul's expense; David was a deserter; David was an outlaw; David was a Philistine mercenary; David murdered Nabal and seized his wife, Abigail, and his property; David was implicated in Saul's death; David was implicated in Abner's death; David was implicated in Ishbaal's death; David annihilated Saul's heirs when he took the throne; David had his own sons, Amnon and Absalom, murdered to preserve his place on the throne.[5]

But the narrator portrays David not only as an innocent man in the killings of his rivals but also as a righteous man who is compassionate toward them. In fact, the narrator claims that David spared Saul's life twice (1 Sam. 24 and 26) and Nabal's life (1 Sam. 25), although both men die without David needing to raise his hand against them. David's display of righteous indignation against the Amalekite messenger, who brought the news of Saul's death, and the Beerothite brothers, who brought Ishbaal's severed head, authenticates his innocence in the deaths of these two men. He shows remarkable compassion toward his enemies, especially the dead ones. David's show of loyalty and kindness to Mephibosheth, who was lame in his feet and posed no threat to David's kingship, for the sake of Jonathan is well known (2 Sam. 9). His presentation of unrestrained emotions to the public through heartfelt lamentations for Saul and Jonathan (2 Sam. 1.19-27) and Abner (2 Sam. 3.33-34) reaffirms his innocence and compassion for these fallen men. Such displays of emotion reach a crescendo when David learns of Absalom's death. The narrator prepares the reader for outbursts of sympathy later in the story by having David instruct the army to deal gently with his rebellious son Absalom (2 Sam. 18.5). Polzin comments on David's instruction with this rhetorical question: 'How can the reader not be attracted to this man, who sends forth his whole army against all Israel with the words, "Deal gently for my sake with the young man Absalom" (18.5)?'[6] This is a very touching, subtle detail that supports the narrator's portrayal of David as a kind and meek father. It prepares the heart of even the most cynical reader among us to feel the father's heart. Upon hearing the report of Absalom's death, our hearts ache with David as he cries out for his son in 2 Sam. 18.33, 'O my son Absalom, my son, my son Absalom! Would I had died instead of you, O Absalom, my son, my son!' Then, as if to leave no doubt about David's feeling toward his son, the narrator (perhaps overstressing at this point) has David lament again in 2 Sam. 19.4, 'O my son Absalom, O Absalom, my son, my son!' How can anyone not be sympathetic to David?

5. S.L. McKenzie, *King David: A Biography* (Oxford and New York: Oxford University Press, 2002), pp. 32-33.

6. R. Polzin, *David and the Deuteronomist: A Literary Study of the Deuteronomic History, Part 3, 2 Samuel* (Bloomington: Indiana University Press, 1993), p. 187.

The narrator's task in the story is not only to defend David's innocence or to promote his righteousness, but also to explain why God chose David over and against Saul. The narrator offers three reasons for God's preference for David: David was a man after God's own heart; David was better than Saul; and David was more faithful to Yahweh than Saul. The attempt to convince the reader that God's choice has something to do with David's heart, moral character, and faith is not as coherent and consistent as the apology for David's innocence. In the end the narrator wants the reader to believe rather than be persuaded that David's heart, character, and faith were better than those of Saul.

First, the narrator argues that God's decision has something to do with David's heart. God warns Samuel not to look at the outer appearance when selecting God's anointed, 'for the Lord does not see as mortals see; they look on the outward appearance, but the Lord looks on the heart' (1 Sam. 16.7). Even before David appears in the narrative, God's heart is set on David because God 'has sought out a man after his own heart' (1 Sam. 13.4). David was God's choice while Saul was still the king. As McCarter puts it, 'In short, says our narrator, David was Yahweh's choice as king of Israel and his assumption of that role...was fully legitimate in the eyes of the highest authority'.[7] With such emphasis on David's heart, one has to wonder what Eliab means when he says: 'I know your presumption and the evil of your heart' (1 Sam. 17.28). Nevertheless, the narrator wants the reader to believe that God selected David because his heart somehow pleased God, whereas Saul's heart did not.

Second, God chooses David because he is 'better' than Saul. Samuel says so: 'The Lord has torn the kingdom of Israel from you [Saul] this very day, and has given it to a neighbor [David] of yours, who is better (*ṭôḇ*) than you' (1 Sam. 15.28). In what way was David better than Saul? Did David have a better (moral) character than Saul? They both committed acts that were questionable. They both sinned. Was Saul a worse sinner than David? It is hard to say. They also reacted similarly when they were found guilty. Both acknowledged their sins and asked for forgiveness (1 Sam. 15.24-25, 30; 2 Sam. 12.13). Saul's confession was ignored and no forgiveness was offered by God; by contrast David's confession was accepted by God and he was forgiven. Saul was rejected because of his sin but David was permitted to continue his rule in spite of his wrongdoing (2 Sam. 12.13).[8] David was neither better nor worse than Saul in terms of moral character. They were men of different personalities, each with his strengths and weaknesses.

7. McCarter, *I Samuel*, p. 30.

8. W. Brueggemann (*First and Second Samuel* [Interpretation; Louisville, KY: John Knox Press, 1990], p. 115) therefore concludes: 'Either the God who forgives is arbitrary or we must acknowledge the bias of the tradition for David and against Saul'.

Saul was a shy, humble, and reserved leader who reluctantly became king of the Israelites. David was a charismatic, cocky, and ambitious leader who wanted to become king from the beginning. The narrator does not really explain in what way David is better than Saul, but the reader is to believe that David was the better person.[9]

Third, the narrator claims that God's preference for David is due to the fact that he is more faithful to God than Saul. Samuel's, therefore God's, favorable evaluation of David is the perception, which the narrator skillfully paints, that he is obedient to Yahweh's instructions. David is presented as a model of Yahwistic piety in contrast to Saul, who is depicted as being disloyal. Twice David spares Saul's life and credits his 'fear of the Lord' for his restraint:

> The Lord forbid that I should do this thing to my lord, the Lord's anointed, to raise my hand against him; for he is the Lord's anointed (1 Sam. 24.6);
>
> Do not destroy him; for who can raise his hand against the Lord's anointed, and be guiltless... The Lord forbid that I should raise my hand against the Lord's anointed (1 Sam. 26.9, 11).

Of course the reader knows that it is Saul who is raising his hand against the anointed, David, and thus against the Lord. Samuel claims that God rejected Saul because 'you have not kept what the Lord commanded you' (1 Sam. 13.14). However, we can easily make a case that Saul is more faithful to Yahweh than David. Yes, he failed, the narrator claims, to carry out fully two dubious instructions, which were purported to be from Yahweh but uttered by Samuel (1 Sam. 13 and 15). Yet Saul wanted to be faithful to Yahweh in all he did. He was always mindful of Yahweh. He was willing to sacrifice either his own life or that of his own son when the oath he invoked was broken (1 Sam. 14).[10] To the very end of his life, he wanted to hear God's instructions (1 Sam. 28). It was not Saul who was unfaithful to God; it was God and Samuel who changed their minds and stopped speaking to him. In contrast, David had no problem getting God's attention even though he was not as mindful of God as Saul was. David repented when he sinned, and he was forgiven each time. Saul repented more, yet he was not forgiven. We

9. Perhaps the narrator is suggesting that David was more loyal to God than Saul, since the Hebrew word *ṭôḇ* is roughly synonymous with the word *ḥesed*, which can be translated with the English word 'loyalty'. I will discuss this point more fully below.

10. Brueggemann (*First and Second Samuel*, p. 107) makes the following comment on this episode: 'How strange—we take Abraham as a model of radical faith but treat Saul as unbalanced or foolhardy... Saul operated with sincere faith... The narrative crafts a no-win situation for Saul, a pious man who makes an oath he thinks is obedience.' Brueggemann rightly questions the reader's bias against Saul; of course, this bias is shaped by the narrator's rhetoric and the reader's willingness to be persuaded by it.

can easily make a case that Saul was as faithful to God as David was, if not more. But once again the narrator wants us to believe that David was the more faithful man and therefore deserved to be God's choice.[11]

The Enduring Image of David Built on the Rock of Success

The image of David portrayed by the narrator of the David story and augmented by later traditions has endured its critics and the test of time because, in my opinion, it is established foremost on the rock of success. David defeated the house of Saul, consolidated disparate groups of people into one kingdom, and established his dynasty, which lasted for four hundred years.[12] His victory over Saul is an undeniable historical fact on which the narrator's image of David is built. Why did David enjoy such success? The narrator gives a simple but powerful answer to this question. The narrator claims that God was with David (1 Sam. 16.13, 18; 17.37; 18.12, 14, 28; 20.13; 2 Sam. 5.10), and no longer with Saul. Upon the anointment of David, the narrator declares that 'the spirit of the Lord rushed upon David from that day forward...but the spirit of the Lord departed from Saul...' (1 Sam. 16.13-14; my translation). The narrator has one of Saul's young men confirm this fact; the young man lists David's credentials, like a résumé, ending with this final description: 'the Lord is with him' (1 Sam. 16.18). McCarter calls this expression—Yahweh is with him/David—'the theological motif of the apology of David' that runs through the stories of David and Saul.[13] The implications of this expression are made explicit in 1 Sam. 18.14: 'David had success in all his undertakings; for the Lord was with him'. After seeing David's success against the Philistines, Saul is in fear and realizes that success comes from the fact that 'the Lord was with David' (1 Sam. 18.28). At the end of the dramatic rise of David, the narrator punctuates the narrative with this expression: 'And David became greater and greater, for the Lord, God of hosts, was with him' (2 Sam. 5.10). Undoubtedly God, the narrator claims, is behind his rise to power and the establishment of his dynasty.

11. According to Frank M. Cross (*Canaanite Myth and Hebrew Epic* [Cambridge, MA: Harvard University Press, 1973], pp. 274-89), David is the symbol of fidelity in the Deuteronomistic History. This theological scheme influences the reader's view of David as 'faithful' and anyone who opposes or is contrasted with David as 'unfaithful'.

12. McKenzie (*King David*, p. 189) argues that the Deuteronomist uses David's victory over Saul to show that 'success proves the approval of God' and 'this principle and its converse [that failure or ruins are signs of divine punishment] are integral to Dtr's theology; though not shared by all biblical writers...'

13. McCarter, *I Samuel*, p. 281.

Relying on the historical fact that David was the victor, the narrator had an easy task in persuading the reader that David was God's choice.[14] Since the history unfolds according to God's will, the narrator seems to reason, the winner must be God's choice. It seems that to take David's side is to be on God's side. Brueggemann seems resigned to this logic:

> The only explanation is that it is the Lord's doing... We are invited to watch while history works its relentless way toward God's intention. History is not a blind force or an act of sheer power. There is a purpose at work that regularly astonishes us. It is a power that disrupts and heals. David is now carried on the wave of this purpose. The ones who trust the story ride atop this flow of history with David. They ride there with David every time they tell or hear the story. The others, like Saul, either die or go mad.[15]

God's attitude toward Saul and David is not explained in the narrative but made clear by what happens to them. Saul loses because God abandons him. David wins because God embraces him. One can argue that the victor in history may not necessarily be as a result of God's will and therefore the winner might not be due to God's providence. But the narrator uses David's success over Saul to establish him as God's choice and then reasons that God selected David because he was a man after God's own heart who was better and more faithful than Saul.

Over the years many readers of the David story have uncritically appreciated its image of David, undoubtedly persuaded by the narrator's rhetoric and the fact that David was the victor. These readers have glossed over unpleasant and unflattering incidents, remarks, and antics in order to sustain the image of David as innocent, faithful, kind, and meek, as a man after God's own heart who was faithful and (morally) good. They have given the benefit of the doubt to the narrator in order to sustain this image of David. The fact that the Deuteronomist has made him the standard of faithfulness by which the kings of Israel and Judah were judged, added to the idea of David as a model of faith, has inspired many believers over the years. The image of David painted by the apologist has such a strong hold on the

14. We are biased against Saul not only because of the way the narrator portrayed him but also because we are comfortable with the logic that God is on the side of the winner. The narrator's rhetoric works because we the readers are willing partners in this logic. We idolize winners, and it makes perfect sense to us that David was the victor because God was on his side.

15. Brueggemann, *First and Second Samuel*, p. 140. McCarter ('The Apology of David', p. 503) expresses a similar sentiment: 'Throughout the narrative Saul is like a man living under a curse. He is caught up in something larger than himself, something in which he cannot extricate himself, and all his devices go wrong. David, too, is presented to us as man caught up in events he cannot control. In his case, however, everything seems inevitably to go well, and he advances step by step toward the kingship almost in spite of himself'.

imagination of the reader because, to put it simply, the apology worked. The later traditions, especially Psalms and Chronicles, have amplified and enhanced the image of David first painted by the narrator of Samuel.[16]

David: A Machiavellian Man

There have, however, always been critics of the apologist's image of David.[17] Whereas the apologist defends David against accusations hurled at him by his enemies, these critics try to reconstruct the opponents' picture of him in order to extract a more realistic picture of David. Halpern states that one of his goals in writing his book on David is 'to give voice to David's opponents'.[18] These readers tend to focus more on facts and actions in the narrative rather than on the narrator's interpretation of these details. They try to penetrate the 'thick' cloud of rhetoric that screens the 'real' David in order to examine David's actions for what they are and see David for who he really is. When one considers David's deeds without the aid of the narrator's explanation, it is not difficult to see why some people view David as a traitor, murderer, or opportunist, among other descriptions.[19]

16. For a balanced treatment of David's portraits in Psalms and Chronicles as well as in Samuel, see M.J. Steussy, *David: Biblical Portraits of Power* (Columbia: University of South Carolina Press, 1999). McKenzie (*King David*, p. 189) summarizes works of later traditions in this way: 'Other biblical writers further elaborated this image such that David became nearly perfect. His major offenses were omitted, as the Chronicler did with the Bathsheba and Absalom episodes. Alternatively, David became the model of penitence, as in Psalm 51'.

17. McKenzie (*King David*, p. 4) mentions several literary works that portray David negatively and gives this summary statement: 'Other modern novelists have described David in a much more negative way, as someone who lusted not just for sexual fulfillment but for power and control'.

18. B. Halpern, *David's Secret Demons: Messiah, Murderer, Traitor, King* (Grand Rapids: Eerdmans, 2001), p. xv. It is interesting that Halpern sees himself as speaking for the voiceless, namely David's enemies, but seems to be a bit irritated by 'contemporary literary theorists' who claim to be speaking for and representing today's 'marginalized' and 'oppressed'. Halpern states: 'But there is nothing marginal about those with the power to express their views, for they at least have the opportunity to persuade others. The truly marginal are those who are not even suffered to speak. And the most marginal of all are those who have passed, silent, from history' (p. xv). On the problem and role of the scholars speaking for the voiceless, see G.C. Spivak, 'Can the Subaltern Speak?', in P. Williams and L. Chrisman (eds.), *Colonial Discourse and Post-colonial Theory* (New York: Columbia University Press, 1994), pp. 66-111. Spivak problematizes the intellectual's role in constructing the marginalized and speaking for them.

19. Halpern's book title, *David's Secret Demons: Messiah, Murderer, Traitor, King*, is a telling example.

I would characterize David as a Machiavellian man who used *realpolitik* and the sword to achieve his goals. There are nine cases of 'murder' that David's opponents could have accused him of having some role in: Nabal, the husband of Abigail, who dies mysteriously; Saul and Jonathan; Abner, the general of Israel's army; Ishbaal, the king of Israel following Saul's death; Saul's other descendants, two sons and five grandsons, whom David handed over to the Gibeonites; Uriah the Hittite, an officer in David's army; Amnon, David's eldest son; Absalom, who usurped David's throne for a time; and Amasa, the commander of Absalom's military force.[20] Whether David played some role, either directly or indirectly, in these deaths sufficient to warrant bloodguilt for them is debatable; however, the fact that David advanced his career and consolidated his power over Judah and Israel through these deaths is indisputable. Even if he was not complicit in these deaths, there is no question that he was an opportunist who pounced on every advantage afforded by them.

When we consider what David ends up with after these deaths, we cannot help but wonder whether David had a role in them. We find Saul's crown and armlet (2 Sam. 1.10) and Ishbaal's severed head (2 Sam. 4.8) in David's possession, and, shortly afterwards, he ends up as the head of Israel, wearing the crown once worn by Saul. David enormously benefited from the timely deaths of Saul, Jonathan, Abner, and Ishbaal; therefore, one has to question whether David could have come to rule over the northern tribes without these convenient deaths.[21] In order to retain his grip on Israel (or to appease God, as the narrator claims) David hands over seven Saulides to the Gibeonites, knowing that they would be killed. In the end, he spares only one Saulide, Mephiboshet, whose legs were crippled, and, therefore, was not a threat to his kingship. Prior to his defeat of the house of Saul, he took advantage of Nabal's death (1 Sam. 25); as a result, he was able to consolidate his power in Judah. Moreover, after Nabal's death, he ended up with Nabal's wife, Abigail, and probably his estate as well. After having Uriah the Hittite killed, he married Uriah's wife Bathsheba. In this case the narrator surprisingly acknowledges that David is guilty of murder.[22] I suspect that there are other cases in which David ordered a hit which but are not acknowledged by the narrator.

20. See Halpern, *David's Secret Demons*, pp. 76-93, for a succinct discussion of these 'murders'.

21. Brueggemann (*First and Second Samuel*, p. 232) makes this observation on the deaths of Saul, Jonathan, Abner, and Ishbaal: 'It is hard to imagine how David could have prevailed in the north without these deaths'.

22. This is one of the reasons why some scholars believe that this episode was inserted into the David narrative sometime later as a polemic against the house of David.

Although the narrator exonerates David from these murders, we still have to wonder about his guilt, especially since the narrator seems to overstress his innocence. One example is the murder of Abner. Many have noted that there are good reasons to suspect that it is David himself who lures Abner to his headquarters by offering the position of the head of the army and then left Joab to take care of the dirty work.[23] But the narrator is successful, perhaps too successful, in concealing David's role in the death of Abner. When David learns of Joab's assassination of Abner (2 Sam. 3), the first thing he says is: 'I and my kingdom are forever guiltless before the Lord for the blood of Abner son of Ner' (2 Sam. 3.28), and then he curses the house of Joab (2 Sam. 3.29). The narrator frames David's speech with the motive for Abner's murder—a private quarrel between Abner and Joab: 'So he died for shedding the blood of Asahel, Joab's brother' (2 Sam. 3.27) and 'So Joab and his brother Abishai murdered Abner because he had killed their brother Asahel in the battle at Gibeon' (2 Sam. 3.30). Then David leads the funeral himself and lifts his voice and weeps at the grave of Abner (2 Sam. 3.32). Moreover, he writes a lament for Abner and refuses to eat, saying, 'So may God do to me, and more, if I taste bread or anything else before the sun goes down' (2 Sam. 3.35). Then the narrator provides an apologetic note in vv. 36-37: 'All the people took notice of it, and it pleased them; just as everything the king did pleased all the people. So all the people and all Israel understood that day that the king had no part in the killing of Abner son of Ner'. But David is portrayed as being uninterested in influencing the people's opinion; he is sad not because he is trying to win the people's approval but because 'a prince and a great man has fallen this day in Israel' and is worried because 'the sons of Zeruiah are too violent for me' (2 Sam. 3.38-39). This is a clear example of overstress, a literary technique in which the narrator repeatedly states, in this case, David's innocence of Abner's murder, because the accusation has some merit. The more the author stresses David's innocence, as is the case here, the more likely the charge is, in fact, valid. Despite his over-the-top public display of sadness and outrage, David does not punish Joab, a fact that supports the opinion that he was involved in Abner's murder.

Later in David's career, Joab also murders Amasa, the general of Absalom's army (2 Sam. 20), but, once again, David does not punish Joab because the fact is that he has eliminated for David a very popular leader of the tribe of Judah. Could it be that David instructed Joab to kill these two generals just as he ordered Joab to kill Uriah? Joab also kills Absalom

23. For example, J.C. VanderKam, 'Davidic Complicity in the Deaths of Abner and Eshbaal: A Historical and Redactional Study', *JBL* 99.4 (1980), pp. 521-39. Later in the narrative, VanderKam suggests, Shimei accuses David of murdering Abner and Ishbaal and David admits to these murders (2 Sam. 16.10-12).

without any chastisement from David. Yes, Absalom was David's son, but he was also a dangerous rival who wanted to overthrow him. Absalom had to be eliminated in order for David to return to Jerusalem as king.

In the subsequent chapters I will discuss the above cases in greater detail and other cases not mentioned here that speak against David's innocence and reveal David as a Machiavellian man of *realpolitik* and the sword. At this point, it suffices to note that there is some truth to Shimei's accusation that David was a man of blood (2 Sam. 16.8). In fact, David acknowledges that Shimei's cursing comes from God and therefore implies that the charge is correct: 'If he is cursing because the Lord has said to him, "Curse David", who then shall say, "Why have you done so?"' (2 Sam. 16.10b); 'Let him alone, and let him curse; for the Lord has bidden him' (2 Sam. 16.11b). David's having ordered his men to kill the Amalekite messenger (2 Sam. 1) and the Beerothite brothers (2 Sam. 4) in front of his eyes confirms the view that he is more than capable of killing men in cold blood. Regardless of what reason the narrator gives for David to slay these men, these killings show that David is not a man who would hesitate to use the sword. It is, therefore, fitting that the last words attributed to David in the narrative are 'with blood to Sheol' (1 Kgs 2.9), words which resonate appropriately with Shimei's accusation of David as a man of blood and which raise some doubt as to David's innocence.

David is a Machiavellian man who cannot be trusted. He is duplicitous. He instructs Jonathan to lie to Saul in order to find out whether Saul has any ill intention toward him (1 Sam. 20.6-7). David has good reason to suspect Saul and wants Jonathan to know of Saul's desire to kill him, but his asking Jonathan to deceive his own father attests negatively to David's character. He does not hesitate to ask his dear friend to compromise his integrity to get what he wants. David's dealing with Mephiboshet is an example of inconsistency in the way he deals with people. He brings Mephiboshet to Jerusalem and gives him the entire estate of Saul (2 Sam. 9). Then David takes the land away from Mephiboshet for failing to follow him out of Jerusalem when he was on the run from his own son Absalom; David gives that land to Ziba (2 Sam. 16.4). On his return trip to Jerusalem he again changes his mind and divides the land between Ziba and Mephiboshet (2 Sam. 19.29). This decision reflects more on David's unreliability than his wisdom.

There are more examples one can find in the narrative which undermine David's credibility. David dupes Achish the Gittite twice: he feigns that he is mad (1 Sam. 21.10-15) and then later he 'pretends', the narrator claims, that he is loyal to Achish (1 Sam. 27.12). He lures Abner to his camp under the banner of peace, but lets Joab kill him in deceit. He orders Amasa to muster the Judeans in three days shortly after they returned home from Absalom's revolt (2 Sam. 20.4) in order to suppress another rebellion led by

Sheba. But he knows he has assigned Amasa an impossible task and when Amasa fails to show up at the appointed time (surely as anticipated by David), then David immediately appoints Abishai, Joab's brother, to lead his army in pursuit of Sheba. Joab takes over the leadership from his brother and then kills Amasa when he meets him. Again, David does not punish Joab for this murder. However, on his deathbed, he instructs Solomon to kill Joab, who has been loyal to him all his life, and Shimei, whose life David swore to spare (2 Sam. 19.23). How can anyone trust his words? With David's track record, who can afford to believe his promises?

In contrast to the narrator's portrayal of David as an unassuming boy who has greatness thrust upon him, he turns out to be an ambitious man who is willing to do anything to acquire the kingship, including risking his life and the lives of others to get what he wants. He is a driven opportunist who is always looking out for himself. He decides to fight Goliath the Philistine after hearing that 'The king will greatly enrich the man who kills him, and will give him his daughter and make his family free in Israel' (1 Sam. 17.25). After slaying Goliath, he again risks his life against the Philistines in order to win the hand of Saul's daughter. His marriage to Michal helps to draw him a step closer to the throne. Later, after years of separation, he demands Ishbaal to send Michal back to him with no intention of continuing their marital relationship but only so that he can control the womb that is able to bear an heir to the house of Saul. He is dismissive of Michal's criticism (2 Sam. 6.21-23) and most likely locked her up in the same way he incarcerated the ten concubines who were left behind in Jerusalem to take care of his house during Absalom's revolt (2 Sam. 20.3). Furthermore, as mentioned above, he puts Jonathan's life in danger when he asks him to lie for him. He admits to putting the lives of the priests of Nob in danger when he recognized the inherent danger of the presence of Doeg the Edomite there: 'I knew on that day, when Doeg the Edomite was there, that he would surely tell Saul. I am responsible for the lives of all your father's house' (1 Sam. 22.22). Finally, his first reported speech in the narrative, which 'according to the general principle of biblical narrative...is a defining moment of characterization',[24] is indicative: 'What shall be done for the man who kills this Philistine?' (1 Sam. 17.26). As Bodner puts it, 'The context of David's first words is the context of reward, and the delineation of dividends that will be heaped upon the successful soldier is unequivocal'.[25] David was indeed an ambitious man.

24. Alter, *The David Story: A Translation with Commentary of 1 & 2 Samuel* (New York: Norton, 1999), p. 47.

25. Bodner, *David Observed*, p. 17.

David as a Machiavellian man who does not hesitate to employ *realpolitik* and the sword and who takes advantage of his men, wives, enemies, and even God to get what he wants is a more realistic image of David, but I am certain that this David cannot hold a candle to the David the narrator portrays. It is the narrator's David who has been cherished by many readers over the years in spite of strong circumstantial evidence to suggest that he was not that innocent or faithful after all. As an Asian American Christian, I have been imbued with lessons and sermons based on this David who, in my opinion, is ultimately grounded on the rock of success. I do not believe that God's choice of David has anything to do with David's heart, character, or faith. There is no significant difference between Saul and David to explain God's preference for David, except for the fact that David was the victor. Saul was probably more loyal to Yahweh than David was, but the knowledge that David defeated Saul prevailed over that fact. Ultimately, God's preference for David testifies to God's freedom. God chose David not because David had something special, 'a man after God's own heart', but God chose David out of freedom of will, 'a man chosen of God's will'.[26] In selecting David, God's sovereignty is demonstrated rather than David's singularity. God's choice may have nothing to do with David's heart, character, or faith.

We are biased against Saul not only because of the way the narrator portrays him, but, more importantly, because David defeats him. We all love the winner. We are comfortable with the logic that God is on the side of the victor. A consequence of following such logic is that we tend to look for some special or outstanding characteristics of the winner that make him or her God's choice. We want to imitate the victor in order to have God on our side. We believe that if we imitate David, then God will be with us and bless us with success just as God has been with and blessed David.

I understand and respect the many teachers and preachers who taught me to cherish the narrator's image of David as a man after God's own heart who was better and more faithful than Saul. I know I have benefitted greatly from following after this David and meditating on his faith, character, and heart. However, the fact that this David fits well with the prosperity or blessing theology of many Asian American Christians, which promises to reward them when they are faithful to God, needs to be noted. We all seek God's

26. McCarter (*I Samuel*, p. 229) translates *'îš kilḇāḇô* (13.14) as 'a man of his own choosing' and comments, 'This has nothing to do with any great fondness of Yahweh's for David or any special quality of David, to whom it patently refers. Rather it emphasizes the free divine selection of the heir to the throne... As its use in 14.7 shows, the expression *klbb*, "according to (one's) heart", has to do with an individual's will or purpose'.

favor and blessing, and this theology seems to resonate perfectly with their desire to succeed in America. The idea that there is a link between God's blessing and David's behavior and faith makes perfect sense to those of us who have been nurtured in some form of retribution theology or of *quid pro quod* principle.

The purpose of my study is not to deconstruct the image of David constructed by the narrator in cooperation with the reader who desires to put David on the pedestal of faithfulness and success as a testament to their theology. The image of David as the Machiavellian man would receive much resistance from many who hold the Bible dear and cherish the narrator's (and their) picture of David. I am certain that I would encounter much resistance from Asian Americans with the portrayal of David as a Machiavellian leader who was no better than Saul in terms of his faith, character, or heart. I do not expect Asian Americans to meditate on the Machiavellian David to edify their faith and guide their lives. Nor do I desire to promote such an image to them. I contend, however, that if readers pay attention only to the narrator's portrayal of David, then their interpretations will be limited by their personal issues, concerns, and desires and they will fail to engage more fully the issues and concerns arising from their socio-cultural context. Moreover, just as the prosperity or blessing theology sometimes blind us from seeing the needs of the people around us, such non-contextual interpretations will hinder us from seeing what I would like to call 'postcolonial features' in David that could and should be highlighted and imitated among people living in the twenty-first century.

It is my wish to encourage Asian Americans to examine their location in North America and to engage David from their own context. As I see it, Asian Americans are living in the ideological landscape shaped by American national or identity discourse that favors some ethnic or racial groups within American society more than other groups. Asian Americans and their historical memories in North America, like other racialized and minoritized Americans, have been ignored or relegated to 'ethnic discourse' for the benefit of constructing a coherent national/identity discourse. In a similar way, context-specific interpretations of the Bible are undervalued as 'ethnic' or 'minority' or 'women's' or 'Third World' interpretations in order to maintain the normative discourse in biblical studies. Such a practice views context-specific readings of the Bible as less rigorous, serious, or academic than 'context-free' readings. We cannot continue to interpret the Bible as before when the interpreter's context was either assumed or hidden, when readings that focused on the past and the text were deemed 'scientific' or 'objective' while readings that focused on the present and the reader were dismissed as 'premodern' or 'uncritical'.

From a postcolonial perspective, the way David is prescribed in the narrative may not be a positive spin on the David of history. Rather, it may be a suppression of some features in David that are relevant and worthy of being practiced in today's context. In this book I want to portray David as a Machiavellian man of *ḥesed* (more on this term below) and examine some of his practices that speak to our time and challenge our habits. My intention here is neither to dismiss the narrator's image of David nor to critique the prosperity or blessing theology. I want to formulate a strategy of reading the Bible from 'a space of their own', from which Asian Americans, like other minoritized and racialized Americans, can interpret the Bible in a way that is relevant to their own context. My goal is to encourage Asian Americans and others to consider a postcolonial David who may appeal to the imagination and heart of those who are often victims of the politics of identity and loyalty in North America.

Why a Postcolonial Reading?

Why am I using postcolonial criticism to do what is basically an Asian American biblical interpretation?[27] The decision to apply a postcolonial reading is a strategy to move Asian American hermeneutics from being framed by the national discourse of the United States, which inevitably favors some normative groups (read, whites) over and against others (read, racialized and minoritized groups). It is critical to recognize that a network of nationalism, religion, and ethnicity/race makes a coherent narrative of American identity seem natural and obvious. Asian Americans, like other minority groups, are familiar with identity politics in which they are viewed as outsiders. I have used the term '*realpolitik* of liminality' in my previous work to describe the process in which those who are located in the in-between space face danger when the dominant culture imposes its will on that space, often with violence, and forces them to choose a single 'authentic' identity to prove their loyalty to the nation. The politics of identity in the United States does not allow hybrid Americans to exist on their own and tries to subsume them under a national or other ideological identity that favors the dominant culture.

In order to do a postcolonial reading of the Bible one must construct a space that cannot be swallowed whole by the space of nation, where one 'real' identity is imposed and an exclusive loyalty to the nation is demanded. How can we imagine a space of in-betweenness where hybrid identities are accepted and welcomed? Homi Bhabha suggests that we need to move away

27. For a succinct description of Asian American biblical interpretation, see the 'Foreword', in M.F. Foskett and J.K. Kuan (eds.), *Ways of Being, Ways of Reading: Asian American Biblical Interpretation* (St. Louis: Chalice Press, 2006), pp. xi-xvi.

from seeing the nation as the center of history and explore new places from which to write histories of peoples.[28] He suggests a new site of narration for the people: the space of liminality. The nation is not a fixed social formation, he argues, and its instability to unite the people/culture and the state/land shows up as self-evident in 'a process of hybridity' and in the space of in-betweenness where people and culture do not simply comply with the script of the national discourse. Somehow the people have survived the homogenization of the nation or the process of purification. Bhabha argues that when we look at the nation from liminality, when we acknowledge that 'the nation is no longer the sign of modernity under which cultural differences are homogenized' and that the nation is an ambivalent and vacillating representation of the people, it 'opens up the possibility of other narratives of the people and their difference'.[29] Bhabha argues that reality does not work according to the narration of the nation. Hybridity in culture and people is reality at the local level. Thus, Bhabha argues that once it is acknowledged that the nation itself is the space of liminality, then 'its "difference" is turned from the boundary "outside" to its finitude "within", and the threat of cultural difference is no longer a problem of "other" people. It becomes a question of the otherness of the people-as-one'.[30] In the space of liminality, different voices of the people emerge and hybrid and multiple identities can co-exist.

The approach I take in my book may not seem relevant or useful to many Asian American Christians who read the Bible. Some may argue that what I problematize hardly poses problems for many Asian Americans when they read the Bible. Asian American Christians, however, are more diverse than enthusiastic converts and the model-spiritual minority who are not all that interested in their racial/ethnic identity and location. There are many who do not behave according to the model-spiritual minority Christian stereotype and who take seriously their identity and location in the United States. In my opinion, as long as Asian American Christians read the Bible without taking into account their location in the American ideological landscape, they are susceptible to the identity discourse of the United States, which privileges whites over and against minority groups. I am advocating for Asian Americans to read the Bible from a place of their own and from there to dialogue with other readers that are reading from their own respective contexts and as equal subjects.

28. Homi K. Bhabha, 'DissemiNation: Time, Narrative, and the Margins of the Modern Nation', in Bhabha (ed.), *Nation and Narration* (London: Routledge, 1990), pp. 291-322.

29. Bhabha, 'DissemiNation', p. 300.

30. Bhabha, 'DissemiNation', p. 301.

Many have pointed out that postcolonial criticism is not a new method of study at all but only offers a different perspective or context, and, as such, it does not add anything new in terms of knowledge to biblical scholarship. Does postcolonial reading or criticism need to be more than different perspectives to be counted as an academic task? Does it need methods of its own? It is correct that I do not introduce new methods per se; however, different perspectives do develop into new methods. In fact, I am willing to argue that different perspectives need to come first before new methods are developed to guide a practitioner and ensure that his or her research is conducted from newly articulated perspectives. Moreover, an intellectual use of the history and experience from one's location to interpret biblical texts may already be a new method just as Black theology, Latino/a theology, Womanist theology, Minjung theology, to name a few, which take into account the history and experience of their respective communities are considered 'new' theologies. We should not underestimate the significance and difficulty of reading the Bible in academia from other than Western perspectives. I am not minimizing the importance of methods. Methods are important and inherently related to the production of knowledge/truth. Perhaps what is needed in order for postcolonial reading or criticism to be accepted as a legitimate task is an institutional location to produce post-colonial knowledge in biblical studies. Until postcolonial reading or criticism has an institutional space from which to participate at the table of biblical scholarship, scholars doing postcolonial reading need to continue to speak and write in order to disrupt the business as usual in biblical studies.

Although I do not think it is necessary to defend why it is necessary to do postcolonial criticism, perhaps an explanation may be helpful. When one reads a book from the nineteenth century, it is not difficult to identify sexism, racism, or Orientalism in it. Of course it is not fair to criticize the author too harshly for his views since he was expressing or assuming things that were considered acceptable at the time in his context. However, many of these books from the past were written by scholars who were instrumental in formulating the discourse for their respective field of knowledge or discipline of study. Objects of study (knowledge), methods of research (publication), and means of dissemination (pedagogy) were articulated from the time when various 'isms', which are so offensive and problematic to us in the twenty-first century, were taken for granted. We need to recognize that modern biblical scholarship emerged during the time when sexism, racism, and Orientalism were in operation, and the discourse that was forged during this period continues to dictate how we talk about knowledge in our discipline. All disciplines, including biblical studies, have domain assumptions that emerged from the time when sexism, racism, and Orientalism were unprob-lematic to many. Gender, race, and nation are some categories that continue to guide the discourse of many a discipline, often uncritically. Critical examinations of domain assumptions that are in operation in biblical studies are essential, and 'new' approaches, like feminist, liberation, and postcolonial readings, are needed to counter biases that are built into the process of producing knowledge in biblical studies.

This is not an easy task. For modern biblical scholarship, in particular, emerged within the context of colonialism and continues to favor the history, experience, and aspirations of the West, and this legacy continues to dictate biblical studies and remains underexamined. One of the unfortunate outcomes of historical criticism is the marginalization of contextual interpretations of non-Western readers of the Bible. Increasingly, however, they are refusing to read the Bible through the eyes of the West. Postcolonial criticism offers a way for these folks to read the Bible on their own terms and challenges those who insist on interpreting the Bible from the perspective of the West, which invariably benefits the West at the expense of the Rest.[31]

Admittedly, it is difficult for those who have never experienced being treated or represented as members of the Other in relation to the West to understand what the problem is. Why can't the Rest just follow the program outlined by the well-meaning folks from the West? Well, for a start, the Rest of the world has suffered greatly in the last five hundred years or so at the hand of the West, justifying its conquest, domination, and exploitation of the Rest as an effort to bring civilization to the Rest—to transform the Rest into the likeness of the West. Unfortunately, the Rest is still suffering from the continuing legacy of colonialism, which has not been adequately addressed. New modes of colonialism (neocolonialism) are forming to maintain the great divide between the West and the Rest. Moreover, knowledge about non-Western peoples and their worlds has been shaped by an epistemological system formed by the West's desire to narrate its own identity—to put itself as the subject of world history—and to represent and manage non-Western folk as the Other.

31. The terms 'West' and 'Rest' like other dyads—First World and Third World or Two-Thirds World, Developed and Under-developed, North and South, Northern Hemisphere and Southern Hemisphere—are artificial, ideological, and certainly inadequate to describe and divide vast numbers of diverse and heterogeneous people living in the world into two categories. However, it is a necessary strategy, what the postcolonial theorist G.C. Spivak calls 'strategic essentialism', to use such a dichotomy in order to acknowledge the existence of unequal relations between two groups of people and to address the problem. Such use of an artificial division is analogous to how race continues to matter and is used in the United States. Some wish to refrain from using the term race since, they argue, it is an ideological construct; therefore, so the argument goes, fighting against racism perpetuates the illusion rather than eliminating it. But the problem is that racism has had a long and devastating effect in the United States. By ignoring its historical and structural legacies that are interwoven into the very fabric of American society, we are in danger of not adequately addressing these effects and legacies and allowing inequitable socio-economic conditions between different races to remain intact.

Even though postcolonialism as a critical theory emerged in the academy about three or four decades ago,[32] it was not until in the 1990s that some biblical critics began to employ critical tools and insights from postcolonialism to interpret the Bible.[33] Biblical scholars who use postcolonial criticism start with the condition and experience of the Rest rather than with the text. They make intellectual use of the experiences of those who have been colonized by the West in the past and of those who are marginalized by neocolonialism in the present. This is not to say that postcolonial criticism ignores the experiences of those who are of the West. The Rest has no choice but to learn about the history and experience of the West, since its history, experience, and aspirations are already built into the Western academic system of knowledge and cultural texts of various kinds. It understands that the West–Rest dichotomy is an ideological construct that needs to be dismantled; yet it utilizes this dyad in order to address the unequal power relation between the West and the Rest that has been shaped by colonialism. Failure to investigate the interrelationship between Western imperialism and the plight of the Rest is to take a position that leaves the status quo intact. Postcolonial interpreters appreciate historical criticism for its contribution to the knowledge of the Bible and the world 'behind' the text. However, they insist that biblical scholars must acknowledge that

32. Some have articulated intellectually their anti-colonial critiques of the West during the time of struggle for liberation of former Western colonies. For example, Franz Fanon's *The Wretched of the Earth* (New York: Grove Press, 1966) and Albert Memmi's *The Colonizer and the Colonized* (Boston: Beacon Press, 1965) were influential texts that eloquently expressed anti-colonial sentiments; see Robert J.C. Young, *Postcolonialism: A Very Short Introduction* (Oxford: Oxford University Press, 2003), for a concise introduction to postcolonialism as a political movement and as a critical theory. But many point to Edward Said's *Orientalism* (New York: Random House, 1978) for paving the way for a new discipline now called postcolonial studies, which examines the effects of colonialism on the world and on cultural texts in particular.

33. The works of R.S. Sugirtharajah, Kwok Pui-lan, and Fernando Segovia in the early 1990s were instrumental in introducing and disseminating postcolonial criticism to biblical studies: Sugirtharajah edited *Voices from the Margin: Interpreting the Bible in the Third World* (New Edition; Maryknoll, NY: Orbis Books, 2nd edn, 1995; [1991]); Fernando Segovia co-edited with Mary Ann Tolbert *Reading from This Place*, I (Minneapolis: Fortress Press, 1995); and Kwok Pui-lan published *Discovering the Bible in the Non-Biblical World* (Maryknoll, NY: Orbis Books, 1995). In addition to the above books, other key works in introducing postcolonialism to biblical studies include Laura E. Donaldson's edited volume *Postcolonialism and Scripture Reading* (Semeia, 75; Atlanta: Society of Biblical Literature, 1996) and Keith Whitelam's *The Invention of Ancient Israel: The Silencing of Palestinian History* (London: Routledge, 1996). See R.S. Sugirtharajah (ed.), *The Postcolonial Biblical Reader* (Malden, MA: Blackwell, 2006), for a collection of articles that were instrumental in introducing postcolonialism to biblical scholars and general readers; see also my review of this reader, 'Time to Walk the Postcolonial Talk', *RRT* 13 (2006), pp. 271-78.

historical criticism emerged in the context of Western imperialism, and, therefore, biblical scholarship accumulated through historical criticism must be used critically.[34] It can be argued that interpretations based on historical-critical methods were basically contextual interpretations of the West, that is, interpretation and investigation were driven by Western experiences and interests. Although biblical scholars conducting historical-critical research claimed that they were not influenced by the interests and concerns of their context, Kwok argues that 'the political interests of Europe determined the questions to be asked, the gathering of data, the framework of interpretation, and the final outcome'.[35] Questions and concerns that emerged from contexts outside of the West and situations faced by racialized and minoritized people in the West were different from those that were considered proper in biblical scholarship. Thus, postcolonial interpreters are not apologetic in raising problems and interests that stem from different locations around the world.

The Bible was an integral part of colonial discourse, which facilitated the exploitation and management of the colonized. Biblical scholars, as Said had argued, were also complicit in the machinations of colonialism. Failure to examine the association between biblical scholarship and colonialism is to become complicit, wittingly or unwittingly, in maintaining the inequitable relationship between the West and the Rest. Therefore, postcolonial interpreters provide a critical focus on how colonialism has influenced and shaped the contours of biblical scholarship and try to put colonialism at the center of biblical scholarship. They take into account the continuing legacy of colonialism in the very fabric of the discipline of biblical studies and colonial habits in the practice of biblical scholars, including non-Western scholars. To disconnect biblical scholarship from current affairs is to treat the Bible primarily as an ancient text that matters only to a small number of specialists and hide its direct impact on today's world. Postcolonial interpreters insist that interpretation of the Bible must address issues and concerns that matter to the world at large, rather than be limited to interests and affairs that count only to the guild of biblical scholars.

Reading from a Space of Liminality: The Processes of Hybridization and Purification

In my previous book, *Decolonizing Josiah: Toward a Postcolonial Reading of the Deuteronomistic History* (Sheffield: Sheffield Phoenix Press, 2005), I

34. Kwok, in *Discovering the Bible in the Non-Biblical World*, goes further and suggests that postcolonial interpreters should not use historical criticism as the primary method in interpreting the Bible.

35. Pui-lan Kwok, *Postcolonial Imagination & Feminist Theology* (Louisville, KY: Westminster/John Knox Press, 2005), p. 63.

articulated a position from which a postcolonial reading of the DH can be conducted. This present study on David is a continuation of that project. Some additional background to my present study is in order. In *Decolonizing Josiah* I questioned the uncritical use of nationalism in interpreting the DH. My evaluation at the time was that too many biblical scholars were appealing to the discourse of nationalism to view the DH as a national history of the people of ancient Israel in the likeness of modern national histories. Such a modern nationalist reading functioned to confirm the connection between the development of ancient Israel as a nation and the rise of nations in the West. Ancient Israel as a nation was viewed as a model that was imitated by modern nations, but I have argued that it is the other way around: the modern nation was the model for ancient Israel. The 'primordial' model of nationalism, which understands nationalism as a result of deep ancient roots (ethnicity, religion, land, and other characteristics that give identity to human communities) that were latent until revived during the modern period,[36] supports this view. I have followed the 'modernist' model of nationalism, which understands nationalism as a distinctly modern phenomenon that could have been possible only under the modern condition,[37] to critique the former model. I felt that the category of nation was being used too carelessly to connect modern nationalism, which I have argued is no more than the identity discourse of the West, with ancient Israel and its narrative of its past in the DH. These two models are not mutually exclusive, and the modern phenomenon of nationalism is a combination of these two models. I have argued that the DH needs to be read from outside of the nation, in the space of liminality, rather than in the space of nation where every narration of people of the Rest must go through the identity discourse of the West. It is in the space of liminality where a narration of a people is possible without always referring to the nation and where using the discourse of nationalism is done critically. I have tried to emphasize the importance of using the 'third' space[38] for Asian Americans and other interstitial people to narrate their own historical memories somewhat independently from the national

36. Ernest Gellner (*Nations and Nationalism* [Ithaca, NY: Cornell University Press, 1983]), calls this model the 'Sleeping Beauty syndrome'.

37. This model emphasizes the role of the elite to manipulate the past and consolidate discrete people into one nation through political means.

38. In terms of space theory the 'third' space represents the 'lived-space' where people actually live and interact, whereas the 'first' (or 'real') space is the physical, geographic space that can be measured with instruments and the 'second' (or 'imagined') space is a space constructed by people's imagination, ideology, and worldview. As I use it the 'third' space is the 'lived-space' but, following Homi Bhabha and other postcolonial theorists, also a space of liminality, the in-between space that represents an alternative to and an independence from the 'national' (or 'second') space.

history and to read the DH from their own context and history rather than through the history and context of the West.

I have found Y. Shenhav's book helpful in advancing my thoughts for the present book.[39] I want to look at his book in some detail since I see many parallels between his situation and work and my context and work. Shenhav is an Arab Jew who is caught in the politics of identity in which he can be considered either (or both) a Jew or (and) an Arab, yet someone who can be considered neither at the same time. He is a hybrid who is always in danger of being seen and treated as one of the Other. He starts his book with a description of his personal cultural site in which his identity as an Arab Jew disrupts the coherent identity discourse of Zionist nationalism, which has constructed an insurmountable divide between Arabs who are not considered Jews and Jews who cannot be imagined as Arabs. He asks, 'Why is the location of Arab Jews in Israel so complex, so emotional, and such dangerous territory?'[40] Moving from his personal story to collective history, from individual analysis to cultural analysis, he demonstrates that the very existence of Arab Jews and how they are treated as 'one of us but not quite' undermines the ideological logic of Zionist nationalism. Shenhav analyzes the mechanisms in which Zionist nationalism acquires a unified logic that incorporates the Arab Jews into the national collective while simultaneously maintaining the difference between European (Ashkenazi/Western) Jews and Arab (Mizrahi/Eastern) Jews. He chooses to examine the interaction between European Jews, who functioned as Zionist emissaries, and local Arab Jews in the region of Abadan (Iraq) a few years prior to the founding of the state of Israel. This move allows Shenhav to view the site as a 'third' space, neither a Jewish space (Israel was not yet established and Abadan was outside of Palestine) nor an Arab space (Abadan was under the aegis of the British empire), in which the encounter between European Jews and Arab Jews is dictated by Orientalism and the politics of race, color, and identity, and he argues that the Abadan case is a microcosm of a far broader phenomenon that characterized the interaction between them.

Shenhav describes how Zionist emissaries were struggling with two conflicting worldviews. As Europeans they saw Arab Jews as 'others', following the script of the oriental discourse that viewed Arabs as 'others' in relation to Europeans. On the other hand, as Jews they viewed the Arab Jews in Abadan as their kin and wanted to incorporate them into the national project that was being realized in Palestine. They wanted to accept Arab Jews as 'one of us' yet sought to find 'difference' between themselves and Arab Jews. Unable to name exactly what the difference was, they went

39. Y. Shenshav, *The Arab Jews: A Postcolonial Reading of Nationalism, Religion, and Ethnicity* (Stanford: Stanford University Press, 2006).

40. Shenhav, *The Arab Jews*, p. 9.

beyond the oriental dichotomy of the West ('us') vs. the East ('other') and moved into a relationship that is characterized by ambivalence. He concludes that Jewish orientalism 'marks the Arabness and simultaneously erases it' and 'defines the Arab Jews as part of the national collective but leaves a "marker" that afterward become an ethnic category within "Israeliness"'.[41]

Shenhav argues that the processes of hybridization and purification were used simultaneously to turn the Arab Jews into hybrids who are considered 'one of us' but always only a step away from being considered 'one of them'. The process of hybridization mixes two distinct peoples—European Jews and Arab Jews—into one national collective by using religion as an ethnic marker to distinguish Arab Jews from Arabs and by imagining Arab Jews as Zionists, those who yearn to go back to Palestine to establish a Jewish nation. However, the process of purification presents Zionism as a project of secular European Jews rather than that of religious Arab Jews and de-Arabizes their Arabness in order for them to partake in the Zionist nation that is purported to be ethnically free. The Arab Jews cannot fully partake in the nation of Israel without giving up or hiding their ethnic or cultural identity. In practice, the Arab Jews are imagined and treated like second-class citizens, and they feel 'unhomely', to borrow Homi Bhabha's term, in their own homeland, in their own cultural or ethnic skin, due to identity politics that views Western Jews as the norm.

In his argument, Shenhav employs Bruno Latour's theory that views the simultaneous process of hybridization and purification as a key characteristic of modernity.[42] Latour asks why is it that anthropologists studying non-Western (so-called premodern) cultures are able to interweave all threads of nature-culture (knowledge about the nature and the exercise of power in society) in any single trait they narrate, yet they do not study the Western peoples and cultures that way. The reason that is given is that the West has become modern. The most important trait in being modern is the division between knowledge of things (nature: knowledge of things-in-themselves) and human politics (culture: socially constructed knowledge). He critiques the principle of modernity that states that two sets of entirely different practices, hybridization and purification, must remain separate if they are to remain effective. The process of hybridization creates and allows entirely new types of beings, hybrids of nature and culture, to proliferate. The process of purification separates nature–culture hybrids into two ontological zones: that of human beings on the one hand and that of non-human on the other. The prevailing view is that non-Western cultures must go through modernization just as the Western cultures have done. If the non-Western

41. Shenhav, *The Arab Jews*, p. 76.

42. B. Latour, *We Have Never Been Modern* (trans. C. Porter; Cambridge, MA: Harvard University Press, 1993).

cultures are not willing to imitate the West, then the Western cultures must help the premoderns to partition nature-culture hybrids either into the domain of objects or to that of society in order to separate themselves from the past and move toward the future and join the West as moderns.[43]

Latour insists that the moderns give too much credit to the process of purification for the success of modernity while ignoring the proliferation of hybrids at the ground level. But Latour argues that the moderns are at a crisis because there are too many hybrids that cannot be categorized exclusively to either nature or culture. Hybrids exist in the real, lived world (the 'third' space), shuttling between or weaving through different 'domains' of knowledge. This is a common, everyday practice, and too many people are recognizing the simultaneity of these two processes. In order to be modern one has to close one's eyes to the role of hybridization and give credit entirely to the process of purification for the success of modernity: 'It is the concurrent effect of hybridization and purification that constitutes the code of modernity; the proliferation of hybrids has saturated our reality, but purification does not allow us to acknowledge it'.[44] Latour argues that now is the time both to acknowledge the existence and proliferation of hybrids openly and officially and to acknowledge that the partitioning has become superfluous and immoral. Therefore he concludes that 'we can no longer be modern in the same way'.[45] Instead of forcing premoderns into a practice which the moderns exercise only in theory but not in reality, it is the moderns who need to change:

> We scarcely have much choice. If we do not change the common dwelling, we shall not absorb in it the other cultures that we can no longer dominate, and we shall be forever incapable of accommodating in it the environment that we can no longer control. Neither Nature nor the Others will become modern. It is up to us to change our ways of changing.[46]

43. Latour (*We Have Never Been Modern*, p. 130) describes this sentiment in this way: 'The process of partitioning was accompanied by a coherent and continuous front of radical revolutions in science, technology, administration, economy and religion, a veritable bulldozer operation behind which the past disappeared forever, but in front of which, at least, the future opened up. The past was a barbarian medley; the future, a civilizing distinction. To be sure, the moderns have always recognized that they too had blended objects and societies, cosmologies and sociologies. But this was in the past, while they were still only premoderns. By increasingly terrifying revolutions, they have been able to tear themselves away from the past. Since other cultures still mix the constraints of rationality with the needs of their societies, they have to be helped to emerge from that confusion by annihilating their past'.

44. Latour, *We Have Never Been Modern*, p. 50.

45. Latour, *We Have Never Been Modern*, p. 142.

46. Latour, *We Have Never Been Modern*, p. 145.

Shenhav employs Latour's insight to expose the contradictions of the Zionist nationalism, which uses the process of purification to narrate a coherent national history and conceals the proliferation of hybrids, like Arab Jews, at the ground level (lived space, third space). The contradictory voices in Zionism become even more profound when one considers the fact that the legitimacy of Zionism depends on its historical continuity with its religious past, yet it addresses the members of the nation and tries to modernize or secularize them by turning its back on the past. A consequence of such a process is that Arab Jews, who as 'primordial/religious' belong to the premodern, according to this logic, because their link to the nation of Israel is through their religious identity, need to become like Western ('modern/ secular') Jews in order to become modern. For Arab Jews the wish to write their own history outside of the nation of Israel is in effect the wish to remain premodern, as if they are looking back toward their past and remaining outside the legitimate history of the nation of Israel. As long as the history of the modern state of Israel is narrated from the space of nation, it will be narrated through the perspective of Western Jews, as their own identity discourse, at the expense of silencing or suppressing historical memories of Arab (Mizrahi/Eastern) Jews.

The fact that the Arab Jews had continued to exist in Palestine and outside of it and had their own history independent from the desire to establish a Jewish political sovereignty in Palestine threatens the coherence of the Zionist historical narrative. Like many histories and voices that have been silenced or subsumed under national narratives, the voices and histories of Arab Jews have been silenced, forgotten, or suppressed from the national narrative of Israel. Shenhav argues that the attempt of the Arab Jews to have their voice and history included in the national history should not be relegated to the 'ethnic' arena; they should be treated instead as subjects who speak and act within that history. The importance of a third space in which Arab Jews and other hybrids can stand and narrate their own historical memories needs to be encouraged.

There are obvious parallels between the politics of liminality, which I have been using to examine the situation of Asian Americans in the ideological landscape in the United States, and the process of hybridization-purification used to describe the experience of Arab Jews in the Zionist national discourse as Shenhav has done. The process of hybridization-purification is in operation in the United States, Israel, and other 'nations' that continue to narrate the people from the space of nation. Asian Americans are also situated in a space of liminality where the simultaneous processes of hybridization and purification are experienced. The process of hybridization creates and allows entirely new types of beings, hybrids of different race, ethnicity, religion, or culture to proliferate. That has been the reality at the ground level throughout the history of the United States. However, the process of purification occurs at the ideological and political level where hybrids are not tolerated and are separated into different racial/identity categories, usually into 'Americans' (read, whites) and minoritized and racialized 'Others'. Then the practice of giving 'Americans' the entire credit for forming this great nation, while placing the existence and the role of minoritized and racialized 'Others' in a footnote, and the resulting long history of violence and discrimination against 'Others', makes those who are placed in that category feel 'unhomely' in their own country. We need to acknowledge and embrace the existence and proliferation of hybrids—Americans with multiple and/or hybrid identities—openly and to stop partitioning them between 'one of us' and 'one of them' at the convenience of narrating one coherent national identity discourse. Simply put, we cannot be Americans in the same way as before.

It is from the space of liminality that we can recognize the process of purification without closing our eyes to the process of hybridization. It is in this in-between space that hybrids thrive, undermine the partitioning of a national discourse, and threaten those who wish to believe that identity is authentic only when it is singular. People with multiple or hybrid identities have survived and are proliferating in spite of the homogenization or purification process of the nation. It is from this space that I will read the David story.

David as a Machiavellian Man of Ḥesed

When we read the David story from the space of liminality, the third space that does not favor the nation over other types of socio-political, ideological space, the process of hybridization-purification is also evident. The process of hybridization is apparent in the way David mixes diverse groups of people into his kingdom. The process of purification becomes apparent when we examine how the people of his kingdom are divided into two identity groups: Israel and the others. In the narrative, such a neat separation comes apart when we consider the way identity and loyalty come into conflict. When we focus especially on hybrid characters, it will become apparent that the identity formation of ancient Israel is nowhere near completion. It is in the process of defining who the Israelites are. Who is an Israelite? is a question the narrative struggles to answer. Clear boundaries as to who belonged to Israel had to be drawn repeatedly in order to construct its identity as a people set apart from others. However, those who are characterized by hybridity pose a threat to Israel by blurring and disrupting the boundaries that are needed to forge a coherent identity.

From a postcolonial perspective, David was a Machiavellian man of *ḥesed* who was willing to cross various boundaries of difference in order to form his kingdom. He was no doubt an ambitious man who did not hesitate to use *realpolitik* and the sword to achieve his goals. But I would characterize him with the concept of *ḥesed* (loyalty and kindness), which allowed him to make connections with others and to treat others equally and fairly. David himself may have had a hybrid identity. He was radically inclusive and an egalitarian. He was open to forming ties with all sorts of people regardless of their ethnic, tribal, or religious identity. In his time, David had hybridized his kingdom and would have disdained the process of purification that the later editors implemented, which characterized him as a nativist and an exclusivist. In our time he would have challenged us to treat one another fairly and generously, regardless of our differences and encouraged us to form a community based on *ḥesed*, rather than on identity.

In Chapters 2 to 4 I will show that the concept of *ḥesed* is a helpful hermeneutical key in understanding the David story. I will suggest that K.D. Sakenfeld's definition of *ḥesed* as loyalty or 'faithfulness in action' practiced within pre-existing close relations[47] should be open to the possibility of *ḥesed* as an act that can create 'unexpected attachments'[48] when there is no such relationship in existence. Sakenfeld's definition suffers from understanding *ḥesed* only as an act of the will and does not pay enough attention to those who have hinted that *ḥesed* can be understood as an act of the heart as well. Abraham Heschel has commented some time ago that the word *yāda'* ('to know') involves the heart (to have sympathy, pity, attachment, care, or affection for someone) as well as the intellect (to grasp abstract concepts), and he cautioned those who translate *yāda'* as 'to know' without considering other words that reflect its meaning more accurately.[49] Similarly, the word *ḥesed* should be understood as an act involving the heart as well as the will, an emotional as well as an intellectual act. Therefore, I argue that the word *ḥesed* can also mean an act of 'affection and kindness' that a person can perform for another for the sake of God or for the sake of human solidarity, irrespective of whether or not there is a close relationship between them. It is the loyalty side of *ḥesed* that maintains and strengthens existing

47. K.D. Sakenfeld, *The Meaning of* Ḥesed *in the Hebrew Bible: A New Inquiry* (HSM, 17; Missoula, MT: Scholar Press, 1978), and *Faithfulness in Action: Loyalty in Biblical Perspective* (Philadelphia: Fortress Press, 1985).

48. B. Britt, 'Unexpected Attachments: A Literary Approach to the Term חסד in the Hebrew Bible', *JSOT* 27 (2003), pp. 289-307. Britt demonstrates that the term *ḥesed*, which is a common term that expresses Yahweh's covenant with Israel and describes the mutuality of many human attachments, is used in unfamiliar ways in narratives often involving foreigners, spies, and women to express the sense in which *ḥesed* can be an unexpected attachment.

49. Abraham Heschel, *The Prophets* (New York: Harper & Row, 1962), pp. 57-60.

relationships and the *jeong* (a rough translation of 'affection and kindness' in Korean) side of *ḥesed* that not only lubricates an existing relationship but also allows new relations to emerge across various identity boundaries. It is this side of *ḥesed* that enables those who are separated by differences to create a bond, a relationship between them. I will read the David story through *ḥesed* to show how David was able to establish his kingdom by relying on the *ḥesed* of people and of God (1 Sam. 1–2 Sam. 5) and to maintain his kingdom and sustain his kingship through the *ḥesed* of his soldiers, allies, and even enemies (2 Sam. 5–1 Kgs 2).

In Chapter 2, 'Understanding *Ḥesed* as a Postcolonial Term', I will discuss the term *ḥesed* and how I will use it to interpret the David story. I will use two words for *ḥesed*. Sakenfeld has suggested the word 'loyalty', and I think it makes a lot of sense to do so. I will suggest that although loyalty is a convenient word that captures many important aspects of the word *ḥesed*, I will propose that another word, *jeong*, supplements the word loyalty in order to understand the other side of *ḥesed* that loyalty does not convey. *Jeong* is a Korean word that I believe captures the idea of 'kindness and affection' produced in human bonding, which I will argue the word *ḥesed* also entails. The word *ḥesed* I think is appropriate for this study because it has postcolonial traits that I would like to highlight and use in interpreting the David story.

In Chapter 3, 'Raising the House of David on *Ḥesed*' (1 Sam. 1–2 Sam. 5), and Chapter 4, 'Sustaining the House of David with *Ḥesed*' (2 Sam. 5–24; 1 Kgs 1–2), I will use *ḥesed* as a hermeneutical key in reading the David story. This will be a reading of the final form of the David story. It will show that *ḥesed* is a key theme in the first half of the David story and that the house of David is established on God's promise and practice of *ḥesed*. Then it will examine how David suffers through trials brought on by betrayals of *ḥesed* but is able to maintain his kingdom through the politics of *ḥesed* and identity.

In Chapters 5 and 6, the hybridization of David's kingdom and the purification of this history by the later editors will be examined. The process of hybridization-purification is evident in the way the house of David is established through the mixing of various groups of people, yet, at the same time, those who are deemed 'different' or 'non-Israelite' suffer elimination and are separated from the house of David. On the one hand, *ḥesed* forges relationships between different identities in the process of hybridization. On the other hand, *ḥesed* is ignored in order to separate 'real' Israelites from the others in the process of purification.

In Chapter 5, 'The Hybridization of David's Kingdom', I will show that the David of history used the process of hybridization to form his kingdom. To build his kingdom, David assembled an eclectic coalition of various identity groups. He worked with Moabites, Philistines, Hittites, and other indigenous populations and 'foreigners' in addition to the people of Judah and the people of Israel. David's coalition went far beyond David's own 'tribe' or 'people'. His success in forming his kingdom rested on his ability to forge *ḥesed* with various constituents. He established his kingdom through marriages and alliances across ethnic, tribal, and religious borders. The heterogeneous composition of his army and leadership clearly suggests that David established his kingdom with the support of non-Israelites who were loyal to him. His army and leadership, which were composed of disparate constituents, mirrored his hybridized kingdom. David was a coalitionist and a pluralist who valued *ḥesed* over identity.

In Chapter 6, 'The Purification of the David Story', we will see that it is the later scribes who will in the end betray him and turn him into a nativist and an exclusivist. They will 'purify' or dehybridize his kingdom and turn the kingdom of all people into a kingdom for 'real' Israelites. The purification of the cult during Josiah's time, the struggle for identity apart from the land, temple, and Davidic monarchy during the Babylonian Exile, and the purification of Israelite identity during the Persian period may have something to do with this. A reason for portraying David as the archenemy of the Philistines is to construct David and Israel in opposition to the Philistines who are the quintessential Other. This tendency to see Israel in contrast to others, especially the Philistines, played a role in mis/portraying David as a fighter of Philistines and a nativist. In this chapter I will also focus on Uriah the Hittite, who has a hybrid identity and demonstrates an uncompromising *ḥesed* in the story, to see how the politics of identity and loyalty victimizes Uriah as a part of the purification of the David story.

In the end, I am striving to imagine some features in David that will show him to be neither the David of the narrator (and faith) nor the David of his enemies (and modern skeptics). The David that I wish to present is a postcolonial David who represents a third way of reading the David story.

2

ERSTANDING *ḤESED* AS A POSTCOLONIAL TERM

The Importance of Ḥesed *in the Deuteronomistic History*

In his influential article, F.M. Cross argued that there are two themes running through the Josianic edition of the DH: the sin of Jeroboam and the faithfulness of David.[1] Jeroboam established the rival shrine of Bethel (and also of Dan) as a countercultus to the Jerusalem temple and this act became 'the sin of Jeroboam' of which all kings of Israel, the Northern Kingdom, were found guilty. The conclusion of this theme is found in 2 Kgs 17.20-23 which proclaims that the Northern Kingdom has been exiled on the account of the sin of Jeroboam. As Cross puts it, 'In Jeroboam's monstrous sin, Israel's doom was sealed'.[2] God had promised to Jeroboam 'an enduring house', but apparently God's promise was conditional: 'If you will listen to all that I command you, walk in my ways, and do what is right in my sight by keeping my statutes and my commandments, as David my servant did, I will be with you, and will build you an enduring house [*bayiṯ ne'ĕmān*], as I built for David, and I will give Israel to you' (1 Kgs 11.38).[3] What really matters to the Deuteronomist is the all-important command to worship God in the place Yahweh chooses to put his name, namely the sanctuary in Jerusalem, which is the only law Jeroboam explicitly disobeys. In the book of Kings Jeroboam is the symbol of infidelity.[4]

The second theme, according to Cross, begins in 2 Samuel 7, where God promises to build David 'an enduring house' after rejecting David's offer to build Yahweh a house and guarantees to 'not take my *ḥesed* from him [Solomon], as I took it from Saul, whom I put away from before you

1. F.M. Cross, 'The Theme of the Book of Kings and the Structure of the Deuteronomistic History', in *idem*, *Canaanite Myth and Hebrew Epic* (Cambridge, MA: Harvard University Press, 1973), pp. 274-89; an earlier version was published as 'The Structure of the Deuteronomic History', in *Perspectives in Jewish Learning* (Annual of the College of Jewish Studies, 3; Chicago: University of Chicago Press, 1968), pp. 9-24.

2. Cross, 'The Theme of the Book of Kings', p. 281.

3. We will see in the next chapter that God makes 'enduring' promises to Eli, Samuel, and Saul but is also quick to withdraw them for disobedience.

4. Cross, 'The Theme of the Book of Kings', p. 281.

[David]' (2 Sam. 7.15). God has taken *ḥesed* from Saul for disobedience but promises it to the house of David forever: 'Your house [*ne'man bêṯĕḵā*] and your kingdom shall be made sure forever before me; your throne shall be established forever' (2 Sam. 7.16). Even though Solomon and the subsequent kings of Judah tolerated other cultic places, particularly the so-called 'high places' (*bāmôṯ*), Josiah and Hezekiah being the exceptions, God does not take away the *ḥesed* from the house of David. Instead God continues to allow Davides to rule over Jerusalem 'for the sake of David my servant' (1 Kgs 11.12, 13, 32, 34, 36; 15.4; 2 Kgs 8.19; 19.34; 20.6). It was, according to Cross, David's establishment of Yahweh's sanctuary in Jerusalem (not the temple Solomon built later) that counted as the faithfulness of David. It was this act that was the crucial event in Judah that differentiated Judah's fate from that of Israel's destiny, which was sealed from the moment Jeroboam displayed his unfaithfulness by establishing the rival sanctuary at Bethel.

In contrast to Jeroboam, David is the symbol of fidelity in the DH. T.C. Römer summarizes how kings of Israel and Judah are judged by the Dtr: 'All subsequent Northern kings will be systematically blamed for what is designated as "Jeroboam's sin". The Southern kings will be compared to their "father" David (1 Kgs 15.3; 11; 2 Kgs 14.3; 16.2; 18.3; 22.2) and be evaluated, for their part, on their *loyalty* to the Jerusalem temple and their condemnation of the other cultic places'.[5] We can easily use the Hebrew word *ḥesed* for the loyalty or faithfulness that God and David have shown to each other. God has sworn *ḥesed* to the house of David on account of David's *ḥesed* to God. God abandoned the Northern Kingdom because of the disloyalty of Jeroboam (and later Ahab who is accused of introducing Baal to Israel) but remained loyal to the Southern Kingdom because of the loyalty of David and Josiah. When Judah also went into exile, the exilic Deuteronomist(s) blamed the disloyalty of Manasseh for this outcome (2 Kgs 21.11-12; 23.26; 24.34).[6]

5. T.C. Römer, *The So-called Deuteronomistic History: A Sociological, Historical, and Literary Introduction* (London/New York: T. & T. Clark, 2007), p. 98 (my emphasis).

6. It is quite remarkable that the DH blames Manasseh for being solely responsible for the disaster of the Babylonian exile, the destruction of Judah, and the termination of the Davidic dynasty. The unreasonableness of scapegoating one man for God's punishment of the entire people reveals the inability or the struggle to articulate logically the reason for the Babylonian exile. M. Sweeney ('King Manasseh of Judah and the Problem of Theodicy in the Deuteronomistic History', in L.L. Grabbe [ed.], *Good Kings and Bad Kings: The Kingdom of Judah in the Seventh Century BCE* [London: T. & T. Clark, 2007], pp. 264-78), argues that although the Deuteronomistic Historian blames Manasseh for God's punishment on Judah, it does not prepare the reader for such judgment. He suggests that this tension is deliberate and points to the idea that it might have been an attempt to grapple with the problem of theodicy posed by the Babylonian exile. See also

All I am suggesting at this point is that the theme of loyalty (*ḥesed*) is important in the DH as Cross argued and that this theme connects the David story to the larger narrative of the DH. In the next two chapters, I will show that the theme of *ḥesed* also runs through the David story as well. It is not only that the word *ḥesed* appears rather frequently;[7] there are other words that are approximately synonymous with it.[8] In addition, the idea of *ḥesed* is evident, or at least reflected, in passages even where the word does not occur. Before we look at the David story through *ḥesed*, we first need to try to understand what *ḥesed* means. What follows is not a study on *ḥesed* but a limited discussion of its meaning as related to the story of David.

Nelson Glueck's Understanding of Ḥesed

Nelson Glueck's work has been a seminal study on the word *ḥesed*.[9] His understanding of *ḥesed* as conduct appropriate to (corresponding to or based upon) 'a mutual relationship of rights and duties' is a definition that subsequent researchers have engaged with. In his definition an act is called *ḥesed* only when the act is performed by one party within a relationship of obligation for another party. He argued, however, that *ḥesed* is not just any act in accordance to a mutual relationship of rights and duties; it 'never means an arbitrary demonstration of grace, kindness, favor or love'.[10] He

E.A. Knauf, 'The Glorious Days of Manasseh' (pp. 164-88), and F. Stavrakopoulou, 'The Blackballing of Manasseh' (pp. 248-63), in Grabbe (ed.), *Good Kings and Bad Kings*, for a favorable view of Manasseh based on archaeological evidence and critical reading of the biblical sources.

7. It occurs in the following places: 1 Sam. 20.8, 14, 15; 2 Sam. 2.5, 6; 3.8; 7.15; 9.1, 3, 7; 10.2 (twice); 15.20; 16.17; 22.26 (twice), 51; 1 Kgs 2.7.

8. For example, *'ahāḇah* ('love') and *ṭôḇ* ('goodness').

9. N. Glueck, Ḥesed *in the Bible* (trans. A. Gottschalk; Cincinnati: Hebrew Union College, 1967; first published in German in 1927). The completion of B.M. Bowen's study, 'A Study of ḥsd' (unpublished PhD dissertation, Yale University, 1938), which was conducted independently of Glueck's work, was delayed in part because of the publication of Glueck's work. Even though Bowen agreed with Glueck's understanding and usage of *ḥesed* as a human quality, he disagreed with Glueck's understanding and usage of *ḥesed* as a divine quality. They both sought to trace the 'evolution' of the concept of *ḥesed* by dating biblical texts according to source critical analyses. In short, Bowen, in comparison to Glueck, expanded on the meaning of divine *ḥesed* and paid greater attention to the development of the concept through source analyses of the biblical texts. I will note Bowen's disagreement with Glueck where it is appropriate.

10. Glueck, Ḥesed *in the Bible*, p. 55. It is, however, unclear as to exactly what acts Glueck considered to be *ḥesed*, and the parameters in which an act can be considered *ḥesed* was not spelled out. Sakenfeld (see below), addressed the latter issue. Here it is sufficient to note that Glueck differentiates *ḥesed* from *'hb* ('love'), *ḥn* ('grace, favor'), and *rḥm* ('mercy').

seemed to view any assistance or aid to a person that requires a sacrifice on the part of the person doing the act as *ḥesed*. Then he qualified it further and considered *ḥesed* as the giving of help or assistance with the expectation that the other will offer assistance when needed. He claimed that within a *ḥesed*-relationship one had to offer protection to whomever one owed an obligation at one's expense and even at risk of one's own life. *Ḥesed* is an obligatory act, an aid or help in time of need, which one person owes to another within certain mutual relationships of rights and duties. That is, a *ḥesed*-relationship involves some principle of *quid pro quod*.[11]

Since *ḥesed* is not employed to refer to the relationship but to an act within the relationship, it is important to understand what types of relationship (or reciprocity) Glueck considered to be a prerequisite for an act to be called *ḥesed*. Namely, they are relationships between relatives and related tribes, between host and guest, between political allies, between friends, and between ruler and subject. One has to wonder if there is any human relationship he left off his list. In fact it seems only those who do not know each other or come in contact with each other do not perform *ḥesed*. Even enemies can request from and do *ḥesed* for each other (see 1 Kgs 20.31-34). Although he qualified '*ḥesed*-relationship' as being characterized by mutuality and reciprocity, it is doubtful whether there are any relationships in ancient Israel that are not characterized to some extent by obligation and reciprocity.[12]

11. Gordon R. Clark (*The Word* Ḥesed *in the Hebrew Bible* [JSOTSup, 157; Sheffield: Sheffield Academic Press, 1993]), in assessing Glueck's work, articulates aptly Glueck's presentation of *ḥesed* in this way: 'The nature of חֶסֶד [*ḥesed*] in such a relationship may be expressed by an adaptation of the ancient adage: One good turn demands another' (p. 17). Bowen ('A Study of ḥsd', p. 414) called this principle of reciprocity '*ḥesed* begets *ḥesed*'. N.P. Lemche ('Kings and Clients: On Loyalty Between the Ruler and the Ruled in Ancient Israel', *Semeia* 66 [1994], pp. 119-32), also understands a *ḥesed*-relationship as a form of *quid pro quod* system. He suggests that *ḥesed* signifies the concept of mutual loyalty in the patron-client relationship, which he argues was a system of social organization operating in ancient Israel. Lemche explains that the patron–client relationship is 'a system in which both parties, the patron as well as the client, are bound together by mutual oaths of loyalty. It is a system, that, in principle, works to the benefit of both parties' (p. 122). After quoting two statements from the summary of Glueck's Chapter 1 ('*Ḥesed* is conduct corresponding to a mutual relationship of rights and duties… *Ḥesed*, when understood as such conduct, explains the previously mentioned fact that only those participating in a mutual relationship of rights and duties can receive and show *ḥesed*' [Glueck, Ḥesed *in the Bible*, p. 54]), Lemche concludes: 'These statements by Glueck, in fact, articulate precisely the very essence of patronage! The rest of his book simply elaborates on this theme; the essentials are all contained in these two first statements' (p. 126).

12. V.H. Matthews (*Studying the Ancient Israelites: A Guide to Sources and Methods* [Grand Rapids: Baker Academic, 2007], p. 152), lists four types of reciprocity practiced

It was also critical to Glueck's definition that obligations under a *ḥesed*-relationship cannot be enforced by law, and a person cannot resort to external forces to compel the other member in the relationship to perform the duty of *ḥesed*. In that sense the *ḥesed*-relationship is different from a covenantal relationship. It is not a contractual relationship; it is, as Glueck said, 'an ethically binding relationship'.[13] It is up to the individual to perform the act of *ḥesed*. *Ḥesed* is an obligatory act of aid or the readiness of members of an ethically binding relationship to help. Therefore, the importance of loyalty in the working of the *ḥesed*-relationship needs to be emphasized. The maintenance of the *ḥesed*-relationship depends on the commitment to the relationship of involved parties. Loyalty is a crucial component of *ḥesed*. In fact, Glueck could have defined *ḥesed* as an act of loyalty of involved parties in a mutual relationship of rights and duties.[14]

In order to better understand Glueck's definition of *ḥesed* and to relate it to the topic of this book, we now turn to his discussion of specific texts that fall under the David story. He listed and described texts, without an in-depth analysis or much discussion, to show that '*ḥesed* is received or shown only by those among whom a definite relationship exists' or, as he puts it in another way, '*ḥesed* exists between people who are in some close relationship to one another'.[15] Glueck used the relationship between David and Jonathan as an example of a *ḥesed*-relationship between political allies. He noted that David entreats Jonathan to show him *ḥesed* as a political ally (1 Sam. 20.8), then Jonathan in turn asks David to promise to show *ḥesed* to him and his house (1 Sam. 20.14, 15). In fulfillment of his duty under the

in ancient Israel: generalized reciprocity (charity, hospitality, gifts given to kin and the circle of friends without expecting immediate return), balanced reciprocity (exchange of gifts or aids with little or no delay as part of the process of building social or political relationships), imbalanced reciprocity (an aggressive tactic designed to shame someone by giving a gift they cannot financially or socially balance in order to intimidate or bribe that person), and negative reciprocity (an aggressive tactic designed to obtain a greater return or even to get something for nothing through barter or theft). Glueck would appear to have had the first two types of reciprocity in mind.

13. Glueck, Ḥesed *in the Bible*, p. 37. There are those who argue that *ḥesed* needs to be perform within a covenantal relationship; for example, N. Snaith (*The Distinctive Ideas of the Old Testament* [London: The Epworth Press, 1944], p. 95) argued that 'Without the prior existence of a covenant, there could never be any *chesed* at all'.

14. For example, Lemche, 'Kings and Clients', understands the notion of loyalty or *ḥesed* to be fundamental to the patron–client relationship; he states, 'Loyalty is a governing concept, and without it the organization will have no chance to survive' (p. 122). We will see that Sakenfeld also understands loyalty to be the crucial component of *ḥesed*, but she does not understand *ḥesed* (an act of loyalty) as something that can be coerced as in the patron–client relationship.

15. Glueck, Ḥesed *in the Bible*, p. 37.

ḥesed-relationship (this is a key qualification for Glueck) David shows *ḥesed* to Jonathan's son (2 Sam. 9.1, 3, 7). David spares Mephiboshet's life, the last remaining male member of Saul's house, restores to him Saul's land, and offers him a seat at his own table. He does these acts because he is obligated to do so.

David's actions are not surprising, since the relationship between allies is equivalent to the relationship between family members. Glueck's description of *ḥesed* between members of the family, especially between father and son, emphasized the obligatory nature of *ḥesed*: 'Every son owed his father love commensurate with the demands of loyalty. Such love was based not only on personal affection but also on duty. It was the only possible conduct of a son toward his father, since they are both of the same flesh and blood'.[16] He continued that 'There were certain fixed rules of conduct for members of a family based on reciprocity, called *ḥesed*, which obligated all members of a family to assist one another'.[17] Based on such an obligatory nature between members of the family, he argued that for 'the members of an alliance, just as between blood relatives, *ḥesed* was the only possible mode of conduct'.[18] The members of an alliance had the same rights and duties as the members of a family. That is, Mephiboshet had the right to request *ḥesed* from David based on his father's *ḥesed*-relationship with David, but, of course, there was no way to force David to fulfill his responsibility. Commenting on this episode, Glueck distinguished *ḥesed* from *ḥēn* (grace, favor) and *raḥămîm* (mercy, compassion): 'The *ḥesed* shown by David to Jonathan's house was neither grace nor mercy; it was brotherliness required by covenantal loyalty'.[19] He called David's action 'covenantal loyalty' because the *ḥesed*-relationship between David and Jonathan was sealed by an oath before Yahweh. That is, David owed Jonathan the act of protection and assistance not only because they were allies but also because they made a pact (covenant) before Yahweh. He was doubly obligated to fulfill his *ḥesed*.

The relationship between David and Jonathan was forged not only by an alliance made before Yahweh but also by friendship. Glueck argued that even if there was no covenant between them, they owed *ḥesed* to each other because they were friends. Their conduct with each other exemplifies *ḥesed*, which is a conduct stemming from the mutual relationship of rights and duties between friends. Glueck again emphasized that *ḥesed* was the proper conduct of a close relationship, in this case, friendship. Then he explained

16. Glueck, Ḥesed *in the Bible*, p. 39.

17. Glueck, Ḥesed *in the Bible*, p. 40.

18. Glueck, Ḥesed *in the Bible*, p. 46.

19. Glueck, Ḥesed *in the Bible*, p. 49. Glueck repeatedly emphasized the obligatory nature of *ḥesed*. For Glueck, *ḥesed* was something members in a close relationship owed to each other. It was a duty, never a gift.

what this meant: 'Each was expected to take heed of the welfare and safety of his friend and to be loyal to him'.[20] Once again, the proper conduct Glueck described was of some importance—'the welfare and safety' of a friend—not a matter of triviality or convenience. In commenting on the friendship between David and Nahash, Glueck believed that *ḥesed* compelled them as friends and allies 'not to war against each other and to be at readiness to lend mutual assistance to one another'.[21] *Ḥesed* is an obligatory act that is expected within a *ḥesed*-relationship between friends and allies in a similar way to the expectation between family members.

As an example of a *ḥesed*-relationship between ruler and subject, Glueck discussed David's command to Solomon to show *ḥesed* to the family of Barzillai (1 Kgs 2.7). David had received aid from Barzillai when he had to flee from Absalom, and now he was obligated to return the *ḥesed* he had received. The main point of Glueck's discussion was that David owed *ḥesed* to Barzillai. To Glueck this was a merited obligation. David was obligated to offer *ḥesed* to the family of Barzillai since Barzillai was not alive to receive *ḥesed* from David, just as he offered *ḥesed* to Hanun son of Nahash who replaced his father, because there existed a *ḥesed*-relationship between David and Nahash. He also performed *ḥesed* to Mephiboshet for the sake of Jonathan after Jonathan passed away. In each case, the person to whom David owed *ḥesed* was no longer alive to receive it from him. But David did not forget his obligation. Glueck's understanding of *ḥesed* comes through clearly when he commented (again distinguishing *ḥesed* from *ḥēn* and *raḥămîm*) that 'Modern commentators translate *ḥesed* as "mercy" or "favor", which is unacceptable. The *ḥesed* which Solomon was to show to Barzillai's house did not emanate from mercy but from obligation. It did not depend upon the mere will of David or Solomon, but was a requirement'.[22]

Another example used by Glueck to discuss the obligatory nature of *ḥesed* between king and subject was the rescue of the body of Saul from the Philistines by the people of Jabesh-gilead. Glueck argued that earlier in the narrative Saul delivered the people of Jabesh-gilead from a threat from Nahash (1 Sam. 11); therefore, the Jabeshites owed Saul *ḥesed.* David commends and blesses the people of Jabesh-gilead for having shown *ḥesed* to Saul (2 Sam. 2.5) and invites them to enter into the *ḥesed*-relationship of ruler and subject with him. We do not know whether or not they accepted

20. Glueck, Ḥesed *in the Bible*, p. 49.

21. Glueck, Ḥesed *in the Bible*, p. 50. Bowen ('A Study of ḥsd', p. 60) after noting the fact that there is no record of a covenant or a tie between David and Nahash, concluded that this is a case where *ḥesed* 'on the part of one inspires a like consideration on the part of the other' and suggested that it is 'a quality in man expressing itself in reciprocal kindness' and called this aspect 'gratitude expressed in action'.

22. Glueck, Ḥesed *in the Bible*, p. 53.

his invitation, but we do know that they risked their lives to fulfill their obligation to Saul. This episode also demonstrates that *ḥesed* is used to designate an act of great importance that often involves a sacrifice from the actor.

Glueck argued that *ḥesed* was performed within a pre-existing mutual relationship of rights and duties. Although he didn't qualify a mutual relationship as being pre-existing, that seems to be the sense. He did, however, leave a space for *ḥesed* as an act or conduct conducive to forging a new relationship. He stated, 'A mutual relationship also emerged among those who rendered help to one another, even if no other relationship existed between them'.[23] He described the process of forging a new *ḥesed*-relationship in this way:

> He who had been given help was obligated to reciprocate in kind. The helper became his brother; i.e., he had to act toward him as toward a blood relative or ally. On the part of the helper, an act of assistance signified readiness to enter into a mutual relationship, as well as his expectation of being received into such a mutual relationship. He who had been rendered assistance had to recognize the necessity of acknowledging a mutual relationship and had to act accordingly. The conduct in accord with such a relationship was likewise called *ḥesed*.[24]

The first act of assistance is considered *ḥesed* because the helper does the act with the expectation of entering into a mutual relationship and the person receiving the aid recognizes the helper's expectation.[25] Yet if the helper renders aid without the expectation of entering into a *ḥesed*-relationship, or the receiver of the aid does not acknowledge the expected mutual relationship to develop, then is the act still considered *ḥesed*? Although Glueck would see it as 'an arbitrary demonstration of grace, kindness, favor or love' and not an act of *ḥesed*, he does, however, leave an opening to interpret *ḥesed* as an act of assistance that is prior to or outside of (the existence or the expectation of) a mutual relationship and therefore can be performed to forge a new relationship. His failure to recognize fully the ability of *ḥesed* to create new relationships in the David story may have something to do with the way he divided the usage of *ḥesed*.

Glueck divided the usage of *ḥesed* into three categories: the secular meaning (people's conduct towards one another), the religious meaning (people's conduct towards God), and the theological meaning (God's conduct towards

23. Glueck, Ḥesed *in the Bible*, p. 52.

24. Glueck, Ḥesed *in the Bible*, pp. 52-53.

25. This may be an example of balanced reciprocity where the helper gives aid with the expectation of immediate return as a process of building new social or political relationships.

people who are in relationship with him).[26] He used all the texts from the David story discussed above as examples of the secular usage of *ḥesed*, thus limiting the occurrences of *ḥesed* as 'people's conduct towards one another' within an existing relationship of rights and duties. He placed the practice of *ḥesed* outside of or prior to the existence of relationship under the religious usage and limited the religious usage to the prophetic literature. Furthermore, he viewed this usage as a considerable expansion of the meaning of *ḥesed* from the secular usage; this opinion was based on the understanding that the books of Samuel were written prior to the prophetic literature. The usage in the prophetic literature was not considered the common usage, which the secular usage represented. He defined the religious usage of *ḥesed* as the reciprocal conduct of men toward one another and, at the same time, explicitly or implicitly toward God; that is, *ḥesed* is not understood on the basis of interpersonal relationships alone but from the point of view of a human–divine relationship. Therefore, Glueck concluded, 'one cannot discuss *ḥesed* as the conduct of men corresponding to a reciprocal relationship without looking at *ḥesed* at the same time as the conduct of men toward God'.[27]

The religious usage of *ḥesed* as developed by the prophets can be understood as reframing rather than expanding the secular usage of *ḥesed*—people's conduct towards one another in the presence of God or for the sake of God. In discussing the book of Hosea, Glueck explained that the religious meaning of *ḥesed* as developed by Hosea and other prophets was the 'proper conduct' in relationship with God, that is, what is the right thing to do for fellow human beings that will be pleasing to God regardless of the existence of a close relationship. In discussing other prophetic books he reiterated this point: 'Every man becomes every other man's brother, *ḥesed* becomes the mutual or reciprocal relationship of all men toward each other and toward God'.[28] Now all humans were to be viewed as members of the same family for the sake of God; this is anticipated by the way Glueck equated friends and members of an alliance with family members. In his words, 'Whoever views all men as members of his own family, and keeps the welfare of the

26. Bowen ('A Study of ḥsd'), divided the usage and understanding of *ḥesed* into a divine quality and a human quality and sought to examine both qualities in all groups of texts he treated. According to Bowen's count, *ḥesed* appeared more than three hundred times, where fifty times the word was used as a human quality, which he called 'a social virtue', and in the remaining occurrences the word was regarded as a divine attribute 'expressed on man's behalf' (p. 6). Glueck also understood *ḥesed* as human *ḥesed* and divine *ḥesed*, but he organized his book in terms of three usages (two belonging to humans and one to God; more on this point below).

27. Glueck, Ḥesed *in the Bible*, p. 56.

28. Glueck, Ḥesed *in the Bible*, p. 61.

whole human family before him, creates his own leading to the kingdom of God...and will achieve communion with God'.[29] The burden to perform *ḥesed* to others, not only to those with whom one is in a close relationship, falls on all humans if one wishes to have a proper relationship with God.[30] He again emphasized the obligatory nature of *ḥesed* even in the religious usage by distinguishing *ḥesed* from *raḥămîm*: '*ḥesed* is very closely related to the concept of mercy, but is distinguished from it in that *ḥesed* is obligatory'.[31] Throughout his discussion of the religious meaning (and through the entire book), Glueck focused on the obligatory nature of the relationship in which *ḥesed* is proper conduct. Humans are obligated for the sake of God to perform *ḥesed* to one another outside of as well as within a mutual relationship of rights and duties. This is a basis for forming new *ḥesed*-relationships across differences and boundaries that separate humans from one another; however, Glueck failed to emphasize this latter aspect of *ḥesed*.

If doing *ḥesed* toward fellow humans for the sake of God is obligatory, then how is God obligated to show *ḥesed* towards humans who are in relationship with God? In his discussion of the theological meaning of *ḥesed* (God's conduct towards people who are in covenant with him), Glueck showed that God expects that a community with which God is in relationship will give aid to fellow human beings in times of need and, in return, God's *ḥesed* is manifest through the giving of aid and deliverance to God's followers in times of need. He argued that a community faithful to God could expect God to give aid in times of trouble because God is obligated to do so within the existence of a *ḥesed*-relationship.[32]

29. Glueck, Ḥesed *in the Bible*, p. 64.

30. Bowen ('A Study of ḥsd', pp. 417-18), summarized that the human *ḥesed* 'began with the thought of a good deed expressed in loyalty to the obligations incurred through some tie or bond', which is tantamount to Glueck's definition of conduct appropriate to a relationship of mutual rights and obligations, but it was developed to include 'the most interesting of these ties', namely, that people who had a relationship with Yahweh were in a *ḥesed*-relationship with one another, even, for example, Israelites and Kenites (non-Israelites). Bowen then noted the significant contribution of Hosea when he used *ḥesed* for 'an ethical expression of one's religious duty' (p. 418). Therefore, *ḥesed*, as a quality of a human being, is an obligation resting on every religious person and not restricted by covenantal or family ties. It is an obligation that a person owes to everyone, not only to kinspeople, a guest in the home, or a covenantee.

31. Glueck, Ḥesed *in the Bible*, p. 69.

32. This implies that the helper who does *ḥesed* for the sake of God can expect God to perform *ḥesed* for him/her if the person receiving the aid is unwilling or unable to return the act. Even if one performs the act within a relationship with the expectation of return but fails to receive it, then God's *ḥesed* serves as an insurance policy. David asks God to do *ḥesed* to the men of Jabesh (2 Sam. 2.6) because Saul was no longer able to fulfill his obligation (2.7) and to Ittai the Gittite (15.20) because David was not sure whether he would survive Absalom's revolt to pay back Ittai's *ḥesed*.

Glueck discussed several passages in the David story when examining the theological meaning of *ḥesed*. He argued that 'The very fact of Yahweh's choosing David, after having rejected Saul, created a relationship entailing *ḥesed*'.[33] The relationship between God and David was the same as between father and son (Glueck once again equates all human relationships to family relationships), 'a mutual relationship of rights and duties, which made necessary the reciprocal practice of *ḥesed*'.[34] In discussing Psalm 89 and 2 Samuel 7, Glueck showed that the relationship between God and David made 'the practicing of *ḥesed* both possible and necessary' because 'Yahweh swore by his faithfulness to show David *ḥesed*, by designating the relationship between himself and David as that which exists between a father and his first-born'. He noted again the difference between *ḥesed* and *raḥămîm* in God's action: 'The *ḥesed* of God is very closely related to His *rahamim* but distinguished from it by its more positive character. The characteristic of loyalty which belongs to the concept of *ḥesed* is alien to the concept of *rahamim*'.[35] Glueck claimed that God's *ḥesed* was limited to those who were in a covenantal relationship with God: 'it is certain that only those who stand in an ethical and religious relationship to Him may receive and expect His *ḥesed*'.[36] Those who are not in a 'covenantal relationship' with God should not expect God's *ḥesed*, that is, God is not obligated to help them in times of need; however, God is free to show *raḥămîm* (mercy) and *ḥēn* (favor) to them.[37]

Glueck's division of the usage of *ḥesed* into three meanings—secular, religious, and theological—is not helpful. This division comes from an

33. Glueck, Ḥesed *in the Bible*, p. 75.
34. Glueck, Ḥesed *in the Bible*, p. 76.
35. Glueck, Ḥesed *in the Bible*, p. 76.
36. Glueck, Ḥesed *in the Bible*, p. 102.
37. Bowen ('A Study of ḥsd', p. 411) expanded the understanding of *ḥesed* as a quality of God, in that God performs *ḥesed* even to those who are not in a covenantal relationship with God because God loves them: 'From these fifteen passages in the prophetic books there emerges the following conceptions of Yahweh's CHESED: 1. It is a mutual obligation between Yahweh and Israel with Israel fulfilling her part in moral social relationships. 2. It is an agent through which Yahweh forgives and redeems. 3. It is shown because Yahweh loves. 4. It is a universal CHESED shown to all the earth, even towards Nineveh'. In his summary, Bowen expressed some dissatisfaction with Glueck's treatment of divine *ḥesed*. He critiqued Glueck's view of limiting God's *ḥesed* to Israel (the covenantal people). He summarized that Glueck ignored all passages in which Yahweh's *ḥesed* is expressed towards non-Israelites (2 Sam. 2.15; Ruth 1.8; Jonah 4.2) and neglected to mention that God extends *ḥesed* to both man and beast (Pss. 33.5-9; 36.6-8; 147.8-10; Job 37.13) and to 'all peoples' (Ps. 117). Bowen acknowledged that Yahweh's *ḥesed* may be reserved for God's covenantal people but claimed that Glueck did not recognize the fact that Yahweh's *ḥesed* was not limited to them.

assumption that somehow God's *ḥesed* is categorically different from human *ḥesed* just as some have argued that God's love (*agape*) is different from human love (*phileo*). God's *ḥesed* is considered a perfect form of *ḥesed*, whatever that may mean. We will see that God is not perfectly faithful in performing *ḥesed*. On several occasions God withdraws *ḥesed* after promising to perform it forever. God is no different from humans when it comes to *ḥesed*. Humans also show incredible *ḥesed*; humans are willing to sacrifice their own lives for the sake of others even when there is no obligation to do so. There can be no greater *ḥesed* than that. There is no difference between divine *ḥesed* and human *ḥesed*. *Ḥesed* is an act that helps to maintain a relationship between God and humans (as well as between humans). God desires the people who are in a covenantal relationship with him to obey specific commands and to do *ḥesed* for one another, but God's *ḥesed* is not limited to the people of the covenant; God has the freedom to extend *ḥesed* to those outside the covenantal relationship. Sometimes there is neither rhyme nor reason to why God shows *ḥesed* to one and not to another. God does not dole out *ḥesed* according to some logical system. God's *ḥesed* does not work in the way God's covenant works. In the covenantal relationship, God requires and expects certain responses from the people, and conditions or actions of the promise or covenant are explicitly stated. God's *ḥesed* anticipates and hopes for certain responses from the people, but conditions or actions of *ḥesed* are not stated. In the end God is not required, in contrast to a covenantal relationship, to show *ḥesed* to those who seek it, but is morally responsible just as humans are. *Ḥesed* is a characteristic of being God as well as of being human.[38]

Glueck's religious meaning of *ḥesed* need not be separated from the secular usage; both belong to the quality of human *ḥesed*. Under the secular usage he left an opening for a use of *ḥesed* that is very similar to the religious usage: 'A mutual relationship also emerged among those who rendered help to one another, even if no other relationship existed between them'.[39] I will explore this point below. The religious usage involves doing *ḥesed* towards another person with whom one may not be in a close relationship for the sake of God or for the sake of human solidarity, since all humans belong to one family. Doing *ḥesed* for the sake of God or for the sake of human solidarity helps to forge a new relationship with fellow humans who are not in a close, mutual relationship with the doer. Showing *ḥesed* maintains and strengthens a relationship between fellow humans and also with God.

38. According to Clark (*The Word* Ḥesed *in the Hebrew Bible*, p. 260) the terms *'emeṯ* and *'emūnah* ('faithfulness', 'steadfastness') are essential components of *ḥesed* when God is the agent as well as when the agent is human.

39. Glueck, Ḥesed *in the Bible*, p. 52.

Katharine Doob Sakenfeld's Understanding of Ḥesed

Sakenfeld's study on *ḥesed*, *The Meaning of* Ḥesed *in the Hebrew Bible*, like many subsequent works after Glueck's book, engages Glueck's understanding of *ḥesed*.[40] Her work is more substantial and extensive than Glueck's work in terms of the extent and depth of exegesis of texts and in dealing with source critical issues. She refines Glueck's definition, 'conduct in accordance with a mutual relationship of rights and duties', by giving greater specificities to the situation (or specific conditions) in which an action performed can be considered *ḥesed*. In short, Sakenfeld focuses on *ḥesed*-situations in which acts performed are considered *ḥesed*, in contrast to Glueck, whose work paid attention to *ḥesed*-relationships in which certain acts can be rendered *ḥesed*.

Sakenfeld agrees with Glueck in principle that *ḥesed* is practiced within a mutual relationship of rights and duties; however, she seems to reject Glueck's idea of obligation or reciprocity, which is central to Glueck's definition of *ḥesed* and his book, by hardly discussing it. In fact, as Clark notes, she scarcely uses terms like 'mutuality' and 'reciprocity', which were so prominent in Glueck's work.[41] She does not, in fact, think that *ḥesed* is an obligation; she disagrees with Glueck that *ḥesed* is something that is owed or a merited obligation. She reasons, '*ḥesed* is not a legal right but a moral right and as such can also be a gift'.[42] *Ḥesed*, therefore, is something that is practiced out of moral responsibility. No external forces can force the individual to do *ḥesed*; it is an act performed out of one's sense of loyalty to the other party. Although Glueck also understood *ḥesed* as a right or duty within an 'ethically binding relationship', he never saw it as a gift, always distinguishing *ḥesed* from mercy, favor, or love. Sakenfeld thinks that Glueck constructed a false dichotomy between obligatory action (*ḥesed*) and action freely done (*ḥēn* and *raḥămîm*) in his work.

Glueck emphasized 'obligation' as an essential component to *ḥesed* throughout his book, while Sakenfeld prefers the word 'responsibility'. It seems as if there is little difference between these two terms until we look at how Sakenfeld qualifies the nature of 'responsibility' in *ḥesed*. For Sakenfeld, it is the combination of responsibility and freedom that distinguishes an

40. Sakenfeld presented her study in a more accessible format and with a theological perspective in *Faithfulness in Action*.

41. Clark (*The Word* Ḥesed *in the Hebrew Bible*, p. 20) in assessing Sakenfeld's work, notes an important difference from that of Glueck's work: 'Sakenfeld pays very little attention to the reciprocity that features so largely in Glueck's study. She leaves the reader in no doubt that she rejects Glueck's idea of mutual reciprocity'.

42. Sakenfeld, *The Meaning of* Ḥesed, p. 3.

act of *ḥesed* from an act of grace, mercy, or love. She can see an act of *ḥesed* as a gift because even though *ḥesed* entails responsibility, the individual is free not to do *ḥesed*. For Sakenfeld, freedom rather than obligation for the individual to act has to be maintained: 'It is only when coercion is possible but is not exercised that the action is called *ḥesed*'.[43]

Sakenfeld points out (as I have done above) that Glueck had defined too broadly what a *ḥesed*-relationship really is so that all sorts of interpersonal relationships and any human relationship of 'rights and duties' could be considered a *ḥesed*-relationship.[44] She states that, just as any relationship can be considered a *ḥesed*-relationship in Glueck's study, his definition of *ḥesed* 'suggests that any and all proper actions with respect to the other party done by individuals or groups in relationship to one another was called *ḥesed*'.[45] Rather than re-examining what types of relationship are considered a *ḥesed*-relationship in which an act of aid can be called *ḥesed*, she focuses her attention on the specific conditions of a situation in which an action can be rendered *ḥesed* and argues that *ḥesed* is employed when certain actions are performed in specific situations.

The thrust of Sakenfeld's work is to define the parameters within which an action performed can be rendered *ḥesed*. There are four elements to the parameters within which to practice *ḥesed*; that is, four conditions that are normally present in a *ḥesed*-situation in which the word *ḥesed* is appropriate to describe an action. First, a pre-existing relationship (covenant can enhance relationship but *ḥesed* is not limited to covenant) or a previous action on which *ḥesed* can be based must exist for a situation to be a *ḥesed*-situation: 'the human actor always has some recognizable responsibility for the person who is to receive *ḥesed*, either because of an obvious personal relationship or because of some previous action'.[46] Second, the existence of a serious situation of need—a matter of life or death, not a matter of convenience, is required to be considered a *ḥesed*-situation. Third, the situation creates a

43. Sakenfeld, *The Meaning of* Ḥesed, p. 12. This is quite different from Lemche's understanding of *ḥesed* within the patron–client relationship.

44. She, however, does not limit *ḥesed* to a formal covenant relationship, in contrast, for example, to Snaith, in *The Distinctive Ideas of the Old Testament*. She limits *ḥesed* to an act performed within a specific situational relationship. *Ḥesed*, to Snaith, was primarily 'determined faithfulness' to a covenant. He argued that the word *ḥesed* appears frequently with the word אמן (*'mn*; 23 times), which supports this meaning. Such understanding of *ḥesed* was also based on his argument that the etymological origin of the word means 'eagerness, steadfastness' and then developed into 'mercy, loving-kindness', but all in connection with the idea of covenant. He states, 'It never meant "kindness" in general and to all sundry' (p. 98).

45. Sakenfeld, *The Meaning of* Ḥesed, p. 3.

46. Sakenfeld, *The Meaning of* Ḥesed, p. 24.

situationally (not necessarily socially) superior person who acts for a situationally inferior person. Fourth, often the actor is the only person who can perform *ḥesed* for the person in need; the act is something which the recipient 'cannot possibly do for himself and often is something which no one but the actor can do for him'.[47] These are indeed rigid conditions, thereby greatly restricting what actions can be rendered *ḥesed* and who can perform it.

Sakenfeld emphasizes that in a *ḥesed*-situation, with the existence of all four conditions, the individual has moral responsibility, but also freedom to not do *ḥesed*. Even in a situation of life or death, the actor is free not to perform the act of *ḥesed*. A combination of 'responsibility and freedom', which are in tension with each other, is crucial in Sakenfeld's understanding of *ḥesed*. She insists that an act must be offered from 'a position of responsibility and freedom' in order for that act to be rendered with the word *ḥesed*.

In order better to understand Sakenfeld's view of *ḥesed*, I will examine her discussion of the secular use of *ḥesed*, focusing on the texts in the David story. She examines the same texts as Glueck in discussing the secular usage in pre-exilic prose. Although she uses the term 'secular usage', it is more appropriate to call it human *ḥesed* since she does not treat the religious usage (people's conduct towards God) of *ḥesed* separately. Human *ḥesed* combines Glueck's secular and religious usages and divine *ḥesed* combines Glueck's theological and religious usages.[48] She divides the secular (human) *ḥesed* into two types: (1) acts of *ḥesed* based on a close personal relationship and (2) acts of *ḥesed* based on some prior action. Here we can see what she means by the first condition of a *ḥesed*-situation. In the first type, no reason or basis for *ḥesed* is explicitly stated since the responsibility is assumed as part of a close relationship. In the second type, the two parties involved are not connected by a close relationship or any tie or bond at all in which to assume the responsibility of *ḥesed*.

In discussing *ḥesed* based on a close personal relationship, Sakenfeld examines several texts from the David story. In 2 Sam. 16.17, Absalom questions the *ḥesed* of Hushai the Archite, David's top adviser: 'Is this your *ḥesed* to your friend? Why did you not go with your friend?' Sakenfeld points out that the basis for Absalom's accusation lies in the close relationship between the king and his adviser in which Hushai has the responsibility and freedom to perform *ḥesed* for David (the first condition of a *ḥesed*-situation). David cannot force Hushai to do *ḥesed* even though he is in serious trouble and needs Hushai's help (second condition), but he puts

47. Sakenfeld, *The Meaning of* Ḥesed, p. 24.

48. She seems to be following Bowen ('A Study of ḥsd'), who divided *ḥesed* into two categories: a quality of God and a quality of humans. In her later work, *Faithfulness in Action*, she discusses *ḥesed* as having two categories: human loyalty and God's loyalty.

Hushai in the position of responsibility and freedom to do so. In this case Hushai is in a situationally superior position to David, who, in spite of the fact that he is socially superior, is situationally inferior (third condition). Unbeknownst to Absalom, Hushai is indeed doing *ḥesed* for David by serving as David's mole inside Absalom's camp. This act is something only Hushai can perform (fourth condition).[49]

One more example will suffice. Sakenfeld thinks that the relationship between David and Jonathan is a special 'mixed' type because the request for *ḥesed* is based on a formal pact as well as a close relationship.[50] This can be viewed as a doubly binding relationship rather than a 'mixed' type, as Glueck also recognized. When David asks for *ḥesed* from Jonathan (1 Sam. 20.8), Sakenfeld notes that Jonathan, who is in a situationally superior position to David in this *ḥesed*-situation, is free to ignore David's request but is morally responsible because of their covenant that was made prior to this situation. In turn, when Jonathan requests *ḥesed* from David in 1 Sam. 20.14-15, David is in a situationally superior position to Jonathan, and, therefore, in a position of responsibility and freedom to fulfill *ḥesed* when the need arises in the future. In 2 Samuel 9, David has the opportunity to exercise his *ḥesed* to Jonathan by extending clemency to Mephiboshet, Jonathan's son, but is also free to execute Mephiboshet if he wishes. There was no one or no system in place to make David live up to his promise or to fulfill his responsibility of *ḥesed*. David's responsibility of *ḥesed* was based not only on his close friendship with Jonathan but also on Jonathan's act of assistance in preserving David's life. Moreover, their acts of *ḥesed* are also partially based on a formal pact they made prior to these acts. Sakenfeld concludes that 'The underlying formal relationship is "secondary" and hence relatively fragile. While *ḥesed* is not exchanged *quid pro quod*, it is rooted in responsibility, and the reference to a prior action concretizes that responsibility'.[51]

49. We need to add that the fact that Hushai performed *ḥesed* to David while putting his own life at risk, even though he was free not to do so, speaks volumes about his character. *Ḥesed* describes not only an act of assistance in time of need but also describes a human attribute; a person of *ḥesed* is someone who is free not to do *ḥesed* but does so consistently so that it becomes part of that person's trait/character.

50. Britt ('Unexpected Attachments', p. 301) describes the *ḥesed*-relationship between David and Jonathan, who are political rivals in reality, and thus make an odd couple, as unusual and surprising: 'In 1 Sam. 20.14-17, David and Jonathan make a pact based on חסד and love. Just as Ruth's attachment to Naomi and Boaz is unexpected, so is the odd couple of David and Jonathan'. Britt includes this episode among those involving 'surprising acts of human חסד in dealings between Israelites and foreigners or among rivals' (p. 301).

51. Sakenfeld, *The Meaning of* Ḥesed, p. 91.

Sakenfeld adds the following point: *ḥesed* is demonstrated by means of a concrete act rather than by an attitude or an abstract quality.[52] When Ishbaal complains about Abner's taking of Rizpah, Saul's concubine, Abner reacts violently: 'Am I a dog's head for Judah? Today I keep showing *ḥesed* to the house of your father Saul, to his brothers, and to his friends, and have not given you into the hand of David; and yet you charge me now with a crime concerning this woman' (2 Sam. 3.8; Sakenfeld's translation). Sakenfeld cautions the reader from understanding *ḥesed* as an abstract quality, because Abner claims to have shown it over a period of time. She suggests that Abner's acts of *ḥesed* are specific and ongoing acts that were necessary to maintain Ishbaal's rule. She, therefore, concludes that 'An attitude is inevitably involved, but the focus of the *ḥesed* is in the concrete action which Abner has taken on Ishbaal's behalf'.[53]

Glueck had argued for the possibility of performing *ḥesed* between those who did not have a prior relationship and the expanded view of *ḥesed* under the religious usage as actions owed to all humans for the sake of God. The initial act, according to Glueck, is performed in anticipation of reciprocal aid from the recipient, whose fulfillment of such expectation completes a *ḥesed*-relationship. A *ḥesed*-relationship can be formed even without the existence of a relationship when two parties exchange acts of assistance in times of need. Although Sakenfeld acknowledges that there are a few texts in which '*ḥesed* might be regarded as the initial act creating a bond', she argues that 'such usage was secondary and exceptional' and maintains that '*ḥesed* was properly used primarily for acts performed within an existing relationship'.[54]

Sakenfeld's second type of *ḥesed* under the secular (human) usage can be viewed as a refinement of Glueck's point made above. The difference between Sakenfeld's argument that *ḥesed* can be based on prior action when there is an absence of a close relationship and Glueck's point that *ḥesed* can be performed to forge a *ḥesed*-relationship is minimal in my opinion. Sakenfeld states that '*Ḥesed* based on prior action has the same characteristics as *ḥesed* based implicitly on personal relationships. Prior actions are identified as the basis for *ḥesed* wherever no intimate personal relationship is

52. Clark (*The Word* Ḥesed *in the Hebrew Bible*, p. 263) agrees with Sakenfeld's conclusion that *ḥesed* is performed for another individual and not for a cause or inanimate object. In his statement, which summarizes the difference between *ḥesed* and *'āhab*, Clark makes the following point: 'אהב [*'hb*] derivatives, but not חֶסֶד [*ḥesed*], are frequently directed to inanimate entities by both Yahweh and human'.

53. Sakenfeld, *The Meaning of* Ḥesed, p. 31. In my opinion she underestimates the importance of attitude or even affection involved or inherent in *ḥesed*. It needs to be understood as an act of the will (loyalty, faithfulness, commitment, responsibility) as well as of the heart (love, affection, kindness, attachment, sympathy). I will discuss this critical element in my understanding of *ḥesed* below.

54. Sakenfeld, *The Meaning of* Ḥesed, p. 13.

apparent'.[55] In Judg. 1.24, the spies from the house of Joseph encounter a man from Bethel/Luz and make the following proposition: 'Show us the way into the city, and we will do *ḥesed* with you'. Glueck saw this as a mutual exchange, but Sakenfeld argues that he overlooked 'the importance of the unevenness in the situation' (condition three of a *ḥesed*-situation: the spies were in a situationally superior position to the man).[56] The spies offered their *ḥesed*, namely, to spare the life of a man from Bethel/Luz, on the condition that he showed them how to enter the city. Once he told them, which is the prior act on which the *ḥesed* of the spies will be based, the spies had the freedom not to keep their word. They could have killed him and not done *ḥesed*. But when they kept their word and spared his life, the sparing of the man's life became an act of *ḥesed*. Sakenfeld, however, would not render the man's help to the spies as *ḥesed*. She argues that *ḥesed* is never used for an 'initiatory' action except 'when it serves as the statement of a basis for a *ḥesed* action by the second party'.[57] For Glueck, the man who gave help to the spies with an expectation of his life being spared initiated a *ḥesed*-relationship. For Sakenfeld, however, it seems the man's initial act cannot become *ḥesed* even if the spies fulfill their responsibility; it can only be a basis for their act of *ḥesed*. The man and the spies cannot form a *ḥesed*-relationship or forge a new relationship; the man's act only puts the spies in a position of responsibility and freedom to act in a *ḥesed*-situation. I believe Sakenfeld's position is too restrictive.

When we consider a negotiation of *ḥesed* between Rahab and the two spies sent by Joshua (Josh. 2.12-14), it is clear that Rahab believed her initial act (hiding the Israelite spies) as an act of *ḥesed* performed in order to form a *ḥesed*-relationship where there did not exist a relationship between them prior to this act: 'Now then, since I have dealt kindly [*ḥesed*] with you, swear to me by the Lord that you in turn will deal kindly [*ḥesed*] with my family. Give me a sign of good faith [*'emet*] that you will spare my father and mother, my brothers and sisters, and all who belong to them, and deliver our lives from death'. The men said to her, 'Our life for yours! If you do not tell this business of ours, then we will deal kindly [*ḥesed*] and faithfully [*'emet*] with you when the Lord gives us the land'. Rahab does not reveal the spies' visitation and ties a crimson cord in the window of her house, which the spies instructed her to tie as a sign of *'emet* (Josh. 2.18). Then, after God gives Jericho to the Israelites, the Israelites spare Rahab and her family (Josh. 6.22-23). Britt comments that in both cases involving Israelite spies and non-Israelites (natives to the land), their decision to cooperate with the Israelites 'reciprocates the offer of חסד in a surprising way. The foreigners

55. Sakenfeld, *The Meaning of* Ḥesed, p. 82.
56. Sakenfeld, *The Meaning of* Ḥesed, p. 50.
57. Sakenfeld, *The Meaning of* Ḥesed, p. 59.

who assist Israelite spies are certainly a case of unexpected attachments... [T]hese stories also underscore the unexpected quality of חסד itself'.[58] In other words, Sakenfeld's position prevents us from seeing the possibility of *ḥesed* to form unexpected connections.

In 1 Kgs 2.7, David commands Solomon to show *ḥesed* to the house of Barzillai: 'Deal *ḥesed*, however, with the sons of Barzillai the Gileadite, and let them be among those who eat at your table; for with such *ḥesed* they met me when I fled from your brother Absalom' (Sakenfeld's translation). David's instruction to assign the family of Barzillai a place on the king's table is called *ḥesed*, not because Solomon is instructed to offer a privilege to them but, Sakenfeld speculates, because they needed protection from opposing factions. Thus she concludes that *ḥesed* generally involves the fulfillment of need rather than the granting of special privilege. Moreover, Solomon was free not to obey David's instruction if he desired. Solomon was in a position of responsibility and freedom to show *ḥesed* to the family of Barzillai. She states, '*Ḥesed* is never performed randomly; a responsibility must always be implicit or explicit'.[59]

Sakenfeld maintains that *ḥesed* is not done outside of a relationship of responsibility even in the case of *ḥesed* based on prior action. She summarizes *ḥesed* as an act performed within a relationship, 'deliverance or protection as a responsible keeping of faith with another with whom one is in a relationship'.[60] She sees an act of assistance outside or prior to a relationship as exceptions to the rule and searches for something (a prior relationship or an act) on which to base a responsibility. She is, in my opinion, trying to avoid the possibility that an act of assistance performed outside of or prior to a relationship can be considered *ḥesed*. In the above episode David's responsibility to Barzillai has to be either implicit (a *ḥesed*-relationship not mentioned in the text) or explicit (based on a prior act called *ḥesed* noted in the text) as is the case here. However, we will never know whether Barzillai's initial *ḥesed* is based on David's prior act of aid or on an already existing relationship between them. There had to be a moment in time when David and Barzillai forged a new *ḥesed*-relationship. How is a new *ḥesed*-relationship ever made?

58. Britt, 'Unexpected Attachments', p. 305. Bowen ('A Study of ḥsd', p. 35) also saw Rahab's initial act as an expression of *ḥesed*, albeit 'a kindness rendered freely and yet not altruistically', but he agreed with Glueck that 'Rahab was only acting under the law of hospitality' and cautioned not to make too much out of this case. Thus, he concluded that Rahab and the spies both expressed *ḥesed* as 'a desire to fulfill a responsibility' (p. 36). Bowen also understood the case in Judg. 1.24 as a case of 'reciprocal kindness' in which 'no tie other than the natural obligation to return kindness for kindness' existed (pp. 37-38).

59. Sakenfeld, *The Meaning of* Ḥesed, p. 82.

60. Sakenfeld, *The Meaning of* Ḥesed, p. 233.

In discussing the *ḥesed* of God, Sakenfeld sees commitment and freedom as being inherent in the *ḥesed* of God similar to the way human *ḥesed* entails responsibility and freedom on the part of the actor. Sakenfeld summarizes that *ḥesed*

> held together in a single expression an emphasis on divine freedom on the one hand and divine commitment on the other, an emphasis on divine power on the one hand and divine care on the other, an emphasis on human need and weakness on the one hand and human responsibility to trust in God on the other.[61]

She maintains that *ḥesed* is a specific divine action or a promise of divine action that fulfills an essential need, not extra blessings or privilege. Here Sakenfeld clarifies what she means by saying that *ḥesed* can be a gift, that is, a voluntary act. She is emphasizing the right or freedom to refuse to do *ḥesed*, which makes *ḥesed* a 'gift' rather than an obligation. The act itself is not a gift or extra blessing or privilege; it is the decision to act that is a gift given from the individual, who has the freedom to refuse to give *ḥesed*.

In commenting on 2 Sam. 2.6 and 15.20 where David blesses the people of Jabesh-gilead and Ittai the Gittite with the phrase 'may Yahweh do *ḥesed* with you', Sakenfeld suggests that the phrase may have been used in a situation in which one party can no longer fulfill the *ḥesed* responsibility. David reminds the people of Jabesh-gilead that their *ḥesed*-relationship with Saul has ended since Saul is dead. David asks God to fulfill the responsibility and also invites them to establish a *ḥesed*-relationship with him. In the case of 2 Sam. 15.20, David is not in a position to protect Ittai and his men and thus invokes God to do his part. This phrase, 'may Yahweh do *ḥesed* with you', Sakenfeld suggests, 'appears to have served as a technical way of bringing a relationship to an end'.[62] Once again, Sakenfeld's understanding is too restrictive.

The two cases above are examples in which God serves as the insurance policy of the principle of reciprocity; to say that no act of *ḥesed* performed within a relationship or outside a relationship for the sake of God will go unaccounted for. God will perform *ḥesed* if the person is no longer able to fulfill his/her responsibility. In the latter case, Bowen argued that God was called upon to show *ḥesed* because of the special relationship between God and his anointed (in this case, David).[63] Bowen understood the former case as 'an expression of Yahweh's desire to act on behalf of his messianic king'

61. Sakenfeld, *The Meaning of* Ḥesed, p. 149. She effectively collapses the difference between divine *ḥesed* and human *ḥesed*. As I have been arguing, there is no need to divide *ḥesed* into two categories: divine and human.

62. Sakenfeld, *The Meaning of* Ḥesed, p. 108.

63. Bowen, 'A Study of ḥsd', p. 108.

as a reward (but more than that) for a kindness that has been shown to an anointed king of Israel (in this case, Saul), and concluded that this act was based on 'appreciation and gratitude on the one hand and on loyalty on the other'.[64] He also noted that there were two sides to the Jabeshites' *ḥesed*: a desire to reciprocate Saul's kindness and a duty to show loyalty to their lord.[65] Bowen came close to articulating *ḥesed* as having two sides: kindness and loyalty. My argument is that rather than understanding *ḥesed* as having two qualities (human and divine), it is more accurate to see two sides (kindness and loyalty) to its meaning regardless of who (either human or God) is performing it.

Sakenfeld also discusses the Dtr's conception of God's *ḥesed* towards the house of David. She gives a succinct description of God's *ḥesed* to the Davidic dynasty based on 2 Sam. 7.15: 'God's *ḥesed* is that which maintains the king on his throne'.[66] God's allowing the Davidic dynasty to continue was God's *ḥesed* to the house of David; compare this to Abner's claim that it is his *ḥesed* that has maintained the house of Saul. She argues that the Dtr uses the phrase 'for the sake of David' to modify possibly the prevalent view of his time that the 2 Samuel 7 passage is an unconditional promise of continual succession of the Davidic dynasty. The Dtr saw the promise as conditional and 'the survival of the dynasty as God's concession to human weakness for David's sake'.[67] Similar to the way David spared Mephiboshet's life 'for the sake of Jonathan' (2 Sam. 9.1), God continues the Davidic line and the survival of the people 'for the sake of David'. She suggests that the Dtr 'prefers to reserve *berith* for a relationship involving all the people in obedience to Yahweh, while he uses *ḥesed* for God's maintenance of the Davidic line, the keeping of a promise because of David's perfect obedience'.[68]

In her subsequent book, *Faithfulness in Action*, Sakenfeld decides to use the word 'loyalty' for *ḥesed*. Her decision to substitute consistently 'loyalty' in place of *ḥesed* appeals to me. I agree in principle that loyalty captures the meaning of *ḥesed* as an act of aid appropriate to being faithful (or responsible), between two human parties in a relationship in some sort of *ḥesed*-situation (a serious situation of need but not restricted by the four conditions outlined by Sakenfeld).[69] Of course, the use of 'loyalty' for *ḥesed* needs

64. Bowen, 'A Study of ḥsd', p. 51.
65. Bowen, 'A Study of ḥsd', p. 55.
66. Sakenfeld, *The Meaning of* Ḥesed, p. 140.
67. Sakenfeld, *The Meaning of* Ḥesed, p. 142.
68. Sakenfeld, *The Meaning of* Ḥesed, p. 143.
69. Snaith (*The Distinctive Ideas of the Old Testament*), would have agreed with Sakenfeld's use of the word loyalty for *ḥesed*, keeping in mind that, for Snaith, *ḥesed* was limited to covenantal relationships. He had argued that *ḥesed* denotes the attitude of

some qualification. Sakenfeld notes that there are some shortcomings in using loyalty in place of *ḥesed* for English speakers. She explains that 'English usage sometimes equates loyalty with the quite negative concept of blind obedience, which we will find is not part of the biblical picture'.[70] In a biblical perspective *ḥesed* (loyalty) is entirely positive. There is no case in which someone's *ḥesed* is objected to or criticized. Loyalty from a biblical perspective, then, is entirely commendable. Sakenfeld also notes that loyalty is 'often used in English for the attitude that a subordinate should exhibit toward a superior, but rarely the other way round'.[71] Sakenfeld has argued in her previous work that *ḥesed* is performed by a situationally superior person for a situationally inferior person in a serious situation of need in which the superior person is often the only person who can render help to the situationally inferior person. In some way, therefore, Sakenfeld can say that 'the biblical notion of *ḥesed*/loyalty refers more often to just the opposite direction of relationship: the powerful is loyal to the weak or needy or dependent'.[72] Sakenfeld's third qualification in using loyalty for *ḥesed* is that the word *ḥesed* encompasses both the attitude and action and takes the verb 'to do'. She explains that *ḥesed* 'keeps its action-connotation even when such a verb is not present'.[73] The word loyalty, however, does not entail this action connotation. It is understood as the attitude, which needs to be tested by action, but then that act, which would be called *ḥesed*, we must refer to as an 'act of loyalty' or 'demonstration of loyalty'.[74] Sakenfeld thinks that as long as the reader keeps these differences in mind, the term 'loyalty' can be used to explore the concept of *ḥesed*, which she describes as 'faithfulness in action'.[75]

loyalty and faithfulness, which both parties to a covenant should observe towards each other. He argued that 'The word means "faithfulness" rather than "kindness", for we find the word to involve, in almost every case, a substratum of fixed, determined, almost stubborn steadfastness' (p. 99). He concluded his study by comparing *ḥesed* with 'favor, mercy, grace' (*ḥen*), which means 'undeserved favour at the hands of a superior, where there is no bond or covenant between the parties, and no obligation on the superior to do anything at all', but, by contrast, *ḥesed* 'presupposes a covenant, and has from first to last a strong suggestion of fixedness, steadfastness, determined loyalty' (p. 130).

70. Sakenfeld, *Faithfulness in Action*, p. 2.

71. Sakenfeld, *Faithfulness in Action*, p. 2.

72. Sakenfeld, *Faithfulness in Action*, p. 2.

73. Sakenfeld, *Faithfulness in Action*, p. 3. Clark (*The Word* Ḥesed *in the Hebrew Bible*, p. 267) agrees with Sakenfeld, 'חֶסֶד is not merely an attitude or an emotion; it is an emotion that leads to an activity beneficial to the recipient'.

74. Sakenfeld, *Faithfulness in Action*, p. 3.

75. An interesting question is: 'Faithfulness to what/whom?' Is it being faithful to a relationship? This question would invite the language of covenant (or theology). Is it being faithful to 'who we are?' This question would invite the language of ontology and

In spite of these differences, I think loyalty does capture the meaning of *ḥesed* in most cases. Loyalty is the attitude and action appropriate to the relationship characterized by responsibility and freedom. It describes the aspect of *ḥesed* that is practiced within a close relationship or a relationship that is being forged by an act in time of need. I will use the word 'loyalty' for an act of assistance performed as a response to a commitment to a close relationship in a *ḥesed*-situation but also as a desire to form a new relationship or as a response for the sake of God or human solidarity in a *ḥesed*-situation.

Understanding Ḥesed *as a Postcolonial Term*

If Glueck's definition is too general and lax, then Sakenfeld's definition is too specific and restrictive. Sakenfeld insists that it is only when a person performs an act within a pre-existing relationship and in specific conditions that the act can be rendered *ḥesed*. Sakenfeld's parameter for a *ḥesed*-situation gives the impression that the word *ḥesed* was used in a technical sense rather than as a concept rendered to describe general human interaction during a time of need. In my opinion, any act can be called *ḥesed* if that act meets the need of a specific *ḥesed*-situation, either to maintain and sustain a pre-existing *ḥesed*-relationship or to forge a new *ḥesed*-relationship or for the sake of God or human solidarity. For Sakenfeld, the principle of 'moral responsibility and freedom' manages a *ḥesed*-situation; for Glueck, the principle of 'mutual responsibility and obligation' guides a *ḥesed*-relationship. It is difficult to discount the fact that some form of *quid pro quod* is involved in *ḥesed* (that is, *ḥesed* begets *ḥesed*) whether one views it as a voluntary moral responsibility or as a required obligation.[76] I agree with Sakenfeld that freedom is a crucial element under which *ḥesed* can be practiced; the actor is morally responsible but is not contractually or legally obligated to help the person in need. It is up to the individual's moral character or sense of loyalty to do *ḥesed* for the other. The person in need can bring up the relationship that the two parties have, a prior act, or the responsibility all humans have for the sake of God or for human solidarity in order to influence the actor to help, but the person in need cannot resort to external forces to compel the actor to do *ḥesed*. However, what the actor decides to do or not do speaks volumes about his/her (moral) character. One can criticize or praise someone

creation. It involves our obligation or duty of being humans, created by God, who has much *ḥesed* and has given us this quality.

76. Clark (*The Word* Ḥesed *in the Hebrew Bible*, p. 261) agrees with Sakenfeld that commitment is an essential feature of *ḥesed* but agrees with Glueck on the importance of 'a mutual, bilateral commitment, unlike the unilateral commitment proposed by both Hills and Sakenfeld'.

for whether the person responds with *ḥesed* or not. *Ḥesed* describes an act but also reflects the actor's quality as a human being. When a person does *ḥesed*, it says a great deal about his/her sense of loyalty. This point is important when we examine the David story.

I agree with Sakenfeld that in most cases *ḥesed* is practiced within a pre-existing *ḥesed*-relationship. She, however, cannot seem to see an act of assistance performed outside of a relationship as an act of *ḥesed*, dismissing a few examples (Josh. 2.12-14; Judg. 1.24; 1 Kgs 20.23) of such scenarios as an exception to the rule on how *ḥesed* was used. There are enough cases to argue that *ḥesed* occurs within as well as prior to or outside of a relationship in the lived-space of ancient Israel. There is no reason to restrict the use of *ḥesed* to the way it is attested most in the text, especially when there are examples to show it was used in another way. The term was not limited by its ordinary or common meaning and usage; it was used in more than one way. It was open to surprises. Britt understands the importance of these 'exceptional' cases involving parties that are not familiar with each other or do not have existing relationships and argues that these exceptional cases that usually form unexpected relationships reveal the unexpected sense of the term that is as valid as the common understanding:

> For many of the biblical authors, חסד was certainly a well-known term in the liturgical and theological life of ancient Israel. By making its appearance surprising, they were developing a notion of the divine–human covenant as something extraordinary, despite its clear resemblance to ancient treaty formulas.[77]

I would add that not only the divine–human relationship but that the human ('us') to human ('them') relationship is open to extraordinary attachment across various differences and boundaries. God's *ḥesed* is not limited to the covenantal people; similarly, a human is not limited to performing *ḥesed* to another human in a relationship.

Furthermore, Glueck mentioned in passing that it is possible for a *ḥesed*-relationship to emerge among those who rendered help to one another, even if they did not have a relationship before. For Glueck, an act of assistance for a person who was not in a relationship with the actor can be rendered with *ḥesed* because the actor performed *ḥesed* for the sake of God or for the sake of human solidarity (brotherhood). There is no reason to view some cases in which *ḥesed* is practiced outside a pre-existing relationship as exceptions to the rule. *Ḥesed* was employed to describe conduct appropriate to a situation of need motivated by a close relationship, a prior act of assistance (which is another way of saying a pre-existing relationship), or for the sake of God or human solidarity.

77. Britt, 'Unexpected Attachments', p. 307.

In my opinion, Sakenfeld has characterized *ḥesed* as an act of the will and does not give enough attention to the side of *ḥesed* that can be understood as an act of the heart. The word *ḥesed* should be understood as an act involving the heart as well as the will; it is an emotional as well as a moral act. Thus it can also mean an expression of 'affection-and-kindness' that a person can perform for another for the sake of God or for human solidarity, irrespective of whether or not there is a close relationship between them.[78] It is the loyalty side of *ḥesed* that maintains and strengthens existing relationships and the 'affection-and-kindness' side of *ḥesed* that not only lubricates an existing relationship but also allows new relations to emerge across various identity boundaries. It is this side of *ḥesed* that enables those who are separated by differences to create a bond, a tie between them.

I will employ the term *jeong*, a Korean word that roughly means 'affection-and-kindness', to express the side of *ḥesed* that enables 'unexpected attachment' between those who are separated by a variety of boundaries.[79] The word *jeong* describes the aspect of *ḥesed* motivated by love, kindness, and affection, even if there are boundaries separating individuals from forming a 'natural' relationship. It is a word that describes the connectivity that is formed between individuals, thereby creating a bond between individuals who would otherwise be separated by various walls. It is the 'in-between' stuff that makes the connected-ness between individuals possible. This is not an attempt to explain and claim that *jeong*, which is as complicated and multifaceted as *ḥesed*, encompasses the multiple meanings of *ḥesed* or even the side of *ḥesed* that it resembles most strongly. I only wish to explore an understanding of *ḥesed* as a postcolonial term, which is capable of transgressing boundaries that separate individuals from making

78. Although Snaith (*The Distinctive Ideas of the Old Testament*, p. 102) would have agreed with Sakenfeld in understanding *ḥesed* as an act or attitude of loyalty in a (covenantal) relationship, he does not deny that it also has the meanings of 'loving-kindness, mercy'. Alter (*The David Story*, p. 240) expresses a similar sentiment, when he comments on 2 Sam. 9.3 that the 'faith' in question for *ḥesed* is 'not creedal but faithful performance of one's obligation in a covenant, a term that also has the connotation of "kindness"'. On his opening comment on 2 Sam. 10, Alter does not choose one meaning but leaves open both meanings: 'This chapter, like the preceding one, opens with a declaration of David's desire to keep faith with, or do kindness to, the son of a father toward whom he feels some prior obligation' (p. 244).

79. Clark (*The Word* Ḥesed *in the Hebrew Bible*, p. 258) reminds us that *ḥesed* is a rich and varied concept and 'in order to resist the leveling out tendency, it must be remembered that insights gained from individual passages do not necessarily apply to each and every occurrence of the word'. In separating *ḥesed* into two aspects—the side of loyalty and the side of *jeong*—I am trying to highlight the difference between these two usages while maintaining the obvious connection between them and the complexity of the word.

connections. I want to use *jeong* to designate the side of *ḥesed* which involves the heart and reflects the transgressive nature of *ḥesed*.[80]

I remember, before I thought about working on this book, whenever I considered the word *jeong*, the word *ḥesed* came to my mind. I had the privilege of delivering a commencement speech at my graduation, which gave me an opportunity to summarize my time as a doctoral student.[81] I characterized the academic community as a place for producing knowledge but also a place where connections and relationships are formed through acts of *jeong*. I described *jeong* as a Korean word that describes 'stickiness' in people relations, and gave an illustration: 'Think of a bowl of rice. It starts out as hard individual grains, but when you add water and heat and wait a few minutes and then you get grains of rice that stick to one another. That is how *jeong* is formed as well. Individuals become connected through shared experiences and frequent contacts'. I explained that acts of *jeong* can be small as well as great. Any act that fosters connected-ness can be called *jeong*. This was my layman's understanding of *jeong*, which, of course, lacked a serious, systematic analysis; the ancient Israelites probably had a layman's understanding of *ḥesed* as well, which also probably lacked a technical, literary analysis of the word. Of course, *jeong*, like any other concepts, has many complex layers of meaning, but it is not my intention to explicate its multiple meanings here. I wish to explain why I think using *jeong* will be helpful in seeing *ḥesed* as a postcolonial term and Joh's work on *jeong* is helpful in articulating this view.

Joh explains that *jeong* 'emerges out of relationships that are not always based on mutuality. Jeong has the capacity to transgress clear and even forbidden boundaries that maintain the separation between Self and Other'.[82] She defends this characteristic of *jeong* by comparing it with *eros*, and notes a trait that is common between these two concepts: 'Just as Western scholars

80. For an articulation of *jeong* as a postcolonial term, see W.A. Joh, 'The Transgressive Power of Jeong: A Postcolonial Hybridization of Christology', in C. Keller, M. Nausner and M. Rivera (eds.), *Postcolonial Theologies: Divinity and Empire* (St Louis, MO: Chalice Press, 2004), pp. 149-63 and *Heart of the Cross: A Postcolonial Christology* (Louisville, KY: Westminster/John Knox Press, 2006).

81. Kim, 'Knowledge and *Jeong* on "Holy Hill"', a speech delivered at the GTU Commencement, 13 May 2004: http://www.gtu.edu/news-events/events/lectures-and-addresses/other-lectures/knowledge-and-jeong-on-holy-hill.

82. Joh, 'The Transgressive Power of Jeong', p. 153. She expounds on this point in her book (*Heart of the Cross*, p. 122) that *jeong* 'often functions to trespass given parameters, boundaries, and norms. Contesting both borders and places of difference, *jeong* is present within the gaps and fissures, and in the uncomfortable and often painful interstitial spaces. Because *jeong* moves freely and is embodied across diverse borders and boundaries, life becomes much more complex. The power of *jeong* lies in its ability to wedge itself into the smallest gaps between the oppressed and the oppressor'.

have often referred to *eros* as "sticky", so too have their Korean counterparts referred to jeong as "sticky"'.[83] She calls *jeong* 'the power of eros' that

> forges its presence in the interval between the Self and the Other. It thus blurs the sharply constructed boundary between the Self and the Other while allowing one to move beyond the edges of the Self into the Other and vice versa. Jeong is a supplement that comes into the interstitial site of relationality.[84]

But she maintains that *jeong* is not love, although it shares some critical characteristics with *eros*. She also notes that it is not 'completely identifiable with compassion alone' but that *jeong* 'connotes agape, eros, and filial love with compassion, empathy, solidarity, and understanding that emerges between hearts of connectedness in relationality. *Jeong* is a supplement that comes into the interstitial site of relationalism. *Jeong* is rooted in relationalism'.[85] It is this trait of *jeong* that reminds us that 'the life of the self is inextricably connected with the well-being of the other and vice versa. We are, in effect, locked into life with the other. We are permeable selves, and this boundary of the permeable self breaches the impossible possible'.[86] It is this trait of *jeong* to forge unexpected connections across various boundaries that, I believe, reflects one side of *ḥesed* that needs to be identified and explicated.

There are some qualifications needed in order to use *jeong* to render the side of *ḥesed* that involves the heart more than the side that involves moral responsibility. First, *ḥesed* takes the verb *'āśah* ('to do, to perform'), whereas *jeong* does not takes the verb 'to do'. *Jeong* takes verbs such as 'to give' or 'to share' but not 'to do'. Therefore, *jeong* denotes acts that are less concrete than *ḥesed*, which may influence me to consider some 'acts' that are not normally concrete enough to be considered *ḥesed* as *ḥesed*. Second, *ḥesed* commonly describes an act, not an attitude or an attribute of the actor, whereas *jeong* is used as much to denote an attribute of a person as to render an act. So, it is high praise to hear Koreans say that someone has much *jeong*, whereas having no *jeong* indicates that the person lacks kindness, humaneness, or even Korean-ness. One can describe an act as a great *ḥesed* but it is not often used to describe the actor as having a great deal of *ḥesed*. However, *ḥesed* is used in a similar sense to *jeong* in the description of the kings of Israel, namely as having *ḥesed* as their attribute: Ben-hadad's servants suggest to him to go and seek mercy from Ahab because 'Look, we have heard that the kings of the house of Israel are kings of *ḥesed*' (1 Kgs 20.31; my translation). Here *ḥesed* is a known trait of the kings of Israel,

83. Joh, 'The Transgressive Power of Jeong', p. 154.
84. Joh, 'The Transgressive Power of Jeong', p. 153.
85. Joh, *Heart of the Cross*, p. 120.
86. Joh, *Heart of the Cross*, p. 64.

including Ahab, and the conclusion of this passage proves it to be true (1 Kgs 20.31-34). It is safe, then, to say that *ḥesed* can be an attribute of God and humans but is used more often to describe an act. Third, *ḥesed* usually stands alone and it is often not obvious with which type of *ḥesed* one is dealing.[87] It is up to the reader to determine whether one is faced with the loyalty side or the *jeong* side of *ḥesed*. *Jeong*, however, is usually qualified by other characters (words) to indicate with which type of *jeong* is mean.[88]

Some may question why I would introduce a term like *jeong*, another 'foreign' term, used in modern Korea, to talk about a complicated term like *ḥesed*, used in ancient Israel and Judah. First, it is to remind readers that they are, in fact, dealing with a term (*ḥesed*) that is 'foreign' and to encourage them to expect the unfamiliar aspects of *ḥesed*. Even though it is a familiar concept and a widely experienced notion even to contemporary readers, I do not wish readers to get too comfortable with words like loyalty, loving-kindness, faithfulness, goodness, and so on, which are too common and familiar to them. Such familiarity or understanding could impede them from recognizing the unexpected and unanticipated quality of *ḥesed*, especially as a notion that facilitates attachments across various differences and boundaries. This strategy of 'defamiliarization' is used so that one can see surprising qualities and attachments in a familiar concept.

Second, I have already made clear that I am going to use the word 'loyalty' to reflect one side of *ḥesed*, but there is another side of *ḥesed*, especially its ability to cross boundaries to form connected-ness, which can be expressed better by the term *jeong* than English words like 'kindness' or 'affection'. It will give readers a pause and perhaps help them to be mindful of this aspect of *ḥesed* whenever they encounter the word *jeong*.

Third, the use of *jeong* opens a postcolonial conversation on the subject and reminds readers that we are moving fast toward, if we are not already here, a global context in which non-Western participants and non-Western terms and ideas are also at the table of discussion. There was a time not long ago when all students of the Bible had to learn to say *Heilsgeschichte*! Is it

87. There are two cases in which *ḥesed* is qualified: *ḥesed* of God/Yahweh and *ḥesed we'emeṯ*. In the former case, it indicates an attribute of God. In the latter case, according to Clark (*The Word* Ḥesed *in the Hebrew Bible*, p. 259), the terms *'emeṯ* and *'emūnah* are essential components of *ḥesed*, emphasizing the enduring strength or stubborness of *ḥesed*. In both cases, however, they alone do not signal which type of *ḥesed* is denoted in the text.

88. Joh ('The Transgressive Power of Jeong', p. 155) notes that there are two different kinds of *jeong*: *mi-uwn jeong* and *go-eun jeong*. 'The former emerges within mutual and satisfactory relationships. The latter emerges out of and in spite of relationships full of discontent.' She also notes that *jeong* has been categorized but not limited to the following relationships: between parent and child, between lovers, and between friends (p. 156).

such a stretch to imagine a time not too long in the future when some students of the Bible from the West will have learned to say *jeong*?

A few more clarifications before we turn to the story. The presence of *ḥesed* is not limited to passages that mention the word *ḥesed*; there are narratives that do not have the word *ḥesed* yet reflect the concept of *ḥesed*. Sakenfeld objects to Snaith's work, which used the concept of *ḥesed* in discussing some narratives even though the word does not occur in them. She argues against 'Snaith's tendency to see *ḥesed* everywhere once a general meaning has been established', even in texts where the word does not occur.[89] She thinks Snaith has made a serious mistake in doing this. I disagree with her view that Snaith's use of *ḥesed* as an idea that was central to texts in which it does not occur is a serious mistake. An idea of *ḥesed* can be communicated without using the word. Obviously the burden of proof falls on the interpreter to convince the reader of the idea of *ḥesed* in a text in which the word does not occur. It is safe to examine only texts that have the word *ḥesed* in them; however, there are passages where an act can be described as *ḥesed* or a situation as a *ḥesed*-situation even if the word does not appear in the text. There are texts where the reader can say, 'That's *ḥesed*!' even without a prompting from the text. Similar to the way biblical interpreters saw ideas of covenant, love, salvation history, and so on in texts that do not mention these words, I see no reason to restrict seeing the idea of *ḥesed* only in texts in which the word occurs.

In his comprehensive study on the word *ḥesed*, Clark notes that the method employed by previous scholars, including Glueck and Sakenfeld, on *ḥesed* was a contextual study of a word, focusing on the word *ḥesed* and investigating it in the various contexts in which it appears but with little attention to other words that frequently occur with it.[90] He reports that his study has confirmed 'insights gained in previous studies' and produced 'insights into the nature and meaning of חֶסֶד that have escaped the attention of previous investigators'.[91] We will look in summary fashion at some of his results in order to recognize the idea of *ḥesed* reflected in the narratives where other words with close approximation of *ḥesed* appear in the texts.

89. Sakenfeld, *The Meaning of* Ḥesed, p. 6.

90. In his work, *The Word* Ḥesed *in the Hebrew Bible*, Clark uses principles of structural linguistics to investigate which words appear in close proximity with *ḥesed* and how these words affect its meaning. He relies on a computer to generate and organize a vast amount of data to present *ḥesed* in relationship with other words. His work examines the linguistic environment in which the word *ḥesed* occurs, which he argues will supplement the situational contexts of these occurrences. His study focuses more on the word itself than on the meanings of the word. He maintains that it is not his desire to supplant the method employed by previous studies but rather to use the lexical method alongside these so that they supplement one another.

91. Clark, *The Word* Ḥesed *in the Hebrew Bible*, p. 256.

Clark's study confirms the suggestion that טוֹב (*ṭôḇ*, 'goodness') is a close approximation to *ḥesed*. His study reveals that 'חֶסֶד and טוֹב can be regarded as synonyms according to the parameters that Sakenfeld set for situations in which חֶסֶד is the expected response'.[92] Clark's study, however, also shows a significant difference between *ḥesed* and *ṭôḇ*: 'a closer examination of passages in which טוֹב is substituted for חֶסֶד in syntagms containing the verb עשׂה reveals a commitment between the parties involved when חֶסֶד, but not when טוֹב, is used'.[93] It is the commitment to each other, not necessarily to the relationship, that sets *ḥesed* apart from *ṭôḇ*. His study also examines the connection between derivatives of *rḥm* ('compassion', 'mercy') and *ḥesed* and shows that they resemble each other closely. But what distinguishes *ḥesed* from *rḥm* is similar to the difference between *ḥesed* and *ṭôḇ*: 'commitment between participants is important with חֶסֶד but not with רַחֲמִים'.[94] Many have noted significant differences between these two terms. Clark's study also supports earlier studies that found several features that distinguish *ḥesed* from *ḥēn*. *Ḥēn* refers to an action that passes from a superior to an inferior, whereas, with *ḥesed*, status of participants does not matter, just as Sakenfeld argued that the situational position of participants is important, not the status of participants. *Ḥēn* is used chiefly of people between whom there is no specific tie or bond, whereas *ḥesed* refers generally to people between whom there is a close relationship. Moreover, Clark reiterates that 'commitment between participants is important with *ḥesed* but not with the *ḥēn* derivatives'.[95]

Clark's study confirms that commitment (or loyalty) to another individual in a relationship is an essential component of situations in which an individual extends *ḥesed* to another. This feature reflects the loyalty side of *ḥesed* and it is appropriate to keep some distinction between *ḥesed* and the words noted above—*ṭôḇ* ('good'), *raḥămîm* ('mercy, compassion'), *ḥēn* ('grace, favor'), and also derivatives of *'hb* ('love') and *'mn* ('faithfulness')—in mind. However, this does not mean that we should refrain from considering these words as reflecting the idea of *ḥesed*. The *jeong* side of *ḥesed* has close affinities with these words even though these words have a noted difference from the loyalty side of *ḥesed*. For the *jeong* side of *ḥesed*, commitment is not necessary to a relationship or to an individual in a relationship but can be to God or human solidarity in which commitment is implicit rather than explicit. Therefore, I will examine with caution these words to see whether they reflect the idea of the *jeong* side of *ḥesed* whenever they appear in the text.

92. Clark, *The Word* Ḥesed *in the Hebrew Bible*, p. 260.
93. Clark, *The Word* Ḥesed *in the Hebrew Bible*, p. 260.
94. Clark, *The Word* Ḥesed *in the Hebrew Bible*, p. 263.
95. Clark, *The Word* Ḥesed *in the Hebrew Bible*, p. 263.

Finally, *ḥesed* is a postcolonial term that can be used to describe practices that foster the crossing of ethnic, tribal, or religious boundaries as well as maintain and strengthen existing relationships. In the following chapters, both the loyalty and *jeong* sides of *ḥesed* will be employed to read the David story.

3

Raising David on *Ḥesed*: 1 Samuel 1–2 Samuel 5

I will begin this chapter with a short summary of the content of the first half of the David story and how I am going to indicate the idea of *ḥesed* in the narrative. First Samuel responds to the problem noted at the end of the book of Judges: 'In those days there was no king in Israel; all the people did what was right in their own eyes' (Judg. 21.25). There are voices for and against the establishment of kingship in 1 Samuel, but the opening story indicates that it is a foregone conclusion that Israel will have its king. First Samuel opens with a petition for a son by a barren woman named Hannah (1 Sam. 1), who praises God with a song when God grants her request (1 Sam. 2.1-11), which proclaims God's king/anointed. Who is Yahweh's king and anointed? Hannah's son Samuel is not the one for whom the people are waiting. He may have been utterly faithful to God, but his sons pervert justice by taking bribes and by seeking gain (1 Sam. 8.3). The failure of his sons to live up to the standards of judges gives the people an opening to ask for a king. Samuel does not want to give in to the people's request, but God instructs him to do so, thereby effectively ending God's 'forever' promise to him. Then God chooses Saul, who stands head and shoulders above the others, as God's anointed and Israel's king but is quickly rejected (1 Sam. 13 and 15). The narrator claims that Saul disobeyed God's instructions, therefore Samuel declares that God will abandon him for another man: 'The Lord would have established your kingdom over Israel forever, but now your kingdom will not continue; the Lord has sought out a man after his own heart; and the Lord has appointed him to be ruler over his people, because you have not kept what the Lord commanded you' (1 Sam. 13.13-14).

It is a ruddy shepherd boy whom God has chosen (1 Sam. 16) and who will eventually shepherd the people of Judah and Israel (2 Sam. 5.2). Once David appears in the narrative, 1 Samuel focuses on why David is God's choice instead of Saul and ends with the ignominious death of Saul (1 Sam. 31). Second Samuel opens with David learning of Saul's death, thus picking up the story where 1 Samuel left off. The people of Judah immediately anoint David their king upon the news of Saul's death (2 Sam. 2.1-4). Several years of war ensue between the house of David and those who remain loyal to the house of Saul. When Abner, the commander of Israel's army, is killed by Joab (2 Sam. 3) and Ishbaal son of Saul is assassinated by his own servants (2 Sam. 4), the people of the northern tribes quickly embrace David as their king, making David king of Judah and Israel (2 Sam. 5.1-5). Then David consolidates his kingdom and builds his house in Jerusalem (2 Sam. 5.6-12), which belongs neither to Israel nor Judah, a space of his own from which to rule the diverse population of his kingdom.

This chapter of the study is divided into five sections: The Selection and Rejection of the House of Eli and the House of Samuel (1 Sam. 1–8); The Selection and Rejection of Saul (1 Sam. 9–15); The Selection of David and the Friendship of David and Jonathan (1 Sam. 16–20); From a Fugitive to a Bodyguard of Achish (1 Sam. 21–30); and From Saul's Death to Becoming King of Judah and Israel (1 Sam. 31.1–2 Sam. 5.12). In each section I will focus on passages in which the idea of *ḥesed* is evident and examine characters who embody some aspect of *ḥesed*. David, of course, will be the main focus throughout these sections. As we read through the narrative, we will be asking whether David is indeed a man of *ḥesed*. We will see that he is a master negotiator of *ḥesed* who receives much loyalty and *jeong* from everyone around him and especially from God without giving much of it in return. It is his remarkable talent in using *ḥesed* from all sorts of people and from God that enables him to establish his kingdom.

In order to see longer thematic threads of *ḥesed* as well as individual narratives of loyalty and *jeong* in the narrative, I will do the following to identify the idea of *ḥesed* in this chapter. First, I will pay attention to passages that contain the word *ḥesed*: 1 Sam. 2.1-10 (the word appearing in v. 9); 15.1-35 (v. 6); 20.1-42 (vv. 8 and 14); 2 Sam. 2.1-7 (vv. 5 and 6). Second, I will explore the passages containing the words *ṭôb* ('good'), *ḥēn* ('grace, favor'), and derivatives of *'hb* ('love') and *'mn* ('faithfulness') to see whether they reflect the idea of *ḥesed* (both loyalty and *jeong* sides) in the narrative. Third, I will indicate some episodes and characters I think reflect the idea of *ḥesed*. I will employ the word 'loyalty' to indicate one aspect of *ḥesed*. In some cases I will indicate the loyalty side of *ḥesed* with 'loyalty (*ḥesed*)' or '*ḥesed* (loyalty)'. In cases where I want to indicate the *jeong* side of *ḥesed*, I will use simply '*jeong*' or sometimes '*jeong* (*ḥesed*)' or '*ḥesed* (*jeong*)'. To give some stylistic variation as well as to make writing less wooden, I will use other English words that reflect the idea of *ḥesed* and indicate them by placing *ḥesed* or *jeong* in parentheses next to them.

The Selection and Rejection of the House of Eli and the House of Samuel (1 Samuel 1–8)

The idea of *ḥesed* runs through the entire narrative of David. Some are loyal and some are not. Some are loyal to one party but not to the other. Some will be betrayed by those who are closest to them. Saul is loyal to God and Samuel, but they think he has betrayed them. Saul extends his *ḥesed* to others, but he is rejected repeatedly. David does not give, but others give him their love and allegiance. God extends *ḥesed* to David but withdraws support (*ḥesed*) from Eli, Samuel, and Saul. But we are getting ahead of the story. Before David appears, the narrator prepares to depict David as a man of *ḥesed* who deserves God's *ḥesed* and people's loyalty and *jeong*.

This section begins with a story of *ḥesed*.[1] Hannah is barren and her rival Peninnah, who has produced sons and daughters, has been pestering her over the years. Perhaps Peninnah and Hannah and their relationship parallel the Philistines and the Israelites and their contentious relationship. The Philistines, who settled along the coast through which the major trade route (the Way of the Sea) runs, are more wealthy and advanced in technology than the Israelites who are living in the highlands, somewhat isolated from the major trade routes (the Way of the Sea to the west and the King's Highway to the east). We will see that the Philistines pose a major threat to the survival of the Israelites.

The text makes it clear that her husband 'Elkanah loved Hannah' (*'et ḥannah 'āhēb*; 1 Sam. 1.5), perhaps more than Peninnah, even though Hannah has not produced a son. God, symbolized by Elkanah, loves Israel despite the fact that she is not productive. God is attached to Israel emotionally as well as politically; God will care for and extend his *ḥesed* to her. For now nothing can console Hannah ('a favored one'). Even her husband's affection (*jeong*) reflected in his words do not comfort her: 'Hannah, why do you weep? Why do you not eat? Why is your heart sad? Am I not more [*ṭôb*] to you than ten sons?' (1.8). These are words arising out of *jeong*, but Elkanah cannot reach out to his wife. God also will speak out of *jeong* to Israel, but God too will discover that his *ḥesed* is not enough for Israel. Elkanah is hurt because he is not good (*ṭôb*) enough to appease her. His affection and loyalty cannot meet Hannah's practical needs, namely to acquire a son. To Hannah nothing can ease her heart until God gives her a son just as Israel will not be satisfied until God gives her a king.[2] God's affection and loyalty do not

1. Brueggemann (*First and Second Samuel*, p. 15) comments that the subject of the first chapter of 1 Samuel is 'Yahweh's astonishing fidelity and Hannah's responding fidelity'.

2. In his reading of the final form of 1 Samuel, R. Polzin (*Samuel and the Deuteronomist: A Literary Study of the Deuteronomistic History*. Part 2. *1 Samuel*. [Bloomington:

satisfy Israel's political needs; they need a king who will deliver them from their enemies all around, especially the Philistines.

Hannah proposes a *quid pro quod* to God. If God gives her a son, she will dedicate her son to God's service (1.11). From the beginning of the narrative, a tension between the outer appearance (what is apparent to the eyes) and the inner motives (from the heart) is evident. This theme of how things appear to the eyes and to the heart will run through the narrative. While Hannah is initiating a *ḥesed*-relationship with God, Eli the priest sees her and mistakes her for a drunk. But he learns that she is, in fact, a sincere woman of *ḥesed*. When Eli acknowledges her pledge (without knowing what the pledge is) and assures her that God will grant her wish, Hannah accepts his acknowledgment as *ḥēn* ('favor'; perhaps a polite way of expressing *ḥesed*) in 'his [Eli's or perhaps God's] eyes' (1.18). For Hannah, Eli's assurance seals the *ḥesed*-relationship between God and herself.

God extends *ḥesed* to Hannah by giving her a son, Samuel, and she is loyal to the *ḥesed*-relationship by loaning (*šā'ûl*) him to God.[3] Elkanah, in turn, understands the arrangement and permits Hannah—'Do what seems good in your eyes' (1.23)—to stay with the baby until he is weaned. In due time Hannah returns God's loyalty (*ḥesed*) with her own act of fidelity by leaving her son Samuel with Eli (1.28). Immediately, Hannah praises God with a song (2.1-10). Just as the story in ch. 1 demonstrates God's faithfulness to Hannah's cry for help, inverting the situation of barrenness to the celebration of birth and life, the song celebrates God's power to turn things upside down (2.4-8). Such reversals anticipate a change in Israel's fortune

Indiana University Press, 1989], p. 25) notes that in the first four chapters of 1 Samuel 'no other specific requests are made of the LORD in these chapters, so that there is a solid basis in the text for suggesting that the story of Hannah's request for a son is intended to introduce, foreshadow, and ideologically comment upon the story of Israel's request for a king'. Therefore, he states, 'the story in chapter 1 about how and why God agreed to give Hannah a son, Samuel, is an artistic prefiguring of the larger story in 1 Samuel about how and why God agreed to give Israel a king' (p. 26). Polzin understands the story of Hannah as a parable that prefigures the larger narrative in 1 Samuel and chs. 1 to 7 which consist of parables, serving as a preview of the entire monarchic history. Moreover, he argues that characters in chs. 1–7 all do double duty: 'Hannah was the mother of Samuel, but she also stood for Israel requesting a king. Elkanah was a slighted but loving husband, but he also introduced us to a God rejected by his people. Eli was the scion of a fallen priestly house, but in addition he was a royal figure falling to his death. Samuel himself was a priest, judge, and prophet certainly, but he also represented Saul (chap. 1), a victorious David (chaps. 2–4), and an idealized judge who would succeed to leadership in exilic times (chap. 7)' (p. 81).

3. Samuel and Saul's lives will be intertwined, often in conflict, throughout the narrative. We see what is to come in this birth narrative. The narrator claims that this is Samuel's birth narrative but the text suggests that it is Saul's name that fits better.

vis-à-vis the Philistines; the Philistines have the upper hand for now but soon the Israelites will have the advantage. The reason God can do this is, 'For the pillars of the earth are the Lord's, and on them he has set the world' (2.8). It is God's world! There is, however, one principle God will honor: 'He will guard the feet of his faithful ones [*ḥăsîdaw*], but the wicked shall be cut off in darkness' (2.9).[4] Surprisingly the song ends with a 'prediction' of God's king and anointed: God 'will give strength to his king, and exalt the power of his anointed' (2.10). God will bring about this reversal through his anointed/king. Who is this anointed/king? Is it Samuel after whose dedication of service this song is being sung? Is it Saul who is actually being loaned (*šā'ûl*) to God? No. We all know, however, that it is David, who will not make his entrance into the narrative until ch. 16, who is God's anointed of this song. David's song toward the end of his story reveals that David himself is God's anointed in Hannah's song: 'He is a tower of salvation for his king, and shows steadfast love [*ḥesed*] to his anointed, to David and his descendants forever' (2 Sam. 22.51). We must wait, however, to see to whom the anointed of this song is referring and to whom God wants to extend *ḥesed*. For now Hannah is portrayed as a faithful woman who honors her promise, and God acknowledges her loyalty and continues this *ḥesed*-relationship by providing more children to her (2.21).

Eli the priest is the incumbent leader of Israel when Samuel is put under his supervision. The text reveals that God has apparently made an eternal promise to the house of Eli to be God's priestly family forever. God sends a man of God and tells Eli, 'I promised that your family and the family of your ancestor should go in an out before me forever' (2.30), but now God qualifies this 'forever' promise with a principle of *quid pro quod*: 'Far be it from me; for those who honor [*kbd*] me I will honor [*kbd*], and those who despise [*bzh*] me shall be treated with contempt [*qll*]' (2.30). The problem is evident in the introduction of Eli's sons: 'Eli's sons were sons of *beliyaal*' (*bĕnê 'ēlî bĕnê bĕlîyā'al*). Throughout the narrative the narrator deliberately contrasts those men who are considered loyal and those who are not. According to McCarter, *bĕnê haḥayil* ('sons of valour') specifically connotes loyalty, warriors or soldiers who 'may be depended upon for loyal service', and *bĕnê bĕlîyā'al* ('sons of worthlessness') suggests 'a traitor or disloyal individual'.[5] It is because Eli's sons have been disloyal to God by taking more than the allotted share of the burnt offering (2.12-17) and the fact that Eli has overlooked their disloyalty and honored (*kbd*) his sons more than God (2.29) that God decides to rescind his promise. Eli's two sons, Hophni and

4. David's song in 2 Sam. 22 reiterates this principle: 'With the loyal [*ḥāsîd*] you show yourself loyal [*titḥassād*]...and with the crooked you show yourself perverse' (2 Sam. 22.26-27).

5. McCarter, *I Samuel*, p. 94.

Phinehas, have shown contempt to God; therefore, God decides to void this promise.[6] God now rejects the house of Eli and delivers a judgment on it through the mouth of young Samuel: 'Therefore I swear to the house of Eli that the iniquity of Eli's house shall not be expiated by sacrifice or offering forever' (3.14). Eli accepts God's decision: 'It is the Lord; let him do what is good in his eyes' (3.18; my translation).

God swiftly moves to dishonor Eli and his family just as they have dishonored him. Hophni and Phinehas are killed in a battle (4.11) and Eli dies upon hearing the news of his sons' death and the capture of the ark (4.18). However, the house of Eli continues to be active in the narrative. We find Ahijah (son of Ahitub son of Phinehas son of Eli) in the service of Saul (14.3). Abiathar (son of Ahimelech son of Ahitub son of Phinehas son of Eli), the sole survivor of Saul's massacre of the priests at Nob, serves as David's priest (22.20), but in the end Abiathar is banished to Anathoth by Solomon for taking the side of Adonijah: 'So Solomon banished Abiathar from being priest to the Lord, thus fulfilling the word of the Lord that he had spoken concerning the house of Eli in Shiloh' (1 Kgs 2.27). Nevertheless, God does not abandon the house of Eli completely. Priests from the house of Eli will rise again from Anathoth and continue to serve God in the larger narrative (the DH) and in the history of Israel.[7]

In place of Eli God chooses Samuel. God says, 'I will raise up for myself a faithful [*ne'ĕmān*] priest, who shall do according to what is in my heart [*bilbābî*] and in my mind. I will build him a sure house [*bayit ne'ĕmān*], and he shall go in and out before my anointed one forever' (2.35). God promises to raise the house of Samuel as the priestly line that will serve God forever.[8]

6. Brueggemann (*First and Second Samuel*, p. 23) states, 'It turns out that Yahweh's promise "for ever" was stringently conditional... In this theological tradition, responsive obedience is required even for God's most sweeping promises'. We will see that God's 'forever' promise to David is different from God's *ḥesed* to the house of Eli (also to the house of Samuel and to the house of Saul) in that there are no strings attached to the *ḥesed* extended to the house of David. God makes a provision to continue his *ḥesed* to the Davidides even if they become disloyal to him (2 Sam. 7).

7. It turns out that Jeremiah was from Anathoth and his father Hilkiah was probably the one mentioned in 2 Kgs 22 who served as the high priest during Josiah's reign. Jer. 1.1 notes that there were priests in Anathoth. It is beyond the scope of this study but it is safe to assume with some confidence that Jeremiah and the priests from Anathoth had some influences on Josiah's reform and the formation of the DH. This shows in my opinion that God's *ḥesed* is 'sticky'. In what seems like a severed relationship due to the unfaithfulness on the part of Eli's family, God's *jeong* continues to reach out to them and desires to maintain a bond. It seems a *ḥesed*-relationship with God cannot be easily severed. God has too much *jeong* to completely disconnect from us in spite of our disloyalty.

8. One can argue that the 'faithful priest' refers to Zadok whose 'house' becomes the priestly line in the service of the house of David; however, in the narrative at this

It looks like Samuel is a good choice. He shows uncompromising loyalty to God throughout the narrative, although we will see that he shows no *jeong* to Saul or the people. He trusts that God will deliver the people from the Philistines even though the Philistines seem to be better organized and have a technological advantage over the Israelites.[9] Samuel's faith (*ḥesed*) in God is steadfast (*'mn*), but his loyalty to God is one dimensional and unforgiving. Samuel witnesses the ark being captured by the Philistines and coming back in glory (4.1–7.2), and this event must have bolstered his confidence in God's *ḥesed* for Israel.

Chapter 7 presents us with a renewal of the *ḥesed*-relationship between God and Israel. Samuel reminds the people of the *ḥesed*-relationship with Yahweh: God will deliver them from their enemies if the people demonstrate loyalty. He demands that the people put away other gods and serve only (*lĕbaddô*) Yahweh so that God can deliver them from the hand of the Philistines (7.3-4).[10] The Israelites are expected to serve only Yahweh and are not allowed to serve other gods or the king; this is the only way to show their *ḥesed* to God in the DH. From Samuel, God demands an uncompromising loyalty from the people, and later from Saul as well. Samuel is utterly obedient to God and expects others to do the same. Samuel is a picture of unyielding loyalty. The people obey Samuel's call for repentance and 'Israel put away the Baals and the Astartes, and they served the Lord only' (7.4). They renew the *ḥesed*-relationship with God, which is tantamount to accepting Samuel to rule over them (7.6); they ask Samuel to pray on their behalf so that God will deliver them from the Philistines. They are negotiating a *ḥesed*-relationship with God, with Samuel as the mediator. They will be loyal solely to Yahweh in return for God's deliverance from the Philis-

juncture, the term refers naturally to Samuel. Therefore, God promises to Samuel 'a sure house', just as he did to Eli and will do to Saul and then to David.

9. In 1 Sam. 4.1, Israel 'went forth to meet to do battle (*wayyēṣē' liqra't... lammilḥāhah*) with the Philistines' whereas the Philistines 'formed ranks to meet (*wayya'arkû liqra't*) Israel' (4.2); this may indicate that the army of the Philistines were more organized than the militia of Israelites. It is not until 17.2 that the Israelites under Saul form ranks for battle to meet (*wayya'arkû milḥāmah liqra't*) the Philistines. Moreover, the Philistines controlled the metal and the technology needed to make swords and spears (13.19-22).

10. Brueggemann (*First and Second Samuel*, p. 49) remarks, 'The demand of Samuel is that Israel belongs only to Yahweh and not be permitted any other loyalty'. Polzin (*Samuel and the Deuteronomist*, p. 74), notes that the addition of *lĕbaddô* ('alone' or 'only') is significant. Although the phrase 'to serve the Lord' occurs frequently in the DH, it occurs with the term *lĕbaddô*, 'to serve the Lord alone', only here in 7.3-4. Polzin states, 'Even when Samuel later recalls Israel's habitual promises to serve the LORD (12.10) and repeatedly admonishes the nation to do so (12.14, 20, 24), he never adds the exclusive term *lebaddo*'.

tines. While Samuel offers up the burnt offering to confirm their commitment to the relationship, the Philistines draw near to attack them, but God makes his presence known—'the Lord thundered with a mighty voice'—and enables the Israelites to defeat the Philistines (7.10-11).

The *ḥesed*-relationship is in place between God and Israel, and Samuel and his family are to rule over Israel. A *quid pro quod* relationship is established with each party having responsibility and freedom to honor it. All Israel has to do is serve Yahweh only and God will deliver them from its enemies through Samuel and his family. There are consequences for failing to live up to the relationship. Unfortunately, Samuel's sons are no better than Eli's sons, and this promise to the house of Samuel is no surer than the one God made to the house of Eli. His sons, Joel and Abijah, who also are judges over Israel, 'did not follow in his ways, but turned aside after gain; they took bribes and perverted justice' (8.3).[11] The people use the failure of Samuel's sons as an opportunity to request a king to rule over them. Samuel is displeased. He seems to take this personally, as a personal attack against him. He thinks the people are being disloyal to him by requesting a king. By revoking their commitment to it they show that they do not want to continue a *ḥesed*-relationship with Samuel and his family. God reassures him that they did not reject him: the Lord said to Samuel, 'Listen to the voice of the people in all that they say to you; for they have not rejected you, but they have rejected me from being king over them' (8.7). Even after Samuel's stern warning about the disadvantages of having a king, the people are determined to have a king over them. God concedes, but Samuel seems unwilling and tells the people, 'Each of you return home' (8.22).[12] Nevertheless, it is certain that the house of Samuel will not continue to serve God as priests and to rule or judge over the people.[13] God does not choose Samuel's sons

11. Eli falls out of God's favor because his sons show contempt to God, and Eli honors his sons more than God. Samuel's 'sure house' is undone by his sons, who being judges (*šōpĕṭîm*) did not practice justice (*mišpaṭ*). Later Saul loses his kingship when his own children 'love' David ('one who is loved') more than him. David's reign almost comes to an end when his son Absalom steals the heart of the people. But God intervenes in David's case and sustains David's reign with *ḥesed*.

12. Polzin (*Samuel and the Deuteronomist*, p. 83) argues that the narrative characterizes Samuel, who appears to be imperceptive in ch. 3, as 'a stubborn, self-interested judge in ch. 8, who for his own reasons is slow to do the LORD's will'.

13. In Samuel's farewell address to the people in ch. 12, he tries one more time to place his sons to rule over Israel: 'I am old and gray, but my sons are with you' (12.2). But the people ignore his hint. Then Samuel rants about how great a sin the people committed by requesting a king, thus severing a relationship with him and his family and effectively ending 'a sure house'. Samuel does not accept this quietly; he calls upon God to send thunder and rain. God obliges, and the people are in a great fear. Samuel comes back to his senses and reassures the people that he will continue to pray for them.

to rule over Israel but will send Samuel to anoint another man to be a ruler over Israel.

A final reflection on this section is needed. It is interesting to note that Hannah is all about the loyalty side of *ḥesed*, a calculatable principle of *quid pro quod* in action, whereas Elkanah reflects *jeong*, the softer, kinder, more affectionate side of *ḥesed*. Eli the priest reflects the *jeong* side of *ḥesed*, a kind and meek man whose fatherly affection and kindness leaves him vulnerable to his children's manipulation (like David in the second half of the narrative), and Samuel represents without any doubt the loyalty side of *ḥesed*. God demonstrates both sides. We will see that Saul gives more *ḥesed* than he receives. It is only David who receives more *ḥesed* than he gives.

The Selection and Rejection of Saul (1 Samuel 9–15)

God now turns to selecting a king. Saul is the man God chooses. Saul's three-fold selection process unfolds in the narrative: Samuel anoints Saul in private (1 Sam. 10.1-2); Saul is taken by lot in front of all the tribes of Israel at Mizpah, but there are some who question Saul's ability to do the job (10.17-27); and Saul's kingship is renewed by Samuel and the people before God in Gilgal (11.14-15).[14] The narrator first introduces Saul's father Kish with a long genealogy, which indicates that he is a man of some standing and pedigree. He is also called *gibbôr ḥayil* ('mighty man of valour'), which the NRSV translates as 'a man of wealth'. I mentioned above a synonymous term, *bĕnê haḥayil*, which connotes loyalty and designates those who may be depended upon for loyal service. Then Saul is introduced as 'a handsome [*ṭôb*] young man'—in fact, 'there was not a man among the people of Israel more handsome [*ṭôb*] than he; he stood head and shoulders above everyone else' (9.2). Saul is no doubt an outstanding physical specimen; his outer appearance must have made a striking impression on the eyes. Of course, this is the point the narrator wants to make, that we should not trust our eyes. We will hear this lesson loud and clear when Samuel is taken in by the physical appearance of David's brothers and wants to anoint one after another. God reprimands Samuel, 'Do not look on his appearance or on the height of his stature, because I have rejected him; for the Lord does not see as mortals see; they look on the outward appearance, but the Lord looks on the heart' (16.7). However, in Saul's case Samuel has nothing to do with his choice. He sees Saul after God chooses him. It is entirely God's decision. Therefore,

14. V.P. Long (*The Art of Biblical History* [Foundations of Contemporary Interpretation, 5; Grand Rapids: Zondervan, 1994], pp. 205-23), rather than seeing these three different 'selections' of Saul as an indication of different sources in the narrative, summarizes the view that these three incidents can be attributed to the author using the narrative art of writing history in ancient Israel.

either God is fooled by Saul's imposing physical stature or there is more to *ṭôb* ('good', translated as 'handsome' here in the NRSV) than meets the eye; there is *double entendre* here. Saul is good looking and, like his father, is also 'a man of valour', who can be counted on for a loyal service. God selects Saul as much for this characteristic as for how he will look to the eyes of the people and Samuel.[15]

We find Saul on a mission to retrieve his father's lost donkeys. Instead of finding the donkeys he comes face-to-face with Samuel, who turns out to be as stubborn as a donkey and will micro-manage his life.[16] Samuel anoints Saul with these words: 'The Lord has anointed you ruler (*nāgîd*) *over his people Israel. You shall reign over the people of the Lord and you will save them from the hand of their enemies all around. Now this shall be the sign to you that the Lord has anointed you ruler (ἄρχοντα)* over his inheritance' (10.1).[17] The words (italicized) in the LXX clearly allude to the book of Judges and God's selection of judges to deliver the people from 'the enemies all around' (Judg. 2.14), indicating perhaps that Samuel wants to view this as a continuation of the period of judges. Moreover, in the Greek version Samuel indicates that Saul will see the sign that he is indeed God's anointed.

Samuel gives Saul long and complicated predictions and instructions for him to follow in order to flaunt his prophetic prowess (10.2-8). Polzin makes the following comment: 'Samuel's series of signs to Saul...amounts to

15. David, too, is pleasing to the eyes of the people as well as to the heart of God. God may care only about the inner content of a person, but there is no question that the outer appearance matters to the people. God understands this and chooses those who appeal to the people as well.

16. In his study of Saul as a charismatic leader, T. Czövek (*Three Seasons of Charismatic Leadership: A Literary-Critical and Theological Interpretation of the Narrative of Saul, David and Solomon* [Regnum Studies in Mission; Milton Keynes: Paternoster Press, 2006], p. 88), argues that Saul's charisma was doomed to failure from the beginning because Saul had a debilitating flaw as a charismata, 'his willingness to listen to and controlled by others', and the unfortunate luck of having Samuel as an overbearing mentor who expected Saul to be totally dependent on him. Moreover, he argues that it was not Saul's arrogance or lack of submissiveness towards Samuel that extinguished his charisma; on the contrary, it was because he failed to act independently from his mentor that he fell short of establishing himself as a charismatic leader. I would characterize Samuel as a man without any *jeong* yet who demands unyielding loyalty from everyone, which is exactly how the Dtr want to portray Samuel—a man who shows uncompromising loyalty to their understanding of God without regard for fellow human beings.

17. The MT omits the italicized words and only has the following: 'Has not the Lord in fact anointed you over his inheritance as a leader (*nāgîd*)?' The LXX also has leader (ἄρχοντα) rather than king. However, in 2 Sam. 17, the MT has: 'Through the hand of David, my servant will deliver my people Israel from the hand of the Philistines and from the hand of all their enemies' (my translation). This suggests that originally a similar saying was also in 1 Sam. 10.1 in the MT.

something like prophetic overkill. Through the use of thirteen predictive verbs... Samuel appears almost to be showing off his prophetic powers'.[18] Who can actually remember and follow them? Saul is to go to Rachel's tomb in the territory of Benjamin at Zelzah, then to the oak of Tabor, then to Gibeath-elohim, and then finally to Gilgal. In the first two stops Saul does not need to do anything but hear a message from two men that the donkeys have been found (v. 2) and receive two loaves of bread from three men (vv. 3-4). At the third stop he is instructed to 'do whatever you see fit to do' since God is with him (v. 7). Then at the fourth and last stop he is instructed by Samuel to do the following: 'And you shall go down to Gilgal ahead of me; then I will come down to you to present burnt offerings and offer sacrifices of well-being. Seven days you shall wait, until I come to you and show you what you shall do' (v. 8). Samuel's last instruction will turn out to be Saul's stumbling block. Even though the text clearly states that 'all these signs were fulfilled that day' (v. 9), however, a surprise awaits Saul. The last instruction does not come into play until ch. 13![19]

After anointing Saul as *nāgîd* over Israel in private, Samuel summons the people at Mizpah for a public selection of Saul (v. 17). First, however, he reprimands the people for rejecting God as their ruler and for requesting a king (v. 19). Samuel is only delaying the irrevocable march to kingship; he cannot stop the process. After some drama and comic relief Saul is chosen by lot to be king in the presence of all Israel (vv. 20-24). Saul is described again as being 'head and shoulders taller' than any other Israelite (v. 23). The people like what they see. They accept Saul and shout, 'Long live the king (*hammelek*)!' (v. 24). They accept the *ḥesed*-relationship between Saul as king (*melek*) and themselves as his subject. God has already committed himself to Saul when he instructs Samuel to anoint him as a ruler (*nāgîd*), but God and Samuel are still reluctant to use the term 'king' (*melek*). However, there are *bĕnê bĕlîyā'al* ('sons of worthlessness' or 'worthless men'), those who have predilection for disloyalty, who are not convinced that Saul can do the job and do not want to be part of this *ḥesed*-relationship (v. 27).

The narrative turns its attention to answer whether or not Saul has the ability or the charisma of past judges to deliver the people in a time of crisis. An opportunity arises. The people of Jabesh-gilead are in danger of being humiliated by Nahash the king of the Ammonites who wants to gauge their right eyes if they want him to spare their lives (11.1-2). The elders of

18. Polzin, *Samuel and the Deuteronomist*, p. 105.

19. One gets the feeling that Saul is being set up to fail. From the beginning of Saul's narrative, Samuel plays hardball. Saul must follow Samuel's multiple instructions just to confirm that he is indeed God's anointed. These signs turn out to be tests, signs/tests designed not to confirm Saul's selection as a leader over Israel but to disqualify him as God's anointed. When Samuel anoints David, there are no instructions, signs, or tests.

Jabesh-gilead negotiate a period of seven days to answer Nahash's terms of surrender and send messengers through all the territory of Israel for help. A crisis comes to the people, and they look for a deliverer. The Jabeshites are in a serious situation of need; they are in danger of being either killed or humiliated. Saul responds according to a *ḥesed*-relationship. When Saul hears the message 'the spirit of God came upon Saul in power when he heard these words, and his anger was greatly kindled' (v. 6). He musters the Israelites and sends a message to the people of Jabesh that 'Tomorrow, by the time the sun is hot, you shall have deliverance' (v. 10). The Jabeshites with confidence tell Nahash, 'Tomorrow we will go out to you and you may do to us whatever is good in your eyes' (v. 10; my translation). But it is not the Jabeshites who go out next day to surrender their eyes; it is Saul and the Israelite militia, who defeat the Ammonites. Saul has now demonstrated his ability to save the people in a time of crisis. Then the people turn to Samuel, who is still considered the leader, and say to him, 'Who is it that said, "Shall Saul reign over us?" Give them to us so that we may put them to death' (v. 12). But it is Saul who answers them, finally wrestling away the leadership from Samuel. Saul does not put anyone to death on this day, for God delivers the people from their oppressors as in the days of the judges. He accepts them into the *ḥesed*-relationship between the king and his people. However, it is not like the days of the judges. A new age has dawned in the history of leadership in Israel. Saul is not a charismatic leader; he is to be a king. Then Samuel says, 'Let us go to Gilgal and there renew the kingship' (v. 14). The people follow Samuel to Gilgal and make Saul king there 'before the Lord'. Finally, a *ḥesed*-relationship initiated by God is accepted by all the people of Israel. This *ḥesed*-relationship is strengthened and ratified by a covenant ceremony at Gilgal with God in attendance.

On this happy occasion Samuel cannot resist delivering another speech on the people's sin in asking for a king (ch. 12). Samuel ends his speech with a warning: 'Only fear the Lord, and serve him faithfully with all your heart; for consider what great things he has done for you. But if you still do wickedly, you shall be swept away, both you and your king' (12.24-25).[20] The message reflects a principle of *quid pro quod*: God delivered them, therefore the people need to serve God; God will punish them if they fail to serve him. This statement reflects the *ḥesed*-relationship between God as one party and the people and their king as the other party. If the people are faithful, then God will continue to extend *ḥesed* to them. We will see that God will offer a promise to Saul to establish his house forever (13.13-14) but, similar to the case of Eli and Samuel, God will renege this promise because of Saul's supposed disloyalty.

20. Brueggemann (*First and Second Samuel*, p. 96) summarizes the rhetoric of Samuel's speech well: 'Samuel proposes a rhetorical world of theological simplicity, sobriety, and sanity in which question may be reduced to the single issue of loyalty to Yahweh'.

Just as there were three selections of Saul as king, there are three rejections of Saul as king as well. Chapter 13 narrates the first rejection. It begins with Jonathan, Saul's son,[21] defeating the garrison of the Philistines at Geba, which results in an all-out offensive from the Philistines. Saul waits for Samuel to come to Gilgal to offer a sacrifice, apparently referring to the earlier instruction from 1 Sam. 10.8, so that he can receive God's blessing before he faces the Philistines. Samuel does not show up at the appointed time, and the soldiers begin to slip away from Saul. He is anxious and cannot wait any longer for Samuel to arrive. He decides to offer the sacrifice himself. As soon as he finishes sacrificing the burnt offering, Samuel shows up, as if he had been hiding behind a bush waiting for Saul to do the very thing he was instructed not to do. Samuel ignores Saul's reasonable and pragmatic explanation.[22] Instead he quickly delivers God's judgment to Saul: 'The Lord would have established your kingdom over Israel forever, but now your kingdom will not continue' (13.13-14).[23] This is comparable to the 'forever' promise God made to Eli and rescinded because Eli's sons have dishonored God; they disobeyed an unwritten expectation of the *ḥesed*-relationship (2.30). God rejects Saul. Moreover, God proclaims that another man will take his place just as God chose Samuel to replace Eli: 'The Lord has sought out a man after his own heart; and the Lord has appointed him to be ruler (*nāgîd*) over his people, because you have not kept what the Lord commanded you' (13.14).[24] The narrative casually ignores the fact that many years have passed since Saul's selection as king and the event in ch. 13 and

21. Surprisingly Saul has a son who is old enough to take up arms. Alter (*The David Story*, p. 70) comments, 'The neophyte king had himself seemed a very young man, but with the casualness about chronology characteristic of the biblical storyteller, Saul now has a grown son'. The text specifically says that Saul is a young man (*baḥûr*) in 9.2.

22. Samuel's reaction to Saul's explanation is puzzling to say the least, unless one acknowledges the fact that the narrative is anxious to bring David into the story. Brueggemann (*First and Second Samuel*, p. 101) explains it in this way: 'Saul's argument and justification were irrelevant and he never had a chance—because the narrative has stacked the cards in the favor of David; because Samuel is so partisan; because the literature is deeply committed to David, even before David explicitly appears in the literature; because Yahweh had committed to David before the literature was ever cast'. Polzin (*Samuel and the Deuteronomist*, p. 125) shares this sentiment: 'However Samuel, Saul, or the people choose to act, the narrator never lets us forget that it is God who is directing traffic... It is difficult to avoid seeing the Lord as the one who ultimately sets up Saul for proximate rejection just as he will Israel for ultimate exile'.

23. What a tease! Why does Samuel even bother to reveal this promise, namely God intended to establish his kingdom forever, when there is no chance of it happening now?

24. In a nutshell, this statement tries to explain why God chose David over Saul. David is already projected as being more loyal to God than Saul. We will see that not only is David a man of *ḥesed* /*ṭôb*, a man after God's own heart, but God's promise to David (2 Sam. 7.14-16) is categorically different from the one offered to Saul. God offers *ḥesed* to David and his house without any strings attached.

does nothing to decrease the gravity of Saul's failure to obey Samuel's last instruction from 10.8. According to the narrative, Saul has proven to be disloyal and that is all it matters.

In ch. 14 Samuel departs from the scene, but Saul has a war on his hands. Saul and the people of Israel are in serious trouble against the Philistines. Jonathan comes to the rescue with God's help. God indeed extends *ḥesed* to Israel through Jonathan, the heir apparent. Jonathan and his armor-bearer surprise the Philistines, causing a panic (an indication of God's activity) in the Philistine camp. The rest of the troops join Jonathan in attacking the Philistines. Saul lays an oath for the entire army: 'Curse be anyone who eats food before it is evening and I have been avenged on my enemies' (v. 24). Fate has it that it is Jonathan who breaks the oath. Upon being told of his father's oath, Jonathan reprimands his father's decision: 'My father has troubled the land' (v. 29). At the end of the day the soldiers are exhausted and hungry. They start slaughtering the animals on the ground and eating them with the blood (v. 32). Saul stops his men from sinning against God by eating meat with the blood, instructs them to kill the animals on a large stone so that the blood is drained from the animals, and then to build God an altar (vv. 33-35). Saul, like his men, must have been tired and starved, but he thought first of obeying God's command in the midst of frenzy. To his credit Saul is a man who is always mindful of God.

Saul now wants to continue to pursue the Philistines through the evening. His men are willing to follow him and they respond, 'Do whatever is good in your eyes' (v. 36). But the unnamed priest says, 'Let us draw near to God here' (v. 40). God refuses to answer Saul's inquiry because someone has not kept the oath. The people know that it is Jonathan who broke the oath but they remain silent. Saul divides the people on one side and Jonathan and himself on the other side. He is willing to sacrifice Jonathan or himself to keep his oath to God. The people do not stop Saul and say to him, 'Do whatever is good in your eyes' (v. 40). When Saul learns by lot that it is his own son who broke the oath, he is willing to sacrifice Jonathan to demonstrate his *ḥesed* to God. Saul's piety should not be questioned.[25] The people, however, intervene on Jonathan's behalf and save him from death. Saul gives in to the wish of his people and does not kill Jonathan for breaking the oath he had

25. Too many readers dismiss Saul's sincere piety. Saul is a man of faith. But influenced by the judgment that David is allegedly more obedient, thus more faithful to God, some readers do not acknowledge Saul's loyalty to God. It is interesting that there are many who defend Jephthah's rash vow to offer anyone who comes out of his house and his subsequent willingness to sacrifice his own daughter as a sign of piety (Judg. 11.29-40), yet only a few see Saul's oath and determination to sacrifice his own son as an act of faith. Brueggemann (*First and Second Samuel*, p. 107) notes this odd reaction: 'How strange—we take Abraham as a model of radical faith but treat Saul as unbalanced or foolhardy'.

made with God.[26] They do not know that they have dishonored their king; they are disloyal to their king and prevent him from displaying his fidelity to God. They show allegiance to Jonathan rather to their king and to their God. Saul's display of *ḥesed* to God is misunderstood and rejected by his own son and his own troops. Saul is rejected for the second time—this time by his own son and his own people.

In ch. 15 Saul is rejected for the third time. As in the latter case, his *ḥesed* to God is misconstrued and rejected in this pericope as well. This incident of rejection is initiated by Samuel who finally calls Saul king (v. 1) but continues to test him. He instructs Saul to put the Amalekites under ban (*ḥerem*). When Samuel comes to the camp, he hears the bleating of sheep in his ears. He again ignores Saul's explanation and delivers God's judgment: 'Has the Lord as great delight in burnt offerings and sacrifices, as in obeying the voice of the Lord? Surely, to obey is better than sacrifice, and to heed than the fat of rams' (v. 22). Samuel claims that God demands an uncompromising *ḥesed* to God. Those who do not show unqualified loyalty to Yahweh are considered rebellious: 'For rebellion is no less a sin than divination, and stubbornness is like iniquity and idolatry. Because you have rejected the word of the Lord, he has also rejected you from being king' (v. 23).[27] Saul acknowledges his part in the failure to carry out *ḥerem* to its full extent: 'I have sinned because I transgressed whatever came out of God's mouth and your words' (v. 24; my translation). One has to wonder whose words Saul has disobeyed, even though the narrator identifies Samuel's words as God's

26. Czövek (*Three Seasons*, p. 87) argues that Saul's willingness to listen to others is a basic flaw as a charismatic leader and questions whether Saul was a good choice. He states that Saul 'was easily influenced and was not determined in decision making and leading the people… Reluctance characterizes him throughout the narrative…and this is a fundamental fault in a person in a leadership position… If a leader is not resolute and firm but rather prone to be easily influenced, he/she is likely to fail. Again this begs the question whether Saul was a good choice'. From a literary perspective, Polzin (*Samuel and the Deuteronomist*, p. 103) expresses a similar sentiment from the moment Saul is introduced in the narrative in ch. 9 as a seeker of his father's donkeys: Saul's 'character zone is filled with doubt and uncertainty. Surrounded by a dubious aura, Saul is the epitome of a questionable choice… Saul, therefore, is a seeker of answers as well as asses, a traveling question mark'.

27. As in Hannah's song (1 Sam. 2) and in David's song (2 Sam. 22), Samuel's poetic oracle divides the people into two camps: those who are loyal and those who are disloyal. Saul falls into the unfaithful camp from the perspective of Samuel's theology, and, of course, Samuel belongs to the loyal camp. Polzin (*Samuel and the Deuteronomist*, p. 153), however, argues that the Deuteronomist's portrayal of Samuel is more nuanced than that: 'Read superficially, as it is usually done, the career of Samuel is of a loyal, if human, advocate of God; the heart of the matter, as the Deuteronomist describes it, is that Samuel remains, to the end, insensitive to the interests of God'.

words. Saul confesses his sin twice and asks for forgiveness but to no avail (vv. 24-25, 30). Saul is rejected—his confession is ignored and no forgiveness is offered. Saul begs Samuel to return with him so that he may worship Yahweh (v. 25). Samuel will not return with Saul: 'I will not return with you; for you have rejected the word of the Lord, and the Lord has rejected you from being king over Israel' (v. 26). Saul is desperate and grabs Samuel's robe because he thinks he needs Samuel's support to be king.[28] Samuel notes that his robe is torn and delivers this judgment: 'The Lord has torn the kingdom of Israel from you this very day, and has given it to a neighbor of yours, who is better [*ṭôb*] than you' (v. 28). We have to wait and see how David is 'better' than Saul.

We can still see that Saul is a man of *ḥesed* in spite of the way he is depicted as a disobedient (disloyal) man, the way Samuel sees him. When he comes to the city of the Amalekites to attack them, he warns the Kenites to escape from the city. In doing so he extends *ḥesed* to the Kenites who showed *ḥesed* to the Israelites when they came up from Egypt: 'Go! Leave! Withdraw from among the Amalekites, or I will destroy you with them; for you showed kindness [*ḥesed*] to all the people of Israel when they came up out of Egypt' (15.6).[29] Thereafter the Kenites withdraw from the Amalekites and save themselves from the *ḥerem* that was placed on the city and its inhabitants. Saul did not have to warn them; he was not obligated to do this. He was free not to extend *ḥesed* to them, but the fact that he did so says much about the man. Even though God rejects Saul and the narrator portrays Saul as disobedient, we will see that there are other episodes later in the narrative that will show that Saul is indeed a man of *ḥesed* (*jeong*). It is David who will receive so much more *ḥesed* from the people and from God than Saul has received. But this should not prevent us from seeing that Saul is a man of *ḥesed* who extended his *jeong* generously.

28. Czövek (*Three Seasons*, p. 88) notes that Saul's failure was caused by his inability to establish himself as an independent charismatic leader; he was unable to move away from Samuel's shadow, therefore, 'His doom and the death of his charisma in turn were caused by Samuel's expectation of total dependence'. He continues, 'I have suggested that Saul's failure consisted not in cultic blunder, self-aggrandisement, arrogance or lack of submissiveness towards Samuel, as commentators are keen to demonstrate, but rather the very opposite. Despite being a charismatic leader as he was he fell short of establishing himself as such, did not demonstrate independence from his mentor but rather subordination as a submissive apprentice to his mentor' (p. 91). Saul did not live up to his calling as a charismatic leader and was unable to assert his independence from Samuel.

29. Bowen ('A Study of ḥsd', p. 67) argues that the *ḥesed*-relationship between the Kenites and the Israelites was formed by a common loyalty to Yahweh and that 'this was the basis for the extraordinary friendliness between the two peoples...[this *ḥesed*-relationship was based] in loyalty to the tie that binds men worshipping the same God'.

The Selection of David and the Friendship of David and Jonathan (1 Samuel 16–20)

The story of David's rise begins with God's unequivocal rejection of Saul: 'I have rejected him from being king [*mimmĕlōk*, "from ruling"] over Israel' (1 Sam. 16.1). God is still reluctant to call Saul 'king' even though he had accepted Saul as ruler over the people of Israel. Then God sends Samuel on a clandestine mission and announces his plan: 'I will send you to Jesse the Bethlehemite, for I have provided for myself a king [*melek*] among his sons' (v. 1). Now God is ready to call a son of Jesse 'king' (*melek*). If it were up to Samuel, he would not have chosen David. Samuel takes one look at Eliab and thinks, 'Surely the Lord's anointed is now before the Lord' (v. 6). The people were impressed with Saul's physical stature and Samuel too relies on his eyes to select God's anointed.[30] But God teaches him a lesson: 'Do not look on his appearance or on the height of his stature, because I have rejected him; for the Lord does not see as mortals see; they look on the outward appearance [*la'ênayim*, "to the eyes"], but the Lord looks on the heart [*lallēbāb*, "to the heart"]' (v. 7). Jesse's seven sons are put before Samuel, but to Samuel's surprise God rejects all of them. Finally, the eighth son of Jesse appears, and God instructs Samuel to anoint this one. In v. 12, this son is described as ruddy with beautiful eyes (*yĕpeh 'ênayim*) and a 'good appearance' (*ṭôb rō'î*).[31] Samuel anoints him in the presence of his brothers and then goes back to his hometown.

The spirit of the Lord rests upon David from then on (v. 13) but from Saul the spirit of the Lord departs (v. 14).[32] Moreover, an evil spirit from God

30. An interesting use of the word 'eye' occurs in this section, keeping the reader off balance since David is more complicated than he appears to the eyes. He has characteristics that are hidden from how he appears to the eyes. The reader is encouraged to trust God's evaluation and election of David, but one has to wonder what God 'sees' in David that is so different from Saul.

31. Although God has warned Samuel not to judge a person through the eyes, David, described as having 'beautiful eyes' and 'good appearance', has a pleasant face. He is introduced again as 'a man of form' (*'îš tō'ar*) in 16.18. He is comparable to Saul in terms of physical form; however, Saul was a tall man ('head and shoulders above everyone else' [9.2; 10.23]) and David was probably a short man (as suggested by McKenzie, *King David*, p. 64). This may explain why God's warning to Samuel is specific about the 'height of his stature' (16.7).

32. In his study of David as a type of charismatic leadership, Czövek shows that during his rise to kingship David, unlike Saul, cannot be mentored, controlled, guided, or restrained by the two people who were in position to do so: Saul and Samuel. Czövek claims that independence from others is a basic characteristic of a charismatic and David is successful in resolving the crises (the Philistine and other external threats) he was commissioned. David's success is a credit to his willingness 'to use every possible means

torments Saul. His servants suggest that a man skilled in playing the lyre be brought to relieve Saul's troubles. Someone in Saul's court introduces David with the following credentials: 'I have seen a son of Jesse the Bethlehemite who is skillful in playing, a man of valor (*gibbōr ḥayil*),[33] a warrior, prudent in speech, and a man of good presence (*'îš tō'ar*);[34] and the Lord is with him' (v. 18). It is indeed an impressive résumé. In spite of what God said to Samuel about the heart of a man being more important than the external appearance, David is an impressive young man with many skills. Here he is not a naïve shepherd boy. God is not naïve. God does not choose a 'nobody'. God chooses someone who could succeed as king. But it is the last credential, 'the Lord is with him', that will differentiate him from Saul.[35] God will extend loyalty to David without any qualifications. David will not be tested as Saul was. He will receive one act of *ḥesed* after another without him asking for them. It is all because God is with him.

Surprisingly no one has yet uttered David's name. The narrator has been saving David's name for Saul. It is Saul who first calls his name—how ironic! Saul sends for David: 'Send me your son David who is with the sheep' (1 Sam. 16.19). Samuel had warned that the king would take young men and put them into military service (8.11-12), and David enters Saul's service. But the text states without any explanation or qualification that Saul 'loves' David greatly and makes him his armor-bearer (16.21). Saul could have done this without asking permission from Jesse, but he initiates in 16.22 a *ḥesed*-relationship with Jesse, David's service in return for Saul's *ḥēn*: 'Let David remain in my service for he has found *ḥēn bĕ'ênāy* ["favor in my eyes"]'. David stays, thus suggesting that Jesse agrees to a *ḥesed*-relationship. Jesse probably received a gift in exchange for David's service. Thus, for Saul, David's 'betrayal' of him is tantamount to severing this *ḥesed*-relationship. This may explain why Saul repeatedly calls David 'a son

to attain his political objectives', a characteristic that Czövek claims 'is not optional but a hallmark of a charismatic, as David was' (*Three Seasons*, p. 116). Moreover, in the narrative, charisma is acknowledged when the narrator notes that God or God's spirit is with the individual and the individual loses charisma when God or God's spirit departs from him.

33. This is the same term, 'man of valour', used to introduce Saul's father Kish (9.1), connoting loyalty.

34. The term 'man of form/appearance' once again shows that David appeals to the eyes.

35. As I mentioned in Chapter 1, this phrase 'Yahweh is with him/David' (1 Sam. 16.13, 18; 17.37; 18.12, 14, 28; 20.13; 2 Sam. 5.10) is a theological motif, which runs through the first half of the David narrative describing his rise, which explains why David is successful in defeating Saul and establishing his kingdom. The last attribute is the one that sets David apart from Saul. Czövek (*Three Seasons*, p. 104) notes that 'Yahweh is with him' is 'the hallmark of a charismatic military leader in the DH'.

of Jesse'. He formed a *ḥesed*-relationship with Jesse and reminds David that he is shaming his father by breaking this honor-based relationship.

Similar to the way Saul demonstrated his prowess as God's anointed by defeating the Ammonites, David spectacularly displays his qualifications as God's anointed in one of the most beloved stories in the Bible: the story of David and Goliath. In this story we learn that David is a very ambitious young man. Indeed David's first speech reveals his aspiration very plainly: 'What shall be done for the man who kills this Philistine, and takes away the reproach from Israel? For who is this uncircumcised Philistine that he should defy the armies of the living God?' (17.26). To be fair, David is very angry that Goliath has insulted God, even though it is his second sentence. This line may attest to his piety, but his very first sentence reveals his ambition. His brother Eliab seems to know something about David, which is not perceivable to the eyes and we the readers are not privy to: 'I know your presumption and the evil of your heart; for you have come down just to see the battle' (17.28). Bodner examines Eliab's direct speech to David and argues that there are at least two levels of meaning: one meaning in the dialogue between Eliab and David and a second meaning directed toward the reader.[36] Eliab's statement indirectly characterizes David and sounds a warning about the heart of David; therefore, the reader should not ignore an insight offered by Eliab on David's heart. In other words, there is a dark side to David's heart of which the reader should be mindful.

What is more striking than Eliab's statement is what David does in response to his older brother's words. David replies, 'What have I done now? It was only a question' (17.29), then he turns his back on his brother and faces another and 'spoke in the same way; and the people answered him again as before' (17.30). David will not be denied any opportunity to advance himself; he will not be deterred from his goals. He knows what he wants, and he knows how to get it. Later the narrative says that 'David was well pleased to be the king's son-in-law' (18.26). He risks his life to kill one hundred Philistines for their foreskins in order to marry Saul's daughter (18.27). Saul was a pious man who wanted to be loyal to God and was reluctant to be king. In contrast, David is foremost an ambitious man and wants to be king from the start.

Goliath is extremely upset to see 'a youth, ruddy and handsome in appearance' to fight against (17.41; cf. 16.12).[37] Of course, looks can be deceiving. David is far more than he appears. Beneath his youthful and innocent

36. Bodner, *David Observed*, utilizes Mikhail Bakhtin's notion of 'double-voiced utterance' and shows that Eliab's statement is double-voiced.

37. The text says that Goliath 'disdained' (*bzh*) David; this is the same verb used to describe how God will show 'contempt' (*qll*) to those who despise (*bzh*) God (1 Sam. 2.30).

appearance lies a deceptive warrior (cf. 16.18). David claims that he comes in the name of God: 'You come to me with sword and spear and javelin; but I come to you in the name of the Lord of hosts, the God of the armies of Israel who you have defied' (17.45). The Philistine has repeatedly reproached God and now David will defend God's honor. His pious words are backed by a clever strategy that makes this battle a mismatch in his favor. Halpern suggests that Goliath, like everyone else, is waiting for a hand-to-hand battle, but David declines the rules and fights from a distance.[38] In military terms Goliath is heavy infantry while David is light infantry (archers, slingers, javelin hurlers). Goliath cannot move quickly enough to draw close to David for hand-to-hand combat. David could have danced around Goliath all day, flinging projectiles at will. Thus, Halpern concludes that 'Goliath never stood a chance'.[39]

Chapter 18 is a text of love, allegiance, and betrayal. The word 'love' has the meaning of loyalty or allegiance in the larger narrative context of David's rise. It seems as if there was no one who did not love or give allegiance to David. Everyone is ready to pledge his or her *ḥesed* to David. One has to wonder what it is about David that attracts so much affection (*jeong*) and loyalty from just about everyone. It may be that he is different and unorthodox in his approach, as shown in his battle against Goliath;[40] perhaps he is 'modern' or even 'postcolonial' in the sense that he is not bound by the tradition or trenched in the status quo. Of course, the narrator would claim that it is because Yahweh is with him. For Saul, however, this chapter is a chapter of betrayal; everyone around him, from his own children and closest servants to the ordinary people of Israel and Judah will choose David over him. They pledge their *ḥesed* to David and show willingness to sever their ties with Saul.

After defeating Goliath, David enters Saul's service for the second time: 'Saul took him that day and would not let him return to his father's house' (1 Sam. 18.2). Jonathan instantly loves David when he sees him: 'the soul of Jonathan was bound to the soul of David, and Jonathan loved him as his

38. Halpern, *David's Secret Demons*, pp. 10-13.

39. Halpern, *David's Secret Demons*, p. 13. This battle reminds me of the dual between Indiana Jones and a bad guy with a scythe in *The Raiders of the Lost Ark*. The bad guy swings his scythe in all different directions to show off his skills, and the crowd is impressed with his display of power. Indiana Jones is relaxed and does not seem too concerned. Then he pulls out his gun and shoots him. The guy had no chance against Indiana Jones.

40. Halpern (*David's Secret Demons*, p. 13) summarizes David's special quality in this way: 'In the Goliath episode, he moves on to reject the etiquette of social relations shared by all around him. This is the pattern that will persist throughout his history. He is not just Yahweh's elect: he is Yahweh's avenger. He is not just destined for greatness: he shapes his greatness by a complete disregard for orthodoxy'.

own soul' (v. 1).[41] Then Jonathan makes 'a covenant with David, because he loved him as his own soul' (v. 3). Incredibly, he strips himself of his robe, armor, sword, bow, and belt and gives them to David (v. 4). Jonathan in effect gives his right to the throne to David. It is hard to believe that Jonathan would relinquish his future as king to someone he had just met. Thompson argues that the fact that both Saul and Jonathan divest their armors and give them to David (17.38, 39; 18.4) and the fact that David takes Goliath's armor (17.54) is another subtle feature in the narrative that suggests a political implication.[42] That is, the passing of arms from the lesser to the greater reflects the transference of power from the house of Saul to David and the future dominance of David over the Philistines.

Saul's daughter Michal also loves David (18.20, 28). Moreover, the women of Israel love David, greeting David with singing and dancing whenever he returns from fighting with the Philistines (vv. 6-7). In fact 'all Israel and Judah loved David; for it was he who marched out and came in leading them' (v. 16).[43] Even Saul's own servants love David (v. 22). These displays of love not only indicate their affection for David but also their political allegiance to him. The people of Israel and Judah and even Saul's closest officers pledge their *ḥesed* to David.[44]

No wonder Saul is nervous about David's popularity. Saul is being betrayed by all. The narrator claims that Saul wants to kill David purely out of jealousy. When he hears the song of the women, he becomes very angry and begins to *eye* him from that day on (v. 9). When he sees that David is more successful than he is, 'this thing was evil in his *eyes*' (v. 8; my transla-

41. McCarter comments on this verse: 'In this and the present case, then, the expression refers to inseparable devotion. Jonathan, in other words, is so taken with David that he becomes vitally devoted to him in *affection and loyalty*' (*I Samuel*, p. 305 [my emphasis]). This is the full meaning of *ḥesed.*

42. Thompson, 'The Significance of the Verb *Love*', p. 335.

43. McCarter (*I Samuel*, p. 313) in commenting on the fact that 'all Israel and Judah loved David', makes this observation: 'The love that the people have for David goes beyond an affectionate response to his personal charisma...[and love] seems to have a political connotation here... In the present case, to Saul's chagrin, it is *all* Israel and Judah who love David. That is, all Israel and Judah have given their loyalty to the young man who leads them in war, and it is partly out of his recognition of this state of affairs... that Saul has come to fear David'.

44. Polzin (*Samuel and the Deuteronomist*, p. 178) notes that although the narrator makes transparent the hearts of these characters, David's heart is completely hidden from the reader's view: 'Jonathan gives everything to David...whereas David is not reported as giving anything in return. Nor does the narrator give us very much intrinsically belonging to David. In contrast to others in the chapter, David's inner life and motivation are almost completely hidden... Chapter 18 tells us a lot about Saul's inner life, but almost nothing about his rival's'. David's heart is hidden from us not only in ch. 18 but also through most of his rise to power.

tion). From this point on Saul tries to kill David. He makes several attempts but fails every time. He twice throws his spear to pin David to the wall but misses (vv. 10-11), and then Saul tries again to pin David to the wall with his spear without success (19.8-10). Later, when David escapes to Ramah, Saul goes there to fetch him but fails again because he falls into a prophetic frenzy and lays naked in humiliation (19.18-24). This time the text clearly indicates that God is behind the protection of David. Saul fails to kill David because, as we will see below, everyone loves (gives *ḥesed* to) him and is on David's side, and, most importantly, God is on his side.

When Saul learns that his daughter Michal loves David he is pleased that he has her as bait to lure David into a situation of danger (18.20). He commands his servants to tell David that 'the king is delighted with you, and all his servants love you; now then, become the king's son-in-law' (v. 22). When David raises a concern about dowry, Saul communicates to David that 'the king desires no marriage present except a hundred foreskins of the Philistines' in order to make 'David fall by the hand of the Philistines' (v. 25). Saul understands David's ambition; he may be jealous of David's popularity, but he is not blind to what David is up to. It seems he is the only one who sees David's aspiration. The text states that 'the thing was pleasing in the eyes of David to be the king's son-in-law' (v. 26; my translation). David immediately assembles his men and kills the Philistines so that he might become the king's son-in-law (v. 27). Saul has no choice but to give his daughter in marriage to David: 'But when Saul realized that the Lord was with David, and that Saul's daughter Michal loved him, Saul was still more afraid of David. So Saul was David's enemy from that time forward' (vv. 28-29). Now Saul realizes that Michal's love involves more than emotional attachment; it involves loyalty that is even stronger than a bond between father and daughter. She is more loyal to David than to her father! Michal's loyalty to David will become evident when she, identified as 'David's wife' in 19.11, helps him escape from his house after learning of Saul's plan to kill him there (19.11-17).[45]

Jonathan, too, is more loyal to David than he is to his father. In ch. 19, Jonathan's loyalty to David is clearly demonstrated when he persuades his father from killing David by making a case that David's deeds are very good (*ṭôb*, 19.1-7).[46] He has already made clear his intention to turn over his right

45. In 1 Sam. 19.11 (also 2 Sam. 3.14) Michal is 'David's wife' rather than 'Saul's daughter' (1 Sam. 18.20, 28; 2 Sam. 3.13; 6.20, 23). This identification reveals where Michal's loyalty lies.

46. McCarter (*I Samuel*, p. 322) notes the significance of the word *ṭôb* as it relates to the idea of loyalty: 'As recent studies of biblical and extrabiblical materials have shown, "good(ness)" is to act as a friend or loyal ally… The things David has done have been good, says Jonathan; that is, he has acted consistently with the loyalty he owes his king… The passage also introduces us to the theme of Jonathan's loyalty to David'.

to the throne to David (18.4). According to the narrative there is no conflict between David and Jonathan. It is Saul who is jealous of David's success and popularity and his knack for winning over everyone's *ḥesed*, including God's. It is Saul who understands that as long as David is around neither Jonathan nor his kingdom will be established (20.31). But Jonathan has no interest in establishing his rule. He is convinced that it is David who will be king over Israel. Moreover, as unlikely as this may sound, he loves David more than his own father. Jonathan chooses a friend over his father! In that sense he is no different from Eli's or Samuel's sons whose disloyalty ended their fathers' reign. Jonathan is a disloyal son who rejected his father's piety to God in 1 Samuel 14 and now rejects his father's love for him.

In ch. 20, Jonathan wants to seal his friendship and political alliance with David with a pledge of *ḥesed* from David. Jonathan wants to make a covenant/pact between himself and his heirs with David and his house. Jonathan uses the term *ḥesed* twice, asking loyalty from David and his house: 'If I am still alive, show me the faithful love [*ḥesed*] of the Lord; but if I die, never cut off your faithful love [*ḥesed*] from my house, even if the Lord were to cut off every one of the enemies of David from the face of the earth' (vv. 14-15). David does not respond; he is silent.[47] Jonathan is taken aback by this lack of response. He becomes anxious and quickly makes a statement directly related to David's future, not his. Therefore, Jonathan speaks again, 'May the Lord seek out the enemies of David' (v. 16). Then the narrator summarizes the *ḥesed*-relationship between two friends and political allies: 'Jonathan made David swear again by his love for him; for he loved him as he loved his own life' (v. 17). Yet, once again, the narrator does not reveal David's heart.[48] Later in the chapter when Jonathan gives a sign that David must depart from Saul (vv. 35-42), David remains silent through the entire episode. David does weep with Jonathan, the narrator noting that David wept more (v. 41), but he never commits to this relationship verbally. Finally, Jonathan says to David: 'Go in peace, since both of us have sworn in the name of the Lord, saying, "The Lord shall be between me and you, and between my descendants and your descendants, forever"'

47. Alter (*The David Story*, p. 107) notes a biblical narrative convention where a speaker speaks again when the addressee remains silent and schematize it as: 'And X said to Y; [no response from Y]; and X said to Y, with the intervening silence being dramatically significant'.

48. Polzin (*Samuel and the Deuteronomist*), points out that this chapter reflects the language of mutual fidelity; however, he questions, 'But how faithful are these men who swear their oaths in behalf of one another? On one hand, Jonathan's love for David…is unquestioned… On the other hand, because of the narrator's practice so far of keeping the inner life of David's opaque, we have only this character's words and actions to go by; author will keep reader in suspense until David's future actions establish or negate the same kind of fidelity we know to be part of Jonathan's persona' (p. 191).

(v. 42). There is a passage in 23.16-18 that seems out of place but is relevant to the discussion at hand. It relates to Jonathan's desperate effort to have David commit to this *ḥesed*-relationship. Jonathan says to David, 'Do not be afraid; for the hand of my father Saul shall not find you; you shall be king over Israel, and I shall be second to you; my father Saul knows that this is so' (23.17). Then the text says that they made a covenant before Yahweh. This time the text explicitly states that they reconfirmed their *ḥesed*-relationship with a covenant before God. Again, though, David is the silent partner in this relationship. The only time David acknowledges verbally Jonathan's love (*ḥesed*) occurs after Jonathan's death: 'I am distressed for you, my brother Jonathan; greatly beloved were you to me; your love to me was wonderful, passing the love of women' (2 Sam. 1.26). But, even then, we do not know whether David is committed to keeping his loyalty to Jonathan.[49]

David's refusal to respond verbally to Jonathan's repeated requests for a pledge of *ḥesed* is quite striking in light of the fact that it is David who comes to Jonathan for help in the first place (ch. 20). David pleads to Jonathan that Saul is after his life for no good reason. Jonathan seems clueless to Saul's ill intention. David explains why Jonathan is unaware of this: 'Your father surely knows that I have found *ḥēn* in your eyes; and he thinks, "Do not let Jonathan know this lest he be pained"' (20.3; my translation). David claims that Saul knows about their *ḥesed*-relationship, and therefore Saul is hiding his plan to kill David from Jonathan. David proposes a test so that Jonathan can see plainly how his relationship with Saul has deteriorated. He will not show up to dinner during the new moon festival. If Saul says 'good' (*ṭôb*), then 'it will be well with your servant; but if he is angry, then know that evil has been determined by him' (20.7). He assumes that Saul will be angry with his absence and continues his speech to Jonathan: 'Therefore, deal kindly [*ḥesed*] with your servant, for you have brought your servant into a sacred covenant with you. But if there is guilt in me, kill me yourself; why should you bring me to your father?' (20.8). David is indeed skilled in speech (see 1 Sam. 16.18) and articulates his case well. He is not silent when he is the one who needs help. Jonathan is not like David; he responds to

49. Perhaps the only exception is when David extends *ḥesed* to Jonathan's son in 2 Sam. 9, but we will see in the next chapter that David may have ulterior motives for doing this. Brueggemann (*First and Second Samuel*, p. 149) readily accepts David as a man of *ḥesed*: 'David is indeed a man of *ḥesed*... David is to be a very harsh winner, but one who will honor his specific commitments and pay his debts'. In reference to David's loyalty to Jonathan, he reiterates this view, 'David is a man of loyalty and will honor his commitment to Jonathan' (p. 150). I am more reluctant to call him a man of *ḥesed*, or at least that term has to be qualified. The term 'a Machiavellian man of *ḥesed*' or 'a man of *ḥesed* and sword' seems more fitting for David. We will see why such qualifications are needed. P.D. Miscall (*1 Samuel: A Literary Reading* [Bloomington: Indiana University Press, 1986]), characterizes David as a man between *ḥesed* and *ḥereb* ('sword').

David's every speech. Their dialogue initiated by David's need is: X said to Y; Y said to X. Jonathan does not remain silent, so David is not anxious. The narrator reveals Jonathan's heart. He agrees to test Saul and says to David, 'By the Lord, the God of Israel! When I have sounded out my father, about this time tomorrow, or on the third day, if he is well disposed [*ṭôb*] toward David, shall I not then send and disclose it to you?' (20.12). We need to remind ourselves that the test is to see whether Saul will honor a *ḥesed*-relationship that is in place between Saul and David/Jesse. When Saul asks Jonathan why David failed to show up to dinner, Jonathan lies to his father: 'Let me go; for our family is holding a sacrifice in the city, and my brother has commanded me to be there. So now, if I have found favor in your sight ("if I have found *ḥēn* in your eyes"), let me get away, and see my brothers. For this reason he has not come to the King's table' (20.29).[50] Saul is furious that Jonathan has taken David's side:

> You son of a perverse woman, rebellious woman! Do I not know that you have chosen the son of Jesse to your own shame, and to the shame of your mother's nakedness? For as long as the son of Jesse lives upon the earth, neither you nor your kingdom shall be established. Now send and bring him to me, for he shall surely die (1 Sam. 20.30-31).[51]

Saul knows, by Jonathan's cooperation in David's escape, that his suspicion of Jonathan's *ḥesed* (loyalty and *jeong*) for David has been reconfirmed.

Jonathan shows uncompromising *ḥesed* to David. Jonathan's *ḥesed* has a characteristic of *jeong* more than loyalty because he pledges and performs *ḥesed* without assurance of David's *ḥesed* in return. He gives, David takes. He is being cheated in some way in this *ḥesed*-relationship, but Jonathan does not mind. Michal also gives and gives *jeong*, and David takes and will continue to take from her. She is being cheated in their *ḥesed*-relationship, but unlike her brother, this bothers her (see 2 Sam. 6). Saul sees David for who he is, but he is unable to stop David's march to his destiny. He will try but will fail. He will learn that like Goliath he never stood a chance to beat David. David is articulate, active, and clever when he needs someone else's *ḥesed* but is silent and disinterested when someone asks for his *ḥesed*. The question that still needs to be answered, in spite of what the narrator claims, is whether David is indeed a man of *ḥesed*.

50. Polzin (*Samuel and the Deuteronomist*, p. 188) recognizes that Jonathan's lie to his father involves the issue of loyalty: 'Jonathan misleads, but only out of an uncompromising loyalty to David; he accommodates himself to David's duplicity, rather than initiating any himself'.

51. McCarter (*I Samuel*, p. 343) comments on Saul's accusation of Jonathan's disloyalty: 'This insult is directed toward Jonathan, not his mother. "Son of" in such a case means "member of the class of", viz, in this instance, of people who forsake those to whom they properly owe allegiance'.

From a Fugitive to a Bodyguard of Achish (1 Samuel 21–30)

David is on the run, running away from Saul and toward his destiny. At the end of this section he will be in the service of Achish the Philistine as his bodyguard, but only a short step away from establishing his own kingship. Until then, David is a fugitive, looking for a safe haven out of Saul's reach. He becomes a leader of a band of men who are discontent with their lot (1 Sam. 22.1-2). David and his men offer protection in return for payment from those who are located between the areas of Saul's influence and those of the Philistines. He is in a business of *quid pro quod*, regardless of whether or not the other party accepts the arrangement. Saul had his chances to kill David but failed because of the disloyalty of those who were close to him and also because of God's *ḥesed* to David. Now in this section, God gives David the chance to kill Saul twice, but he refuses to do so because he honors the *ḥesed*-relationship between God and Saul even though God and Samuel have severed that relationship (chs. 24 and 26). David takes his men to Gath and decides to serve Achish as the captain of a raiding band and later as his bodyguard, supposedly to get away from Saul (ch. 27). The narrator justifies David's decision to join the Philistines and rationalizes why David is God's choice instead of Saul. Saul is disconnected from and out of touch with God. In contrast, David is in constant communication with God, always ready and willing to obey God's every word. As Saul is about to march toward his death, David extends his *ḥesed* to his friends in Judah and patiently waits for Saul's demise (chs. 28–30).

Now we will pick up the story where we left off in the previous section. After departing from Jonathan, David flees to the priestly city of Nob (21.1-9). There David acquires the sword of Goliath of Gath and provisions from Ahimelech son of Ahitub son of Phinehas son of Eli, and then surprisingly he goes to the Philistine city of Gath. When the servants of Achish, the ruler of Gath, recognize David as the hero of Israel, David feigns madness before them (21.10-15).[52] He escapes to the cave of Adullam and attracts those who are discontent with the status quo: 'everyone who was in distress, and everyone who was in debt, and everyone who was discontented gathered to him; and he became captain over them' (22.2). Interestingly, David leaves his parents with the king of Moab, perhaps indicating that there is some truth to David's genealogy in the book of Ruth (Ruth 4.18-21) and his actions may point to the existence of a *ḥesed*-relationship between David's family and

52. Polzin, *Samuel and the Deuteronomist*, reminds us that David's continual use of deception now undoubtedly becomes a salient element in his character zone. He notes that 'such details as David feigning madness before Achish to save his own life underline the dissembling and deception that continue to fill the character zone of David, even at this early stage in his career' (p. 198).

the king of Moab (1 Sam. 22.3-5). More importantly, David becomes captain over these men and their households, and they will be loyal to him through his wilderness period and beyond. He must have promised them something concrete in return for their service since they were unhappy with the status quo ushered in by Saul. Samuel had warned the people that the king will take things from them (1 Sam. 8.10-18), and one of the incentives Saul offered to the one who fights Goliath is to make his family free from paying taxes in Israel (17.25).[53] Moreover, Saul questions his kinsmen's loyalty by asking, 'Hear now, you Benjaminites; will the son of Jesse give every one of you fields and vineyards, will he make you all commanders of thousands and commanders of hundreds?' (22.7). These words may reflect what David has been offering to recruit people to himself and away from Saul.

Saul is correct when he implies that it is he who is providing all these perks to his kinsmen, not David. They owe him *ḥesed*, but he claims that they have betrayed him. Surprisingly, it is a foreigner who shows *ḥesed* to Saul. It is Doeg the Edomite, a non-Israelite, who discloses that Ahimelech was the one who helped David escape: 'I saw the son of Jesse coming to Nob, to Ahimelech son of Ahitub; he inquired of the Lord for him, gave him provisions, and gave him the sword of Goliath the Philistine' (22.9-10).[54] Upon learning that Ahimelech helped David escape from his hand, Saul interrogates him. Ahimelech in his defense argues that he had no reason to suspect David's loyalty to Saul. He claims that there is no one who is as loyal to Saul as David: 'But who of all your servants is as trustworthy [*ne'ĕmān*] as David, the king's son-in-law and the commander of your bodyguard [*śār 'el mišma'tekā*], who is honored [*kbd*] in your house?' (v. 14; McCarter's translation).[55] He states two facts about David: that David is Saul's son-in-law and the captain of his bodyguard. Based on these two positions there is no reason to suspect David's loyalty (*ne'ĕmān*) to Saul and his importance (*kbd*) to Saul's family. Saul knows, however, that David is honored (*kbd*) more than he is in his own house, even by his own children!

53. With the permanent army, which is perhaps the most important difference of monarchy in comparison to the ad hoc militia of the charismatic leadership of judges, there are costs that come with maintaining it; for example, taxes the people had to bear. One of the promises Saul made to anyone who killed Goliath was to give relief from this tax burden (17.25).

54. Bodner (*David Observed*, p. 34) notes that it is Doeg the Edomite who first reveals to the reader that Ahimelech is connected with the house of Eli and makes the following observation: 'The fall of Eli's house thus intersects with the rise of David. In 1 Samuel 21–22, Ahimelech, a member of the doomed priestly line, is acting in a manner that promotes the interests of the Davidic house over and against other rejected dynastic alternatives, namely: Eli and Saul'.

55. McCarter (*I Samuel*, p. 364) suggests that the term *mišma'at* can 'refer to a city or state giving special allegiance to a king…or to an intimate circle of royal retainers, i.e. a king's bodyguard'.

For Saul to be as faithful (*ne'ĕmān*) as his servants is equivalent to being disloyal (vv. 7-8; see above). Therefore, Saul does not waste time refuting Ahimelech's defense; he simply makes a decision to kill him in v. 16: *môt tāmût 'aḥîmelek 'attah wĕkol bêt 'ābîkā* ('You shall surely die, Ahimelech; you and all who belong to your father's house'). Saul orders the guard (*rûṣîm*) who stood around him (secret service agents, if you will) to kill the priests of Nob, but his servants refuse to raise their hands against them (v. 17). Again, his own servants disobey him (cf. 14.45-46); his servants, like his own children, are not loyal to him. Doeg is the only one who is willing to perform an act of loyalty to Saul; Doeg the Edomite, a non-Israelite, is the only one who obeys Saul.

Abiathar is the sole survivor of this massacre and joins David and serves as his priest (vv. 20-23). He tells Abiathar, 'I knew on that day, when Doeg the Edomite was there, that he would surely tell Saul. I am responsible for the lives of all your father's house. Stay with me, and do not be afraid; for the one who seeks my life seeks your life; you will be safe with me' (vv. 22-23). It turns out that Ahimelech and the priests at Nob knowingly risked their lives to save David's life.[56] They showed a remarkable *ḥesed* to David but betrayed their own king. We are to applaud their loyalty to David and refrain from scolding their disloyalty to their own king who, after all, was anointed by God and accepted by all the people of Israel and Judah.

David, now with his men who have pledged *ḥesed* to him, and Abiathar the priest, who brings the ephod (23.6) and thereby helps to open the communication between God and David, is ready to flex his muscles. When he hears that the Philistines are raiding the town of Keilah, David first asks God whether or not he should go and help. After receiving God's approval he goes to Keilah and rescues its inhabitants (vv. 1-6). They did not ask David for help, but David volunteers to deliver them, perhaps in the hope of forming a *ḥesed*-relationship with them, thereby expanding his support base. But surprisingly the people of Keilah do not wish to form a *ḥesed*-relationship with him. They are quite willing to turn David their savior over to Saul (v. 12). It is God who tells him that the people of Keilah will turn him over to Saul. David has no choice but to go into hiding, this time in the Wilderness of Ziph. The narrator notes that Saul 'sought him every day, but the

56. Bodner (*David Observed*), examines in Chapter 3 of his book the possibility that David and Ahimelech are partners in 'collusion' in deceiving Doeg the Edomite when David was visiting Ahimelech at Nob. Bodner uses Bakhtin's literary technique of 'delayed exposition' to argue that Ahimelech communicated to David that Doeg was in the sanctuary that day. Moreover, he suggests that Ahimelech, like Michal and Jonathan, protected David's life while risking his own because the narrator used his action as an example of what Bodner calls the 'motif of deceptive alliance'. Bodner suggests that Ahimelech's motivation for participating in the 'motif of deceptive alliance' is to fulfill the prophecy of judgment against the family of Eli.

Lord did not give him into his hand' (v. 14). A group of Judahites, namely Ziphites, goes to Saul and informs him of David's whereabouts (vv. 19-24; again in 26.1). They are willing to cooperate with Saul in capturing David. Saul is elated when the Ziphites offer to help him, for there seems to be no one on his side, no one who remains loyal to him. He exclaims in v. 21, 'May you be blessed by the Lord for showing me compassion!' David would have expected *ḥesed* from his own kinsmen, but the Ziphites do not extend *ḥesed* to him. Saul nearly catches David with their help but has to stop pursuing him when he hears that the Philistines are raiding the land (vv. 27-28). God saves David again. God's loyalty to David is steadfast; God's *ḥesed* to David is infuriating for Saul.

This incident shows that, on the one hand, at this point in time David was not yet strong enough to win the allegiance of his own kinsmen over against Saul, contrary to the narrator's claim that everyone 'loves' David. On the other hand, in spite of what the narrative says about the lack of support for Saul, it cannot completely overwrite the fact that Saul draws affection and loyalty from some people, even among the people of Judah. The narrator controls the narrative on David's behalf yet there are moments when people's *ḥesed* for Saul cannot be concealed. The people of Keilah and the Ziphites, David's own kinsmen, want to turn David over to Saul. David could not stay in the region of Judah probably because he did not have enough support from his own people. They are still loyal to Saul.

God gives David two chances to kill Saul (23.29–24.22 and 26.1-25); perhaps this is his test of loyalty, and he refuses to raise his hand against Saul, God's anointed. He refuses to kill Saul not because he 'loves' Saul but in order to win over God's and the people's (the reader's) heart. The narrative makes clear that it is God who has given David the opportunities to kill Saul. In 24.4 David's men utter what sounds like a prophetic oracle to David: 'Here is the day of which the Lord said to you "I will give your enemy into your hand, and you shall do to him *whatever is good in your eyes*"' (my translation). For David 'whatever is good in your eyes' (*yiṭab bĕ'ênêkā*), or 'what is considered an act of loyalty in your eyes', is to spare Saul's life. Then, in 26.8, Abishai, Joab's brother and one of David's fiercest warriors, delivers another prophetic oracle to David, 'God has given your enemy into your hand today; now therefore let me pin him to the ground with one stroke of the spear; I will not strike him twice'. Moreover, in ch. 26 the narrator explains why David and Abishai are able to sneak into Saul's camp undetected: 'No one saw it, or knew it, nor did anyone awake; for they were all asleep, because a deep sleep [*tardēmat*][57] from the Lord had fallen

57. This term is used to describe sleep induced by supernatural agency (God), as, for example, when God puts 'the earthling' to sleep in order take out a rib from him (Gen. 2.21) and Abraham falls into deep sleep during the making of the covenant with God (Gen. 15.12). Here it is clear that the soldiers are asleep due to supernatural activity.

upon them' (26.12). It is unmistakable that God is the one who has handed Saul over to David, perhaps as a sign of God's *ḥesed* to David.

The narrator seems to be arguing that the fact that David does not kill Saul, even though he had two opportunities to kill him, clears David from any suspicion of his role in Saul's death later in the narrative and also shows that there is no reason to suspect David's *ḥesed* to Saul. This is enough to prove his innocence. David demonstrates his loyalty by not raising his hand against Saul. He calls Saul 'my father', reminding Saul of their *ḥesed*-relationship, and reasons, 'For by the fact that I cut off the corner of your cloak, and did not kill you, you may know for certain that there is no wrong [*rā'ah*] or treason [*peša'*] in my hands. I have not sinned against you, though you are hunting me to take my life' (24.12). He claims that he has not harbored 'evil' (*rā'ah*) or 'transgression against' (*peša'*) Saul; his deeds of goodness and faithfulness speak for themselves. Furthermore, David argues that he has prevented other men from slaying Saul (24.7; 26.8-9), and he also reprimands Abner for not doing his job: 'This thing that you have done is not good [*ṭôb*]. As the Lord lives, you deserve to die, because you have not kept watch over your lord, the Lord's anointed' (26.16).[58] The narrator claims that David has always been loyal to Saul; it is only Saul's paranoia that has pushed him to see David as disloyal.

But David's loyalty to Saul is ambivalent. Saul suspects that David has been disloyal to him for good reason. There may be some truth to the suspicion that David has tried to overthrow Saul (more on this point in Chapter 5). Saul complains that everyone has taken David's side and even his own children have given their allegiance or love to David. He claims that his servants have conspired against him and questions their *ḥesed*. Interestingly, David does acknowledge that there is a rumor that he wants to harm Saul in 24.9: 'Why do you listen to the words of those who say, "David seeks to do you harm?"' He claims that this is a fabrication by those who wish to harm his relationship with Saul. He accepts the role of God in this matter and proclaims that he will not take the matter into his own hands but leaves it up to God to judge between him and Saul (24.11-15). Then he skillfully argues that Saul is the wicked, and he is the righteous: 'Out of the wicked comes forth wickedness; but my hand shall not be against you' (24.13). God will reward 'everyone for his righteousness and his faithfulness [*'mn*]; for the Lord gave you into my hand today, but I would not raise my hand against the Lord's anointed' (26.23).

The narrative overstresses David's innocence and his loyalty to Saul. The narrator even has Saul admit that David is innocent and more righteous than

58. Polzin (*Samuel and the Deuteronomist*, p. 207), commenting on this verse, remarks, 'The reader of ancient or modern times can scarcely imagine a more powerful means of conveying David's fidelity' toward the Lord's anointed.

he is (24.17-21; 26.21). After learning that David spared his life the first time, Saul acknowledges that David is loyal to him: 'You are more righteous than I; for you have repaid me good [*ṭôb*], whereas I have repaid you evil' (24.17). Saul expresses his wrongdoing in light of his violation of a *ḥesed*-relationship. He specifies David's *ḥesed* to him; it is an undeserved *ḥesed* in light of his recent actions: 'Today you have explained how you have dealt well [*ṭôb*] with me, in that you did not kill me when the Lord put me into your hands' (24.18). He continues, 'For who has ever found an enemy, and sent the enemy safely away? So may the Lord reward you with good [*ṭôb*] for what you have done to me this day' (24.19). He may feel that he is not in a position to repay David for his *ḥesed*. He does not trust himself, and for a good reason. Evil spirits have been tormenting him; he has more than once unexpectedly gone into a prophetic frenzy. Therefore, he asks God to do *ḥesed* on his behalf for David's act of loyalty to him.

Between these two stories of David's *ḥesed* to Saul is the intriguing story of the marriage of David and Abigail (25.2-42). This also is a story of *ḥesed*.[59] Just as David had argued above that he has performed good (*ḥesed*) even though Saul returned evil for his loyalty, he will face another case in which his good (*ḥesed*) will be not be honored. According to David he has been protecting Nabal's men and his flocks; therefore, he wants to collect what is due to him. He makes a request based on a *ḥesed*-relationship between his men and Nabal's men. He sends his men to Nabal with the following message: 'Ask your young men, and they will tell you. Therefore let my young men find favor [*ḥēn*] in your sight; for we have come on a feast day. Please give whatever you have at hand to your servants and to your son David' (1 Sam. 25.8).[60] The phrase 'to find *ḥēn* in your eyes', as we have seen before, functions as confirmation of a *ḥesed*-relationship and a polite way of asking for *ḥesed*. But Nabal rejects David's claim that he owes *ḥesed* and insults David: 'Who is David? Who is the son of Jesse? There are many servants today who are breaking away from their masters' (v. 10). Nabal has the freedom not to do *ḥesed*. But he does not understand David. David does not take 'no' for an answer. He is used to getting his way.

David is furious and prepares his men for an attack on Nabal. One of Nabal's servants tells Abigail, Nabal's wife, how Nabal treated David's men

59. This story is framed by two notes: Samuel's death (25.1) and David's marriage to Ahinoam of Jezreel and Michal's marriage to Palti (25.43-44). Perhaps ch. 25 is a series of incidents involving ending and forming relationships: Samuel's relationship to the people of Israel and the living ends; Nabal and Abigail's relationship is disconnected; Abigail and David form a new relationship; David and Ahinoam form a new relationship; David and Michal are disconnected; and Michal and Palti form a new relationship.

60. VanderKam ('Davidic Complicity', p. 525) suggests that David deliberately provoked an incident with Nabal in order to gain access to Nabal's fabulous wealth.

and explains, 'Yet the men were very good [*ṭôb*] to us, and we suffered no harm, and we never missed anything when we were in the fields, as long as we were with them' (v. 15). The servant confirms that David and his men did provide protection for Nabal's livestock, albeit unbeknownst to him. Now David is coming toward Nabal's estate, thinking to himself, 'Surely it was in vain that I protected all that this fellow has in the wilderness, so that nothing was missed of all that belonged to him; but he has returned me evil for good [*ṭôb*]' (v. 21). Nabal, in David's opinion, has violated the principle of *quid pro quod*, a foundation of a *ḥesed*-relationship. Nabal's wife Abigail prevents a massacre; she meets David and persuades him to refrain from shedding blood. In her speech to David, Abigail summarizes two pillars that will support the house of David: David's righteousness and God's loyalty will build 'a sure house' (*bayit nĕ'emān*) for David (vv. 28-29). Then she eloquently proposes a *ḥesed*-relationship with him:

> When the Lord has done to my lord according to all the good [*ṭôb*] that he has spoken concerning you, and has appointed you prince over Israel, my lord shall have no cause of grief, or pangs of conscience, for having shed blood without cause or for having saved himself. And when the Lord has dealt well [*ṭôb*] with my lord, then remember your servant (25.30-31).

She claims that she has done *ḥesed* for David by saving him from shedding blood, and when God extends *ṭôb* (mentioned twice) to David, she anticipates that David will extend his *ḥesed* to her. He happily obliges and calls for her to be his wife immediately after Nabal's mysterious death. Abigail gladly accepts, jumps on a donkey, and rides into the sunset with David as his wife (25.40-42).

One has to wonder about Abigail's eagerness to be David's wife, jumping into David's arms on the day her husband died. She is not a woman of *jeong* from Nabal's point of view; that is, she has no legal duty to stay with the dead man, but she shows no affection or kindness to her husband, even if her husband was a foolish man. From David's perspective, however, she is a woman of loyalty; she gladly took David's side from the beginning of this episode.

In ch. 27 David, along with his wives and his six hundred men and their families, goes back to Achish of Gath and enters the service of Achish (27.1–28.3). The narrator explains that he has no choice but to escape to the Philistine territory since Saul is still determined to kill him. The narrative is clear that David goes to the Philistine lord in order to stay alive. There may have been two factors in David's decision to enter into Achish's service: the people of Judah are still loyal to Saul, and David now is strong enough to form an alliance with Achish against Saul (more on this point in Chapter 5). It is evident that David negotiates a *ḥesed*-relationship with Achish. He says to Achish in 27.5, 'If I have found favor (*ḥēn*) in your sight, let a place be given me in one of the country towns, so that I may live there; for why should your servant live in the royal city with you?' David forms a *ḥesed*-relationship with Achish by offering his service in return for a town. He is initiating a *ḥesed*-relationship, using *ḥēn* as a polite term to request *ḥesed* from someone of higher social status (or from a situationally superior person). The narrator continues to play on the tension between the outer appearance (to the eyes) and the inner motives (of the heart). Achish gives him the city of Ziklag in good faith, believing that his *ḥēn* will be returned with David's *ḥesed*. David's act of loyalty to Achish is to raid towns in Judah and share the spoil with Achish, but unbeknownst to Achish, the narrative claims, David and his men raid non-Judahite towns (the Geshurites, the Girzites, and the Amalekites), though David tells Achish that he has been taking spoils from the region of Judah (against the Negeb of Judah, the Negeb of the Jerahmeelites, and the Negeb of the Kenites). He makes sure no one is alive from the sacked towns in order to hide his duplicity from Achish (27.11). He maintains a *ḥesed*-relationship with Achish through lies and with the elders of Judah through gifts (30.26-31).[61]

Achish is so convinced of David's loyalty to him that Achish makes him his own bodyguard for life (28.1-2).[62] He believes that David can never go back to the people of Judah after what David alleges to have done to them. Then the Philistines gather their forces for an all-out war against Saul's forces. After an interesting story about Saul's encounter with the medium at Endor (28.3-25), which we will examine below, the story leading to the war between the Philistines and the Israelites picks up in ch. 29. David and his men join the Philistines at Aphek to do battle against Saul and the Israelites (v. 2).[63] The Philistine lords recognize David and recite the proverb of David's heroism (for the fourth time in the narrative), 'Saul has killed his

61. Polzin (*Samuel and the Deuteronomist*, p. 217) notes a lingering question related to David's continual use of duplicity to get what he wants: 'the reader's recognition of Achish's foolishness carries a corresponding realization of David's growing duplicity. One continues to wonder whether David's dealings with various Israelites might not conceal similarly self-serving motives'.

62. Perhaps it is at this time that David acquired the Cherethites and the Pelethites, who are fiercely loyal to David, for his service. They will serve as David's bodyguard for the remainder of his life. They will play an important role during David's reign.

63. David's loyalty to his men is questionable. He puts his men's lives in jeopardy by putting them in the service of Achish. Achish thinks David and his men are completely loyal to him. Are they privy to David's duplicity? Do they know that they are to feign loyalty to Achish? Not surprisingly, Achish, like everyone else, 'loves' David. His men 'love' him, but he has put his men's lives in jeopardy. Moreover, he is prepared to send his men into battle against the Israelites. As Brueggemann (*First and Second Samuel*, p. 226) notes, 'The odd tension between loyalty and betrayal is not foreign to David, for that has been his story, implicitly with Saul and explicitly with Achish (1 Sam. 27)'.

thousands, and David his ten thousands', and refuse to let David and his 'Hebrews' go to war with them (vv. 4-5). They are afraid that David and his Hebrews will turn against them.[64] Achish vouches for David's *ḥesed* to no avail; therefore, he asks David to go back to Ziklag: 'As the Lord lives, you have been honest, and to me it seems right ["good in my eyes"] that you should march out and in with me in the campaign; for I have found nothing wrong in you from the day of your coming to me until today. Nevertheless the lords do not approve of you ["in the eyes of the lords you are not good"]' (v. 6). When David protests, Achish replies, 'I know that you are as blameless in my sight ["you are good in my eyes"] as an angel of God; nevertheless, the commanders of the Philistines have said, "He shall not go up with us to the battle"' (v. 9). Achish relies on his eyes to discern David's motives. Many have assumed or misconstrued David's motives, and they have paid dearly for such mistakes. Luckily for Achish, the Philistine lords are not convinced of David's loyalty to them.

Upon returning to Ziklag David learns that it has been burnt to the ground and everything in it has been taken (30.1-6). David's men, who have been following him since ch. 22, are loyal to David. However, when they discover that their home is burned and loved ones have been taken captive, they are ready to stone David (v. 6). David is a realist. He knows that their *ḥesed* can be counted on only when things are going well. They can betray him just as they have betrayed Saul.[65] For now, David does what he has done whenever he is in trouble or has important decisions to make: he inquires of Yahweh. After receiving a positive answer to pursue the culprits, he and his men pursue the raiders and are successful in recovering all that belonged to them and more (vv. 7-20). The four hundred men do not want the two hundred men to have a share in the spoil 'except that each man take his wife and children, and leave' (v. 22). The text calls the four hundred men *'îš rā' ûbĕlîya'al* ('men of evil and worthlessness'), which indicates that their proposal is an act of disloyalty. They are unfaithful to their fellow comrades and to David. Yet David calls them 'my brothers' (*'eḥāy*) and gives credit to God for the successful raid (v. 23). He upholds the *ḥesed*-relationship of the community, wins them over with his words, and divides the spoil from the Amalekites between the four hundred men who pursue the Amalekites and the two hundred men who stayed behind to guard the equipment (vv. 24-25). He is a master of acquiring and maintaining the *ḥesed* of his people. Moreover,

64. This has happened before: 'Now the Hebrews who previously had been with the Philistines and had gone up with them into the camp turned and joined the Israelites who were with Saul and Jonathan' (14.21). More on the 'Hebrews' in Chapter 5.

65. This may be the reason why he will rely more on the loyalty of the Chrethites, the Pelethites, and the Gittites who are loyal exclusively to him, and less and less on the 'Hebrews' whose loyalty can be divided.

David sends gifts from the spoil 'to his friends, the elders of Judah' (v. 27). He has been trying to woo the allegiance from the leaders of Judah since the beginning of his wilderness period in order to establish his base there.

We now need to go back to ch. 28 and discuss this story as it relates to this section and specifically to the theme of *ḥesed*. Saul is afraid when he sees the Philistines encamped for battle. He inquires of Yahweh, but God does not answer. God has not communicated with Saul for some time now. Saul is desperate and goes to the medium at Endor. He asks to speak to Samuel, who had tormented Saul's life while he was alive. Even in death Samuel stays true to his character. He is blunt and harsh. He has no sympathy for Saul. The man has no *jeong*. He condemns Saul's unfaithfulness to God, names David as the neighbor to whom God will give his kingdom, and delivers an oracle of judgment: 'Moreover the Lord will give Israel along with you into the hands of the Philistines; and tomorrow you and your sons shall be with me; the Lord will also give the army of Israel into the hands of the Philistines' (28.19). After hearing Samuel's oracle, Saul falls to the ground, completely spent from lack of food and full of anxiety. The woman of Endor wants to set food for him (28.20-22). He refuses, but his servants join her in urging him to eat (28.23). Saul is moved by their *jeong* and complies in the end. He shows his appreciation for the woman's and his servants' display of *jeong* (kindness and affection). Then she goes out of her way to prepare a meal fit for a king. Their *ḥesed* lifts him from the ground and gives him the strength to go on and face his death.[66]

From Saul's Death to Becoming King of Judah and Israel (1 Samuel 31.1–2 Samuel 5.12)

This section begins with the ignominious death of Saul (1 Sam. 31.1-10) and the inspiring *ḥesed* of the people of Jabesh-gilead (31.11-13). An Amalekite brings the news of the death of Saul and Jonathan and also Saul's crown and armlet to David (2 Sam. 1.1-11). David immediately has the bringer of the bad news killed and composes a heartwrenching lament for Saul and Jonathan, a brilliant display of his *ḥesed* to them (2 Sam. 1.11-27). The people of Judah anoint David as their king, and David lauds the *ḥesed* shown by the people of Jabesh-gilead to Saul (2 Sam. 2.1-7). From 2 Sam. 2.8 to 5.5 the narrative recounts how the house of David triumphs over the house of Saul and how David wins over the loyalty of the elders of Israel, who are

66. When David fasts after his son born of Bathsheba is taken ill, his servants ask him to get up from the ground and have food, but he refuses (2 Sam. 12.17). His servants do not ask him again. Their *ḥesed* is limited to their duty (loyalty). They have no *jeong* for David.

by and large still faithful to Saul and his house. David is the king over Judah but not over Israel. Abner, the commander of Saul's army takes Ishbaal, son of Saul, and makes him king over all Israel (2.8-9). War between the house of David and the house of Saul lasts many years, but 'David grew stronger and stronger, while the house of Saul became weaker and weaker' (3.1). The turning point of the war occurs when Abner defects to David and promises to bring the entire house of Israel over to him (3.21). The reason for his defection is that Abner has shown *ḥesed* to the house of Saul but feels that he is not appreciated by Ishbaal. His overture of *ḥesed* to David is not appreciated by Joab, whose brother Asahel had been killed earlier by Abner, and Joab murders Abner (3.27). Now David's victory is a foregone conclusion. When the news of Abner's death reaches Israel, Ishbaal's 'courage failed, and all Israel was dismayed' (4.1). Then Ishbaal is betrayed by his own servants (4.2-8). They bring Ishbaal's severed head to David, expecting a reward, but David has them killed, showing his respect to Ishbaal (4.9-12). Then all the tribes of Israel come to Hebron and anoint him king over Israel (5.1-5). He then conquers Jerusalem with his own men and there builds for himself a house worthy of a king (5.6-11). Finally, he perceives that God 'had established him king over Israel, and that he had exalted his kingdom for the sake of his people Israel' (5.12).

David and his men are successful in defeating the Amalekites (1 Sam. 30), but Saul and the Israelites are defeated by the Philistines. Saul dies along with Jonathan on Mt. Gilboa (31.1-7). At the final battle against the Philistines, Saul is badly wounded. He asks his armor-bearer to finish him off, but his armor-bearer refuses to thrust his sword through him (31.4). Saul thrusts himself with his own sword; when his armor-bearer sees him dead, he also falls on his own sword and dies with Saul (31.5). This incident attests again to the ambivalent relationship between Saul and his servants: the fact that Saul's servants do not obey him, but they show their *jeong* to him. The armor-bearer demonstrates his *ḥesed* to his king, the only way he could under the circumstances. He refuses to kill his king, but he is willing to die with him. Then Saul's body is mutilated and put on display for all to see in a Philistine town. Saul is dishonored. But the men of Jabesh-gilead honor Saul with their heroic deed. They risk their lives to retrieve the bodies of Saul and his sons from the Philistines. They give Saul and his sons a proper burial and fast for seven days (31.8-13). They show remarkable *ḥesed* to a man who delivered them from the Ammonites. Their action reflects more than their duty or obligation (the loyalty side of *ḥesed*) to their king; it exemplifies their affection and kindness (the *jeong* side of *ḥesed*) to their beleaguered leader.

David hears the new of Saul's and Jonathan's death from an Amalekite, not an Israelite, who also brings the spoil (Saul's crown and armlet) from his scavenging after the battle. He even claims that Saul had asked him to finish him off and that he complied with his request (2 Sam. 1.10). The Amalekites! They were Saul's stumbling block who brought God's final rejection of him (1 Sam. 15). Saul, a man of *jeong*, spared King Agag the Amalekite (1 Sam. 15.8); Samuel, a man of unyielding loyalty, hacked Agag to pieces before the Lord (1 Sam. 15.32-33). The Amalekites! They had burned Ziklag and took captive all the people in it (1 Sam. 30). David pursued them, attacked them, and took their spoil. And here stands an Amalekite before David, expecting a reward for bringing Saul's crown and armlet. He will get a reward he deserves. But David does not know the messenger's ethnic identity; first David tears his clothes, mourns and weeps, and fasts until evening for Saul and his son Jonathan.[67] Then David asks where he is from. The man answers, 'I am the son of a resident alien [*gēr*], an Amalekite' (2 Sam. 1.13). He is not a foreigner after all: or is he? What if he were an Israelite? David orders him killed. Would David have killed an Israelite in such a manner? The reason for his killing: the Amalekite messenger has killed Yahweh's anointed. David repays him with evil because he has done evil against Yahweh's anointed.

David's show of *ḥesed* to Saul is extravagant. He overstresses his faithfulness to Saul and Jonathan when he composes a lament for them (2 Sam. 1.17-27). He calls them 'the beloved' (*hanne'ehābîm*) and 'the delightful' (*hannĕ'îmim*). He claims that 'in life and in death they were not divided' (2 Sam. 1.23), contrary to the way their relationship was depicted. He is distressed for Jonathan whom he calls 'my brother' (*'āḥî*) and 'a dear friend to me' (*nā'amtā lî mĕ'ōd*). He acknowledges Jonathan's love for him: 'your love to me was wonderful, passing the love of women' (2 Sam. 1.26). Yet he does not explicitly express his love for Jonathan. He never does; he never overcommits to a relationship.

After reciting his heartfelt lament for Saul and Jonathan, David immediately inquires of Yahweh whether he should move out of Ziklag and enter any of the cities in Judah. He obviously knows what is at stake. Saul is dead. There is a power vacuum to be filled. God tells him to go up to Hebron. This is not surprising, since Hebron is recognized as the capital city of Judah, and he has been courting it for a while.[68] He enters Hebron with his entire

67. Although this messenger gives a conflicting report on Saul's death, Brueggemann (*First and Second Samuel*, p. 213) observes that 'the narrative is perhaps not concerned with who killed Saul. It is rather preoccupied with David's faithful, magisterial response to Saul's death. David grieves and acts for the sake of Saul's honor'. Polzin, however, suggests that both David and his double (the Amalekite messenger) 'outwardly mourn the death of Saul, but perhaps both secretly rejoice over it. *Neither actually kills Saul but both look forward to profiting from his death*' (*David and the Deuteronomist*, p. 7, emphasis original).

68. He also has a connection to Hebron via his marriage to Abigail. More on this point in Chapter 5.

entourage, flanked by Abigail on one arm and Ahinoam on the other. There the people of Judah come and anoint him king over the house of Judah.

David's first act as king of Judah is to send a message to the people of Jabesh-gilead (2.4-7). He is impressed with the *ḥesed* shown to Saul by the men of Jabesh and now wants to negotiate a *ḥesed*-relationship with them. He says (2 Sam. 2.5-6a), 'May you be blessed by the Lord, because you showed this loyalty [*ḥesed*] to Saul your lord, and buried him! Now may the Lord show *steadfast love and faithfulness* [*ḥesed wĕ'emet*] to you!' He reframes this *ḥesed*-relationship between Saul and the Jabeshites by having God take Saul's place. Then he invites himself into this *ḥesed*-relationship by acting as God's agent. He says that 'I will do for you this goodness [*ṭôb*] just as you have performed this deed' (my translation; 2.6b). Here *ṭôb* is in parallel with *ḥesed wĕ'emet*; therefore, David's *ṭôb* is equivalent to God's faithful loyalty [*ḥesed wĕ'emet*]. He now wants them to join him and reminds them to whom they should show *ḥesed*: 'Therefore let your hands be strong, and be valiant; for Saul your lord is dead, and the house of Judah has anointed me king over them' (2.7).[69] He wants to take Saul's place in the *ḥesed*-relationship. Is this a threat to impose himself on them or an invitation to renew the *ḥesed*-relationship they already have? David is indeed a heavy-handed negotiator of *ḥesed*.

There is no word on whether the Jabeshites accept his offer or continue to be loyal to the house of Saul. David may have won over the loyalty of the house of Judah, but it will not be an easy task to win over the *ḥesed* of those who are still devoted to the house of Saul. This is evident by the fact that while David rules from Hebron for seven years and six months, the text acknowledges that 'there was a long war between the house of Saul and the house of David' (3.1). The Israelites probably would not have embraced David if not for the fact that Abner, the commander of Israel's army, and Ishbaal, the king of Israel, are murdered. These deaths, in addition to the death of Saul and Jonathan, made it possible for David to win over the loyalty of the elders of Israel. They really had no choice since there was no viable heir to the house of Saul.[70]

69. Brueggemann (*First and Second Samuel*, pp. 220-21) comments on David's tactic in this way: 'It is as though David reminds the city that it can expect no more *ḥesed* from Saul, who is dead and has no more *ḥesed* to give, but may find adequate *ḥesed* in the enduring inclination of Yahweh. In a skillful move, David then promises he will do "good" for them... Moreover, David's offer of "good" is a way through which Yahweh's *ḥesed we'emet* are mediated. David, according to his own words, is an offer of Yahweh's solidarity. David is Saul's rightful successor as the vehicle of *ḥesed*'.

70. There is a note in 2 Sam. 4.4 about Mephibosheth son of Jonathan who is crippled in his feet. The survival of Mephibosheth will give David an opportunity to display his *ḥesed* to Jonathan and the house of Saul later in the narrative (2 Sam. 9). Brueggemann (*First and Second Samuel*, p. 234) comments on the importance of this note in the larger

Second Samuel 3 is a chapter of betrayal and unfaithfulness. Abner could have easily swayed the Israelites to join David once Saul and Jonathan die; however, he stays devoted to the house of Saul by placing Ishbaal as king over Israel. At some point Abner acquires a desire to become king himself: 'While there was war between the house of Saul and the house of David, Abner was making himself strong in the house of Saul' (3.6). The fact that Abner takes Rizpah, Saul's sole concubine, attests to his desire to take over the kingship from Ishbaal. Bodner notes that by attempting to acquire Saul's concubine, Abner is adopting the same strategy as David, who is described in 3.2-6 as 'becoming strong and partially gaining mastery over the house of Saul by means of wives and sons'.[71] David will continue his strategy by repossessing Michal, daughter of Saul, in order gain control over the house of Saul just as Abner tried here to possess another woman belonging to the house of Saul.

In the following verses, Abner's taking of Saul's concubine becomes an issue for Ishbaal because Ishbaal recognizes Abner's intent to gain control over the house of Saul.

Ishbaal is weak but he is not stupid. He realizes this and confronts Abner, who reacts violently to Ishbaal's accusation: 'Am I a dog's head for Judah? Today I keep showing loyalty [*ḥesed*] to the house of your father Saul, to his brothers, and to his friends, and have not given you into the hand of David; and yet you charge me now with a crime concerning this woman' (3.8).[72] Moreover, he rants that he will turn over Saul's kingdom to David (3.9-10). Ishbaal is speechless because he fears Abner. He has forfeited Abner's *ḥesed* over Rizpah. However, if he does not confront Abner for this action, it would be only a matter of time before Abner took over the throne as well.

Abner sends messengers to David and proposes a *ḥesed*-relationship: 'To whom does the land belong? Make your covenant with me. Behold, my hand is with you to bring over all Israel to you' (2 Sam. 3.12; my translation). Abner wants to form a bond (*ḥesed*) with David in return for his act of

narrative: 'In terms of the total David plot, this verse stands midway between I Samuel 20.14-17 and II Samuel 9.1-8. The subject of these two passages is the kindness (*ḥesed*) of David toward Jonathan. In the former, David promised Jonathan that he would not cut off his "loyalty" to the house and name of Jonathan. In the latter, David now keeps that promise by asking if there is anyone left of the house of Saul to whom the king may show kindness. David promises *ḥesed* and fulfills that promise. Mephiboshet is the channel for the fulfillment of the promise. Thus this verse sets the stage for the affirmation that David is a man of *ḥesed* who keeps vows, honors friends, and shows mercy to those with whom he is bound'.

71. Bodner, *David Observed*, p. 45.

72. Bodner (*David Observed*, p. 48) makes the following observation: 'Abner does not directly answer Ishbosheth's question, but circuitously turns his response toward his avowed loyalty (חסד) to the house of Saul… Abner expresses anger only over the charge within the context of his חֶסֶד ("loyalty"), not an acknowledgment or denial of the charge'.

loyalty, which is to turn the allegiance of Israel to David. David likes the proposal; he answers *ṭôb* ('good'), 'I will make a covenant with you' (v. 13). But David is a master negotiator of *ḥesed*, and he wants Abner to add something more to the deal: 'But one thing I require of you: you shall never appear in my presence unless you bring Saul's daughter Michal when you come to see me' (v. 13). Then David reminds Ishbaal (and the reader) that he had paid for 'my wife Michal' (v. 14). David asks for 'Saul's daughter' because she is 'my wife' (cf. 1 Sam. 19.11). Michal is again placed in the 'in-between' space of competing loyalties. David does not love Michal; he only wants what belongs to Saul. Similar to Jonathan's case he never says he loves her. He does not renew their marriage or 'love'. It is a strategy to gain mastery over the house of Saul and to have someone who can produce a Saulide under his control, and, of course, to test Abner's commitment to the proposal. Abner obliges and sends Michal to David (v. 16).[73] He transfers Saul's daughter to David. Then he speaks to the elders of Israel, 'For some time past you have been seeking David as king over you' (v. 17). He reminds them that they too love David (cf. 1 Sam. 18), and then transfers God's words to Saul to David: 'For the Lord has promised David: Through my servant David I will save my people Israel from the hand of the Philistines, and from all their enemies' (v. 18).[74] Then he speaks directly to the Benjaminites, who are the staunchest followers of their kinsman, Saul. Now Abner has done his part and reports that 'Israel and the whole house of Benjamin' are ready to embrace David as their king. He has now betrayed Ishbaal and the house of Saul. David is ready to benefit from this act of disloyalty.[75]

Abner comes to David in order to seal a *ḥesed*-relationship. Then David welcomes Abner and his twenty men and gives them a feast. David is pleased with this turn of events. Abner pledges his loyalty to David again: 'Let me go and rally all Israel to my lord the king, in order that they may make a covenant with you, and that you may reign over all that your heart desires' (3.21). David sends him on his way, and Abner leaves in peace (*šālôm*). Joab arrives; the narrator notes again that David has sent Abner in *šālôm* (v. 22). Joab too learns that David has send Abner in *šālôm* (v. 23). Joab calls back Abner, without David's knowledge, and takes him aside for a private talk (v. 27). Joab betrays Abner's trust, the narrator adds David's

73. Bodner (*David Observed*, p. 50) sees this demand as a message for Abner to ponder: 'In light of Abner's alleged appropriation of Rizpah, David's demand for Michal illustrates the political power of a royal wife and his own superior claims to the throne. This may be a veiled message that Abner should be content with a subordinate status in David's kingdom'.

74. God does not utter these words to David but only to Saul (1 Sam. 10.1).

75. Brueggemann (*First and Second Samuel*, p. 226) remarks that 'David is a highly complex, not to say ambiguous, character, who benefits from the shattering ugliness of betrayal, which is a convenient contrast to his own innocence'.

trust as well, by killing him in broad daylight in a public place. Joab does the killing; David, however, is also responsible. Abner's *šālôm* was David's responsibility. It is David who betrays Abner's trust as well. The word *šālôm* ('peace') also appears three times when David hosts Uriah the Hittite (2 Sam. 11.7). Uriah drinks and eats in David's presence (11.13) before being sent away from Jerusalem. David threw a banquet for Abner (3.20). In the case of Uriah, David instructs Joab to kill him. In the case of Abner, the narrator strongly denies that David had any part in Joab's murder of Abner.

David is extremely upset when he learns of Joab's killing of Abner. Abner was ambushed; he had no clue. The narrator, however, has prepared the readers for this murder by citing the fact that Abner had killed Asahel, Joab's brother, earlier in the narrative (2.18-23), making it clear that Joab has a reason to kill Abner, while David does not. The narrator blames Joab for killing Abner out of vengeance for his brother's murder. Joab is an unsavory character but is completely loyal to David. David will benefit immensely from Abner's death, yet he laments over Abner's death and asserts his own innocence (vv. 31-39). The narrator overstresses David's grief and innocence; the first words that come out of David's mouth upon learning of Abner's death are: 'I and my kingdom are forever guiltless before the Lord for the blood of Abner son of Ner. May the guilt fall on the head of Joab, and on all his father's house' (vv. 28-29). Then he orders Joab and the people to 'tear your clothes, and put on sack cloth, and mourn over Abner' (v. 31). He weeps at Abner's grave and utters a lament. The people observe his conduct and weep with him. They are convinced that 'the king had no part in the killing of Abner son of Ner' (v. 37). Then he reprimands and curses the sons of Zeruiah again (v. 39), but surprisingly he does not punish them. David's response demonstrates his *ḥesed* to Abner, but there is still a lingering doubt about his role in Abner's death.[76]

Upon hearing of Abner's death, Ishbaal loses courage and becomes a lame duck waiting for his expiration. Again David does not have to stain his hands with blood. The story of betrayal and disloyalty that brings down the house of Saul, which started in ch. 3, continues in ch. 4. Ishbaal's two captains of raiding bands (the position David held while he was in Achish's service), Rechab and Baanah (Gibeonites who were resident aliens; cf. the Amalekite messenger in 2 Sam. 1), assassinate him in his own bedchamber. They betray Ishbaal in his own house. They come to David carrying Ishbaal's severed head, expecting a reward. We have seen this before; we know what will happen. David makes another pious speech:

76. Bodner (*David Observed*), argues the narrator gives the opinion of the people but the narrator's actual opinion is not stated. There is an air of doubt as to David's innocence; David's dramatic change in his opinion of Abner is unconvincing. Bodner summarizes, 'David is successful insofar as public relations are concerned. Yet as the episode concludes, there are more questions than answers about David's knowledge' (p. 62).

> As the Lord lives, who has redeemed my life out of every adversity, when the one who told me, 'See, Saul is dead', thought he was bringing good news, I seized him and killed him at Ziklag—this was the reward I gave him for his news. How much more then, when wicked men have killed a righteous man on his bed in his own house! And now shall I not require his blood at your hand, and destroy you from the earth? (2 Sam. 4.9-11).

David repays the assassins, whose deed will enable him to acquire Saul's kingdom, with their own blood. They were opportunists who thought they were performing *ḥesed* for David. They just happened to be dealing with the ultimate opportunist. David wants to make them an example of those who are disloyal to their king. He has them killed and their hands and feet cut and their bodies hung in Hebron for all to see. He shows his *ḥesed* to Ishbaal and the house of Saul by taking vengeance on them, but he also confirms his innocence in Ishbaal's death and sends a warning against those who are not loyal to the king.[77]

The assassination of Ishbaal is the last hurdle David needs to clear in order to become the king of Israel. All the elders of Israel come to David at Hebron and say to him: 'Look, we are your bone and flesh. For some time, while Saul was king over us, it was you who led out Israel and brought it in. The Lord said to you: It is you who shall be shepherd of my people Israel, you who shall be ruler over Israel' (5.1-2).[78] The narrator uses the shepherd metaphor to summarize David's rise from shepherd boy (1 Sam. 16.11) to shepherd king. The mission is accomplished; David finally is anointed king over Israel and becomes king of Judah and Israel. The narrator reports that he reigned over all Israel and Judah for thirty-three years.

Yet there is one more thing David wants to do to secure his kingship. He immediately turns to acquiring his own city to build his own house. He

77. Brueggemann (*First and Second Samuel*, p. 236) makes the following comment on the fate of these two men: 'These less discerning, less cunning ones must die in the service of David's overriding destiny. David's destiny advances precisely through their misdeeds. They pay—and David moves a great step toward fulfillment and power. The narrative constructs a powerful interface between such cunning destructiveness by lesser characters and David's firm resolve to do *ḥesed*. Their destructiveness does not nullify David's resolve'.

78. McCarter (*II Samuel: A New Translation with Introduction, Notes, and Commentary* [AB, 9; Garden City, NY: Doubleday, 1984], pp. 133-34), notes: 'To this end he has presented David throughout as a man innocent of overweening ambition, whose extraordinary successes result less often from self-interested undertakings of his own than from the willing deeds of others—the men of Judah (2.4), Achish of Gath (I Sam. 27.5; cf. 29.6), Jonathan (I Sam 19.4; 20.9; 23.16; etc.), Michal (I Sam 19.11-17), Saul himself (I Sam 16.21-22), and still others—whose affection and loyalty he seems to command naturally—or rather supernaturally, by the will of Yahweh. The present episode is not an exception to this pattern'.

conquers Jerusalem, a city belonging neither to Israel nor to Judah but to the Jebusites, turns it into the capital of his kingdom and then builds his house there (5.6-12). Rather than staying at Hebron, which is the capital of Judah, or moving to Gibeah, which was the seat of Saul's kingdom, David chooses to establish his seat of power in a 'third' city. He also establishes a tie with Hiram of Tyre who sends him builders and supplies for David's house. This is perhaps David's first inter-regional alliance with powers outside of the Palestine region. Through this diplomatic relation he now is recognized by other powers as king like those of other kingdoms. Upon building his house and establishing his status in the inter-regional political arena, David perceives that 'the Lord had established him king over Israel, and that he had exalted his kingdom for the sake of his people Israel' (5.12).

Conclusion

David's rise to kingship can be attributed to acts of *ḥesed* extended to David from all sorts of people, who love him, and most importantly from God, who chose him. Everyone partook in raising David to this position. Now his house is firmly established on the rock of God's faithfulness for the sake of his people; in the future God will maintain his loyalty to the people for the sake of David. During David's journey to the top, there have been many memorable characters who provided him with loyalty and *jeong*: Jonathan, Michal, Abigail, Samuel, Achish, Abner, Joab, even Saul, among others. There have been many intriguing moments of *ḥesed*. There also have been those who have been discarded for the sake of David: Saul, Abner, the Amalekite messenger, the Beerothite brothers. For a man who received so much loyalty and *jeong*, it is still uncertain whether David is indeed a man of *ḥesed*. He is a complex character, and he is an ambiguous man of *ḥesed*. He is a calculating and tough negotiator of loyalty. He takes what others give; he does not give when it is not to his advantage. In the next chapter we will see the *jeong* side of David's persona, for until now David has not needed to compromise. He has been riding on God's *ḥesed* to the top.

4

SUSTAINING DAVID WITH *ḤESED*: 2 SAMUEL 5–24; 1 KINGS 1–2

In this chapter, I will examine the narrative from 2 Samuel 5 to 1 Kings 2 with the focus on the theme of *ḥesed*. This is not a difficult task since the narrative has a strong concern for *ḥesed*.[1] In Chapter 3, we have seen that *ḥesed* is a hermeneutical key in the first half of the David story that explains how David was able to establish his house on the *ḥesed* of people who love him and of God who chose him. In this chapter, we will see how David establishes his house on God's *ḥesed* but then suffers greatly due to his own unfaithfulness and his children's disloyalty. He, however, maintains his rule, and his kingdom is sustained by the *ḥesed* of some unlikely allies and the ever-dependent God.

A brief summary of the content of the second half of the David story is in order. David makes his home in Jerusalem and acts like a typical monarch of the ancient Near East, building his harem and producing children (5.13-16). The Philistines are taken aback by David's swift rise to power over Israel and try to curtail his influence over the region. David is victorious over the Philistines (5.17-25). Now he has delivered Israel from the hands of the Philistines. Then he, who is from the tribe of Judah, secures the loyalty of the northern tribes by bringing the Ark of the Covenant, which is associated with the northern religious tradition, into Jerusalem (2 Sam. 6). In ch. 7, David offers to build God a temple/house, a final 'building' project that will elevate his status among his fellow kings of the ancient Near East, but God refuses the offer. Instead, Yahweh promises to build him a sure house on

1. J.W. Whedbee, 'On Divine and Human Bonds: The Tragedy of the House of David', in G.M. Tucker, D.L. Petersen, and R.R. Wilson (eds.), *Canon, Theology, and Old Testament Interpretation* (Philadelphia: Fortress Press, 1988), pp. 147-65. Whedbee demonstrates that the theme of divine and human bonds is central and crucial for understanding the David story during his reign in Jerusalem (2 Sam. 5–1 Kgs 2). He convincingly shows that 'the theme of bonding animates the action of this story from start to finish' (p. 150). I disagree with his idea of bonding as 'the creation of covenantal relationships', since I have argued in Chapter 2 that 'bond' or *ḥesed* is not limited to a covenantal relationship; however, I agree with Whedbee that *ḥesed* creates 'bonding' between individuals.

God's *ḥesed*. God offers *ḥesed* to David and his house forever. This section ends with David's victories over the surrounding nations (8.1-14); thus David has saved his people from the enemies all around (cf. 1 Sam. 14.47-48, which also credits Saul with sweeping victories over enemies on every side). A list of names of David's officers appears to indicate that his house is firmly established and his kingdom is enjoying stability and peace (8.15-18).

David is generous with his *ḥesed*, extending it to Mephiboshet son of Jonathan (2 Sam. 9) and Hanun son of Nahash the Ammonite (2 Sam. 10). Yet surprisingly Hanun suspects David's loyalty and insults David's envoy, which results in a war between David and Hanun and his Aramean allies (2 Sam. 10–12). This is a sign that not all is well in David's kingdom and his heart. David then eyes a woman from a distance and commits a serious breach of trust and loyalty when he 'knows' Bathsheba and kills her husband, Uriah the Hittite, along with a score of David's servants (2 Sam. 11). God is not pleased. David's unfaithfulness must be punished. The illegitimate son of David dies, but God sustains David and his house by extending *ḥesed* to David and his (and Bathsheba's) legitimate son Solomon/Jedidiah (2 Sam. 12). Like father, like son—David's eldest son Amnon desires a woman he is forbidden to take, his half-sister Tamar, sister of Absalom (2 Sam. 13). Amnon betrays his father's *jeong* and his sister's trust and rapes Tamar and then sends her away in dishonor. David does not punish Amnon but two years later Absalom betrays David's *jeong* and Amnon's trust and kills Amnon (2 Sam. 14).

Unhappy with the way he is treated by David after David's return from exile, Absalom tests the loyalty of the people, deciding to usurp the throne when he realizes that the people are willing to give their loyalty to him (2 Sam. 15). From Absalom's wooing of the people (2 Sam. 15) to David's return from exile (2 Sam. 20), everyone's *ḥesed* is tested. The Israelites, the Judahites, the Cherethities, the Pelethites, the Gittites, and the servants of David are called upon to show their *ḥesed* to David. Ahithophel and other defectors gather in Hebron to show support to Absalom (2 Sam. 15.7-12). Ziba accuses Mephiboshet of betraying David (15.30-31). Shimei son of Gera, a Benjaminite, curses David (16.5-14). Sheba son of Bichri, a Benjaminite, leads the people of Israel in rebellion against the house of David (2 Sam. 20). However, many, including some unlikely allies, continue to show their *ḥesed* to David. The testing of *ḥesed* ends with the kingdom again firmly in the hands of David. A roster of David's officials, longer than the previous list, ends this section, which may indicate that his rule and kingdom are stronger than before (20.23-26).

We see why David was able to survive troubles from outside as well as from inside his house. A collection of stories in 2 Sam. 21.15-22 and 2 Sam. 23.8-39 shows how loyal his men are to him. The adventures of David and his men of *ḥesed* frame songs attributed to David (2 Sam. 22.1–23.7). David has all reason to praise God. He has been sustained by the *ḥesed* of God and of his people even though sometimes he is unfaithful to his people and to his God (2 Sam. 21 and 24).

Finally, David's last days are recounted in 1 Kgs 1.1–2.12. David is old and frail and is beguiled by Bathsheba and Nathan into designating Solomon as his successor. At the end he returns to his old self and instructs Solomon to take care of business concerning three individuals according to his judgment of their *ḥesed*.

This chapter is divided into five sections: Establishing the House of David on God's *Ḥesed* (2 Sam. 5.13–8.18); The Practice and Betrayal of *Ḥesed* in David's House (2 Sam. 9–14); Sustaining David with *Ḥesed* (2 Sam. 15–20); David's Confidence and his Men of *Ḥesed* (2 Sam. 21–24); and David's Last Days and Judgment of *Ḥesed* (1 Kgs 1–2). Each section will have a chiastic structure, except the last section, and this will guide our discussion.

Establishing the House of David on God's Ḥesed (2 Samuel 5.13–8.18)

The following chiastic structure will guide the discussion in this section:

1a. David builds his harem and sires more children (5.13-16)
  2a. David delivers Israel from the hands of the Philistines (5.17-25)
    3a. David brings the ark of the 'old covenant' to Jerusalem (6.1-20)
    3b. David receives the 'new covenant' from God (7.1-29)
  2b. David delivers Israel from its enemies all around (8.1-14)
1b. David builds his administration (8.15-18)

1a. *David builds his harem and sires more children (5.13-16)*

The narrator notes that David takes more concubines and wives, a sign of a successful monarch in the ancient Near East, and lists the names of the sons born to him in Jerusalem, including Solomon, who will be his successor.[2] David not only has his house built in Jerusalem but adds more sons to his offspring from Hebron (3.2-5); they will assure the success of his dynasty. God shows *ḥesed* to David just as God showed it to Hannah by providing her with many children (cf. 1 Sam. 2.21). He has more children than the previous leaders—Eli, Samuel, and Saul—but they will eventually become a source of troubles and much heartache for him.

2. Solomon's name appears among other sons without added significance, but the fact that the narrator reveals his existence prior to his birth story in 2 Sam. 11–12 shows his significance in the narrative. The narrative from 2 Sam. 5 to 1 Kgs 2 can be viewed as Solomon's succession narrative, as many have argued since L. Rost, *Die Überlieferung von der Thronnachfolge Davids* (BWANT 3/6; Stuttgart: Kohlhammer, 1926).

2a. *David delivers Israel from the hands of the Philistines (5.17-25)*

The Philistines seem to have miscalculated David, like so many people in the story. They are caught off guard by David's meteoric rise to power over Israel, thus consolidating two peoples into one kingdom. They may have allowed him to rule over Judah but not over Israel; now he has become a big threat to their hegemony over the region. They come to attack David (vv. 17, 22). In this war against the Philistines, David is in constant communication with God, always asking God first before setting off on military actions (vv. 19, 23). He exactly follows God's instructions, and the narrator praises David for his faithfulness in observing God's word: 'David did just as the Lord had commanded him' (v. 25). Therefore, the narrative seems to reason, David is able to defeat the Philistines from Geba all the way to Gezer (v. 25). The credit for David's success lies not only in his obedience to God's commandments but also in God's direct involvement in that success. It is Yahweh who does the fighting on his behalf. God breaks forth against the Philistines (v. 20). The Philistines abandon their idols and David's men carry them away (v. 21). These details certainly follow the script of the old divine battle myth; in this case it is Yahweh who is the champion, and defeats the enemy deity (the gods of the Philistines). In the second battle, Yahweh gives a sign to indicate exactly when he will fight against the Philistines; the texts says, 'for then the Lord has gone out before you to strike down the army of the Philistine' (v. 24). It is Yahweh who leads and fights the Philistines; David follows and collects the spoil.

3a. *David brings the ark of the 'old covenant' to Jerusalem (6.1-20)*

The procession of the ark in 2 Samuel 6 continues (from v. 2a) God's involvement in David's march to establish his kingdom and dynasty.[3] Here it is David who leads the ark in a ritualized procession, reenacting the victory of Yahweh as the divine warrior and his consequent accession as king. David's rise to kingship parallels the divine warrior's rise to supremacy: David (like Yahweh/Baal/Marduk) defeats the enemies (5.17-25), marches to the mountaintop/throne (6.1-16), and then ends with the banquet as a celebration of his accession (6.17-19).[4] For David, as well as for his descendants, 'the procession marked a turning point in history. David had succeeded in

3. Many scholars have noted the significance and genius of David's installment of the ark in Jerusalem; it marks an important point in the history of Israelite religion and politics. C.L. Seow (*Myth, Drama, and Politics of David's Dance* [HSM, 46; Atlanta: Scholars Press, 1989], p. 1), remarks that 'scholars hail David's initiative as a brilliant maneuver that effectively galvanized the loose confederation of Israelite tribes into a monarchical state. The procession was, first and foremost, of great political significance inasmuch as it legitimated David and his successors'.

4. Seow (*Myth*, p. 142) states that 'the climax of the celebration was a ritual banquet', which 'corresponds to the victory banquet which the victorious warrior hosts'.

establishing a place for YHWH and, in doing so, had assured a place for himself and his posterity'.[5] In addition to legitimating David as the ruler of Israel and Judah, this act inaugurates the new city and legitimates Jerusalem as the center of David's kingdom and Israelite cult.[6]

With this move, David is able to secure the loyalty of the northern tribes and consolidate the two distinct peoples, Israel and Judah, into one kingdom. The narrator, however, quietly disconnects David's reliance on and attachment to the house of Saul in 6.16-23. Michal 'the daughter of Saul' confronts David for his antics before the people, especially in front of the women.[7] She does not think his behavior is appropriate for a king. David completely dismisses her with these acerbic words: 'It was before the Lord, who chose me in place of your father and all his household, to appoint me as prince over Israel, the people of the Lord, that I have danced before the Lord' (v. 22). Then the narrator brings God's judgment upon her and the entire house of Saul: 'And Michal the daughter of Saul had no child to the day of her death' (v. 23).[8] The triumph of the house of David over the house of Saul is now complete. The tie between the two houses is completely severed. Moreover, the ark, which represent the 'old' covenant associated with the northern tribes, will be replaced by a 'new' covenant specifically tied to David and his dynasty in the next episode.

3b. *David receives the 'new covenant' from God (7.1-29)*

Now, to David's surprise, God will put David and his 'house' on a surer foundation than relying on the house of Saul or even on the old religious artifact from the north. God has made other 'forever' promises to Eli, Samuel, and Saul in the past; however, they did not last more than one generation. Now God makes one for David and his house. When David offers to build God a house/temple, a more permanent and secure place for God to dwell in, Yahweh declines the offer. The narrator plays on the word 'house' and focuses the chapter on building a 'house' (dynasty) for David. God offers an enduring house/dynasty for the sake of David, for his supposed fidelity to God: 'I will not take my steadfast love [*ḥesed*] from him [i.e. Solomon],[9] as I

5. Seow, *Myth*, p. 210.

6. C.L. Seow, 'Ark of the Covenant', in *ABD*, I, pp. 386-93.

7. Michal is referred to as 'Saul's daughter' in v. 20 (cf. 1 Sam. 18.20, 28; 2 Sam. 3.13) rather than 'David's wife' (1 Sam. 19.11; 2 Sam. 3.14). She symbolizes the house of Saul, therefore she has no part in David's future.

8. Note again, Michal 'the daughter of Saul'. Brueggemann (*First and Second Samuel*, p. 252) observes, 'The rhetoric of David's response (vv. 22-23) evidences complete reliance on Yahweh and, at the same time, a disdainful dismissal of Michal and an end to any reliance on Saulide legitimacy'.

9. This offspring from David who will build the house for God and to whom God promises enduring *ḥesed* is none other than Solomon (see 1 Kgs 5.5).

took it from Saul, whom I put away from before you. Your house ["your enduring house"; *ne'man bêtĕkā*] and your kingdom shall be made sure forever before me; your throne [*mamlaktĕkā*] shall be established forever' (vv. 15-16). Brueggemann observes that 'David (and Solomon) are thus contrasted with Saul. Saul could lose Yahweh's *ḥesed*, but David, David's son, and David's line can never lose Yahweh's loyalty. Yahweh has made an unconditional promise'.[10] This 'unconditional'/'forever' promise is different from the ones God made to Saul, Samuel, and Eli. There are no strings attached to God's commitment (*ḥesed*) to David and his house. This is granted unconditionally—the house of David can never lose God's *ḥesed*. Here the relationship between God and David moves beyond the relationship between God and other leaders. It is more intimate, more secure than any other relationships. Their relationship is that of father and son, 'I will be a father to him [David's son], and he shall be a son to me' (v. 14a). Of course, God has expectations and will punish like a parent when David's sons fail to meet those expectations—'When he commits iniquity, I will punish him with a rod such as mortals use, with blows inflicted by human beings' (v. 14b)—but God promises not to sever the relationship with the house of David.

David, in his response to God's promise, repeats God's word several times in his prayer (vv. 18-29). It reads like a strategy to hold God to his pledge; he tries to close any loop-holes that might give God a way to compromise or rescind it. David wants to make sure God knows what he is getting into: 'And now, O Lord God, as for the word that you have spoken concerning your servant and concerning his house, confirm it forever; do as you have promised' (v. 25). David claims that God's reputation and honor are attached to and dependent on the success of this promise: 'Thus your name will be magnified forever in the saying, "The Lord of hosts is God over Israel"; and the house of your servant David will be established before you' (v. 26). David attaches the promise to God's identity: 'And now, O Lord God, you are God, and your words are true [*'emet*], and you have promised this good thing [*haṭṭôbah*] to your servant' (v. 28). It seems as if David is anxious to have the promise written down so that God cannot take it back: 'now therefore may it please you to bless the house of your servant, so that it may continue forever before you; for you, O Lord God, have spoken, and with your blessing shall the house of your servant be blessed forever' (v. 29). In his prayer David uses *'ôlām* ('forever') five times (vv. 24-29), *bêtî* ('my house' or equivalent) six times, *dĕbārĕkā* ('your word' or equivalent) eleven times, and addresses God as *'adōnāy yhwh* ('O my lord Yahweh') eight times. Why is David so anxious? Perhaps it is because he has seen God renege other 'forever' promises made to Eli, Samuel, and Saul.

10. Brueggemann, *First and Second Samuel*, p. 255.

David, too, will sin and fall short of God's expectations like his predecessors; the question is whether God will take away *ḥesed* from David as he has done from Eli, and from Samuel, and from Saul.

2b. *David delivers Israel from its enemies all around (8.1-14)*

David changes after his prayer to God. Chapter 8 summarizes David's military campaigns. This time it is David who attacks the Philistines (v. 1). It is not much of a battle. David takes what he wants from the Philistines; they are no longer a match for him. Hannah's song of reversals becomes a reality. Then David attacks two regional powers, the Moabites and the Arameans, on the other side of Jordan (vv. 1-8) and other neighboring kingdoms (vv. 9-14). David acquires tributes from other kingdoms without much effort (vv. 9-12). They submit to him based on his reputation alone. Those who resist him he puts to the sword and makes his slaves (vv. 13-14). He is the aggressor now.

Another critical change occurs during this time. Even though his relationship with God should be more intimate than ever before, he no longer overtly depends on or communicates with God. In his battle against enemies and neighbors all around, David does not communicate with God. He does not inquire of God anymore. He goes to battle on his own and is successful. The narrator does note that it is God who gives him success, 'The Lord gave victory to David wherever he went' (vv. 6, 14), but God is no longer directly involved in David's battles. One gets the sense that David can take care of himself and the people on his own.

1b. *David builds his administration (8.15-18)*

At the end of this section (8.15-18) a list of David's officials appears, attesting to the stability of his kingdom and a more organized 'administration' to rule over his people. Compared to a similar list for Saul in 1 Sam. 14.29-51, David has more wives, more sons, and more officials. It seems God has blessed David more than Saul, indicating what is so obvious to the reader by now: God loves David more than Saul. The caption on the list also attests to the peace and security the people are enjoying now that David is in charge: 'so David reigned over all Israel; and David administered justice and equity to all his people' (8.15). Whereas Saul's administration had to deal with the Philistine problem, which it never was able to solve, David's administration manages the everyday affairs of the kingdom so that David could 'do justice and righteousness for all his people' (*'ōśeh mišpāṭ ûṣĕdāqah lĕkol 'ammô*).

All is good for David. David has his house in Jerusalem, the new capital of his kingdom; he acquires more wives and sires more children (1a) and expands his administration (1b). The people of Israel are able to enjoy peace, justice, and prosperity because David finally eliminates the Philistine threat

(2a), expands his kingdom, and removes the threat from the enemies all around (2b). This is possible because David unites the peoples of Israel and Judah into one kingdom by bringing the old cultic object associated with the northern tribes to Jerusalem but permanently cuts ties with the house of Saul (3a). Now David will base his kingdom and dynasty on a new covenant: God's promise of eternal *ḥesed* to him and his descendants (3b). What can possibly go wrong for David now?

The Practice and Betrayal of Ḥesed *in David's House (2 Samuel 9–14)*

The following chiastic structure will guide the discussion in this section:

1a. David extends *ḥesed* (loyalty) to Mephiboshet ([21.1-14+] 9.1-13)
  2a. The Betrayal of David's *ḥesed* (loyalty) by Hanun (10.1-19)
    3. God extends *ḥesed* (loyalty and *jeong*) to David (11.1–12.25)
  2b. The Betrayal of David's *ḥesed* (*jeong*) by his son (13.1-22)
1b. David extends *ḥesed* (*jeong*) to Absalom (13.23–14.33)

1a. *David extends* ḥesed *(loyalty) to Mephiboshet ([21.1-14+] 9.1-13)*
I will read 2 Sam. 9.1-13 and 21.1-14 together at this point; later I will also read 21.1-14 as part of chs. 21–24. By doing this I am following the opinion that these two stories were originally one story but separated from each other through editorial decisions.[11] Chapter 9 begins with the question that presupposes that the execution of Saulides had already taken place, which is reported in 21.1-14, and is concerned that the house of Saul is in danger of extinction; David asks, 'Is there still anyone left of the house of Saul to whom I may show kindness [*ḥesed*] for Jonathan's sake?' (9.1). Therefore, we will examine 21.1-14 first before looking at 9.1-13.

11. We can, of course, understand these two pericopes as independent stories, which the editors did not try to put together. We will see that 21.1-14 makes perfect sense as part of 2 Sam. 21–24. McCarter (*II Samuel*, p. 264) summarizes the view that 21.1-14 was originally a prequel to 9.1-13 in this way: 'II Sam 21.1-14 + 9.1-13 displays a literary and thematic completeness in itself. It has a clear beginning ("There was a famine in the time of David...", 21.1) and end ("so Meribbaal [Mephiboshet] ate at David's table like one of the sons of the king", 9.11b), followed by a concluding summary (9.12-13). It contributes to the succession question ("Why did Solomon succeed David to the throne?") only in the most general way, but it addresses another question ("Why did David execute the seven Saulids and summon the eighth to Jerusalem?") directly and succinctly. For these reasons it seems preferable to think of 21.1-14 + 9.1-13 as deriving from an originally independent document taken up by the author of I Kings 1–2 in support of his work'. See D.M. Gunn, *The Story of King David* (JSOTSup 6; Sheffield: JSOT Press, 1978), for an argument against this view.

There is a *ḥesed*-relationship between the Gibeonites and the Israelites (see Josh. 9) that the story in 2 Sam. 21.1-14 assumes. The Gibeonites claim that Saul has broken this relationship, citing that Saul has tried to wipe them out from Israel (vv. 1-2).[12] Even though Saul's alleged action was to benefit the people of Israel and Judah—Saul acted 'in his zeal for the people of Israel and Judah' (v. 2)—the *ḥesed* relationship between the Israelites and the Gibeonites, albeit a non-Israelite people, takes precedence. The text acknowledges the Gibeonites as non-Israelites: 'Now the Gibeonites were not of the people of Israel, but of the remnant of the Amorites' (v. 2). Saul's zeal for Israel does not excuse his wrongful deed against those who were connected to Israel through the *ḥesed*-relationship, which placed the Israelites in a position of responsibility to protect the Gibeonites in times of trouble. The *ḥesed*-relationship does not recognize political, ethnic, and religious boundaries. It functions to facilitate the process of hybridization, forging disparate groups into close relationships.

The narrator gives this breach of the *ḥesed*-relationship as the cause of a three-year famine in the land.[13] Upon learning this, David approaches the Gibeonites in order to expiate the bloodguilt from the land. Saul has betrayed the *ḥesed*-relationship and now David has to make it right. David invites the Gibeonites to come up with the terms under which they would be appeased. After some negotiation, they ask David to hand over seven sons of Saul as a sacrifice to God. David agrees to turn them over without any hesitation. Two sons of Rizpah, Saul's concubine, and five sons of Merab, Saul's daughter who is married to the son of Barzillai, are given to the Gibeonites to be impaled (21.8-9).

The corpses are left exposed on the ground in their shame, and God does not act immediately. Rizpah demonstrates one of the most profound acts of *ḥesed* in the David story: a mother's *jeong* for her children has no equal. She makes a tent for herself and camps near the corpses in order to protect them from birds by day and wild animals by night. She does this throughout the summer months.[14] Rizpah's *jeong* for her sons is remarkable and attracts the attention of the narrator, David, and even God; later a father's *jeong* will be

12. If this allegation is true, then this is out of character for Saul. He spared the Kenites, even though they lived among the Amalekites, because of the *ḥesed*-relationship between them and the Israelites (see Chapter 3). If Saul did persecute the Gibeonites, then it is because of David's connection to them (see Chapter 5).

13. This indicates that David's decision to wipe out the Saulides took place soon after Saul's death; no more than one to three years lapsed between Saul's alleged offense against the Gibeonites and the time David used it as a pretext for his action against the Saulides.

14. Thus Alter (*The David Story*, p. 331) says: 'The bereaved Rizpah then watched over the corpses throughout the hot months of summer, until the rain returned—heralding the end of the long famine—in the fall'.

manipulated by David's sons to move David. After being told of Rizpah's action, David is touched by her display of *jeong* and shows proper respect to the house of Saul. He gathers the bones of Saul's seven sons and the bones of Saul and Jonathan that were retrieved by the people of Jabesh-gilead and gives them a proper burial in the tomb of Saul's father Kish. Only then does God heed the supplications for the land (21.14).

The note in 21.7, which states that David spares Mephiboshet from being sacrificed to God because of the oath made between David and Jonathan, is most likely a later insertion. The Gibeonites probably wanted all of Saul's 'sons' and David likely handed the surviving Saulides to them. Mephiboshet was not among the known Saulides because he was taken to an unknown place by his nurse upon hearing of the death of Saul and Jonathan (2 Sam. 4.4). This is why David asks whether there is still anyone left of the house of Saul because he thought he was rid of all the Saulides. Then he adds, 'For I wish to do *ḥesed* with him for the sake of Jonathan'.[15] He summons Ziba, a servant to the house of Saul, and asks the same question, 'Is there anyone remaining of the house of Saul to whom I may show the kindness [*ḥesed*] of God?' To his surprise, there is someone left—Mephiboshet son of Jonathan is still alive. To his good fortune, Mephiboshet is crippled and therefore is not a threat to David. Mephiboshet comes to David, but he is afraid. He is afraid because David has a reputation of using the sword liberally and has just handed over his cousins and uncles to be impaled. David assures him that he will not die: 'Do not be afraid, for I will show you kindness [*ḥesed*] for the sake of your father Jonathan' (9.7).

David extends *ḥesed* to Mephiboshet for the sake of Jonathan his friend. Ziba, the servant of the house of Saul, becomes the facilitator of *ḥesed* just as Rizpah was instrumental in moving David to show *ḥesed* to the house of Saul in ch. 21. Ziba tells David where Mephiboshet is. He is in the care of Machir son of Ammiel at Lo-debar (9.4). David uses the word *ḥesed* three times in this passage (vv. 1, 3, and 7) as if to amplify his desire to show *ḥesed* for Jonathan's sake (vv. 1 and 7). He calls it the *ḥesed* of God in v. 3, perhaps because Jonathan and he made a pact before God. He proclaims that Mephiboshet will eat at his table in Jerusalem always (vv. 7, 10). The narrator repeats this arrangement twice, namely, that Mephiboshet is in Jerusalem and always eats at the king's table (vv. 11, 13).[16]

15. Polzin (*David and the Deuteronomist*, p. 95) states, 'By the time David comes to question whether there is anyone left...in Saul's house, the reader cannot help but wonder whether David's loyalty (*ḥesed*) for the sake of Jonathan counts for anything'.

16. Many critics have argued that David has an ulterior motive for having Mephiboshet under his 'care'. Alter (*The David Story*, p. 243), for example, suspects that this arrangement, repeated by the phrase 'at the king's table he would always eat', gives a greater advantage to David than to Mephiboshet and remarks that 'it is really a kind of luxurious house arrest'.

It is intriguing that the last sentence in this passage is: 'He was lame in both his feet'. The last word is *raglâw* ('his feet'). The narrative already went out of its way to mention this fact before (2 Sam. 4.4). Ziba also introduces Mephiboshet as, 'a son of Jonathan; he is crippled in his feet' (9.3). Why this emphasis on Mephiboshet's feet unless this explains why he survived? How ironic that the injury he suffered while trying to escape from an unreported danger (from David?) upon the death of his father and grandfather would invite David's *ḥesed.*

Many have argued that David's desire to bring Mephiboshet into his house is to keep a close eye on the last male heir to the house of Saul, and the fact that Mephiboshet is crippled in his feet made him less of a threat to David. Therefore, one can argue that David's *ḥesed* to Mephiboshet is no more than a convenient means of fulfilling his oath to Jonathan without any political cost to himself. Nevertheless, David's action deserves some credit.[17] He could have had Mephiboshet killed along with other 'sons' of Saul if he wished, but he does not. He values the relationship he had with Jonathan and wants to honor it by sparing the life of Jonathan's son. David practices *ḥesed* not only for political reasons but also for the sake of the relationship he had forged with Jonathan.

2a. *The Betrayal of David's* ḥesed *(loyalty) by Hanun (10.1-19)*

This story presupposes a prior *ḥesed* relationship between David and the house of Nahash, the same Nahash who terrorized the people of Jabesh-gilead. Upon hearing of Nahash's death, David thinks to himself, 'I will deal loyally [*ḥesed*] with Hanun son of Nahash, just as his father dealt loyally [*ḥesed*] with me' (10.2). Then he sends his servants to give his condolences to Hanun. David wants to perform *ḥesed* to Hanun just as he has done with Nahash. He wants to continue the same cordial relationship with Hanun as he had with his father. Hanun's servants, however, do not trust David's intention. They accuse David's servants of being spies sent to reconnoiter their city. They suspect the emissaries' 'walking about' (from the same word as *rgl*, 'foot') as a ploy to overthrow the city. Hanun is convinced of this and rejects David's envoys because of their 'spying' ('wandering feet'), whereas

17. Brueggemann (*First and Second Samuel*, p. 267) sees David's action as an act of *ḥesed* and David as a man of *ḥesed*: 'David is a man of loyalty (*ḥesed*). He is not "kind" to everyone, but he is loyal to those to whom he has obligation. To outsiders he can be brutal and ruthless (cf. 8.2, 5), but to those in the scope of his promise he is gracious and steadfast'. Polzin (*David and the Deuteronomist*, p. 105) is less enthusiastic about David's (and God's) *ḥesed* toward Mephiboshet but acknowledges it as such: 'Mephiboshet's continued existence, however reduced and subservient it may be, testifies to David's and the LORD's continuing *ḥesed* or kindness toward him. A permanent reminder of the LORD's rejection, Mephiboshet is a continual sign of his kindness also'.

David invited Mephiboshet to his house because of Mephiboshet's crippled 'feet' (*rgl*). Thus Hanun decides to sever the *ḥesed*-relationship between his father and David. Hanun shames the envoys by shaving half of their beards and cutting their garments in the middle at their hips (10.4). David does not invite them back to Jerusalem but commands them to stay in Jericho until their beards grow back.[18]

Hanun now realizes that he has become odious to David and hires various groups of Arameans for help. The Ammonites stand ready by their city gate for a war, and the Arameans are out in the open fields facing the Israelites, who find themselves in the middle of two armies. Joab, who is in charge of the Israelite army, sees the danger his men are in and tells his troops, 'Be strong, and let us be courageous for the sake of our people, and for the cities of our God; and may the Lord do what seems good [*ṭôb*] to him' (10.12). God is 'our God' to Joab, and based on that relationship he asks for God's *ḥesed*. The text does not mention God's action or response at all. God stays more and more in the background. Nevertheless, Joab and his brother Abishai are successful in defeating the Ammonites and their allies. The Ammonites return to their city, shutting themselves inside Rabbah (10.14). Joab is satisfied with the result and returns with the people to Jerusalem.

Soon after, a larger coalition of Arameans attempts again to defeat Israel, but David strikes a heavy casualty on the coalition. The Aramean coalition signs a peace treaty with Israel and serves David (10.19). Now the Ammonites are left on their own to defend themselves. There is a delayed consequence for Hanun's rejection of David's *ḥesed*. We learn that Joab and the army go back to Rabbah to lay a siege against it (11.1), but it is not until 12.26-31 that Rabbah is conquered.

Furthermore, the narrator portrays David as a man of *ḥesed* in 12.26-31 without having David lift as much as a finger. In this passage, David receives a positive characterization as a man of loyalty by the action of Joab. Joab honors David by giving him the opportunity to receive the glory for conquering Rabbah even though it is Joab himself who has done all the work (12.28). He has been faithful in his duty at Rabbah while David has been disloyal to his servants and subjects and unfaithful to God in Jerusalem (chs. 11–12). He could have set himself as a rival to David as David did to Saul after his military successes, but instead he defers to David in a remarkable

18. Brueggemann sees this as a positive action on the part of David. He understands David as a man of *ḥesed* and makes the following observation: 'Before the war narrative opens, David displays his remarkable sensitivity toward his humiliated men (v. 5). He gives them a chance to regrow their beards and recover their signs of manhood before making a public appearance in Jerusalem. This verse is a nice aside, indicating why David could command such tenacious loyalty. He was characteristically able to attend to the human dimensions of power transactions' (*First and Second Samuel*, p. 270).

display of loyalty. This says much about who David is: he is a man who commands profound loyalty from his men.[19]

3. *God extends* ḥesed *(loyalty and jeong) to David (11.1–12.25)*

There are many *ḥesed*-relationships that will be betrayed in 2 Samuel 11: king and subject; king and his officers; between officers; husband and wife; king and God.[20] In this section, it is David who betrays the trust and loyalty of several people. The matter of David's disloyalty to Bathsheba, Uriah, and other officers will be discussed in greater detail in Chapter 6. The *ḥesed*-relationship between David and God will be the primary focus of this section.

David stays in Jerusalem and sends Joab and the army to lay siege against the Ammonites at Rabbah.[21] He commits two wrongs according to Nathan's oracle (2 Sam. 12.9): he murders Uriah the Hittite with the sword (of the Ammonites) and takes Bathsheba from Uriah to be his wife. Nathan the prophet makes it clear that there is a special place for David in God's heart. God would have given David whatever he wished for. God already gave to David all that belonged to Saul: 'I gave you your master's house, and your master's wives into your bosom, and gave you the house of Israel and of Judah; and if that had been too little, I would have added as much more' (v. 8). Then God characterizes David's sin in a way that is similar to the way Eli's sons' actions were described (with the use of *bzh*, 1 Sam. 2.30) and

19. We will see more examples of David's ability to attract the uncompromising loyalty from his men later in the narrative.

20. Whedbee ('On Divine and Human Bonds', p. 152) notes that the David–Bathsheba–Uriah affair (2 Sam. 11–12) 'determines the rest of the story of David's reign; it is absolutely crucial for understanding the second half of David's career'. He comments that 'Here in microcosm we see all the significant bonded relationships under severe pressure, as the king violates one bond after the other... The king breaks his bond with the army and subjects by a triple act of criminal irresponsibility. He stays home when he should have been at war, he sleeps with another man's wife, who becomes pregnant by him, he has the loyal, innocent third party murdered' (p. 153).

21. Czövek (*Three Seasons*, p. 118) argues that after David establishes his house in Jerusalem he wavers between two forms of leaders: a charismatic military king who considers deliverance his call and relies on Yahweh's intervention and an oriental (absolutist) king who is keen on controlling everything by centralizing power. In 2 Sam. 11 there is no question that he is behaving as a sedentary monarch who sends his servants to do his bidding. Czövek notes that David has become 'an oriental monarch dealing with his subjects, women and troops as he likes... Samuel's nightmare (1 Sam. 8.17) has been fulfilled' (p. 131). I am not sure why Czövek uses the term 'oriental monarch' to designate a king who rules from his palace with near absolute power. He does not explain the term in any detail, thus he seems to assume that there is a common understanding of 'oriental kingship' shared by his readers. The term 'oriental' brings too much excess meaning for me.

promises to punish David's family (just as God punished the house of Eli): 'Why have you despised [*bzh*] the word of the Lord, to do what is evil in his sight... Now therefore the sword shall never depart from your house, for you have despised [*bzh*] me' (vv. 9-10). David has dishonored and disrespected God and betrayed the *ḥesed*-relationship with him. In addition to the murder of Uriah and the theft of Bathsheba, David also causes the deaths of a number of his servants who die along with Uriah, as well as the death of the child of David's liaison with Bathsheba. God is not pleased. God rescinded His promises to David's predecessors on lesser accounts. One would expect God to withdraw his *ḥesed* from David just as God took it away from Eli, Samuel, and Saul.

However, the *ḥesed*-relationship between God and David continues; the bond between God and David can be stretched, but it cannot be broken or cut. It can be detached for a moment, but the disconnection is not permanent. Nathan functions as the facilitator of *ḥesed*, providing an opportunity for David to reconnect with God (v. 13). David confesses his sin to God: 'I have sinned against the Lord' (v. 13). David does not apologize to or ask forgiveness from humans. This is strictly between David and his God. God forgives David without any drama, in contrast to Saul's case. Whedbee notes a difference in God's response between David's confession and Saul's confession in this way: 'The divine–royal bond has been violated as have all the other bonds. But in sharpest contrast to the damning response to Saul's confession (1 Sam. 15.26-29), God mysteriously forgives David, who is spared the death sentence for not one but two capital crimes: adultery and murder'.[22]

Nathan pronounces that God will spare his life, but someone has to pay for his sin; it is going to be the child who will bear the burden. David behaves strangely from the perspective of servants when he eats after learning of the child's death. They have been urging him to rise and eat; he has not eaten or arisen from the ground for seven days while the child was ill. Yet they could not move David the way the witch at Endor and Saul's servants moved him to rise and eat (1 Sam. 28). David is not easily moved by someone's *jeong*. He uses others' *ḥesed* for his benefit but does not let himself be influenced by others' *jeong*. Later, his sons will take advantage of his fatherly *jeong* for them. In v. 22, David explains his behavior, 'While the child was still alive, I fasted and wept; for I said, "Who knows? The Lord may be gracious (*ḥēn*) to me, and the child may live?"' David is a pragmatic man. He knows that there is always hope of *ḥēn* in a *ḥesed*-relationship. God has the freedom and responsibility to perform *ḥesed* or the freedom to extend *ḥēn* (comparable to *jeong*). God has a pragmatic side too; God does not save the child, thus not showing *ḥēn*, but does forgive and extend *ḥesed* to David.

22. Whedbee, 'On Divine and Human Bonds', p. 156.

God does not remove *ḥesed* from David and his house. When David reaches out to Bathsheba after the death of the child, a rare occasion when David shows his *jeong*, God extends *ḥesed* to him through Solomon (vv. 24-25): 'Then David consoled his wife Bathsheba, and went to her, and lay with her; and she bore a son, and he named him Solomon. The Lord loved him, and sent a message by the prophet Nathan; so he named him Jedidiah, because of the Lord'. It is Bathsheba who names him Solomon,[23] which may mean 'his replacement' (that is, Solomon is a replacement for either the dead infant or her dead husband),[24] but God overrides her decision with the name Jedidiah, 'Beloved of Yahweh' (v. 25), which is related to the name David. This child has two names (Solomon/Jedidiah) representing two bonds (to his mother Bathsheba and to his God) just as Bathsheba is introduced with two bonds (to her father Eliam and to her husband Uriah). We have already met Michal, who had two competing relationships: daughter of Saul and wife of David. In the next episode we will be introduced to Tamar, who also has two bonds (to her brother Absalom and to her father David). Is the text trying to tell us something? It may attest to a conflict between loyalty and identity.

God loves Solomon for no apparent reason. Perhaps the reason is more than to show God's commitment to the forever promise God made to David through his offspring (2 Sam. 7.12)—perhaps it is an expression of a father's *jeong* for David and his offspring. God in effect promises to continue David's dynasty because God loves David like a parent would. God shows both sides of *ḥesed* (loyalty and *jeong*) to David and his house as he promised to do.[25]

2b. *The Betrayal of David's* ḥesed *(*jeong*) by his son (13.1-22)*

Some time has passed since the events in chs. 11–12 and now the narrative sets up a scenario for another story of betrayal of *ḥesed* (this time, its *jeong* side). It says, *ûlĕ' abšālôm ben dāwid 'āḥôt yāpah ûšĕmāh tāmār way-ye'ĕhābehā 'amnôn ben dāwid* ('To *Absalom son of David* belonged a beautiful sister and her name was *Tamar*. And [he] loved her *Amnon son of David*' (13.1; my translation). Tamar is beautiful just as Bathsheba was

23. Following the *qere*: 'she called' (*wattiqrā'*) rather than 'he called' (*wayyiqrā'*).

24. Halpern (*David's Secret Demons*, pp. 401-402) speculates that Solomon was not the son of David but in fact the son of Uriah the Hittite.

25. Whedbee ('On Divine and Human Bonds', p. 158) summarizes this episode as follows: 'The second son (Jedidiah-Solomon), however, is a sign of Yahweh's equally enigmatic love that is now unexpectedly revealed... The child who will bear both a human and divine name signals the healing of the bond between Yahweh and king, showing that Yahweh accepts the chastened couple as forming a new and legitimate marital bond... Yahweh fulfills his pledge to maintain his bond with the house of David—but he does so in the sordid, savage world of betrayal, violence, and bloodshed'.

described as very beautiful (11.2).[26] This attracts unwanted attention from men who should not look at them in that way. Bathsheba belonged to two men: Uriah the Hittite her husband and her father Eliam (11.3). Tamar also belongs to two men: Absalom, her brother, and her father, David. She is forbidden to Amnon just as Bathsheba should have been forbidden to David. Yet David desired Bathsheba in spite of the fact that she was attached to two men just as Amnon will seek to have Tamar even though she is connected to two men.

Surprisingly, she is introduced as Absalom's sister rather than as David's daughter through his wife Maacah. Amnon also refers to Tamar not as a sister or the king's daughter when he responds to Jonadab: *wayyōmer lô 'amnôn 'et tāmār 'aḥôt 'abšālōm 'āḥi 'ănî 'ōhēb* ('*Amnon* said to him, '*Tamar*, the sister of *Absalom* my brother, I love', 13.4). These two verses (vv. 1, 4) suggest textually that she is caught figuratively between two sons of David. Unbeknownst to David he will play a crucial role in the betrayal of trust between David's children. David's two sons will manipulate his fatherly *jeong* to betray each other and their sister.

There are two betrayals of *ḥesed* to be addressed in this story.[27] Amnon desires Tamar and manipulates David in order to get her to lie with him. David unwittingly becomes part of Amnon's scheme to have Tamar come to his house. Amnon pretends to be ill and waits for David to come and see him. He tells David that he wants Tamar to come and prepare food for him (13.6). David consents to do this and sends Tamar to Amnon's house. Ironically, he unwittingly plays the same role as the messengers who fetched Bathsheba and brought her to his house (11.4). Here Amnon betrays his father's *jeong* to fool his father. David relies on his eyes and falls for

26. Tamar's brother is also described as beautiful, 'Now in all Israel there was no one to be praised so much for his beauty as Absalom; from the sole of his foot to the crown of his head there was no blemish in him' (2 Sam. 14.25; cf. 1 Sam. 9.2 for a description of Saul's appearance, 1 Sam. 16.12, 18 for David's, and 1 Kgs 1.6 for Adonijah's). Good looks indicate divine favor but in the narrative they often foretell bad fortunes or tragic endings to their lives.

27. Whedbee ('On Divine and Human Bonds', p. 158) remarks, 'After the David–Bathsheba affair, the attention increasingly shifts to David's sons and we will again be struck by the fragile character of family bonds—especially the bond between father and sons'. He summarizes the rest of the David story in this way: 'The narrative is often terrifying in its depiction of violated bonds, moving and even magnificent in its accounts of bonds upheld. Though all the significant relationships in David's kingdom come into the field of vision, the spotlight falls on the relationships between father and sons. The house of David in all its metaphoric extent is the central theater for action. David's sons, who embody all the hopes and fears of the future of David's house, become partial incarnations of their complex father, possessing some of his strength but also some of his fatal weaknesses' (p. 164).

Amnon's ruse. Then again, how can we blame David for caring for his sick son and for accommodating his son's request?

Tamar comes to Amnon's house not knowing what is in store for her. When she discovers what Amnon wants to do, Tamar tries to reason with him (13.12-13):

> No, my brother, do not force [*'nh* 'to humble, afflict'] me; for such a thing is not done in Israel; do not do anything so vile [*nbl*]! As for me, where could I carry my shame [*ḥrp*]? And as for you, you would be as one of the scoundrels [*nbl*] in Israel. Now, therefore, I beg you, speak to the king; for he will not withhold me from you.

Such a senseless deed [*nbl*] is not done in Israel, Tamar claims. The Levite whose concubine was raped and murdered also claimed that such a thing had never happened in Israel (Judg. 19.30), though it was, in fact, the Israelites (Benjaminites) who committed this crime. The Levite bypassed Jebus/Jerusalem because he felt unsafe in a city that did not belong to Israel. He chose to stay in a city (Gibeah) belonging to Israel because he thought it would be safe. He believed that only foreigners would do such a thing. Tamar also seems to suggest that Amnon is behaving like a foreigner.

Tamar's term (*nbl*) for Amnon also reminds us of Nabal who screamed (*'yṭ*) at David's messenger (1 Sam. 25.14) and therefore insulted David, and here God protected David's honor by slaying Nabal: 'Blessed be the Lord who has judged the case of Nabal's insult [*ḥrp*] to me' (1 Sam. 25.39). God removed the insult from David but will not remove it from Tamar. Amnon, however, will die like Nabal during the sheep-shearing while being drunk on wine (cf. 1 Sam. 25.2, 36; 2 Sam. 13.23, 28).

Goliath also insulted (*ḥrp*) Israel (1 Sam. 17.25), which prompted Saul the king to make the following offer: 'Have you seen this man who has come up? Surely he has come up to defy [*ḥrp*] Israel. The king will greatly enrich the man who kills him, and will give him his daughter, and make his family free in Israel' (1 Sam. 17.25). David responded with these words, 'What shall be done for the man who kills this Philistine, and takes away the reproach [*ḥrp*] from Israel? For who is this uncircumcised Philistine that he should defy [*ḥrp*] the armies of the living God?' (1 Sam. 26). It was David who removed the shame (*ḥrp*) from Israel and eventually acquired the king's daughter, but now one of his sons will behave like a foreigner, a foolish, senseless man who will put shame (*ḥrp*) on the king's daughter by doing this foolish thing (*nbl*).

The dialogue between Tamar and Amnon could have been a dialogue that might have occurred between David and Bathsheba. Bathsheba perhaps tried to persuade the king that it was not right to do such a thing in Israel and that he could have any available woman he wanted in Israel. Perhaps David ignored her plea just as Amnon ignores Tamar's plea and overpowers her.[28] Then he rapes (*'nh*) and lies (*škb*) with her (2 Sam. 13.14). What is worse for Tamar is what Amnon does to her after the rape. In v. 15, Amnon 'was seized with a very great loathing for her; indeed, his loathing was even greater than the lust [*'hb*] he had felt [*'hb*] for her. Amnon said to her, "Get out!"' She protests that this deed is more evil (*r'h*) than the former act of humiliation. But he has his servant push her out the house and lock the door behind her. She is totally humiliated and now walks about in mourning. She dies as a woman this day.

The latter act adds insult to her humiliation. First he breaks her trust, and then he shames and sends her way just as Hanun betrayed David's envoys and had them sent away in shame; again, Amnon is portrayed as a foreigner, like Hanun. Hanun tore their garments in the middle at their hips; now Tamar tears the long robe that she is wearing (13.19). Absalom consoles her and instructs her to remain in his house similar to the way David instructed the envoys to stay in Jericho until their beards regrew; Absalom, like David, will also wait for the right time to avenge this insult (see below). We do not hear from her again. Whedbee comments concerning Tamar's tragic fate: 'Like Jephthah's daughter, like Michal, Tamar will suffer the curse of child–lessness. Hers will be that terrible destiny of enduring a life that is a form of living death; she is thereby denied opportunity for the bond of wife and mother'.[29] David is upset but does not punish or shame Amnon the way he punished Hanun and the Ammonites. The narrator notes, 'When King David heard of all these things, he became very angry, *but he would not punish his son Amnon, because he loved him, for he was his firstborn*' (v. 21).[30] Amnon is spared from punishment by David because of a father's *jeong*. But there is a delayed consequence for Amnon by Absalom who has no *jeong* for his half-brother like he has for his sister. Just as there was a delayed conquest of Hanun's city, Amnon will be killed by Absalom two years later (v. 29).

28. Cf. Judg. 19.25. 'He [Amnon] was not willing to listen to her voice and he seized her [Tamar]' (*wĕlō' 'ābah lišmōa' bĕqôlāh wayyeḥezaq mimmennah*, 2 Sam. 13.14); 'The men [of Gibeah] were not willing to listen to him [the Levite] and the man [the Levite] seized his concubine' (*wĕlō' 'ābû hā'anāšîm lišmōa' lō wayyaḥazēq hā'îš bĕpîlagšô*, Judg. 19.25). It is hard not to connect Amnon's rape of Tamar with other 'such a thing that is not done in Israel' incidents, including what happened to the Levite's concubine and to Bathsheba.

29. Whedbee, 'On Divine and Human Bonds', p. 159.

30. The MT lacks the italicized words. McKenzie (*King David*, p. 162) suggests that 'David does not, as is sometimes alleged, ignore the crime. He is furious at Amnon. It is just that he loves his firstborn son so deeply he cannot bring himself to punish him... This fits the apologetic portrayal of David as "a loving father who was victimized by his rebellious son"'.

1b. *David extends* ḥesed (jeong) *to Absalom (13.23–14.33)*
Two years after Amnon betrayed the trust of Tamar and manipulated David's *jeong*, Absalom now exploits the same *ḥesed*-relationship between father and son to force David to send Amnon to the sheep-shearing feast just as Amnon convinced David to send Tamar to his house. Absalom first requests that David come to the feast (13.24).[31] When David declines, he presses his father without success (v. 25). Then Absalom asks David to send Amnon to the feast. David questions him, but Absalom insists and David reluctantly gives in to his request. A father's *jeong* makes David vulnerable. A Machiavellian man has a soft spot after all—it is his *jeong* for his children.

Absalom betrays his father's trust, duping his father into sending Amnon just as Amnon tricked David into sending Tamar to him. How ironic! David was a master at deceiving people; now he is the fool. Absalom instructs his servants: 'Watch when Amnon's heart is merry with wine, and when I say to you, "strike Amnon", then kill him. Do not be afraid; have I not myself commanded you? Be courageous and valiant [*bĕnê ḥāyil*]' (v. 28). He encourages his men to act like 'sons of valour' (*bĕnê ḥāyil*) who exemplify *ḥesed*. He wants his men to be loyal to him. His servants follow the instruction and kill Amnon.[32] Then Absalom flees to Talmai, king of Geshur, his maternal grandfather. Upon hearing the report that all the king's sons have been murdered, David tears his robe and cries. Then he learns that only Amnon, in fact, has been murdered. He mourns for Amnon, and it is three years before he is consoled over his death (v. 39).

Joab reads David's heart correctly that David yearns for Absalom; a father's *jeong* cannot hold a grudge forever. Surprisingly it is David's henchman who sees David's heart rather than his appearance. David wants to reconnect with his exiled son Absalom but is unwilling to show it. Joab acts as a facilitator of *ḥesed*. Joab sends a woman from Tekoa and tricks (again!) David into seeing his fault just as Nathan the prophet fooled (ditto!) David into indicting himself of charges against Uriah the Hittite and his wife Bathsheba. The story told by the woman from Tekoa is of a broken *ḥesed*-relationship, in which a man kills his brother. As a result, his clan wants to avenge the murder by demanding the perpetrator's life. This logic does not work for the woman from Tekoa who pretends to be the mother of the two

31. Did Absalom anticipate David's refusal? Or, was David the original target of Absalom? Perhaps Absalom blames his father for his sister's humiliation and for not punishing Amnon. His *jeong* for his sister is very evident; he names his daughter after his sister (2 Sam. 14.27). His daughter is described like her aunt: 'one daughter whose name was Tamar; she was a beautiful woman' (14.27).

32. Brueggemann (*First and Second Samuel*, p. 289) comments that Absalom's servants 'are deeply loyal and ready to obey… We only know they were unquestioningly loyal to Absalom'.

brothers. She claims that she thought she would put the case before the king because 'for my lord the king is like the angel of God, discerning good and evil' (14.17), and later she adds, 'my lord has wisdom like the wisdom of the angel of God to know all things that are on the earth' (14.20). But she is not relying on David's judgment or wisdom, which has been lacking lately. She is relying on a father's *jeong* for David to make a decision according to her (Joab's) wish, just as David's sons used it to put their father in a position of vulnerability.

The woman from Tekoa is working with the logic of *jeong*, not the logic of law. *Jeong* is not contained inside a *quid pro quod* system. Taking a man's life is not a consequence of a strict retribution system. It takes into account the mother who is part of this case. She is part of this *ḥesed*-relationship, and her feelings and needs are to be included in the equation. David understands this and commits himself to saving the son who murdered his brother. David finally sees (until now, he was blind) and realizes that Absalom can be brought back to Jerusalem and that he can reconnect to Absalom. He is not constrained by an inflexible *quid pro quod* system, in which Absalom must die for Amnon's death, but works within a system of *ḥesed*, in which a father's feelings and needs are part of the equation.[33] He acknowledges Joab's effort and instructs him to bring Absalom back to Jerusalem. Joab is grateful for David's acknowledgment of his *ḥesed*: 'Today your servant knows that I have found favor [*ḥēn*] in your sight, my lord the king, in that the king has granted the request of his servant' (14.22).

David, however, is still reluctant to reconcile with his son Absalom. David refuses to see Absalom for two years after his return to Jerusalem. It would take Absalom's initiatives to overcome a grudge between them. Absalom takes the matter into his own hands by instructing his servants to burn Joab's field. Once Absalom gets Joab's attention, he demands that he be allowed to see David. Joab takes the message to David, and David extends his *ḥesed* to Absalom; David's fatherly *jeong* overcomes his grudge toward his son and he kisses Absalom (14.33).[34]

33. Brueggemann (*First and Second Samuel*, p. 295) puts it in this way: 'If the king is wise, he will not decide Absalom's case on routine judicial grounds. He will know more than quid pro quod. Retribution will keep Absalom away from his father forever, but such uncaring retribution is not what life is about. Life is about breaking the cycle of fear and resentment and welcoming him home, denying blood to the thirsty ones'.

34. There are those who question the sincerity of David's display of acceptance. For example, Alter (*The David Story*, p. 282) notes the use of the noun 'king' rather than 'David' and suggests that 'this is more a royal, or official, kiss than a paternal one'. Brueggemann (*First and Second Samuel*, p. 298), however, sees a genuine reconciliation between father and son: 'There can, however, be little doubt that this scene of welcome and restoration is a genuine one. Absalom is home! Joab is vindicated. David is satisfied'. Whedbee ('On Divine and Human Bonds', p. 160) is a bit more cautious than

1a and 1b

Passages 1a and 1b form the outer bracket around the central passage 3. All five episodes have pre-existing *ḥesed*-relationships. In section 1a, the pre-existing *ḥesed*-relationships are between the Gibeonites and the Israelites and between David and Jonathan. The relationship between the Gibeonites and the Israelites is recounted in the book of Joshua and the relationship between David and Jonathan is narrated in 1 Samuel. In section 1b, the *ḥesed*-relationship between father and son is assumed. After establishing or assuming *ḥesed*-relationships each section describes how they are disrupted and broken. And there are consequences to these betrayals. In 1a, David hands over seven sons of Saul to the Gibeonites and they are subsequently impaled. David spares Mephiboshet for the sake of Jonathan. In 1b, David hands over his sons, including Amnon, to Absalom and the first message to David reports that all the king's sons are murdered. It turns out that only Amnon is killed. There are facilitators of *ḥesed* who encourage David to reconnect with Mephiboshet and Absalom. In 1a, Ziba aids David in his effort to show *ḥesed* to Jonathan by telling him where Mephiboshet is. David extends *ḥesed* to Mephiboshet by bringing him to live in his house in Jerusalem. In 1b, Joab and the woman from Tekoa are the facilitators who help David to reconcile with Absalom by persuading David to bring him back to Jerusalem. David finally extends his *ḥesed* (*jeong*) to Absalom when he invites Absalom to his house and kisses him.

2a and 2b

Sections 2a and 2b form the inner bracket around section 3. Once again, pre-existing *ḥesed*-relationships are assumed or noted. In 2a, the pre-existing relationship between David and the house of Nahash is noted. In section 2b, the relationship between father and sons is assumed. In 2a and 2b, David sends the victims to their humiliation. In 2a, David sends the envoys to Hanun; in 2b, David sends Tamar to Amnon. There are several interesting similarities between the way the victims are treated. The envoys and Tamar are sent away after their humiliation. The garments of the envoys are cut just as Tamar tears her robe. David tells the envoys to remain at Jericho; Absalom tells Tamar to remain at his house. Then there are delayed consequences to the broken trust. Hanun's city, Rabbah, is ravaged in 12.26-31 (section 3); Absalom kills Amnon in 13.29 (section 1b). The damaged relationships are not fixed. David does not extend *ḥesed* to Hanun; Absalom does not extend *ḥesed* to Amnon.

Brueggemann: 'the reconciliation finally takes place and is sealed by a father's kiss of his son. A fragile bond is seemingly restored, and once again a delicate balance is achieved in David's kingdom'.

1a-2a and 2b-1b

There are contrasting details between sections 1a and 2a (prior to section 3) and sections 1b and 2b (after section 3). The word *ḥesed* is explicitly used in 1a-2a but not in 1b-2b. 1a-2a deals with David's preexisting relationships external to his house, namely, to the house of Saul and the house of Nahash; 1b-2b deals within the house of David. 1a-2a recounts David's relationship to sons outside his house; 1b-2b tells David's relationship to his own sons. In 1a-2a, David initiates the action; in 1b-2b, David is fooled into taking actions. 1a-2a presents the loyalty side of David's *ḥesed* whereas 1b-2b shows the *jeong* side of his *ḥesed*.

Section 3 is the center of this block of narrative that focuses on *ḥesed*. Structurally it follows sections 1a and 1b: *ḥesed*-relationships assumed; betrayals of *ḥesed*-relationships; the consequences of these betrayals; facilitators who help David to reconnect; practices of *ḥesed*. In section 3, there is a *ḥesed*-relationship between God and David. It is David who betrays this relationship when he has Uriah the Hittite killed and takes Bathsheba as his wife. In the process, a score of officers becomes innocent victims. Moreover, Bathsheba's first son dies as a result of David's sin. Nathan plays the role of the facilitator who helps David to reconnect with God. But, ultimately, it is God who shows both the loyalty and *jeong* sides of *ḥesed* to David and their relationship is reconciled.

Sustaining David with Ḥesed *(2 Samuel 15–20)*

All is not well after the reconnection between David and Absalom (14.33). Starting in ch. 15, Absalom launches a rebellion against his father that will test everyone's resolve to stay loyal to David. Some will take the side of Absalom; others will stay loyal to David. Absalom's usurpation took many years of planning and is realized rather easily when he enters Jerusalem unopposed (15.1-12, 37; 16.15). Sensing the danger, David quickly leaves Jerusalem with those who are still faithful to him. On his journey from Jerusalem to Mahanaim (15.13–17.29), the old capital of Ishbaal, he encounters several characters who demonstrate their *ḥesed* to him. But not all are displeased with his plight. Some gladly display their hatred for and grudges against him. His escape from Jerusalem becomes a journey of *ḥesed*, in which David is sustained by the *ḥesed* of his followers and of God. Even though Absalom's rebellion is short-lived when he is killed in the battle between Absalom's army led by Amasa and David's army led by Joab, Abishai, and Ittai the Gittite, his death leaves his father's heart forever broken. Joab disobeys David's heartfelt plea not to harm Absalom and kills him mercilessly. Upon Absalom's death, David returns to Jerusalem on another journey of *ḥesed* (19.8b-40), in which David acknowledges and judges the *ḥesed* of those he encounters. The Israelites and the Judahites argue over who were more loyal to David, a dispute that leads to another rebellion against David, and this time by the Israelites with Sheba as their leader (19.41–20.26). Sheba's rebellion is quickly crushed but not before Joab again displays disrespect to David.

The following chiastic structure will guide the discussion in this section:

1a. The rebellion of Judah with Absalom as the head (15.1-12; 16.15–17.23)
  2a. Sustaining David with *Ḥesed*: David flees from Jerusalem (15.13–17.29)
    3. Absalom's death breaks David's heart (18.1-19.8a)
  2b. Sustaining David with *Ḥesed*: David returns to Jerusalem (19.8b-43)
1b. The rebellion of Israel with Sheba as the head (20.1-26)

1a. *The rebellion of Judah with Absalom as the head (15.1-12; 16.15–17.23)*
Absalom tests the people's *ḥesed* toward David. Like a modern presidential candidate, Absalom steals the heart of the people with unrealistic promises. He would say to those seeking to see David, 'see, your claims are good and right; but there is no one deputed by the king to hear you' (15.3). He implies that David does not care about them. He questions David's heart for the people. Then he makes 'campaign' promises: he will grant all of their wishes (15.4). He would reach out to them and kiss them. Apparently this works. He steals 'the hearts of the people of Israel' (15.6). The people, like other characters in the narrative, are swayed by the outer appearance and do not look at the heart; Absalom is a very good looking man (14.25-26), but he lacks sound judgment.

Absalom goes down to Hebron and prepares to take over his father's throne from there. The fact that he starts his rebellion with Hebron as his base, just as his father, David, was king of Judah at Hebron before becoming king over Israel, indicates that he is relying on his kinsfolk, the Judahites, to be his primary supporters. He attracts defectors from throughout Israel to Hebron, including the most important defector of all, Ahithophel, David's most influential adviser (15.12). Absalom enters Jerusalem unopposed (15.37 and 16.15) with Ahithophel by his side (16.15), but Hushai the Archite enters the city at the same time (15.37). Hushai is the friend of David who returns to Jerusalem as a mole, sent by David to frustrate the counsel of Ahithophel (15.34). Hushai is God's answer to David's prayer, 'O Lord, I pray you, turn the counsel of Ahithophel into foolishness' (15.31). This is God's *ḥesed* to David in time of need. Husahi will deceive Absalom and frustrate Ahithophel's good counsel for David's sake.[35]

35. Czövek (*Three Seasons*, p. 173) makes the following point about David's strategy of deception as viewed from the perspective of charismatic leadership: 'I have pointed out that deception, as the weapon of the weak against the powerful, is essential in his emergence. David is deceptive when powerless—both under Saul and in the Absalom

Absalom questions Hushai's *ḥesed* to David, but Hushai convinces him that he will be loyal to him just as he was loyal to David.

Absalom's rebellion becomes irreversible when he follows Ahithophel's counsel and enters David's ten concubines. What David did in secret with Bathsheba, Absalom does in broad daylight, thus fulfilling Nathan's prediction that a neighbor from David's own house will lie with his wives (2 Sam. 12.11-12). Absalom makes himself odious to his father. Now his relationship with his father is irreparable (16.20-23).[36] Absalom, however, does not follow Ahithophel's second counsel to let Ahithophel pursue David immediately. Ahithophel's second plan is defeated when Absalom asks for Hushai's opinion, thus giving him an opportunity to undermine Ahithophel's plan. Hushai claims: 'This time the counsel that Ahithophel has given is not good [*ṭôb*]' (17.7). Is he questioning Ahithophel's loyalty to Absalom? Ahithophel did say that he himself wanted to pursue David, 'Let me choose twelve thousand men, and I will set out and pursue David tonight' (17.1). But Hushai rebuts Ahithophel's plan and argues that it is not a good idea to pursue David immediately because David is surrounded by *bĕnê ḥayil* ('men of loyalty') and that Absalom should gather a large army himself and 'you go to battle in person' (17.11). Hushai strokes Absalom's ego, and he and his servants are persuaded by Hushai's counsel: 'The counsel of Hushai the Archite is better [*ṭôb*] than the counsel of Ahithophel' (17.14a).[37] The narrative acknowledges that Ahithophel's counsel is good [*ṭôb*], but it is God who 'had ordained to defeat the good counsel of Ahithophel, so that the Lord might bring ruin on Absalom' (17.14b). Then Hushai sends a warning

revolt, when he recovers his charisma. Deception seems to be a means of emerging charismatics to establish themselves in the face of the powerful. Once in power, however, David does not resort to deception, but is often deceived himself. It follows that a powerful leader, not deceiving but being deceived, cannot be charismatic by definition'. Czövek acknowledges that David's misuse of power violates the call and role of a charismata, a major impediment to maintaining his charisma. It is troubling, however, that he seems to understand the use of deception as an inherent characteristic of a charismatic leader.

36. If Ahithophel is Bathsheba's grandfather, then it makes sense that he defects to Absalom because of what David has done to his granddaughter and her husband Uriah. His advice to Absalom to sleep with his father's concubines, which alludes to what David did to Bathsheba and God's punishment for it in 2 Sam. 11–12, and his desire to lead the army in order to kill David himself reveals a grudge toward David. As Bodner (*David Observed*, p. 129) observes: 'Ahithophel is not the least bit cautious of severing the bond between father and son, and it is at this point where a reader might begin to sense something "personal" emerging in his directive to Absalom'.

37. Bodner (*David Observed*, p. 129) sees a stark contrast between Hushai's speech and Ahithophel's second advice: 'Hushai's speech is to be heard in the context of his loyalty to David and his subterfuge here. In contrast, the discourse of Ahithophel has a much more vindictive accent, and in his first portion of counsel it is evident that he is pushing for David's complete and irrevocable displacement'.

via the intelligence network, made up of those still loyal to and setup by David. Hushai tells Zadok and Abiathar, who send a servant girl to their sons Ahimaaz and Jonathan who relay the message to David. Ahithophel, David's most reliable but treacherous counselor, commits suicide when his counsel is not followed (17.23).

2a. *Sustaining David with* Ḥesed*: David flees from Jerusalem (15.13–17.29)*
Upon learning that 'the hearts of the Israelites have gone after Absalom', David flees Jerusalem (15.13). Who will go with David? Who will stick by his side? Who will remain loyal to him? His journey out of Jerusalem becomes a test of *ḥesed* for many of his constituents. His servants (v. 15), his household (v. 16), and his 'foreign' soldiers (v. 18)—the Cherethites, the Pelethites, and the Gittites—follow him. David is surprised that Ittai the Gittite decides to leave Jerusalem and follow him. He instructs Ittai to go back and wishes God's *ḥesed* on him and his people (vv. 19-20):

> Why are you also coming with us? Go back, and stay with the king; for you are a foreigner [*nokrî*], and also an exile [*gōleh*] from your home. You came only yesterday, and shall I today make you wander about with us, while I go wherever I can? Go back, and take your kinsfolk with you; and may the Lord show *steadfast love and faithfulness* [*ḥesed we 'emet*] to you.

Ittai, however, affirms his *ḥesed* to David, 'As the Lord lives, and as my lord the king lives, wherever my lord the king may be, whether for death or for life, there also your servant will be' (15.21).[38] Here is a striking statement of allegiance from the mouth of a foreigner, reminiscent of a similar statement of loyalty in the mouth of Uriah the Hittite, another 'foreigner' (2 Sam. 11.11). David is impressed and allows Ittai and six hundred Gittites and their families to escort him. He trusts Ittai to the extent that he appoints Ittai as one of three generals over his army (18.2). It is people like Ittai, with their unswerving *ḥesed*, that will sustain David during this dangerous time.[39]

38. Alter (*The David Story*, p. 287) observes that Ittai utters 'death' before 'life' in his statement, indicating Ittai's uncompromising loyalty to David: 'Given the grim circumstances, this loyal soldier unflinchingly puts death before life in the two alternatives he contemplates'. Whedbee ('On Divine and Human Bonds', p. 160) notes this paradox: 'the king who was always so successful in attracting the loyalty of his followers could not retain the loyalty of his own sons'.

39. Polzin (*David and the Deuteronomist*, p. 151) suggests that the figure of Ittai points to a larger theme involving loyalty: 'The narrative role of Ittai, therefore, whose very name suggests "loyalty" or "companion", is *to be with David wherever he goes*... Moreover, if we look at the larger story of Absalom's revolt, we notice that the occurrences of *'et*, "with", in these five chapters are much more frequent than anywhere else in the book. It is safe to suggest, therefore, that wordplay involving the meeting of David and Ittai in 15.19-22 points to aspects of the narrative that transcend a merely aesthetic connection of the name of Ittai to his abiding desire to be *with* David'.

David encounters several characters in his flight from Jerusalem. Some will show *ḥesed* to him, and others will not. Abiathar and Zadok and their sons Jonathan and Ahimaaz, along with the Levites and 'the ark of the covenant of God', follow David. But David instructs them to go back to Jerusalem with the ark, hoping he will see the ark and Jerusalem again (15.25): 'Carry the ark of God back into the city. If I find favor [*ḥēn*] in the eyes of the Lord, he will bring me back and let me see both it and the place where it stays'. This sounds more like, 'if God keeps his *ḥesed*, then I will return to Jerusalem'. There is a *ḥesed*-relationship between God and David; therefore, David could ask God to extend *ḥesed* to him, but, of course, God has the freedom not to act in David's favor. That seems to be the case here. David acknowledges God's freedom not to do *ḥesed*, but if God says 'I take no pleasure in you', then David will appeal to God's *jeong*, 'Here I am, let him do to me what seems good to him' (15.26). He trusts God's *ḥesed* but is also a practical man, always looking for an advantage. He sends back those who came with the ark to Jerusalem so that they can act as spies for him.

When David learns that Ahithophel is among the conspirators supporting Absalom, he realizes that it will not be easy to defeat the rebellion counseled by Ahithophel. As I have noted above, David prays to God for an intervention: 'O Lord, I pray you, turn the counsel of Ahithophel into foolishness' (15.31), and his prayer is immediately answered when Hushai the Archite appears to meet him. David instructs Hushai to return to Jerusalem and serve as a mole in cooperation with Zadok and Abiathar. When Hushai comes to Absalom in Jerusalem, Absalom questions Hushai's *ḥesed*: 'Is this your loyalty [*ḥesed*] to your friend? Why did you not go with your friend?' (16.17). Hushai deceives Absalom with a false statement of allegiance to him: 'No; but the one whom the Lord and this people and all the Israelites have chosen, his I will be, and with him I will remain. Moreover, whom should I serve? Should it not be his son? Just as I have served your father, so I will serve you' (16.18-19). Hushai shows his *ḥesed* to David by risking his life. We do not hear from Hushai again after he defeats Ahithophel's counsel; this may indicate that he is executed when his treachery is discovered. It is ironic that Ahithophel, who is loyal to Absalom, kills himself when his counsel is not followed by Absalom, and Hushai, who is loyal to David, is probably killed by Absalom when his plan is followed. Hushai indeed honored his *ḥesed* to David with his own life.

After sending Hushai to Jerusalem, David encounters Ziba, the servant of the house of Saul. He demonstrates his *ḥesed* to David by bringing supplies of food and drink for David and his followers (16.1-2). Ziba has made a strong statement of loyalty to David with this lavish gift; however, David is not fully convinced and asks him, 'Why have you brought this?' (16.2). After hearing Ziba's explanation, David seems to be satisfied, but then

David asks Ziba about Mephiboshet.[40] Ziba accuses Mephiboshet of betraying David's kindness (16.3). Convinced of Ziba's allegation and to show appreciation for Ziba's *ḥesed*, he gives all that belongs to Mephiboshet to Ziba (16.4).[41] Polzin points out David's inconsistency in showing his *ḥesed*: 'The kindness (*ḥesed*) David shows Mephibosheth for Jonathan's sake in 2 Samuel 9, he now retracts in 2 Samuel 16—only to backtrack once more in 2 Samuel 19. Whether the LORD always shows steadfast love to his anointed, as David sings in 22.51, God's anointed is clearly inconstant in demonstrating *hesed* to friend and foe alike'.[42]

This incident shows again that David is indeed a master negotiator of *ḥesed*. Ziba replies (16.4), 'I do obeisance; let me find favor [*ḥēn*] in your sight ["eyes"], my lord the king'. David and Ziba already have a relationship, king and subject, but Ziba initiates a *ḥesed*-relationship by assisting David in a time of need, and David responds favorably. To Ziba, this is 'favor' (*ḥēn*), an appropriate term for *ḥesed* when it is extended by a person of superior rank.

Then David encounters Shimei son of Gera, a Benjaminite, who comes out of the town of Bahurim and is gloating over David's plight. He throws stones at David and curses him (16.7-8): 'Out! Out! Murderer! Scoundrel! The Lord has avenged on all of you the blood of the house of Saul, in whose place you have reigned; and the Lord has given the kingdom into the hand of your son Absalom. See, disaster has overtaken you; for you are a man of blood'. Abishai son of Zeruiah wants to cut off Shimei's head. We have already seen Abishai's eagerness to kill anyone for David (1 Sam. 26), and we will see this again when Abishai volunteers to kill Shimei on David's return journey to Jerusalem (2 Sam. 19). These incidents show Abishai's unquestionable loyalty to David (he benefitted from Abishai's *ḥesed* before,

40. In the conversation, according to Brueggemann (*First and Second Samuel*, p. 306), David 'alludes to the fact that Ziba has belonged to the Saulide party, and David has ample reason to doubt Ziba's sudden loyalty. Moreover, David does not want Ziba to forget that David knows about this old loyalty, which is not eradicated by a simple assertion of new loyalty. David's question to Ziba about Mephibosheth is not about the physical location of Saul's grandson. More likely it is about Mephibosheth's political sympathies. Whose side is he on? The gifts of Ziba...make clear where Ziba is. The loyalty of Mephibosheth, however, is at this point not clear'.

41. McKenzie (*King David*, p. 170) notes that the way David handled the estate of Saul must have appeared offensive to some: 'The land in question was the heritage of the household of Saul that was never supposed to leave his line. David had no right to confiscate it or parcel it out to someone else. This was a flagrant breach of one of the oldest and most revered traditions in Israel. Such acts of tyranny had brought success to Absalom's revolt and were another source of continuing resentment against David and his dynasty'.

42. Polzin, *David and the Deuteronomist*, p. 162.

e.g., 2 Sam. 21.17), even though David rejects it in this case. David restrains him and shows his practical side again; he wants to put himself in the best position to receive God's *ḥesed*. He reasons that God will show *ḥesed* to him on the account of being cursed by Shimei: 'Let him alone, and let him curse; for the Lord has bidden him. It may be that the Lord will look on my distress, and the Lord will repay me with good [*ṭôbah*] for this cursing [*qll*] of me today' (16.11-12). He appeals to a principle of *quid pro quod*; he hopes for God's *ḥesed* for his endurance of such a display of disrespect (*qll*). He assumes that God knows what he is going through since God reacts, often violently, whenever anyone shows disrespect (*qll*) to God. He hopes God will be sympathetic to his situation, give him credit for not responding himself, and act on his behalf. Incidentally, this incident takes place in Bahurim (from the root 'to choose'), the same town where Ahimaaz and Jonathan hide from Absalom's men when they try to deliver the message of Hushai to David (17.18). This probably indicates that the loyalty of the town of Bahurim, like the rest of Israel, is divided between David and Absalom.

When David finally arrives at Mahanaim he is greeted by three men: Shobi son of Nahash from Rabbah of the Ammonites, Machir son of Ammiel from Lo-debar, and Barzillai the Gileadite from Rogelim. They bring food supplies for David and his people (17.28-29). Shobi is probably another son of Nahash whom David placed on the throne after he defeated Hanun when he rejected David's *ḥesed*. He helps to sustain David by staying loyal to him. Machir is the man who housed Mephiboshet until David brought him to his house. When he turned over Mephiboshet to David, he was changing his allegiance from the house of Saul to David. Here he maintains his *ḥesed* to David even though this crisis would have been an ideal time to switch sides. He also sustains David with his *ḥesed*. Remarkably, Barzillai shows loyalty to David even though David handed over his grandsons to the Gibeonites (21.8). We will see that Barzillai has a special place in David's heart. These three men could have taken advantage of the situation and not honored David with their *ḥesed*, but they choose to remain faithful to David and sustain him during this time of desperate need. David's journey from Jerusalem to Mahanaim, the old capital of Israel under Ishbaal, is a series of encounters with characters whose *ḥesed* is tested, but his march also displays the tenacious loyalty of the followers who sustain David during Absalom's revolt. David is saved once again by the *ḥesed* of many people who would risk their own lives in order to deliver David to safety. In the background God is always there to show *ḥesed* to David (e.g. sending Hushai in response to David's prayer). David also wishes, hopes, and perhaps expects God to extend *ḥesed* to him.

3. *Absalom's death breaks David's heart (18.1–19.8a)*
Absalom and the Israelites encamp in the land of Gilead with Amasa as the head of his army. David divides his army into three divisions headed by Joab, Abishai, and Ittai the Gittite. He wants to go out with the army, but his men insist that he stay in the city (18.3; cf. 2 Sam. 21.17). He acquiesces to his men's wishes. David also has a wish with which he wants his men to comply. He orders the three generals not to harm Absalom: 'Deal gently for my sake with the young man [*na'ar*] Absalom' (v. 5). Moreover, all the people hear David's instruction to the commanders (v. 5). David still cares deeply for Absalom; a father's *jeong* is irrepressible and his heart desires to reconcile with his son. In a *ḥesed*-relationship, reconnection is always possible; disconnection is never permanent.

Absalom's army, which is more like a militia made up of untrained volunteers, has no chance against David's well-trained and disciplined men of war. His militia is easily routed by David's army, and he finds himself suspended in the air by his hair caught in a tree (v. 9).[43] An unnamed soldier discovers Absalom and reports to Joab, 'I saw Absalom hanging in an oak' (v. 10). Joab reprimands the soldier for not killing Absalom in v. 11: 'What, you saw him! Why then did you not strike him there to the ground? I would have been glad to give you ten pieces of silver and a belt'. But the soldier remains faithful to David's wish: 'Even if I felt in my hand the weight of a thousand pieces of silver, I would not raise my hand against the king's son; for in our hearing the king commanded you and Abishai and Ittai, saying: "For my sake protect the young man [*na'ar*] Absalom!"' (v. 12). Joab becomes impatient and dismisses the soldier's commitment (*ḥesed*) to obey David's instruction. He goes to where Absalom is and then thrusts (*tq'*) three sticks 'into the heart of Absalom while he was still alive in the heart of the oak' (*bĕlēb 'abšālôm 'ôdennû ḥay bĕlēb hā'ēlah*, v. 14). Absalom falls to the ground, and Joab orders his armor-bearers to finish him off: 'And ten young men, Joab's armor-bearers, surrounded Absalom and struck him, and killed him' (v. 15). With Absalom killed there is no need to continue the war (cf. Ahithophel's plan called for killing David only; perhaps killing Absalom only was Joab's plan). Joab shows remarkable restraint against the people who rebelled against David. Immediately Joab blows (*tq'*) the trumpet to restrain his troops from pursuing Israel (v. 16). He shows *jeong* to Absalom's group but not to Absalom, David's young man/son. His action is a

43. Absalom was a very good looking man (2 Sam. 14.25) just like his father and Saul. His hair was a source of his pride and honor (*kbd*; cf. Samson whose hair was the source of his physical strength, Judg. 13–16), 'When he cut the hair of his head (for at the end of every year he used to cut it; when it was heavy [*kbd*] on him, he cut it), he weighed the hair of his head, two hundred shekels by the king's weight' (2 Sam. 14.26). It is his 'crown' of glory (*kbd*) on his head that will bring about his humiliating death.

blatant disregard for David's instructions. This betrayal will hurt David more than any other affliction, and Joab will pay for this with his own life.

Ahimaaz son of Zadok volunteers to take the news that 'the Lord has delivered him from the power of his enemies' to David (v. 19). Joab knows well what can happen to those who bring bad news to David (cf. 2 Sam. 1). He restrains Ahimaaz from going, 'You are not to carry tidings today; you may carry tidings another day, but today you shall not do so, because the king's son is dead' (v. 20). Instead, he sends a Cushite, a foreigner, without any warning: 'Go, tell the king what you have seen' (v. 21). The Cushite, like a good soldier, runs to deliver the news of Absalom's death. Ahimaaz still wants to be the messenger. Joab again tries to stop him, showing an unexpected *jeong* toward Ahimaaz in v. 22: 'Why will you run, my son, seeing that you have no reward for the tidings?' But Ahimaaz insists and Joab gives in. This exchange between Joab and Ahimaaz shows the tender side of Joab's tough persona. He actually cares about Ahimaaz's life and wants to protect him from potential harm. On the other hand, he shows no concern for the Cushite's life, a foreigner's life.

A sentinel sees Ahimaaz first because he has outrun the Cushite: 'I think the running of the first one is like the running of Ahimaaz son of Zadok' (v. 27a). David assumes, 'He is a good [*ṭôb*] man, and comes with good [*ṭôbah*] tidings' (v. 27b). This may indicate the loyalty of Ahimaaz and his father Zadok to David during Absalom's rebellion. Ahimaaz and his father will stay on the good side of David during Solomon's succession as well. He tells David that God has delivered him from the men who rebelled against him but does not report the bad news of Absalom's death (vv. 28-30). His speech is incoherent, but that works out to his advantage. David will remember the house of Zadok for bringing the good news of his victory. It is the Cushite who reports to David the fate of his son/young man (v. 31), 'May the enemies of my lord the king, and all who rise up to do you harm, be like that young man [*na'ar*]'.

Upon hearing his son's death, David is deeply hurt and weeps loudly, lamenting with these words (18.33): 'O my son Absalom, my son, my son Absalom! Would I had died instead of you, O Absalom, my son, my son!' It is fortunate for the Cushite that David is overwhelmed with grief, otherwise David might have had him killed. The Cushite might have been puzzled that he does not receive a prize for delivering good news, but for a father, the death of a son, no matter the circumstances, is not good news. Whedbee notes that 'a father's compassion transcends the law and the king attempts to uphold the bond between himself and his son, even at the expense of his bond with God and the nation'.[44] While David mourns for Absalom,

44. Whedbee, 'On Divine and Human Bonds', pp. 160-61. He continues that 'The scene of David's mourning over his fallen son Absalom is one of the most poignant in

dramatically displaying a father's *jeong*, the people steal away (*gnb*) into the city like those who sneak (*gnb*) into a city in shame after a defeat in battle (19.3). Absalom started his revolt when he 'stole (*gnb*) the heart of the men of Israel' (15.6) from David; now, in his death, he steals David's heart in a way that causes the people to depart from him. David does not care; he cries aloud again in 19.4, *bĕnî 'abšālôm 'abšālôm bĕnî bĕnî* ('My son, Absalom, Absalom, my son, my son!').

Joab is not pleased. Joab's allegiance belongs foremost to his king and his people. Absalom is someone who was disloyal to David. Joab is upset that David has demoralized the people, and he questions David's *jeong* for the people who risked their lives for him. He delivers a stinging indictment (19.5-6):

> Today you have covered with shame the faces of all your officers who have saved your life today; and the lives of your sons and your daughters, and the lives of your wives and your concubines, for love of those who hate you and for hatred of those who love you. You have made it clear today that commanders and officers are nothing to you; for I have perceived that if Absalom were alive and all of us were dead today, then you would be pleased.

Joab demands that David show his face and speak kindly to the people in order to acknowledge their *ḥesed* to him; otherwise, Joab claims, they will abandon him. Joab is someone who cannot be ignored.[45] David has to consider the consequences of his public display of *jeong* for his son without any acknowledgment of the people's loyalty. David complies with Joab's demand and takes his place above the gate; he shows his face but does not speak a word. He is sad but acknowledges his people's *ḥesed*. The people see him and reconfirm their loyalty to him by coming before him (19.8).

2b. *Sustaining David with Ḥesed: David returns to Jerusalem (19.8b-43)*

David's trip back to Jerusalem begins with a dispute among the peoples of Israel and Judah over whether to bring David back as king and, later, who will be the first to bring him back (vv. 9-10). It is interesting that there

literature and brings to a climax the whole theme of bonded relationships in the story of David's reign and the tragic rupturing of those bonds' (p. 161).

45. One has to wonder who is running the show: Joab or David. There are several incidents to indicate that it is Joab who is in power rather than David (cf. the relationship between Abner and Ishbaal). This passage can be considered the lowest point of David's life. Czövek argues that David's charisma is manifested during his rise when the narrative shows his independence from both of his mentors, Samuel and Saul, but loses his charisma when he becomes more and more dependent on Joab. He notes that after he established his kingship, 'David gradually loses independence and becomes overshadowed and controlled by his general' and 'his charisma becomes inactive, so he cannot be considered charismatic in most of 2 Samuel' (*Three Seasons*, p. 174).

would be such a dispute. This indicates that Absalom's revolt had popular support; perhaps David did not rule his kingdom with justice and equity for all his people (contrary to 2 Sam. 8.15). Even after Absalom's death, many are still reluctant to have David as their king. Who will renew their *ḥesed*-relationship with David? Remarkably, the tribe of Judah does not make a move to bring David back. This again shows that Absalom had the support of Judah; he planned his revolt in Hebron, probably with the support of the elders of Judah. David sends Zadok and Abiathar with the following message: 'Why should you be the last to bring the king back to his house? The talk of all Israel has come to the king. You are my kin, you are my bone and my flesh; why then should you be the last to bring back the king?' (vv. 11-12).[46] It seems that David had to make a compromise with the rebellious party, for he promises to keep Amasa as the head of the army: 'Are you not my bone and my flesh? So may God do to me, and more, if you are not the commander of my army from now on, in place of Joab' (v. 13). Amasa is son of Ithra the Ishmaelite, who married Abigail daughter of Nahash, sister of Zeruiah, Joab's mother (according to 17.25).[47] So David replaces one nephew with another nephew as the commander of the army. He needs the support of his own people to sustain his kingship even if that means he has to replace Joab with the commander of the opposing army. It is this arrangement that persuades the people of Judah to welcome David as their king. The people of Judah send a message to the king: 'Return, both you and all your servants' (v. 14). Then they go to Gilgal to escort David back to Jerusalem. Based on this incident, it is not surprising that the people's *ḥesed* to David will be tested again in 2b.

As David is crossing the Jordan, Shimei, accompanied by a thousand men from Benjamin, and Ziba, accompanied by his entire household, come to greet him along with the people of Judah (vv. 16-18). David, with his entire household, is crossing the Jordan *la'aśôt haṭṭôb bĕ'ênāw* ('to do what is good in his eyes', v. 18). He will evaluate the loyalty of those who come to meet him. Shimei son of Gera is the first one to be judged.

46. The elders of Israel also used this phrase, 'your bone and your flesh', to embrace David as their king (2 Sam. 5.1-7).

47. J.D. Levenson and B. Halpern ('The Political Import of David's Marriages', *JBL* 99 [1980], pp. 507-18), argue that Amasa was son of Abigail and Nabal (Ithra the Ishmaelite being his real name). This would explain, they argue, why Absalom appointed Amasa as the head of his army: Amasa, being of Calebite descent, 'was essential to Absalom's receiving Hebronite support for his *coup*' (p. 511). This would also explain 'David's effort to appease the Judeans by replacing Joab with Amasa—an otherwise baffling move in light of Amasa's key role in the rebellion just quashed' (p. 511). They also speculate that Amasa's mother (Abigail, wife of Nabal) and David's sister (also named Abigail) were one and the same person.

Shimei asks for forgiveness (vv. 19-20). He claims that he is the first one from the house of Joseph to greet David on his way back to Jerusalem: surely this demonstrates his loyalty to David? Abishai again wants to kill him, but David reprimands Abishai and extends his *ḥesed* to him with an oath, 'You shall not die' (v. 23). It is important to note that David is upset not only with Abishai but also with 'sons of Zeruiah' (v. 22).[48] The fact that Shimei comes with a thousand men from Benjamin, a formidable force indeed, might have swayed David to forgive him. In his decision to forgive Shimei, 'David clearly intends his affirmation of Shimei as a larger strategic gesture to reclaim the loyalty of the north'.[49] He needs Shimei's support to sustain his kingship. For now, David is pleased with the fact that he can return as the king of Israel and Judah. Once again, David shows his practical side. He is undoubtedly a Machiavellian man of *ḥesed*.

Mephiboshet is the next person to be evaluated by David. David's first words are: 'Why did you not go with me, Mephiboshet?' (v. 25).[50] Mephiboshet makes a case that he remained loyal to David throughout the insurrection and was prevented by Ziba's ruse from being with David. He accuses Ziba: 'He has slandered your servant to my lord the king. But my lord the king is like the angel of God; do therefore what seems good to you ["good to your eyes"]' (v. 27; cf. 14.17, 20). Contratry to Ziba's claim that he was hoping to recover Saul's kingdom, Mephiboshet tries to convince David that he never had such a desire and was grateful that David spared his life. However, David is not fully convinced of his *ḥesed* and decides to divide the land between Ziba and Mephiboshet. David may have failed to discern the truth in this case; he is not like the angel of God who can discern

48. McKenzie (*King David*, p. 166) summarizes David's need–hate relationship with Joab, Abishai, and Asahel, sons of Zeruiah: 'He needs them to do the dirty work, but they are difficult to handle. He benefits from their violent nature, but they have jeopardized his innocence and broken his heart when they killed Absalom. But it is important to keep in mind that the historical David was probably a great deal more like the sons of Zeruiah than he was different from them'.

49. Brueggemann, *First and Second Samuel*, p. 327.

50. Polzin (*David and the Deuteronomist*, p. 193) notes that in order to show loyalty to David one had to accompany David in his journey from Jerusalem and now one has to accompany him in his return trip to Jerusalem: 'When he left Jerusalem, David measured personal loyalty by a person's willingness to accompany him as he fled. He certainly was impressed with Ittai for wanting to go with him ("Why will you also go with us?" [15.19-20]), but now condemns Mephibosheth for not having done so ("Why did you not go with me, Mephibosheth?" [19.26]). In chs. 15–19, this continuing emphasis on being with the king, on accompanying him, provides a wider context for the repeated wordplay concerning Ittai's name, already discussed. This foreigner personifies a central aspect of the story: *being with the king* in a physical sense pictures forth for us larger themes of siding with him in terms of loyalty, devotion, and allegiance'.

good and evil. Mephiboshet does not care to have a share in the land and is happy with the fact that David has returned: 'Let him take it all, since my lord the king has arrived home safely' (v. 30). This statement proves that he was, in fact, loyal to David during Absalom's revolt. It may also be, as Alter suggests, 'an implicit judgment on the unwisdom of David's decree'.[51] Yet David does not care about Mephiboshet's loyalty. He does not need Mephiboshet's or the house of Saul's support to sustain his kingship.

David, however, is fully convinced of Barzillai's *ḥesed* to him.[52] Similar to the way he extended *ḥesed* to Mephiboshet earlier (2 Sam. 9) he wants to invite Barzillai to live with him as a 'guest' in his house,[53] but Barzillai declines, citing his old age. In his place he asks David to take Chimham, presumably his son, to Jerusalem. David promises to do whatever Barzillai desires, 'Chimham shall go over with me, and I will do for him whatever seems good to you ["good in your eyes"]; and all that you desire of me I will do for you' (v. 38). Then he kisses and blesses Barzillai (v. 39). This is a touching moment of *ḥesed* between two men who probably have been through a great deal together. They probably have mixed feelings toward each other. But at this moment David sincerely appreciates Barzillai's service to him.

This section ends with another dispute among the people: this time between the people of Judah and the people of Israel. The Israelites and the Judahites argue over who are more loyal to David and who have more rights over David. Now all the people of Israel, even though at first only half the people of Israel accompanied him during his return trip (v. 40), claim that the people of Judah have 'stolen' him from them: 'Why have our kindred [*'aḥênû*, "our brothers"] the people of Judah stolen [*gnb*] you away, and brought the king and his household over the Jordan, and all David's men with him?' (v. 41). Absalom began his rebellion by 'stealing' the hearts of the people; the people were 'stealing' away from David when he showed greater love for his rebellious son than to those who risked their lives to save him. After Joab's admonishment David wins back the people's loyalty by reaching out to his people. Now the people of Israel claim that the people of

51. Alter, *The David Story*, p. 317. David was able to discern the case brought to him by the woman from Tekoa in 2 Sam. 14 and showed his wisdom. In this episode, David makes judgment without probing the case.

52. Alter (*The David Story*, p. 318) makes the following observation: 'David's three encounters at the ford of the Jordan form a progressive series on the scale of loyalty: first Shimei, who has heaped insults on him and now pleads for forgiveness; then Mephibosheth, whose loyalty, though probably genuine, has been called into question by Ziba; and then the unswerving devoted old man, Barzillai'.

53. Many critics have suggested that this, like the case of Mephiboshet, may have been David's attempt to put Barzillai under house arrest to ensure that Barzillai's people remain loyal to him (more on this point in Chapter 5).

Judah are 'stealing' David away from them. The people of Judah answer that 'the king is closer to us' (*kî qārôb hammelek 'ēlay*). How is David closer to them? The narrative claims that David is from the tribe of Judah and therefore is closer kin to the people of Judah than to the people of Israel. David calls the elders of Judah 'my brothers' and 'you are my flesh and my bone' (v. 12). He also calls Amasa 'my bone and my flesh' (v. 13). Yet the people of Judah don't use these terms to refer to David; it is the Israelites who use them to indicate their connection to David, 'We are your bone and flesh' (2 Sam. 5.1). Besides, the Israelites counterclaim that they have ten shares in David and that they were the first ones to decide to bring him back (v. 43).

Here is a conflict of identity and loyalty. To whom does David owe greater loyalty? Should he side with the people of Judah who are supposed to be his kinsmen but do not seem to recognize him as such? Or, should he side with the people of Israel who wanted to bring him back first and are a larger constituent than the Judahites? David is silent during this dispute, in contrast to the earlier dispute when he used blood relation to sway the Judahites to take him back. Perhaps this silence sends a wrong message to the Israelites. He does not acknowledge that indeed it was the Israelites who first decided to bring him back and that he is also related to them, perhaps not through blood relationship but through *ḥesed*-relationship. David's *ḥesed* to the people of Israel is ambiguous and the people of Israel suspect the genuineness of his *ḥesed*.

1b. *The rebellion of Israel with Sheba as the head (20.1-26)*

The people of Israel follow Sheba son of Bichri, a Benjaminite, and rebel against David. Sheba declares, 'We have no portion in David, no share in the son of Jesse! Everyone to your tents, O Israel' (20.1). But the people of Judah 'cling (*dbq*) to their king from the Jordan to Jerusalem' (20.2; my translation); here *dbq* is used to express 'loyalty and affection' (*ḥesed*) to David. They extend their *ḥesed* to him. Interestingly, the first thing David does upon entering his house at Jerusalem is to give his attention to the ten concubines who were left behind to take care of the house and later became victims of Absalom's political move. He provides for them but never has conjugal relations with them again. Moreover, they are placed in a house under guard, living the rest of their lives as if in widowhood (cf. Michal's case).

Then David turns his attention to Sheba. He instructs Amasa, who replaced Joab as the commander of the army, to muster the men of Judah in three days. David's instruction to Amasa functions in a similar way to Samuel's instruction to Saul: to test the instructed person and then to give the job to someone else. Amasa fails to show up at the appointed time

(20.4); the failure is expected since this is an impossible task coming so soon after the battle in which the men of Judah (a militia, not a standing army) suffered a great loss! David sends Abishai with his servants to take care of Sheba, but it is Joab whom 'Joab's men, the Cherethites, the Pelethites, and the warriors' follow (v. 7). The narrative describes these servants as 'Joab's men' rather than 'David's men'.[54] It appears that these men are loyal to Joab as much as they are to David. Along with Joab's men, the Cherethites and the Pelethites, who owe allegiance to David only, go with Joab. Joab is in charge again.

Amasa finally shows up 'at the large stone in Gibeon' (20.8) to his peril.[55] Joab grabs Amasa's beard to kiss him and with his left hand thrust his sword in Amasa's belly. Joab kills Amasa by ruse (v. 10) just as he killed Abner by surprise. The men who came with Amasa do not know what to do. They do not know whom to follow. They do not know with whom their allegiance rests. Then one of Joab's men stands by Amasa's body and challenges them, 'Whoever favors Joab, and whoever is for David, let him follow Joab' (v. 11). He equates their *ḥesed* to Joab with that to David. He claims that to follow Joab is to be faithful to David. The men who were mustered by Amasa decide to follow Joab.

In the meantime, Sheba and his men lock themselves inside Abel of Beth-maacah. A wise woman from the city prevents Joab from destroying the city. She speaks to Joab and asks why he is laying a siege on her city. Joab replies that Sheba has raised his hand against David. She convinces her people to cut off Sheba's head (another Benjaminite loses his head; Saul and Ishbaal are the other two Benjaminites who lose their heads) and throw it to Joab, thus showing their loyalty to David. Joab is pleased and goes back to Jerusalem.[56]

54. Alter (*The David Story*, p. 323) comments that 'the fact that they are here called "Joab's men" suggests where the real power is, and where Joab's brother Abishai assumes it must be. The clear implication is that the supposedly dismissed Joab is actually leading his men in the pursuit'.

55. Saul used a large stone as an ad hoc altar to kill animals in order to avoid eating meat with blood (1 Sam. 14.31-35). Abimelech killed his seventy brothers on top of one stone (Judg. 9.5) as a perversion of a sacrificial act. In the next chapter (2 Sam. 21), the Gibeonites will sacrifice Saul's seven sons in Gibeon. In this incident, in light of the narrative noting the large stone and Gibeon, we could see Joab's killing of Amasa as a sacrifice. This brings us back to how Samuel condemned Saul for offering a sacrifice himself and not waiting for Samuel. Here Amasa is late and is offered as a sacrifice by Joab.

56. Alter (*The David Story*, p. 329) remarks, 'Joab comes back to Jerusalem, not to his house…in nearby Bethlehem. The implication…is that he now resumes his post as David's commander. David evidently has little say in the matter, being controlled with a *fait accompli* of military power'. Of course, one can argue that this is precisely what

This section ends with a list of David's administrators (20.23-26). Joab appears first on the list as the commander of the army of Israel. We can assume that the rest of the names on the list remain loyal to David during Sheba's revolt. Some, however, will end up on the wrong side, as we will see in 1 Kings 1–2.

To summarize this section, 1a and 1b form the outer bracket around section 3. In both 1a and 1b the people's *ḥesed* to David is tested. Absalom steals the heart of the people and Sheba leads the people of Israel in revolt against David. Absalom is supported by both the tribe of Judah and the tribes of Israel. Nevertheless, he sets up his revolt from Hebron, the center of Judah, just as his father launched his war against the house of Saul from there. Ahithophel, from the city of Giloh which is near Hebron, is his top counsel. Amasa, son of David's sister, is the commander of Absalom's army, and later Amasa is remembered as 'the commander of the army of Judah' (1 Kgs 2.32). After Absalom's death, Judah was reluctant to accept David back, indicating that there was a serious strain in the relationship between David and Judah. It was not until David promised to appoint Amasa as the head of his army in place of Joab that Judah agrees to take back David as its king. In 1b it was only the people of Israel that supported Sheba's revolt. The text says that 'every man of Israel went from following David to following Sheba son of Bichri' whereas 'every man of Judah clung to their king' (20.2). 1a and 1 b show that the people's *ḥesed* to David was tenuous.

2a and 2b form the inner bracket around section 3, which reveals that the *ḥesed* of David's followers sustains his kingship. 2a shows that his soldiers were loyal to him, especially the non-Israelite soldiers—the Cherethites, the Pelethites, and the Gittites. Ittai the Gittite's statement of allegiance summarizes the unswerving loyalty of those who clung to David. They want to be with David and to support him in any way they can. Hushai, Zadok, Abiathar, Ahimaaz, Jonathan, and the unnamed servant girl risk their lives in order to deliver David to safety. Ziba, Shobi son of Nahash, Machir son of Ammiel, and Barzillai provide necessary food supplies for David and his followers. On his journey back to Jerusalem even his toughest critic, Shimei, pledges his loyalty to David. Shimei brings his clan to greet David and is the first in the house of Joseph to receive David back as king. Shimei uses the words 'king' and 'lord' three times each in his short speech to David (19.19-20). Likewise Mephiboshet, in his speech to David (19.26-28), uses the word 'king' six times and the word 'lord' four times. Upon hearing David's decision he says, 'Let him take it all, since my lord the king has arrived home safely' (19.30). Mephiboshet's *ḥesed* is sincere. Finally, the narrator

David had planned when he appointed Amasa over Joab. It was a convenient way to get rid of Amasa (cf. the way Abner was eliminated).

highlights Barzillai as a man of *ḥesed par excellence*. In spite of the fact that David handed over Barzillai's five grandsons to the Gibeonites, Barzillai shows *ḥesed* to David during the time when David is in danger of losing his kingdom and his life. Barzillai shows gratitude for David's invitation to dwell in the king's house but declines to be a burden to the king.

In section 3, Joab's *ḥesed* to David is ambivalent and David's *ḥesed* is torn between loyalty to his people and *jeong* to his son Absalom. Joab blatantly disobeyed David's instruction not to harm Absalom. The unnamed soldier refused to kill Absalom because he heard David's order. He showed his loyalty to David. One has to wonder where Joab's loyalty lies. Is it to David or to himself?[57] Perhaps his loyalty lies with his soldiers. The soldiers who pursued Sheba were called 'Joab's men' (20.7). When David was mourning over Absalom, Joab questions David's *ḥesed* to his core followers. Joab accused David of shaming the faces of 'all your servants' (19.5) and of choosing to love those who hate him and to hate those who love him (19.6). He admonished David that he would have preferred the death of 'commanders and servants' over the death of Absalom (19.7). He demanded that David go out and speak to his servants. Joab's accusation questions where David's loyalty is. Is it to his family, to the people, to God, or to himself? David's loyalty should be with the people first. David also realizes that Joab's advice makes sense, but his fatherly *jeong* knows no logic.

David's Confidence and his Men of Ḥesed *(2 Samuel 21–24)*

This section has been considered mere appendices to the David narrative proper, as a collection of writings that does not add much to the preceding narrative and also with significant differences from it. In recent years, however, scholars have identified intricate connections to the rest of the narrative.[58] The following chiastic structure will guide the discussion in this section:

1a. David seeks God's *ḥesed* (21.1-14)
 2a. David's men of *ḥesed* (21.15-22)
  3. David's songs of *ḥesed* (22.1–23.7)
 2b. David's men of *ḥesed* (23.8-30)
1b. David seeks God's *ḥesed* (24.1-25)

57. There are those who argue that Joab was probably following rather than disobeying David's orders when he killed Absalom.

58. Alter (*The David Story*, p. 329) summarizes a change in understanding of chs. 21–24: 'Recent critics have abundantly demonstrated the compositional coherence of chs. 21–24 and have argued for some significant links with the preceding narrative. For that reason, it may be preferable to think of this whole unit as a coda to the story rather than as a series of appendices'.

1a (21.1-14) and 1b (24.1-25): *David seeks God's* ḥesed

These two stories begin with a sin committed by a king: in the first story by Saul and the second story by David. In 1a, Saul has broken an agreement between the Israelites and the Gibeonites (see Josh. 9.15), resulting in three years of famine in the land. In 1b David orders a census and realizes that he has committed a sin against God, resulting in three days of pestilence against the people (24.13, 15). David chooses this punishment from the three options God presents to him: three (MT has 'seven') years of famine, three months of being pursued by his enemies, or three days of pestilence. The reason for David's choice is God's mercy, 'I am in great distress; let us fall into the hand of the Lord, for his mercy [*raḥămîm*] is great; but let me not fall into human hands' (24.14). Here mercy (*raḥămîm*) is synonymous with the *jeong* side of *ḥesed*. David appeals to God's mercy because God is known for *jeong*. We have seen how David's fatherly *jeong* makes him vulnerable to his sons' requests; David uses his understanding of *jeong* to put his life in God's hand.[59] Seven thousand people die, but David's life is spared again (cf. the number of casualties caused by David's sin in 2 Sam. 11). Brueggemann summarizes the interaction between God and David in this episode in this way: 'Yahweh repents of anger (v. 1) and remembers mercy; David repents of foolish arrogance (vv. 10, 17) and remembers trusting, submitting faith. The simultaneous action of the two makes new interaction and new mutual fidelity possible'.[60]

Thus in each story a sin brings a disaster to the land. In order to appease God, David offers a sacrifice in each case. In 1a David offers the seven sons of Saul to the Gibeonites; they sacrifice Saul's sons 'before God' at Gibeon on the mountain of the Lord (21.6).[61] In 1b, David makes burnt offerings and offerings of well being at the altar he builds on the plot of land in Jerusalem, which he purchases from Araunah the Jebusite (24.24-25). Araunah wishes to give to David the supply for sacrifice as a gift: 'Let my lord the king take and offer up what seems good [*ṭôb*] to him; here are the oxen for the burnt offering, and the threshing sledges and the yokes of the oxen for the wood. All this, O king, Araunah gives to the king' (24.22-23a). When David does not respond, Araunah continues, 'May the Lord your God respond favorably to you' (24.23). David says, 'No, but I will buy them from you for a price; I

59. This is comparable to Ben-hadad, king of the Arameans, who asks for mercy from Ahab because of the reputation of the kings of Israel as being merciful. His servants advise him in this way: 'Look, we have heard that the kings of the house of Israel are merciful [*ḥesed*] kings; let us put sackcloth around our waists and ropes on our heads, and go out to the king of Israel; perhaps he will spare your life' (1 Kgs 20.31).

60. Brueggemann, *First and Second Samuel*, p. 354.

61. Alter (*The David Story*, p. 331) claims that the use of the phrase 'Before the Lord' is 'an explicit indication of the sacrificial nature of the killings'.

will not offer burnt offering to the Lord my God that cost me nothing' (24.24). He purchases the threshing floor and the oxen, builds an altar, and offers sacrifices. After the sacrifices have been made by David, God accepts David's supplications in 1a and 1b: 'God heeded supplications for the land' (21.14) and 'so the Lord answered his supplication for the land' (24.25).

2a (21.15-22) and 2b (23.8-30): *David's men of* ḥesed

These two reports recount the feats of David's warriors probably during his early years as a captain under Saul's service. It must have been a time of camaraderie, forging enduring connections through shared experiences of battles and hardships. It was during this early period of his career when he was able to form a deep *ḥesed*-relationship with his men. They trusted him and were willing to sacrifice their own lives for him. These reports of adventures show the bond between David and his men. It shows how much his men care for and love him. It clearly displays both the loyalty and *jeong* sides of *ḥesed* that David's men had for him.

In 2a four of David's warriors kill four giants from Gath. Abishai son of Zeruiah, who shows an unswerving loyalty to David in the narrative, is one of the four men whose heroic deed in recounted. He saves David's life when one of the giants attacks him: 'But Abishai son of Zeruiah came to his aid, and attacked the Philistine and killed him' (21.17). Abishai performs an act of loyalty (*ḥesed*) when David is in a situation of a serious need. After this incident, David's men forbid David from fighting: 'You shall not go out with us to battle any longer, so that you do not quench the lamp of Israel' (21.17). This statement may reflect their affection (*jeong*) for their dear leader.

In 2b, the deeds of David's top five most notable warriors are recounted (23.8-23), followed by a list of the names of thirty warriors (vv. 24-39). Another heartfelt story of *ḥesed* is noted in this collection. When David yearned to have a drink from the well of Bethlehem, 'the three warriors broke through the camp of the Philistines, drew water from the well of Bethlehem that was by the gate, and brought it to David' (v. 16).[62] David was not in a situation of a serious need, but they risked their lives to bring the water from Bethlehem. This is not an act of loyalty (*ḥesed*) per se, but this act of *jeong* reveals their affection and care for him. David is moved by their display of *jeong*. He refuses to drink the water himself but offers it as a sacrifice to God. He acknowledges their deed and offers their *ḥesed* to God as a devotional offering: 'The Lord forbid that I should do this. Can I drink the blood of the men who went at the risk of their lives?' (v. 17). He returns

62. Cf. 1 Sam. 31.8-13; all the 'loyal men' (*kol 'îš ḥayil*) of Jabesh-gilead risked their lives to take the bodies of Saul and Jonathan from a Philistine city.

their *ḥesed* through a deep solidarity (*jeong*) with them by connecting their deed with God's loyalty to him. These men are indeed models of *ḥesed* and serve as examples for all David's people to emulate. They exemplify their singular loyalty to David which his men later in his career will be asked to demonstrate.

3. *David's songs of* ḥesed *(22.1–23.7)*

The center of this section is David's two songs, which express David's confidence in himself and God's *ḥesed* while praising God for saving him from all his enemies and from the hand of Saul. The song can be divided in the following way according to the content: God delivers him from his enemies (vv. 2-20); the reason for God's special favor is because David deserves it (vv. 20-28), with an emphasis on God's *ḥesed* to the faithful—'With the loyal [*ḥesed*] you show yourself loyal [*ḥesed*]; with the blameless you show yourself blameless; with the pure you show yourself pure, and with the crooked you show yourself perverse' (vv. 26-27);[63] he describes how God has trained and guided him to conquer his enemies all around (29-46); then he blesses God (vv. 47-51), while underlining God's eternal *ḥesed* to him—'He is a tower of salvation for his king, and shows steadfast love [*ḥesed*] to his anointed, to David and his descendants forever' (v. 51). Whedbee characterizes it as 'a poetic celebration of the mutual loyalty between God and king in upholding their divine–human bond'.[64] Polzin states, 'By the end of the song, we cannot help but see the basis for David's gratitude: God has transformed him into a miniature of himself—a quasi-god in royal garb'.[65]

The above song is juxtaposed with 'David's last words' (23.1-7), which, according to Whedbee, shows 'the inner connection between just rule and Yahweh's covenantal bond with the house of David'.[66] But it is far more than that. The second song reaffirms the notion that David has become God's 'mini-me'. It is difficult to tell God and David apart in this song. God's will is David's will; God's word is David's word. Nevertheless, the main point of these words is that God has made an everlasting covenant with David but the godless (i.e. whoever opposes him) will be destroyed (vv. 5-7). No doubt this assertion refers to God's 'eternal' *ḥesed* promised in 2 Sam.

63. Brueggemann (*First and Second Samuel*, p. 343) understand David's songs and the rest of chs. 21–24 as a critique of the official portrayal of David in the narrative. He comments on the contradiction between David's claim of innocence and his known misdeeds from the narrative: 'For David to make such a claim is odd and incongruous, for Israel knows better… Israel knows enough about David that the claim of "blameless" can only be heard ironically'.

64. Whedbee, 'On Divine and Human Bonds', p. 163.

65. Polzin, *David and the Deuteronomist*, pp. 203-204.

66. Whedbee, 'On Divine and Human Bonds', p. 163.

7.14-16. David is confident that God is on his side. His confidence comes from his alleged faithfulness to God, but, more importantly, he is confident because God has promised God's *ḥesed* to him, or as Brueggemann puts it: 'The Davidic house is not a tenuous historical institution but an ontological structure based in God's decree'.[67]

David's Last Days and Judgment of Ḥesed *(1 Kings 1–2)*

The men who had remained faithful to David during Absalom's revolt and later during Sheba's uprising face another test of *ḥesed.* Their king has advanced in years and is only a shell of the man he used to be. Upon learning of David's impotency (1 Kgs 1.4), Adonijah, the oldest of David's living sons, thrusts himself to kingship (1.5).[68] Adonijah and his actions are eerily similar to those of Absalom that led to his revolt. Adonijah is described as *ṭôb tō'ar mĕ'ōd* ('a very handsome man', 1 Kgs 1.6; cf. 1 Sam. 16.12, 18 for David and 1 Sam. 9.2 for Saul). In describing Absalom the narrator states, 'Now in all Israel there was no one to be praised so much for his beauty as Absalom; from the sole of his foot to the crown of his head there was no blemish in him' (2 Sam. 14.25). They both take similar steps to usurp the throne. At the outset, Adonijah prepares for himself 'a chariot and horsemen, and fifty men to run before him' (1.5) just as Absalom got himself 'a chariot and horses, and fifty men to run ahead of him' (2 Sam. 15.1). Then Adonijah brings his supporters to a sacrifice outside of Jerusalem, similar to the way Absalom gathered his supporters at Hebron. And just as Absalom started his revolt with the support of Judah, Adonijah invites 'the men of Judah' to his sacrifice to launch his kingship. Absalom took over David's harem (2 Sam. 16.20-23) whereas, after his first attempt to take the throne failed, Adonijah asks Solomon, via Bathsheba, for Abishag the Shunammite, David's last woman (1 Kgs 2.13-18). Bathsheba agrees to this: 'Very well [*ṭôb*], I will speak to the king on your behalf' (1 Kgs 2.18). This, however, is not a way to show loyalty to Solomon. Solomon exclaims in 2.22, 'And why do you ask Abishag the Shunammite for Adonijah? Ask for him the kingdom as well! For he is my elder brother; ask not only for him but also the priest Abiathar and for Joab son of Zeruiah!' He orders Benaiah, who will replace

67. Brueggemann, *First and Second Samuel*, p. 346.

68. McKenzie (*King David*, p. 177) understands Abishag the Shunnamite's role as a test of David's manhood: 'The intent of the servants was not really to keep the old king warm but to test his virility... The test proved that the king was impotent. This was intolerable. The king was the symbol of his nation, its strength and fertility. Israel simply could not have an impotent king. In short, it was time to choose a replacement for David... Abishag's true function as a test of David's potency is made clear in v. 5. At the news that David failed the test, Adonijah declared himself king'.

Joab as the commander of the army, to kill Adonijah (1 Kgs 2.25) just as Absalom was killed by Joab, the commander of the army at the time (2 Sam. 18).

David's inner circle of men who remained loyal to him during two revolts becomes divided. Joab and Abiathar support Adonijah, but Zadok, Benaiah, and Nathan do not side with him. Adonijah invites his supporters to a sacrifice, which is a thinly disguised ceremony to anoint him as king. Adonijah does not invite Benaiah, Zadok, and Nathan to this celebration. Moreover, he invites all his brothers except Solomon. Bathsheba, in her speech to David, reiterates that Adonijah invited all the sons of the king, Joab, and Abiathar to his sacrifice but not Solomon (1.19). She mentions only Solomon among those not invited. Nathan, in his speech to David, confirms that Adonijah invited all the king's sons, Joab, and Abiathar but names Nathan, Zadok, Benaiah, and Solomon among those who are not invited (1.26). Now David has a choice to make. Does he side with Adonijah and his supporters or with Solomon and his supporters? But we know from 2 Sam. 12.24-25 that God has already formed a *ḥesed*-relationship with Solomon and has decided to put him on the throne. David only makes God's decision a reality. Once he decides in favor of Solomon, the Cherethites and the Pelethites, David's most loyal soldiers, escort Solomon, riding on the king's mule, to his coronation (1 Kgs 1.38-40). As soon as Adonijah and his guests hear the noise from Solomon's coronation, Jonathan son of Abiathar arrives. Adonijah asks, 'Come in, for you are a worthy man and surely you bring good news' (1 Kgs 1.42; cf. 2 Sam. 18.27). It is good news for Solomon but not for Adonijah and his supporters.

What happens to Joab and Abiathar after Solomon becomes king cannot be explained adequately by the *realpolitik* of succession. Of course, it would have been politically expedient for Solomon to eliminate those who supported his rival, but Solomon spares Abiathar's life for the sake of the *ḥesed* he showed to David over the years (2.26): 'Go to Anathoth, to your estate; for you deserve death. But I will not at this time put you to death, because you carried the ark of the Lord God before my father David, and because you shared in all the hardship my father endured'. He could have spared Joab's life for the *ḥesed* he showed to David. More than anyone in David's career, Joab stood by David through toughest times. He served as David's henchman and the commander of his army. Solomon, however, shows no mercy and has him killed inside the tent of the Lord. The narrator claims that Solomon is merely following David's words (1 Kgs 2.5-6).

After Solomon takes the throne, David gives Solomon his last instructions (1 Kgs 2.1-9). David exhorts Solomon to follow God's ways and invokes God's promise to give *ḥesed* to his house: 'If your heirs take heed to their way, to walk before me in faithfulness [*'emet*] with all their heart and with all their soul, there shall not fail you a successor on the throne of Israel' (2.4).[69] God's *ḥesed* will support the continuation of the Davidic dynasty and promises to sustain it just as God has promised in 2 Sam. 7.12-16. Yet this promise is surrounded by, rather swallowed whole by what appears to be qualifications or conditions they must abide by in order to receive God's *ḥesed*. This passages ends with the following words: 'if your sons observe their ways to walk before me in faithfulness' (*'im yišmĕrû bānêkā 'et darkām lāleket lĕpānay be'emet*, v. 4). God's unconditional *ḥesed* (2 Sam. 7.12-16) comes with a stipulation after all. Even if a Davidide sincerely attempts to be faithful to God by keeping 'the charge of the Lord your God, walking in his ways and keeping his statutes, his commandments, his ordinances, and his testimonies, as it is written in the law of Moses, so that you may prosper in all that you do and wherever you turn' (1 Kgs 2.3), who decides whether he is doing it with all his heart and with his soul (2.4)? In other words, God can take *ḥesed* from the house of David just as God took it away from the house of Saul, and from the house of Eli, and from the house of Samuel. We see that David is indeed a man after God's own heart; just as David is a master negotiator of *ḥesed* and will demonstrate this again in the next passage, God also renegotiates the *ḥesed*-relationship with David's house.

David gives orders to Solomon concerning three individuals. His orders are based on their *ḥesed*. He instructs Solomon to kill Joab for murdering two generals, Abner and Amasa: 'Act therefore according to your wisdom, *but do not let his gray head go down to Sheol in peace* [*wĕlō' tōrēd śêbātô bĕšālōm šĕ'ōl*]' (1 Kgs 2.6). Joab will be executed for the betrayal of the trust of these two men, even though their deaths greatly benefitted David. Joab did what he thought was best for his king; he was being loyal to David, but that is not how David sees it now. He did not punish Joab when he committed these murders, but now he wants Joab dead. Of course, this serves Solomon's interests, since Joab supported Adonijah. Although David does not mention it, he must have had Absalom's death on his mind as well. It was Joab who disobeyed David's order and had Absalom killed, leaving an indelible wound in David's heart. For all that Joab has done for him over the years, David has a grudge against him because he broke a father's heart. Yes, his son Absalom wanted to kill him, but his *jeong* for his son would have spared his life.

69. Acknowledging the fact that these two verses (2.3-4) are from the Deuteronomist, Alter (*The David Story*, p. 374) wonders why the Deuteronomist decided to insert these words: 'Why did the Deuteronomistic editor choose to intervene at this penultimate point of the David story? It seems very likely that he was uneasy with David's pronouncing to Solomon a last will and testament worthy of a dying Mafia capo: be strong and be a man, and use your savvy to pay off all my old score with my enemies'.

Sandwiched between two men (Joab and Shimei) with whom David has a grudge, Barzillai is once again praised for his *ḥesed*. David instructs Solomon to extend *ḥesed* to Barzillai's house: 'Deal loyally (*ḥesed*), however, with the sons of Barzillai the Gileadite, and let them be among those who eat at your table; for with such loyalty they met me when I fled from your brother Absalom' (2.7). David as a man of *ḥesed* deals with individuals with kindness, affection, faithfulness, and loyalty when he judges them to have helped him to establish and sustain his kingship and kingdom. David judges people according to how they have shown *ḥesed* toward him. Moreover, he also understands a father's heart. Barzillai would have wanted his sons to be protected; if he were alive he would have asked for David's *ḥesed*. As a father, David gave his *jeong* to his children without any reservation, which often put him in a position of vulnerability. It was to his children that David displayed his *jeong*, and now he wants his son to show *ḥesed* to the children of a man who has shown so much love to him.

However, that is not the last image of David. David also orders Solomon to kill Shimei for cursing him on the day he left Jerusalem. He has a grudge against Shimei even though he swore to not kill him (2 Sam. 19.23). He instructs Solomon, 'Therefore do no hold him guiltless, for you are a wise man; you will know what you ought to do to him, and *you must bring his gray head down with blood to Sheol* [*wĕhôradtā 'et śêbātô bĕdām šĕ'ōl*]' (2.9). David whose first words were, 'What shall be done for the man who kills this Philistine?', which revealed his ambition, has as his last words *bĕdam šĕ'ôl* ('in blood to Sheol'), which summarizes his bloody legacy.[70] Indeed Solomon, like his father, manipulates words to kill Shimei (2.36-46). David was a violent man who was skillful in using the sword of other men to do his bidding. David was a man of *ḥesed* who utilized *realpolitik* and the sword until the very end. This is the last image of David the narrative leaves with us.

70. Whedbee ('On Divine and Human Bonds', p. 164) summarizes David's legacy in this way: 'Thus Yahweh has his way, keeping his word of promise, and Israel has her second Davidic king. But what price success and succession? For David's house a frightful price indeed! Adultery, murder, rape, vengeance, conspiracy, rebellion, assassination, and plague have cut their grim course through the Davidic kingdom. Thousands of dead soldiers and four dead sons litter the stage of David's court. Yahweh's promise of a Davidic rule continues to be fulfilled, but at the price of shattered bonds and bloody acts'.

5

THE HYBRIDIZATION OF DAVID'S KINGDOM

As we have seen, the concept of *ḥesed* is a useful hermeneutical key to understanding the David story. In 1 Samuel 1 to 2 Samuel 5, David rises to the top by riding the *ḥesed* of God, who chooses him over Saul, and the support of the various constituents who give him their unswerving loyalty and *jeong*. *Ḥesed* explains how David is able to establish his kingdom. It continues to play a key role in 2 Samuel 5 to 1 Kings 2 where David's *jeong* is manipulated by his sons and his kingship is threatened by disloyalty of his own people, but he is able to maintain his kingdom and kingship by the *ḥesed* of his eclectic group of followers and of his God. I have also noted some conflict of identity and *ḥesed* in the narrative and hinted at the role of the transgressive power of hybridity in consolidating David's kingdom, but I have kept these discussions to a minimum because I wanted to show first the importance of *ḥesed* in understanding the David story. In the following two chapters I will be more deliberate in showing the politics of identity and *ḥesed* in the narrative and in demonstrating how David's kingdom and story reflect the processes of hybridization and purification.

In this chapter we will look at a historical David with a postcolonial imagination. Rather than seeing the narrator's apology as a positive spin on the David of history with his faults and misdeeds, we will see that there are positive features in David that are worth recovering for postcolonial subjects. At the historical level David's actions can be understood as part of the process of hybridization through which he was able to form his kingdom. To build his kingdom, David called together a striking coalition of ethnic, tribal, and regional groups. He worked with Moabites, Philistines, Ammonites, Hittites, and other non-Israelites in addition to incorporating two distinct peoples, the Judeans and the Israelites, into one kingdom. David's coalition went far beyond David's own 'tribe' or 'people'. His success in forming his kingdom rested on his ability to forge a *ḥesed*-relationship with various constituents across boundaries and differences. Therefore, the house of David was not built on the *ḥesed* of the people of Judah and Israel alone. It was built also on the *ḥesed* of non-Israelites whose loyalty to David made it possible.

First, it is important to understand Saul as a fighter of the Philistines and his policy of nativism in order fully to appreciate David's unorthodoxy. The biblical texts, especially Judges and 1–2 Samuel, and archaeological evidence suggest that the Philistines were the external threat that compelled the highlanders/Israelites to form a political organization geared toward resisting the Philistines. In tandem with political development, the formation of highlanders as an ethnic group can also be attributed to the appearance of the Philistines and the threat they posed to the heterogeneous group of highlanders. Avraham Faust describes the ethnogenesis of Israel in a nutshell with this statement: 'The Philistines seem to have been the anvil on which Israel's identity was forged'.[1] The emergence of Saul and his policy can be explained by the historical context of the late Iron Age I (eleventh century BCE; Iron Age I: 1250–1000; Iron Age II: 1000–586), in which the highlanders organized and identified themselves as a distinctive group in contrast with the Philistines. Saul became a leader of highlanders/Israelites to fend off the threat from the Philistines. He consolidated his kingdom, with his own tribe of Benjamin as its core, in opposition to the Philistines. Yet remarkably, David rejected Saul's policy and went against the historical reality of that time and worked with the Philistines and other 'non-Israelites' to establish his kingdom. In fact, Philistines made up the bulk of his army and David included them in his kingdom. The heterogeneous composition of his army and leadership, in contrast to Saul whose inner circle was made up mostly of Benjaminites (1 Sam. 22.6-8), suggests that David established his kingdom on the backs of non-Israelites based on their *ḥesed* rather than on their identity. David's success owes as much to his ability to use the transgressive power of hybridity to form ties with disparate groups in the region as to God's providence.

This chapter is divided into three sections. *The Philistines as Israel's Other* will discuss the Philistines' role in the formation of highlanders/Israelites as an ethnic/political group and as Israel's enemy/other in the narrative. *The Hybridization of David's Kingdom* will describe how David was able to form his coalition of disparate groups and establish his hybrid kingdom. *Postcolonial Features in David* will highlight those characteristics, inspired in part by postcolonial imagination, that are needed in the world in our time.

The Philistines as Israel's Other

The Philistines as the Other in the Text

It is evident that the Philistines were the archenemy of the Israelites during the late Iron Age I. This conclusion is supported by the way the Philistines

1. Avraham Faust, *Israel's Ethnogenesis: Settlement, Interaction, Expansion and Resistance* (London: Equinox, 2006), p. 148.

are viewed in the Hebrew Bible. According to Gitin, 'out of 919 biblical references to Israel's foes, 423 (46%) refer to the Philistines', and Gitin concludes that 'Philistia is clearly considered ancient Israel's most significant enemy'.[2] Faust states that the term 'uncircumcised' refers overwhelmingly to the Philistines and adds that 'they refer to the Philistines in such a negative manner *only* in texts that are meant to describe the reality during the late Iron I'.[3] In the DH the Philistines are clearly portrayed as Israel's enemy/other. Before David appears in the narrative, the Philistines are already typecast as Israel's worst enemy/other. In the book of Judges there are enemies all around, but it is the Philistines who emerge as the main enemy toward the end of the book (chs. 10; 13–16). When Samson wants a Philistine woman for his wife, his parents ask him (Judg. 14.3), 'Is there not a woman [*bĕnôt*, 'daughters'] among your kin [*'aḥêkā*, 'your brothers'], or among all our people [*'ām*], that you must go to take a wife [*'iššah*] from the uncircumcised [*hā'arēlîm*] Philistines?' This verse sets up a dichotomy between Israel as 'us' and the Philistines as 'them'—the daughters of our brothers (read, 'our people') on the one hand and on the other hand the women from the uncircumcised (read, 'unclean') Philistines who are not 'our people'. This contrast runs through Judges and into the David narrative: Israelites ('brothers') and Philistines ('uncircumcised'). The Philistines are labeled with the term 'uncircumcised' (Judg. 14.3; 15.18; 1 Sam. 14.6; 17.26, 36; 18.25, 27; 31.4; 2 Sam. 1.20; 3.14), and they are the only ones to be branded as such in the DH. The practice of circumcision became an identity marker when a cultural practice that was common in Canaan was selected as a 'difference' that could distinguish Israelites from the Philistines who did not practice circumcision at that time. The Philistines were their archenemies during the period of Judges and in the days of Saul and David. In turn, the Philistines used the term 'Hebrews' to belittle the Israelites. The term 'Hebrews' is not an ethnic term or associated exclusively to the Israelites, even though the term is used to refer to the Israelites by the Philistines.[4] Both terms were derogatory names used by these two groups to refer to each other, so the narrative claims. The Israelites were poking fun at the cultural practice of the Philistines, the 'uncircumcised', who were expanding into

2. Quoted in Faust, *Israel's Ethnogenesis*, pp. 145-46.

3. Faust, *Israel's Ethnogenesis*, p. 88 (original emphasis). He suggests that 'The disappearance of the term "uncircumcised" as a designation for the Philistines in the Iron Age II reflects…an interesting but simple fact: the Philistines started to circumcise during this time' (p. 88).

4. McCarter (*I Samuel*, p. 106) explains that the term 'Hebrews' was 'evidently a generalized designation and not entirely synonymous' with 'Israelites' as reflected in 1 Sam. 14.21, where the Philistines differentiate Hebrews and Israelites. He continues, 'Characteristically it was used of Israelites by foreigners, but the origin and precise significance of the term are disputed' (p. 106).

their territory; and the Philistines saw the people from the highlands as 'Hebrews' (similar to 'hillbillies') who were culturally backward and economically poor.[5]

The Philistines are portrayed as having one definite goal in the DH: to oppress the Israelites. From the time of the Judges to the opening scenes in 1 Samuel, the Philistines are the biggest threat with which the Israelites have to deal. There is no need to revisit 1 Samuel in detail to see this idea. Even a cursory reading of 1 Samuel impresses this upon the reader. Eli the priest dies when he hears the news that the Philistines have captured the Ark of the Covenant and the Israelites are routed. Samuel is depicted as being successful at thwarting the Philistine threat but the people still desire a king. Samuel could offer only temporary relief from the Philistines, and the people desired a permanent solution to the Philistine problem. Saul is successful in confronting the Philistines directly even though the Philistines are better organized and have superior weapons. He establishes a permanent army to engage the Philistines in long-term conflict. In the end Saul is unsuccessful in removing the Philistine threat; he dies in battle against the Philistines and his body is fastened on the wall of a Philistine city. It is when David appears in the narrative that a savior to the Philistine problem can be imagined. It is not until 2 Samuel 8 that David finally removes the Philistine threat for good. It is David who removes the enemies all around Israel, particularly the Philistines, who have been trying to place the Israelites under their hegemony.

The Philistines: The External Threat that Forged Israel's Identity

Now we turn to the view that the archaeological evidence supports the narrative's depiction of the Philistines as Israel's enemy/other. I found Faust's work, *Israel's Ethnogenesis*, very convincing. He demonstrates that the archaeological evidence indicates that the Philistines were the group that may have made possible the formation of Israel's ethnic identity. In other words, the animosity and/or competition between the Israelites and the Philistines was real, and the text reflects this reality; namely, it was the Philistines who pushed the Israelites into demanding a different political

5. Faust (*Israel's Ethnogenesis*, pp. 151-52) comments that 'It is common for a dominant group to relate to all "others" as one, usually in a denigrating way… It can be supposed that the Philistines treated all of highlanders in the same disparaging manner, viewing them as backwards, paltry, or primitive, with no care taken to notice their internal distinctions'. This is similar to the way the term 'Israel' is used in the Merneptah stela to refer to the highlanders living in the interior of Canaan. J.M. Miller and J.H. Hayes (*A History of Ancient Israel and Judah* [Louisville, KY: Westminster/John Knox Press, 2nd edn, 2006], p. 114), remark, 'Merneptah's scribe may have had little specific information about Israel and seems to have used the name in a generalized fashion to encompass all the peoples of the Palestinian interior'.

organization and forming an ethnic identity for the highlanders.[6] In his book, Faust argues that the Israelites or highlanders (those who were living in the central hill regions at the time) began to identify themselves as an ethnic group (Israelites), thus 'the ethnogenesis of Israel's ethnic identity' came toward the end of Iron Age I when the Philistines imposed an external threat to them.

I will examine Faust's interpretation of archaeological evidence to support this view in greater detail. Faust's work traces artifacts and specific behaviors of the highlanders during the Iron Age I that became Israelite ethnic traits, and then he concludes that the historical contexts in which they became such was the late Iron Age I, in the eleventh century BCE. He argues that the formation of Israel's ethnic identity was a long and complex process, which covers the entire Iron Age I and beyond, but it was during the late Iron Age I that Israelites defined themselves in relation to, and in contrast with, the Philistines, and that their ethnic identity was forged. Faust follows the work of Frederick Barth on understanding ethnic identity[7] and accepts the notion that 'groups define themselves in relation to, and in contrast with, other groups' and therefore an ethnic group is formed when it has 'an ability to be identified and distinguished among others'.[8] It is important to Faust's argument that 'the ethnic boundaries of a group are not defined by the sum of cultural traits but by the idiosyncratic use of specific material and behavioral symbols as compared with other groups'.[9] Thus it is not the artifacts or behaviors themselves that necessarily carry any ethnic importance or traits, but the use or the constructed meaning of these artifacts that is potentially important to ethnic identity. According to Faust, two most important factors in the ethnogenesis of Israelites are the following: the Philistines served as the external force, the so-called enemy/other from whom the Israelites wanted to distinguish themselves; and 'an ethos of egalitarianism and simplicity', which was a characteristic of the highlanders that made certain artifacts and behaviors likely choices to become ethnic markers as contrasting symbols to the Philistines.

6. Miller and Hayes (*A History of Ancient Israel and Judah*, p. 115) also suggest that fighting against common enemies, particularly the Philistines, was one of the primary factors in forming a solidarity among the highlanders: 'Common enemies (such as the Philistines) would have required the emerging "Israelite" tribes to join together in warfare from time to time, and this in turn would have encouraged a sense of solidarity'.

7. F. Barth, 'Introduction', in *idem* (ed.), *Ethnic Groups and Boundaries: The Social Organization of Culture Difference* (Long Grove, IL: Waveland Press, 1969), pp. 9-38. Barth understand ethnic groups not as a matter of groups of people connected by blood relations or defined by 'cultural stuff', but as 'a matter of self-ascription and ascription by others in interaction'; Barth defines an ethnic group as a form of social organization of cultural difference.

8. Faust, *Israel's Ethnogenesis*, p. 15.

9. Faust, *Israel's Ethnogenesis*, p. 15.

I will examine the Philistines factor first. Faust summarizes that certain traits and behaviors—like the practice of circumcision, the avoidance of pig meat, a limited ceramic repertoire, unpainted and undecorated pottery, a lack of imports, four-room houses, among others—were chosen by the highland population because they contrasted particularly with the traits and behaviors of the Philistines. His point is not that the highlanders began to practice them during their interaction with the Philistines; he acknowledges that these traits and behaviors were practiced prior to their interaction with the Philistines. His argument, however, is that in the highlanders' effort to distinguish themselves from the Philistines, they used their own repertoire of traits and behaviors to serve as a 'difference' from the repertoire of traits and behaviors belonging to the Philistines. An additional meaning and significance was added to these traits and behaviors in interaction with the Philistines, resulting in their becoming ethnic traits.

Pork avoidance, for example, was likely practiced by the highlanders and other groups in Canaan prior to the Philistines. According to Faust, there is evidence of moderate to low consumption of pork at Bronze Age sites in the highlands and lowlands, indicating that the consumption of pork was not a 'difference' that functioned to draw boundaries among the people living in Canaan prior to the arrival of the Philistines. One can argue that Israelites, who may have been Canaanites living in the highlands, practiced to some extent the avoidance of pig meat, but once the Philistines showed up on the scene with one of their prominent traits being the consumption of pig meat in large quantities, the Israelites went from low consumption to no consumption to distinguish themselves from the Philistines. Faust states that 'The importance of the pig taboo for the Israelites is well known, and likely received much of its importance due to interaction with and in contrast to the pork-eating Philistines'.[10] He argues that the archaeological evidence clearly supports this view: 'The height of Philistine pork consumption according to the archaeological record was during the Iron Age I, thus giving us a clear indication of the time and context in which pig avoidance could have become so ethnically important'.[11] It became a 'difference' for the Israelites in contrast to high consumptions of pork by the Philistines. In their effort to define themselves in contrast to the Philistines, this practice was given additional meaning at the time and eventually was used to inscribe their identity.

Surprisingly, the Philistines lowered their consumption of pork during the Iron Age II, and, as expected, the Israelites continued to avoid pig meat during this period. Whether the Philistines became acculturated to the cultural

10. Faust, *Israel's Ethnogenesis*, p. 39.

11. Faust, *Israel's Ethnogenesis*, pp. 39-40.

practice of the Israelites is unknown. In the Iron Age II, it is no longer possible to distinguish between the Philistines and the Israelites based on pork consumption. The difference in the amount of pork consumption between the Israelites and the Philistines was relevant only to the Iron Age I; this practice of avoiding pork could only have served as an ethnic behavior then. Therefore, Faust concludes, the avoidance of pork became a 'difference' precisely during the late Iron Age I when the Philistines began to expand their hegemony into the highlands.

An Ethos of Egalitarianism and Simplicity

The second major factor in the highlanders choosing certain practices from their reservoir of habits, according to Faust, was 'an ethos/ideology of egalitarianism and simplicity'. Faust credits this ethos/ideology to be responsible for some of these traits becoming ethnic markers, especially in conjunction with the fact that 'an interaction with the Philistines, who...appear to have been the outside pressure that caused the Israelite to resist and to form an ethnic identity'.[12] He does not discount the fact that these traits may have been the result of economic hardship in the highlands, which was the reality of life there at the time, but he argues that it was an ethos of egalitarianism and simplicity that made these traits meaningful or functioned as a 'difference' in contrast to other groups, especially the Philistines, at that time.

Israelites, for example, were known to have produced undecorated pottery in contrast to the decorated pottery from the lowlands during the Iron Age I. This may have something to do with the hardship of life in the highlands. Faust notes that, surprisingly, Israelites continued to produce undecorated pottery during the Iron Age II. Faust argues that hardship had nothing to do with the lack of decoration on Iron Age II pottery but results from interactions with the Philistines during the Iron Age I. He reasons that 'since the Philistine pottery was highly decorated, it is possible that the Israelites chose not to decorate their pottery as part of their ethnic negotiation with the Philistines, and that this tradition continued into the Iron II'.[13] The most important factor in the selection of the practice of not decorating pottery as an ethnic trait had to do with an ethos of egalitarianism and simplicity that influenced the worldview of the highlanders.

The Israelites were certainly reacting against the Philistines. It is not that the Israelites first began to produce plain pottery when they encountered the Philistines—they left their pottery undecorated prior to the appearance of the Philistines, in Canaan during the closing years of the Late Bronze Age in reaction to the Egyptio-Canaanite culture in the lowlands—but it was during

12. Faust, *Israel's Ethnogenesis*, p. 138.
13. Faust, *Israel's Ethnogenesis*, p. 46.

the encounter with the Philistines that a prior practice, like leaving pottery undecorated, was 'canonized' as an Israelite marker. After examining a lack of imported pottery, a limited pottery repertoire, and the four-room house, Faust suggests that these traits were chosen by the highlanders as their identity markers not only because they offered differences from those belonging to the Philistines, but also because artifiacts produced and practiced by the Philistines represented a different worldview, a world indicating hierarchy and luxury.[14]

Israelites developed a negative view of the Philistines' products and practices because of their ethos of egalitarianism and simplicity. Undecorated pottery fit their worldview. An ethos of egalitarianism and simplicity is a critical component of their worldview and served as a channel through which the Israelites formed their self-identity in contrast to the Philistines. Therefore, Faust argues that undecorated pottery as well as the lack of elaborated cult, the lack of any observable burials (individuals were buried in simple inhumations without tombs and burials), the limited repertoire of pottery, the four-room house, among other traits practiced by the highlanders, reflect this ethos. He summarizes his argument in this way:

> The egalitarian ethos became for the Israelites an important part of their distinct identity *vis-à-vis* other groups... It is even likely that in Israel, more than in many other similar societies, the ethos had some impact on social reality... It is also clear that this ethos had an impact on many facets of material culture that were discussed earlier, both during the Iron Age I, when the discrepancy between the ethos and social reality was small, and Iron Age II, when the disparity was great.[15]

Faust is not claiming that Israelites created an egalitarian society, as the final sentence above notes. There is obviously a clear differentiation between having an egalitarian ethos and implementing egalitarian practice. Faust cautions that an egalitarian practice 'never truly exists, and only relatively so in regard to some simple societies'. Faust, however, argues that 'an egalitarian ethos...can exist even in extreme hierarchical societies'.[16] That is, the ethos had some impact on Israel's social reality even though it remained hierarchical. When I argue below that David's actions reflect an ethos of simplicity and egalitarianism, I am not arguing that David's kingdom was an egalitarian society—far from it! His policy of inclusivism and some of his actions, however, may have been influenced by or compatible with an egalitarian ethos that was characteristic of the highlanders/Israelites.

14. Faust (*Israel's Ethnogenesis*, p. 146) indicates that 'The archaeological evidence, in accordance with the written sources, seems to indicate that the Philistines were the most complex society during the Iron Age I'.

15. Faust, *Israel's Ethnogenesis*, p. 107.

16. Faust, *Israel's Ethnogenesis*, p. 69.

The Historical Reality at the Time

The books of Judges and Samuel give a picture of several groups of people in the land of Canaan whose competition for the land results in the formation of states and ethnic identities. The Israelites were primarily located in the central highlands between areas along the coast and lowlands inhabited by the Canaanites and the Philistines and areas controlled by emerging Transjordan kingdoms like Midian, Moab, and Ammon on the eastern front. What we see in the region is a competition among the Israelites and other peoples fighting over the land once populated by the local Canaanites, the natives or indigenous people of the land, if you will. Other 'outsiders' wanted a piece of Canaan just as much as the Israelites did. Different parts of the land experienced different patterns of settlement or occupation. At some sites, the Israelites, depicted as outsiders of the land, displaced the local Canaanites. At other sites, foreigners, like the Philistines, displaced the Canaanites. The Israelites and the Philistines were among several groups of people who competed over the land. What the text reflects is a formation of states and ethnic groups in Canaan due to such competition.[17]

There is archaeological evidence to support the picture presented in the text. Faust draws attention to major shifts in the settlement patterns in Canaan during the transition from the Iron I to the Iron II:

> Most excavated Iron I rural settlements throughout the country, and especially in the highlands, were either abandoned or destroyed before the transition to the Iron Age II, or during the first decade of this period. The relatively few excavated Iron I villages that did not cease to exist turned into central settlements, i.e., towns or cities.[18]

He continues that 'the fact that the vast majority of Iron II rural sites were not located on Iron I sites, and that none of the Iron I villages continued to exist as a village into the Iron II, supports the view that major shifts in the settlement patterns occurred during or around the tenth century BCE'.[19] The population became more concentrated among fewer sites, leading to a formation of a state. Faust credits the Philistines for forging a state in the highlands:

17. Faust (*Israel's Ethnogenesis*, p. 138) based on archaeological evidence suggests the following scenario: 'When there is interaction and/or competition between groups, each will find ways to demarcate its boundaries more clearly. Whether the villagers discussed here had an ethnic consciousness earlier or not, they *must* have developed one when facing another group on such terms. The external threat created a dichotomy of "we" as opposed to "them", therefore defining the sense of togetherness ("we-ness"), so necessary for the formation and existence of ethnic groups. The inhabitants of the settlements discussed here had to develop some sort of common ground that united them against those who threatened them'.

18. Faust, *Israel's Ethnogenesis*, p. 117.

19. Faust, *Israel's Ethnogenesis*, p. 120.

> External pressure on the highland area pushed its inhabitants to leave most of their settlements and gather in several centers... The concentration of a large population in one place in resistance to a threat probably caused a sharp increase in the leadership's power and a gradual growth in organization and the administration, which eventually lead to the formation of a state in the highlands.[20]

Thus, he names the Philistines as the external threat that instigated changes in the settlement patterns in Canaan, resulting in the concentration of populations into larger but fewer settlements than before.

A case in point is the rise of Saul and his kingdom. According to 1 Samuel, Saul's kingdom emerged in the land of Benjamin, and this is corroborated by archaeological evidence. Faust observes that 'the first massively fortified settlement in the highland (of the late eleventh century BCE) was built in the land of Benjamin on a site that was probably not agricultural'.[21] Faust notes that 'the land of Benjamin appears to have had the most elaborate and complex social structure in the highland during the eleventh century BCE, particularly its latter part'.[22] Saul was a fighter of the Philistines and tried to lead the newly organized group of highlanders against the Philistines. Saul's policy of nativism can be explained by the historical context of the late Iron Age I (eleventh century BCE), from which Saul emerged as a leader of the Israelites to fend off the threat from the Philistines.[23] He favored his own kinsmen over others and may have redistributed acquired lands to them at the expense of others (see 1 Sam. 22.7 and 2 Sam. 4.2-3).[24]

20. Faust, *Israel's Ethnogenesis*, pp. 124-25.

21. Faust, *Israel's Ethnogenesis*, p. 130. Miller and Hayes based on careful reading of the biblical text, agree that it was the people of Ephraim/Benjamin and their satellite clans who formed the core of the emerging identity of Israel. In fact, they suggest (*A History of Ancient Israel and Judah*, p. 117) that at this early stage of the development of Israel's ethnic identity, 'Ephraim' may have been essentially synonymous with 'Israel'.

22. Faust, *Israel's Ethnogenesis*, p. 131.

23. Miller and Hayes (*A History of Ancient Israel and Judah*, p. 119) summarize Saul's career in this way: Saul was 'a Benjaminite who gained notoriety by challenging the Philistine hold on the hill country and by managing to keep them at bay for a time. In the process, he emerged as a local warlord of sorts, who ruled Ephraim and the north-central hill country tribes closely associated with Ephraim. It may have been first under Saul that the name "Israel" came to be associated with this cluster of tribes, rather than with Ephraim alone'.

24. In 1 Sam. 22.7, Saul questions the inner circle of his servants, made up mostly of Benjaminites: 'Hear now, you Benjaminites; will the son of Jesse give every one of you fields and vineyards, will he make you all commanders of thousands and commanders of hundreds?' The implication is that the Benjaminites benefitted from Saul's policy of land distribution. Saul's policy is perhaps reflected in the note that reports that the Hivites had to flee their home town and the Benjaminites settled there (2 Sam. 4.2-3); moreover, this

Saul was absolutely anti-Philistine and depended on the loyalty of the Benjaminites, his own kinsmen, to consolidate his kingdom in opposition to the Philistines.

Remarkably David went against this historical reality and Saul's policy. He discontinued Saul's tribal-centric or ethnocentric policy and practiced a policy of ecumenism, which allowed him to be radically inclusive and to forge a hybrid kingdom that was based on *ḥesed* rather than on identity. He was open to making connection with all sorts of people regardless of their ethnic, tribal, or religious identity. He worked with the Philistines, the arch-enemy of Israel, and other 'foreigners' and indigenous people to establish his kingdom.

The Hybridization of David's Kingdom

The formation of David's kingdom as the 'greater' Israel based in Jerusalem emerged through personal union (or bond or relation) characterized by *ḥesed* with disparate populations. David was able to consolidate his kingdom by attracting the loyalty of various groups to himself. He fostered alliances with other powers, regardless of their tribal, ethnic, or religious identities, based primarily on *ḥesed* rather than on ethnic or other identity ties. In the end, David does not take over Saul's kingdom, which was based on the support of the highlanders/Israelites who wanted to differentiate themselves from others in general and from the Philistines in particular, but creates a hybrid kingdom, which was composed of people across various identity boundaries, including the Philistines, and established on *ḥesed* rather than on identity.

The Wilderness Period: David as a Captain of Hebrews

David was in line to Saul's throne after his marriage to Saul's daughter, Michal, and due to his remarkable successes on the battlefield; hence the proverb 'Saul has killed his thousands, and David his ten thousands' (1 Sam. 18.7; 21.11; 29.5). Saul, who, the narrator claims, loved David from the moment he laid his eyes on him, became jealous of David's popularity and wanted to kill him. But Saul was also very afraid of David. Why was he so afraid of David? Why would he want to kill him, his own son-in-law? David was a successful military leader who had the loyalty of the army, attested by the fact that all members of Saul's court and kingdom loved (read, 'pledged political allegiance to') David. Saul was afraid that David would lead a coup and overthrow him. Perhaps David attempted a coup but failed; we can only speculate and many have done so. For example, McKenzie suggests, 'I suspect that David was actually involved in a plot to usurp the kingship. Saul

policy may be the background against which the Gibeonites/Hivites complained to David that Saul had tried to wipe them out from Israel (21.2).

was forced to go on the offensive while he still had the upper hand. But before Saul could have him arrested him [*sic*] and executed, David escaped'.[25] In David's long protest of innocence to Saul in 1 Sam. 24.8-15, David acknowledges that there was at least a rumor that he wanted to harm Saul in v. 9: 'Why do you listen to the words of those who say, "David seeks to do you harm?"'

When he either failed to overthrow Saul or fell out of favor with him, David had no choice but to give up his aspirations to replace Saul as king and flee from Saul's court. His family, as expected, immediately joined him upon his escape (1 Sam. 22.1). This is not surprising, since David already had articulated such a plan. When Jonathan told Saul that David had gone to his hometown of Bethlehem to join his family, specifically his brothers, for a sacrifice, Saul scolded Jonathan for not recognizing what David was really up to, namely, planning to take over Saul's kingdom (20.29-31): 'For as long as the son of Jesse lives upon the earth, neither you nor your kingdom shall be established' (20.31). It turned out that the words David put into Jonathan's mouth were not a ruse after all but a warning to Saul that the game was on. After this episode, Jonathan recognized that Saul wanted to kill David but failed to understand that David wanted to overthrow his father. Jonathan remained clueless and such a thought never entered his mind, according to the narrative.

David probably was hoping to gather supporters in Bethlehem, especially the soldiers and members of Saul's court (cf. Absalom's revolt), but this failed to materialize. After abandoning his plan to launch his coup from Bethlehem, he then went to Nob, but failed to gather support from that city as well, and was unable to strike an alliance with Achish in Gath (1 Sam. 21). He finally went to the cave of Adullam because he was not strong enough to take on Saul head on. His entire family, including his brothers who served in Saul's army, met him at the cave of Adullam to support his rebellion against Saul. The first constituency outside of his family to gather around David was 'everyone who was in distress, and everyone who was in debt, and everyone who was discontented' (22.2). The point of this notice, McCarter explains, 'is that David becomes the leader of all those men who have suffered some kind of loss or deprivation that has left them embittered; he is now champion of the discontented, the disenchanted, and the mis-treated'.[26] We can be more specific and say that among these men were those who suffered under Saul's policy of 'tribalism' and those who were dissatis-fied with Saul's rule and perhaps were also on the run from Saul. Saul distributed 'fields and vineyards' to the inner circle of Benjaminite servants; these land grants must have been possible at someone's expense. Those who

25. McKenzie, *King David*, p. 88.
26. McCarter, *I Samuel*, p. 357.

were displaced from their land probably were among the men who joined David. The establishment of a monarchy entailed centralization of the economic surplus, which benefitted those with wealth more than those who were poor. Saul was from a powerful family (look at his genealogy), and other wealthy people may have wanted to establish a monarchy in order to increase their share of the economic surplus. At Saul's public anointment (10.27) there were those who did not approve of him (perhaps monarchy itself as well) and did not bring tribute to him. Moreover, an important part of the award for slaying Goliath was for the hero's family to be 'free of taxes in Israel' (*ḥopšî bĕyiśrā'ēl*, 1 Sam. 17.25). Perhaps those who joined David either could not afford or refused to pay the 'taxes' required by the newly established monarchy.

These four hundred men are not identified in terms of ethnic, tribal, or regional identities. The term 'Hebrews', however, may be an appropriate name for them. This term is often used to refer to 'those who are socially marginal and economically disadvantaged, who pose a constant threat to the society'.[27] The Philistines called David's group 'Hebrews' (1 Sam. 29.3) and did not allow them to participate in the battle against Saul and the Israelites, even though, at the time of this remark, David's group consisted of disparate groups, including Philistines. The Philistines feared that David's 'Hebrews' would turn against them during a battle against Saul's men (29.4). They had had such an experience before when another group of Hebrews turned against them by joining Saul's army: 'Now the Hebrews who previously had been with the Philistines and had gone up with them into the camp turned and joined the Israelites who were with Saul and Jonathan' (14.21). The Hebrews may have had some association with the Israelites, but it is safe to assume that the term represents groups of people who were socially and politically on the outside. In David, these Hebrews found a captain around whom they could rally. A *ḥesed*-relationship was formed between them and David. David forged a personal union with this motley group and its households.

One of the first things David did after his escape from Saul was to place his parents out of harm's way. He went to the king of Moab and asked, 'Please let my father and mother come to you, until I know what God will do for me' (1 Sam. 22.3). The king of Moab must have agreed to provide protection for his parents, because David 'left them with the king of Moab, and they stayed with him all the time that David was in the stronghold' (22.4).

27. Brueggemann, *First and Second Samuel*, p. 197. Miller and Hayes (*A History of Ancient Israel and Judah*, p. 113) suggest that if the term 'Hebrew' is related to the Akkadian term *Apiru/Habiru*, then it 'would have referred to a social class rather than to any particular ethnic group. A Hebrew was someone who, for one reason or another, was considered marginal to established society—transient, minorities, outlaws'.

The question is: Why would the king of Moab assist the captain of a band of Hebrews? There is no mention of animosity between Saul and Moab except for the summary statement in 1 Sam. 14.47, which states that he fought against all his enemies on every side, including Moab. It is highly unlikely that Saul would have tried to expand his influence into southern Transjordan when 'there was hard fighting against the Philistines all the days of Saul' (14.52). Therefore, there is no reason for the king of Moab to help David for 'nothing'. There must have been 'something' that allowed David to ask for help and for the king of Moab to respond in the affirmative. There seems to be some truth to the notion that David's ancestors included a Moabite (namely, Ruth), and this may indicate that David himself was not of pure Israelite stock (more on this point below). No matter what the connection was between David and the king of Moab, what matters is that David felt it was appropriate and safe to leave his family there. David asked for *ḥesed* from the king of Moab, and the king honored it without any display of reservation. It clearly shows that there was a personal tie between David and the king of Moab. The king of Moab could have assisted David in more ways than just giving a safe haven for his parents during his wilderness years, but we are not privy to such details.[28]

During the wilderness years, David and his men must have formed a close relationship while experiencing all sorts of hardships and adventures together. Foremost, they had to sustain themselves by finding basic necessities like food and shelter. Moreover, they had to do this without having a base, that is, a town from which to operate and receive support. This may explain why he took his men to save the city of Keilah from the Philistines (1 Sam. 23). His men seemed puzzled by this decision (23.3): 'David's men said to him, "Look, we are afraid here in Judah; how much more then if we go to Keilah against the armies of the Philistines?"' David was hoping to use Keilah as his base, but the residents of Keilah rejected him even though he rescued them from the Philistines (23.12). A likely scenario could have been that David tried to form a patron–client relationship with them but they rejected him in favor of keeping Saul as their patron.

David's attempt to acquire gifts from Nabal in 1 Samuel 25 and his endeavor to form a *ḥesed*-relationship with the people of Keilah in the story mentioned above give us a glimpse of how David and his band of Hebrews made a living during this period. David may have tried to form a patron–client relationship with those who were on the fringe of Saul's areas of influence, providing 'protection' for payment and a base, but he may not have had much success even on the southeastern fringe of Saul's area because the

28. In the summary report of David's campaigns (2 Sam. 8) David reversed his policy toward Moab at some point during his reign and it states that David conducted a brutal attack on the Moabites (8.2).

people in the region maintained their loyalty to Saul.[29] They saw no reason to switch their patron. Thus, when David's men asked for the 'payment' for their protection of Nabal's shepherds and livestock, Nabal scoffed at them: 'Who is David? Who is the son of Jesse? There are many servants [*'abādîm*] today who are breaking away [*hammitpārĕṣîm*] from their masters' (1 Sam. 25.10). Nabal berated David for proposing a *ḥesed*-relationship with him. Moreover, by Nabal's description of David and his men as runaway slaves, Nabal was referring not only to David's escape from Saul but also noting the fact that David had gathered around himself 'Hebrews', who were no more than a group of violent thugs in Nabal's eyes. These 'slaves' (*'abādîm*) 'break forth' (*prṣ*) from their masters. The word *prṣ* connotes force and violence. David was a leader of a band of runaway servants/slaves, a band of Hebrews, involved in a racketeering ring.

They survived on what they were able to plunder from local populations regardless of their tribal, religious, or ethnic allegiance. After hearing Nabal's insult, David was about to slaughter all the males of Carmel (1 Sam. 25.13, 34), whose people were considered part of the tribe of Judah, and then he certainly would have plundered Nabal's property after the massacre. Thanks to Abigail's quick thinking, according to the story, such a breach of ethnic loyalty was thwarted. Even though the narrator claims later in the narrative that David did not do such a thing (27.8-12), this episode shows that David disregarded such allegiance.

David's encounter with Nabal, which resulted in his marriage to Abigail, was probably the biggest break for David during his wilderness years. This good fortune was instrumental in consolidating his power in Judah. Nabal's death in conjunction with David's marriage to Abigail probably enabled him to acquire the estate of Nabal in Carmel and the allegiance of the Calebites, a non-Israelite group, whose capital was Hebron.[30] The notion that David's possession of Abigail somehow entitled him to leadership in Caleb is well founded in Israel (2 Sam. 3.6-10; 16.20-23; 1 Kgs 2.13-25).[31] Moreover, he

29. Miller and Hayes (*A History of Ancient Israel and Judah*, p. 165) describe David's situation in this way: 'Fleeing Keilah, David and his men sought refuge in the barren southeastern slopes of the southern hill country, primarily the area between the villages of Ziph, Carmel, and Maon…and the Dead Sea. This was on the southeastern fringe of Saul's area of influence. Saul had set up a monument for himself in Carmel (1 Sam. 15.12), and…persons such as Nabal of Maon seem to have recognized Saul's authority in the area'.

30. McCarter (*I Samuel*, p. 396) understands the Calebites to be non-Israelites: 'Evidently, however, the Calebites were a people of non-Israelite origin (Num. 32.12; Josh. 14.6, 14; cf. Gen. 36.11, 15, 42) later incorporated into Judah (Josh. 15.13); their territory included the region around Hebron (Josh. 14.13-15; cf. Judg. 1.10-20), where the present story takes place, and apparently certain tracts further S (cf. 30.14)'.

31. Levenson and Halpern, 'The Political Import of David's Marriages', p. 508.

was already married to Ahinoam from Jezreel (1 Sam. 25.43), which was a village in the vicinity of Maon, Ziph, and Carmel, the same region as David's newly acquired base.[32] His marriage to Ahinoam and Abigail paved the way to Hebron (and later the control of the entire region of Judah). This must have propelled him to prominence in the heartland of Judah. McCarter summarizes the importance of these two women:

> Now we find him marrying the widow of a high-ranking member of the clan that controlled Hebron...as well as another woman from nearby Jezreel (v 43). His marriage to Ahinoam and Abigail, with Nabal's property in his control, gave him respectability among the leaders of the towns in Judah and its neighboring Philistine territory of Gath. He is becoming a prominent figure in the heartland of Judah and a force to be reckoned with.[33]

David, however, was still in danger from Saul, and he was not strong enough to confront Saul directly. He did not have the support of the local population (cf. 1 Sam. 23.12, 19), including the people from Keilah and Ziph, as he had with the Hebrews and perhaps the Calebites.[34] A significant segment of Judah must have remained loyal to Saul up to the time of his death. Therefore, David makes a risky decision to form an alliance with the Philistines, which will lead him to form a coalition with Israel's archenemy, remarkably disregarding the enmity between the two groups of people and moving him toward using *ḥesed* as the most important criterion for inclusion in his army and kingdom.

The Ziklag Period: David as a Philistine Vassal/Ally

When David stopped at Gath the first time (1 Sam. 21.10-15), he was alone and did not have any leverage to negotiate a relationship; therefore, he was no use to Achish. Then David came to Achish the second time with his men and as a notable leader in the area of Judah (thanks to his marriage to

32. There are those, including Halpern and McKenzie, who accept J.D. Levenson's argument in '1 Samuel 25 as Literature and as History' (*CBQ* 40 [1978], pp. 11-28), that Ahinoam is the same woman as Saul's wife. This would make Ahinoam, the mother of David's first son Amnon, the former wife of Saul. Levenson and Halpern ('The Political Import of David's Marriages', p. 515) suggest an intriguing scenario, 'Behind the textual veil lies only the figure of Ahinoam—Saul's only known wife, and, it is not unreasonable to assume, a prize carried off by David... David's theft of Saul's wife is suggested.' McCarter and others argue that David's Ahinoam had nothing to do with Saul's Ahinoam'.

33. McCarter, *I Samuel*, p. 402. In fact, the Philistines refer to him as 'the king of the land' (1 Sam. 21.12) long before David becomes king of Judah in 2 Sam. 2.

34. The towns of Keilah and Ziph are perfectly willing to turn over David, supposedly their tribesman, to Saul. McKenzie (*King David*, p. 93) makes this stinging remark: 'They do not exhibit the loyalty one would expect to find if David had indeed freed them from oppression and plundering'.

Ahinoam and Abigail). He was in a position of some power, and Achish recognized this. Achish agreed to enter into a type of *quid pro quod* relationship, perhaps a patron–client relationship, with David (1 Sam. 27). Achish gave the city of Ziklag to David, from which David and his men engaged in raids against the local populations of the Negeb. The narrator claims that David and his men, while under Achish's service, never raided towns belonging to Judah (27.8-12), but this claim is unrealistic. As McKenzie puts it, 'These ethnic distinctions were not clear-cut, and David would not have had time to check them anyway. Besides, he and his men were concerned with survival. Their targets were chosen based on economic considerations, not ethnic ones'.[35] David continued to do what he had been doing prior to joining Achish's service, namely, plundering goods from various people in the region or receiving gifts from them in exchange for protection. He must have been very good at it. He quickly earned Achish's trust and was promoted to being his bodyguard (28.2). David served as Achish's bodyguard, a position in the ancient Near East that affords 'easy access to the king, and control of a considerable force of elite soldiers'.[36] David took full advantage of this position (he always does!) by forming a very close relationship with the Gittites and other Philistine soldiers, including the Cherethites and the Pelethites who were from this region as well.[37] These three contingents of soldiers gave their unswerving loyalty to David throughout his career and proved to be a critical factor in establishing and sustaining his kingship and kingdom.

The narrator is understandably anxious to defend David's decision to enter Achish's service as a captain of a raiding band and later as a bodyguard by blaming Saul's relentless pursuit of him as leaving David no choice but to seek asylum from Achish and the Philistines. The narrator resolves this awkward situation by having David spare the towns of Judah during his raids and by crediting David with deceiving Achish into believing his apparent stratagem. However, the fact that the narrator went to such extremes to justify this embarrassing element in David's career leaves no doubt that the

35. McKenzie, *King David*, p. 104. See 1 Sam. 25.21-22 where David desired to destroy the males of Carmel, who were considered part of the tribe of Judah.

36. Halpern, *David's Secret Demons*, p. 79. David may also have been Saul's bodyguard (see 1 Sam. 22.14). If that is the case, then David is continuing his position, albeit under a different patron.

37. The Cherethites and the Pelethites were most likely Philistine contingents; see U.Y. Kim, 'Cherethites and the Pelethites', in *NIB*, I, pp. 585-86. McCarter (*I Samuel*, p. 435) notes that the Negev of the Cherethites 'was that part of the southern desert controlled by the Philistines or, perhaps, a subdivision of it in the vicinity of Ziklag. The presence later on in King David's army of a contingent of Cherethites, who showed a particular loyalty that continued into Solomon's reign, suggests that David won their allegiance decisively in his days at Ziklag'.

relationship between David and Achish was a historical fact and that this relationship was based on more than David's ruse alone.

At the same time, David also maintained a personal bond (*ḥesed*-relationship) with the elders of various towns in Judah, especially Hebron. David was playing it safe, sharing the spoil of his raids with both Achish and the elders of Judah. He wanted to maintain ties with both Gath and Judah. We see this in 1 Samuel 30 when he attacked the Amalekite camp after the Amalekites took the spoil from Ziklag. After he recovered all his belongings and a lot more, he sent part of the spoil to his friends, the elders of Judah. Then the text lists all the towns, namely, 'all the places where David and his men had roamed', including Hebron, to which he sends the spoil (1 Sam. 30.31). David was diligent in maintaining a *ḥesed*-relationship with the leaders of these places.

It was during this Ziklag period, one year and four months according to the text, that David's army became professionalized. His army was not a collection of bandits any longer but was made up of professional Philistine soldiers as well as the Hebrews who had followed him from the start of his uprising. He formed a strong solidarity with his men through shared acts of loyalty and *jeong* during this time of hardship and exploits. Even after David became king of Judah and Israel, he continued to use his standing army as the main source of his military muscle rather than relying on ad hoc militia or conscripted soldiers from his kingdom. This was a significant change in the character and makeup of the military from the days of judges and even from the time of Saul who relied primarily on the Benjaminites. The Cherethites and the Pelethites in particular gave unswerving loyalty to David throughout his life, serving as David's bodyguards until his death. David's army also must have included Gittites, another Philistine force he probably commanded at Ziklag. Later in David's career, we find Ittai and six hundred Gittites in David's service in Jerusalem (2 Sam. 15.19). Moreover, David probably maintained a partnership with Gath throughout his reign, a critical alliance that the narrative downplays but that cannot be denied due to his many connections to Gath and the Gittites. In addition to having connections to Achish, Ittai, and Gittite soldiers, David decided to leave the ark with Obed-edom the Gittite rather than at an Israelite's house (2 Sam. 6.10-11).[38]

38. McCarter (*II Samuel*, p. 170) summarizes this embarrassing connection between David and the Gittites: 'Obed-edom is probably another partisan whose loyalty dates to David's days in Gath and Ziklag, a man upon whom David can rely. Later tradition, perhaps troubled by the consignment of the ark to the care of a foreigner, ascribed to Obed-edom a Levitical genealogy and remembered him as a musician (I Chron 15.21; 16.5, cf. v. 38) and gatekeeper (I Chron 15.18, 24)'. Polzin (*David and the Deuteronomist*, p. 86) notes that 'the house of Obed-edom the Gittite is the only house of any kind that the LORD is said to bless' in the entire DH.

In spite of the narrator's defense, it is certain that there was a close alliance between David and the Gittites. As Halpern put it, the text 'discloses that throughout his reign he had Gittite allies'.[39]

His army, made up of Hebrews, Philistines (Gittites, Cherethites, and Pelethites) and others (including Gibonites; more below), is bound to him by *ḥesed*, not by their ethnic, regional, or religious ties. His men do not owe their allegiance to their own 'people' but to him. He prepared the people of the Judahite territory to receive him as their king now, since he controlled the region, especially the Calebite region, with his army and through his marriages. McCarter summarizes the Ziklag period in this way:

> Indeed the entire Ziklag pericope may be said to demonstrate a historical basis for a bond between David and the people of the Judahite Negeb as surely as the preceding stories do for the Wilderness of Judah and specifically the area east of Hebron. Taken together these materials prepare us for II Sam 2.1-4, the proclamation of David as king of Judah in Hebron.[40]

Now the cast is ready and the stage is set for David's grand entrance to Hebron.

The Hebron Period: David Consolidates his Power from Hebron

Upon Saul's death, David consolidated the 'people' of Judah into one people under his kingship. He entered Hebron with Ahinoam and Abigail by his side, no doubt also accompanied by his army. The text states in 2 Sam. 2.2-3: 'So David went up there, along with his two wives, Ahinoam of Jezreel, and Abigail the widow of Nabal of Carmel. David brought up the men who were with him, every one with his household; and they settled in the town of Hebron'. How did he settle in the town of Hebron? Halpern thinks that 'this signifies the invasion of the Judean hill country by the Gittite contingent supporting David'.[41] While David's men may have provided the muscle, if you will, in conquering territories for David, we should not underestimate the role David's women played in paving the way for him to establish his kingship. His marriages to Ahinoam and Abigail were instrumental in assembling his kingdom. David's good fortune was in acquiring *ḥesed* from men and also from women, but his genius was being open to every connection available to him. As Levenson and Halpern observe, 'To judge from his marriages...David's talent lay in availing himself of every connection. In this connection, his early marriages seem to have played an enormous part'.[42]

Although the text describes David's 'settlement' in Hebron as being brought about through the invitation of the people of Hebron, a more likely

39. Halpern, *David's Secret Demons*, p. 154.
40. McCarter, *I Samuel*, p. 437.
41. Halpern, *David's Secret Demons*, p. 297.
42. Levenson and Halpern, 'The Political Import of David's Marriages', p. 518.

scenario of his 'conquest' of Hebron is due to his superior military strength, the allegiance of the Calebites through his marriages, and his good relationship with some leaders in the region that he had nurtured during his Ziklag period. The text is probably correct in that David's takeover of Hebron was likely a peaceful one. Upon taking up residence in Hebron, the people in this region had no choice but to acknowledge David as their lord, especially since their patron, Saul, was dead. The text describes their 'voluntary' acceptance of David as their lord in this way: 'the people of Judah came, and there they anointed David king over the house of Judah' (2 Sam. 2.4). David was able to unify various groups of people living in this region under his leadership after Saul's death had left a power vacuum in this region. It was not the people of Judah who legitimized David's kingship; it was David who created the 'people' ('tribe' or 'house') of Judah. Rather than basing his kingdom on the tribe of Judah, he founded his kingdom in Hebron on the *ḥesed* of his supporters.

David formed a kingdom from Hebron with his eyes on the greater prize, namely, to rule over the people of Israel still loyal to the house of Saul. Saul's kingdom was now under the leadership of Ishbaal and his general, Abner, in the city of Mahanaim, which was located in Gilead. David's strategy was to put pressure on the house of Saul by forming alliances with its surrounding political entities in the Transjordan. He tried to woo the people of Jabesh-gilead over to his side (2 Sam. 2.4-7) by inviting the Jabeshites to establish a *ḥesed*-relationship with him against the house of Saul. He was probably unsuccessful in persuading the Jabeshites to abandon their loyalty to the house of Saul, but he was able to win over two powerful leaders in the region of Gilead: Barzillai, who was probably an Aramean, and Machir, leader of Lo Debar. Barzillai, who had an alliance with Saul through marriage (his son was likely married to Merab, Saul's daughter), decided to form an alliance with David instead. He handed over his Saulide grandsons to David (2 Sam. 21), and Machir also gave up Jonathan's son, Mephiboshet, to David (2 Sam. 9). It seems that Saul's former allies in Gilead, except Jabesh-gilead, switched their allegiance to David's side early in his years at Hebron. This was a striking blow to the house of Saul.

David formed an alliance with Geshur, north of Gilead, through a marriage to Maacah, daughter of Talmay, king of Geshur, and mother of Absalom (2 Sam. 3.3). Halpern recognizes the importance of this alliance in relation to the time of David's career: 'No king, and no king of a city-state in the Golan, would commit a daughter in marriage to David before David was himself a king in prospect. The presumption is that the alliance took place after David proclaimed himself king of Judah, in Hebron'.[43] This would have been another blow to Ishbaal's kingdom if we read 'Geshurites' for

43. Halpern, *David's Secret Demons*, p. 233.

'Ashurites' in 2 Sam. 2.9: Abner made Ishbaal 'king over Gilead, the Geshurites, Jezreel, Ephraim, Benjamin, and over all Israel'.[44] The Geshurites also changed their loyalty shortly after David took over Hebron.

David also formed an alliance through a *ḥesed*-relationship with Nahash, the king of the Ammonites. Nahash's son, Shobi, maintained this relationship after a brief interruption during the reign of Hanun, another son of Nahash. Ammon was located south of Gilead. There was a good possibility that David formed a *ḥesed*-relationship with Nahash after acquiring the allegiance of the Calebites upon Nabal's death and his marriage to Abigail. This alliance must have also remained strong throughout David's career, since Solomon's chief wife and his heir, Rehoboam's mother, was Naamah from Ammon, most likely the daughter of Shobi son of Nahash. When David was on the run from his son, Absalom, he received greater support and loyalty from these Transjordan allies, Shobi, Machir, and Barzillai, than from his own people (2 Sam. 17.24-29).

It was during the Hebron period that David formed alliances with political forces surrounding Israel that eventually led to the collapse of the house of Saul and further developed his military and administration that allowed him to unify two distinctive peoples into one kingdom. McCarter notes the importance of David's time in Hebron toward unifying Judah and Israel under his leadership in this way: 'David's reign as king in Hebron seems to have been an important stage in the development of the bonds and institutions that eventually made possible the unification of Judah and Israel under a single ruler'.[45]

David Conquers Israel and Incorporates it into his Hybridized Kingdom

It was no accident that the first battle between David and the house of Saul occurred in Gibeon (2 Sam. 2.12-32). McCarter notes that the location of Gibeon 'suggests that the city had considerable strategic importance in the struggle that emerged between David and Ishbaal', and the fact that there was an ill feeling between Gibeon and the house of Saul (2 Sam. 21) made it an ideal place for Joab and his troops to find 'Gibeonite sympathy or even open support in the showdown that occurred here'.[46] The Gibeonites were not Israelites, but were an indigenous population who had an agreement that allowed them to live in peace within the territory of Israel (Josh. 9). The

44. In arguing for reading 'Geshurites' for 'Ashurites', Miller and Hayes (*A History of Ancient Israel and Judah*, p. 139) note the following: Geshur 'makes better historical sense, on the assumption that Saul expanded his influence beyond Gilead into northern Transjordan. No texts associate Saul in any way with Galilee. And why would the tribe of Asher be singled out and the other Galilean tribes ignored?'.

45. McCarter, *II Samuel*, p. 89.

46. McCarter, *II Samuel*, p. 95.

Gibeonites were the Hivites according to Josh. 9.7. Gibeon, Chephirah, Beeroth, and Kiriath-jearim formed the terapolis of the Hivites (Josh. 9.17). They were 'outsiders' living 'inside' Israel's land; they were interstitial 'non/Israelites'. I use this term to note the ambiguity in their identity. Are they Israelites or non-Israelites? They are hybrids or interstitial being who are considered Israelites (cf. Calebites and Kenites were non-Israelites who became 'real' Israelites over time) but, at the same time, they are only a step away from being treated as non-Israelites. They are Israelites but not quite. They can be differentiated from 'real' Israelites whenever there is a need for it, as Saul's nativist policy demonstrates. Saul apparently implemented his policy of nativism against the Gibeonites: 'Now the Gibeonites were not of the people of Israel, but of the remnant of the Amorites; although the people of Israel had sworn to spare them, Saul had tried to wipe them out in his zeal for the people of Israel and Judah' (2 Sam. 21.2). The text claims that Saul tried to exterminate them because they were considered non-Israelites living in the midst of Israel. Saul's decision to persecute the Gibeonites would have been very uncharacteristic of Saul. He honored a *ḥesed*-relationship with the Kenites by giving them an advanced warning before he attacked the Amalekites (1 Sam. 15.6). Why would he not honor this bond between the Israelites and the Gibeonites? It may be that Saul persecuted them because they were David's supporters. The Gibeonites turned to David for retribution, and he agreed to their wish without much hesitation or protest.

Moreover, for Halpern, there is a more interesting reason for the importance of Gibeon in the war between David and the house of Saul. He claims that the relationship between the Gibeonites and David was more than a political alliance formed by their common enmity toward the house of Saul: 'David's relations with the Gibeonites, his depending on them to eliminate Saul's house, and his integration of them into his kingdom represent signs of a thoroughgoing collaboration'.[47] He argues that David, in fact, was a Gibeonite and that some of David's Gittites may also have been Gibeonites. He suggests that Ittai the Gittite and Ittai son of Ribai from Gibeah of the Benjaminite (2 Sam. 23.29) were probably the same person who was part of a Philistine garrison that was in Gibeah until Saul was able to push the Philistines out (13.2-3). The fact that David's hometown was Bethlehem, which also hosted a Philistine garrison and was situated in the same Gibeonite region, and the fact that David is repeatedly referred to as 'son of Jesse', which may indicate that Jesse was the head of a prominent Bethlehemite family, even a local chieftain, enabling David to use this connection to win the support of the Gibeonites in the region, supports Halpern's hypothesis. Halpern states that 'While Saul focused on driving the Gibeonites out

47. Halpern, *David's Secret Demons*, p. 332.

of the Ayyalon Pass, David incorporated them into his coalition'.[48] Therefore, it is not surprising that Ishbaal's assassins, Baanah and Rechab, were Gibeonites; they were from Beeroth, a town belonging to Gibeonites.[49] We will never know for certain whether David ordered the hit on Ishbaal, but based on the fact that David had a very close connection with Gibeonites, it is a distinct possibility that Rimmon's sons acted in corroboration with David.

After the assassination of Ishbaal, the people of Israel had no choice but to accept David as their king. They were surrounded by David's kingdom in the south and his allies on all sides—Geshur, Gilead, and Ammon in the Transjordan and the Philistines to the north and the west of Benjamin. David conquered Israel and accepted the people of Israel into his kingdom. In spite of what the narrative says, the people of Israel were not related to the inhabitants of the territory of Judah. As Halpern concludes, 'before David's time, there is no evidence of an ethnic affiliation of a "tribe" of Judah to Israel'.[50] Even in the text, the idea that the people of Israel and Judah were of one people is contested: the Israelites remind David, 'Look, we are your bone and flesh' (2 Sam. 5.1), but the converse cry rallies them to rebel against David: 'We have no portion in David, no share in the son of Jesse!'[51] Yet the people of Israel and the people of Judah became part of one kingdom through a personal union with David.[52]

48. Halpern, *David's Secret Demons*, p. 310.

49. The text states that the assassins were 'the sons of Rimmon the Beerothite' (2 Sam. 4.5) but were also called 'sons of Rimmon a Benjaminite from Beeroth' (4.2). So, were they Benjaminites or Gibeonites from Beeroth? The text adds a parenthetical remark to explain why Rimmon is also called a Benjaminite, 'for Beeroth is considered to belong to Benjamin. Now the people of Beeroth had fled to Gittaim and are there as resident aliens to this day' (4.2-3). That is, the original population fled and was replaced by Benjaminites. McCarter (*II Samuel*, p. 127) remarks, 'Thus it is somewhat surprising to find a Beerothite called a Benjaminite, unless the designation is merely formal, based on the official assignment of Beeroth to Benjamin in Josh. 18.25'. There is no reason for Rimmon to be called a Beerothite if he was a Benjaminite. His sons were Gibeonites from Beeroth. The confusion arises from the fact that they were interstitial non/Israelites.

50. Halpern, *David's Secret Demons*, p. 275.

51. 2 Sam. 20.1; this cry is repeated in 1 Kgs 12.16 when Israel under Jeroboam's leadership becomes liberated from Judah.

52. S. Hermann ('"Realunion" und "Charismatisches Königtum". Zu zwei offenen Fragen der Verfassungen in Juda und Israel', *Eretz-Israel* 24 [1993], pp. 97-103) summarizes the debate on whether David's kingdom was formed, as A. Alt had argued, through a 'personal union' where Israel and Judah as two originally independent powers felt tied to David, each retaining its own character under David's rule, or, as A. Malamat had argued, through a '*Realunion*' where Israel and Judah combined themselves into one administrative body. Hermann argues that Judah and Israel only for a time were prepared to accept a shared exercise of power through a 'personal union' with David, but not for a

David's strategy had always been to conquer Israel by uniting with peripheral powers in contact with Israel and forming a circle around Saul's kingdom. He 'did not divide his conquest. He engulfed it whole'.[53] A more important point for our purpose, however, is to see the difference between David's and Saul's policies. Saul's base of power was the people of his tribe, the Benjaminites, and his kingdom was based on ethnic, tribal, and religious ties. Halpern summarizes David's strategy of 'ecumenism' in contrast to Saul's policy of nativism: 'There is every indication that David reversed the policy of nativism, and in fact allied with all the surrounding non-Israelite communities in order to exert pressure on Israel itself... In modern Western categories, one might regard David as an ecumenist'.[54] David wanted to isolate, conquer, and then incorporate Israel into his kingdom.

From the beginning of his career, David was not interested in following Saul's policy of nativism, and his power was not based on the people of the tribe of Judah but on a coalition of various constituents who had suffered due to Saul's policy of nativism. David's kingdom was made up of all sorts of people, including Israelites, various inhabitants of the territory of Judah, Gibeonites, Gittites, Hittites, Cushites, Ammonites, Moabites, Gileadites, Hebrews, and others not mentioned in the text. As Halpern puts it, 'David, it would seem, never wrote off a single possible constituency'.[55] David created a kingdom that was based on *ḥesed* rather than on the ethnic, tribal, or religious identity; his kingdom was based on loyalty, not on identity.

David's policy of hybridization came to full fruition when he decided to establish the capital of his new hybridized kingdom in Jerusalem.[56] This was one of the most brilliant political moves of his career. Jerusalem was an excellent strategic position from which to rule Judah and Israel, two large independent political forces. It was centrally located between Israel and Judah but outside of any territory belonging to the tribes of Israel and Judah.

long-term '*Realunion*'. Therefore, Hermann concludes that the kingdom constructed under David is better called a '*Personalunion*' than a '*Realunion*'.

53. Levenson and Halpern, 'The Political Import of David's Marriages', p. 518.

54. Halpern, *David's Secret Demons*, p. 312.

55. Halpern, *David's Secret Demons*, p. 390.

56. We must keep our imagination of Jerusalem in check; a city-state that served as the center of political and religious affairs of ancient Judah during the late monarchic period. It was no more than a town with a mixed population at the time of David's conquest. Miller and Hayes (*A History of Ancient Israel and Judah*, p. 160) describe it at that time in this way: 'Jerusalem seems to have been a small settlement, centered around a stronghold, with a mixed population including people of Amorite, Hurrian, and Hittite stock. In the immediate vicinity of Jerusalem were Gibeon and other Hivite villages'. They opine that 'Surely the most important move of David's career was his conquest of Jerusalem and choice of this city as his residency' (p. 169).

It belonged to the Jebusites, near Bethlehem, and the Gibeon tetrapolis where David had a strong personal connection. All he had to do was to conquer it. Here, too, David made another smart move. He conquered Jerusalem with his own men; 'the king and his men' (2 Sam. 5.6) the text tells us, without the use of troops conscripted from Judah or Israel.[57] Therefore, Jerusalem became David's personal city—'the city of David' (5.7)—a place from which he could rule over his kingdom with little interference from any constituents.

Next, he incorporated Jebusites and other local populations, including Hittites, Hurrians, and Hivvites, into his kingdom now centered in Jerusalem. They were certainly not exterminated; he did not practice a policy of nativism. This is indicated by the fact that David buys the threshing floor from Araunah the Jebusite that would become the future site of Solomon's temple (2 Sam. 24.18-25). The person from whom David acquires the threshing floor may have been the Jebusite king of Jerusalem. N. Wyatt, after noting the fact that the name 'Araunah' in 2 Sam. 24.16 appears with the definite article (*h'wrnh*: K; *h'rwnh*: Q), argues that the term is not an individual personal name but a Hittite or Hurrian term used for the designation of a king.[58] Wyatt sees the negotiation between Araunah and David over the price of the threshing floor as the formal transference of the sacred place from the last king of Jebusites to his successor, David, citing 24.23 as crucial evidence of this.[59] The acquisition of the sacred place (the threshing floor) belonging to the king of Jebus/Jerusalem was an important event in the consolidation of David's control over Jerusalem/Jebus; this was the place that was to become the site of the temple, the holiest place in Jerusalem. Wyatt argues that the 'sale' of the threshing floor may not be an

57. McCarter (*II Samuel*, pp. 154-55), after citing occurrences of 'David and his men' (1 Sam 23.5, 24, 26; 24.3, 4, 23; 25.20; 27.8; 29.2, 11; 30.1, 3; etc.), comments on the force used by David to conquer Jerusalem: 'The Israelite force here is David's personal militia, recruited during his days as a fugitive from Saul's court (cf. I Sam 22.2)... The same force was used for the capture of Jerusalem (5.6)'.

58. N. Wyatt, '"Araunah the Jebusite" and the Throne of David', in *'There's Such Divinity Doth Hedge a King': Essays on Royal Ideology in Ugaritic and Old Testament Literature* (SOTS Monograph Series; London: Ashgate, 2005), pp. 1-14; first published in *ST* 39 (1985), pp. 39-53.

59. Wyatt, '"Araunah the Jebusite" and the Throne of David', pp. 1-2. In 2 Sam. 24.23, the Hebrew text has the following: *hakkōl nātan 'arawnah hammelek lammelek* ('all this Araunah the king give to the king'). He agrees with G.W. Ahlström that the sentence requires the formula *'arawnah hammelek* which should be read as a unity, but he modifies Ahlström's point by suggesting that the term's first three consonants are *ʾwr* (rather than *ʾrw*) and that it should be read, in light of v. 16, as *hʾwrnh* ('the lord/king'; a title of office rather than a personal name), 'clearly meaning "king" in the present context, and the following *hmlk* ["the king"] is simply a gloss translating the foreign term into Hebrew for the reader's benefit' (p. 2).

indication of the transfer of royal power occurring at the moment of the sale. David may have delayed the final removal of the Jebusite king by first agreeing to co-regency in order to make the final transition more legitimate and smooth. Wyatt summarizes this scenario:

> But it may be that by virtue of his purchase of the threshing-floor, David was effectively granted co-regency with the 'Jebusite' king over the city, and afterwards had his co-regent removed so that he should exercise complete authority himself. The devious way by which this was done would simply be a further example of the way in which people who were obstacles to David's advancement were continually coming to an early grave, while David remained ostensibly aloof and innocent of any complicity (except that in this case he was directly accused by Nathan).[60]

Wyatt also suggests that Zadok may have been a son of the king of the Jebusites and a priest by the virtue of his royal birth (cf. David's sons as priests, 2 Sam. 8.18). Zadok may have played 'an important though unspecified role in assisting David to gain control of the city, being subsequently rewarded for his treachery'.[61] Wyatt argues that Zadok's defection to David was 'the spearhead of wholesale acceptance of David as overlord by the whole city administration. These officials would all the more readily accept David as co-regent than as successor to their previous lord'.[62] David's decision to co-regency rather than sole rule over the conquered city may have something to do with David's identity or his lack of royal pedigree. Wyatt summarizes this point well:

> So far as more far-reaching ideological purposes were concerned, the whole point was David's complete lack of any royal pedigree, and even the relative lack of any royal tradition either among the Judahite tribes, for whom David was the first king, or among those of Israel, for whom Saul was the first. By at first a co-regency, and then by sole kingship over Jerusalem, David was able to appropriate the ancient royal traditions of the city, and graft them onto his united kingship over the tribes of Palestine. The indirect means by which he achieved the Jerusalem kingship would—ideally—have scotched any suspicions that he gained it by improper means, and would represent him in the eyes of his people as a true king, whose every successive advancement was a sign of divine favour.[63]

60. Wyatt, '"Araunah the Jebusite" and the Throne of David', p. 10.
61. Wyatt, '"Araunah the Jebusite" and the Throne of David', p. 3.
62. Wyatt, '"Araunah the Jebusite" and the Throne of David', p. 10.
63. Wyatt, '"Araunah the Jebusite" and the Throne of David', p. 10. Miller and Hayes (*A History of Ancient Israel and Judah*, p. 160) conclude that David should be called 'king' rather than 'chieftain' especially after he established himself in Jerusalem because 'Jerusalem had a tradition of kingship, and the pluralistic population over which David ruled would have required a more complex administrative structure than Saul had employed'.

David's brilliant and patient strategy to conquer Jebus/Jerusalem and to win over the people of Jebus/Jerusalem is consistent with the David we have learned to know and even to 'love'. David, following his inclusive policy, from the beginning of his career incorporated all constituents, including the Jebusites, into his kingdom. Moreover, David secured the loyalty of the northern tribes by bringing the Ark of the Covenant, which is associated with the northern religious tradition but perhaps more importantly with Saul,[64] into Jerusalem (2 Sam. 6), and by appointing Zadok to serve as the chief priest, continuing the religious tradition of the Jebusites and securing their loyalty. Miller and Hayes suggest that 'David seems to have retained the indigenous Jerusalem priesthood, the Zadokites, and allowed the Jerusalem cult to become, in effect, incorporated into the state cult'.[65] Now David has finished with the hybridization of his kingdom.[66]

Postcolonial Features in David

David's success in amalgamating his hybrid kingdom rested on his ability to forge a *ḥesed*-relationship across ethnic, regional, or religious boundaries. He was open to forming connections with all sorts of people and built an eclectic coalition that went far beyond his own 'tribe' or 'people', including the Philistines, in order to establish his kingdom. The heterogeneous composition of his army and leadership, in contrast to Saul whose army was

64. Miller and Hayes suggest that Saul had a close relationship with the Elides from Shiloh and used the ark, which was stationed there, as the cultic symbol of his kingdom. They note (*A History of Ancient Israel and Judah*, p. 177) that by bringing the ark to Jerusalem, David wanted to show that his regime in Jerusalem was a continuation of Saul's Israel: 'David brought the ark, the old religious symbol of the Shilonite cult and the Elide line, to Jerusalem and had it placed in a special tent erected for that purpose (2 Sam. 6.17)'. Halpern speculates that the ark was associated with the Philistines, particularly with the Gibeonite and the Gittite constituents with whom David had an alliance. He states, 'But as David knitted together a coalition of non-Israelites against the Israelites whom he ruled, an icon with appeal to his real allies was particularly necessary' (*David's Secret Demons*, p. 292). However, the theory that the ark was associated with the northern tribes long before the emergence of monarchy is well founded; see Seow, 'Ark of the Covenant', pp. 386-93.

65. Miller and Hayes, *A History of Ancient Israel and Judah*, p. 178. Abiathar, who along with Zadok were David's two chief priests, also came from nearby Nob.

66. The success of the formation of David's kingdom was a significant moment in the history of ancient Israel, some would even say in the history of the world. McKenzie (*King David*, p. 139) articulates this sentiment in this way: 'It was David who first united it into a nation... What had been at most a loose confederation of tribes under Saul gained national status under David. In the language of one anthropological model, the chiefdom became a state'.

made up mostly of highlanders and whose inner circle was made up of Benjaminites, suggests that David secured his kingdom on the support of non-Israelites who extended *ḥesed* to him. He relied more on the *ḥesed* of his disparate constituents, even with all sorts of differences among them, than on their ethnic, cultural, or religious identity to construct his hybrid kingdom. This notion is the basis of my postcolonial imagination. What follows is inspired partly on the known facts and educated conjectures I have discussed in this book and partly on imagination from a space of liminality.

I have already elaborated on how David demonstrated the transgressive power of hybridity by his crossing of various boundaries, making unlikely allies as well as maintaining 'old friends', in order to establish his kingship and kingdom. The composition of David's army reflects in microcosm the nature of his policy of inclusivism. The success of David's kingship and the founding of his kingdom owe much to his men. They carried David on their back to his kingship and sustained his kingdom through their *ḥesed* at the most critical times in his career. The Hebrews and David's kinsmen, including perhaps some Gibeonites, came together to form David's original band and stayed with David during his wilderness years. Their livelihood was dependant on the 'gifts' they received and sometimes coerced from those who requested and, in some cases, were forced to accept their protection service. At the same time, they had to elude Saul's pursuit. They formed a strong bond with David through common experiences of hardship and danger. David was able to combine his band of Hebrews and the professional Gittite soldiers into his personal army while he was serving as the captain of a marauding band in Achish's service and later as Achish's bodyguard. Probably during this period he was able to attract the loyalty of the Cherethites and the Pelethites as well. These men, together with their families, marched into Hebron with David and his two wives, establishing a kingdom for him. Their crowning achievement was to conquer Jerusalem for him. When David was on the run from his son, Absalom, it was his personal army that stood by him. It was his personal army that quashed Sheba's rebellion (2 Sam. 20.7). It was his personal bodyguard, the Cherethites and the Pelethites, who escorted Solomon to the throne (1 Kgs 1.38, 44).

The makeup of David's army was as diverse as the people of his hybridized kingdom. He included in his army the following: Hebrews; the Philistines, including Gittites, Cherethites, and Pelethites; the Hittites, including Uriah the Hittite and Ahimelech the Hittite (1 Sam. 26.6); at least one Cushite (a messenger who brings the news of Absalom's death); at least one Egyptian who was once a slave of the Amalekites that raided Ziklag; the Gibeonites who were interstitial non/Israelites ('outsiders' living 'inside'), including Joab's armor-bearer who is from Beeroth, which indicates that he is a Gibeonite (2 Sam. 23.37); the Israelites; the Benjaminites; the Calebites (interstitial non/Israelites who eventually become 'real' Israelites); and the men of Judah. Moreover, two of the most profound statements of *ḥesed* in the David story were uttered by Uriah and Ittai, two men who are labeled as non-Israelites. Ittai states, 'As the Lord lives, and as my lord the king lives, wherever my lord the king may be, whether for death or for life, there also your servant will be' (2 Sam. 15.21).[67] Uriah states, 'The ark and Israel and Judah remain in booths; and my lord Joab and the servants of my lord are camping in the opened field; shall I then go to my house, to eat and to drink, and to lie with my wife? As you live, and as your soul lives, I will not do such a thing'.[68] His army was made of this type of men—*bĕnê haḥayil* ('men of loyalty'); he relied on their loyalty. With such an army he was able to forge a hybridized kingdom based on *ḥesed* across ethnic, regional, and religious boundaries and refused to play the politics of 'difference' to separate 'real' Israelites from non-Israelites. This feature can be explained partly by David's ethos of egalitarianism and simplicity and perhaps also by his hybrid identity. We will now turn our attention to these two factors.

David practiced his version of an ethos of egalitarianism and simplicity to distinguish his hybrid kingdom from others. It is well known that David did not build a temple to Yahweh, but he did build his house in Jerusalem with the help of King Hiram of Tyre, who 'sent messengers to David, along with cedar trees, and carpenters and masons who built David a house' (2 Sam. 5.11). This house is modest compare to Solomon's house, which took thirteen years to build (1 Kgs 7.1). Solomon constructed other buildings and, of course, he spent eight years building the temple. Solomon was no different from other monarchs of the ancient Near East. But David was different. Solomon claims that his father, David, was unable to build the temple for God because he was too preoccupied with fighting against enemies all around (1 Kgs 5.3). This may be true, but we must also consider whether an ethos of egalitarianism and simplicity played a role in his decision not to construct the temple.

Faust notes that there is a lack of fortification and monumental buildings in the highland but such structures existed in the lowlands during the united monarchy. He suggests that the difference is partly due to 'the fact that the highland was populated by Israelites with a strong egalitarian ethos' whereas

67. Brueggemann (*First and Second Samuel*, p. 303) makes this comment on Ittai's statement: 'The foreigner, however, expresses passionate loyalty to and solidarity with David, promising to stay with David in every circumstance (v. 21)'. Alter (*The David Story*, p. 286) makes this comment, 'Ittai's expression of loyalty suggests that they were more than mere mercenaries'.

68. 2 Sam. 11.11. Brueggemann (*First and Second Samuel*, p. 275) comments on Uriah's loyalty in this way: 'Uriah the Hittite, a foreigner, is not even a child of the torah. But he is faithful. It is a stunning moment of disclosure and contrast'.

the lowlands 'were populated to a large extent by non-Israelites'.[69] The Israelites constructed such buildings in the lowlands in order to consolidate their control over that area and as symbols of power but 'without constituting a palpable contradiction to the "egalitarian ethos", given the ethnic composition of the region'. Therefore, Faust concludes that 'the relative absence of monumental fortification in the highland should...be viewed not only as a result of the lack of a real threat, as the area was populated by more "loyal" Israelites', but also as the pervasive presence of the egalitarian ethos there, which would have looked down upon the erection of such monumental buildings.[70] Following this argument, the reason for a lack of a temple for God and a monumental house for David in Jerusalem is not because David was unable carry out these projects but because he was acting according to an egalitarian ethos. In addition to the lack of monumental buildings, the absence of royal inscriptions commemorating David's deeds is puzzling. One would expect the founder of the Jerusalem dynasty to commemorate his accomplishments through display inscriptions. Faust suggests that the absence of Israelite royal inscriptions 'cannot be a result of mere chance, but should be attributed to an egalitarian ethos...where such a direct display of royal power would not be looked upon favorably'.[71] David's policy was influenced by an ethos of egalitarianism and simplicity that he shared with his people rather than succumbing to imitating other kings and their kingdoms (like Solomon). This ethos could have played a significant role in David's decisions not to construct monumental buildings (including a temple) and to display inscriptions, which symbolize and display power and an ethos of hierarchy, as a self-identification of his kingdom in contrast to other kingdoms of that region.

This ethos may have influenced David's dealing with his people as well. David gave equal opportunities to all his constituents. As the composition of his army shows, David did not distinguish between Israelites and non-Israelites. Perhaps he was not in a position to choose who to accept into his military force and had no option but to include whoever came to him; nevertheless, he was fair to his men. When he had to muster (*pqd*) his men (*'ām*) to fight against Absalom's forces, he set 'commanders of thousands' (*śārê 'ălāpîm*) and 'commanders of hundreds' (*śārê mē'ôt*) over them (2 Sam. 18.1). Here there is no mention of dividing his men or choosing 'commanders' according to their group identity. Moreover, David sent forth his army (*'ām*) with one third in the hand of Joab, one third in the hand of Abishai,

69. Faust, *Israel's Ethnogenesis*, p. 230. At this point I will only note Faust's practice of separating the 'real' Israelites from non-Israelites during the 'united' monarchy and attributing different characteristics to them.

70. Faust, *Israel's Ethnogenesis*, p. 231.

71. Faust, *Israel's Ethnogenesis*, p. 95.

and one third in the hand of Ittai the Gittite (2 Sam. 18.2). He let a Philistine command one third of his men. One can argue that Ittai was commanding the six hundred Gittites he brought with him, but the text does not distinguish David's army according to the ethnic or any other identity of his men, except the Cherethites and the Pelethites who served as his bodyguard. Ittai and other non-Israelites had an equal opportunity to serve and thrive in David's army.

We see a clear example of David's egalitarian ethos in action when he divides equally the spoil recovered from the Amalekites (who had raided Ziklag while David and his men were away) between the four hundred men who continued with David to the Amalekite camp and the two hundred men who stayed behind because they were too exhausted to continue the pursuit (1 Sam. 30.21-25). Some of the four hundred men who had gone with David to the end of the raid complained to him, 'Because they did not go with us, we will not give them any of the spoil that we have recovered, except that each man may take his wife and children, and leave' (30.22). They wanted to expel the two hundred men from David's community because they did not partake in the actual raid against the Amalekites. Surprisingly, these men who complained are called *'îš rā' ûbĕliyya'al* ('men of evil and worthlessness'), which identifies them as disloyal. The text implies that these men are not following the ethos of David's community. Even though these men were loyal to David in that they had remained with him until the end of the raid, they were deemed disloyal for trying to push those who stayed behind out of David's community. Yet David would have none of it and declares to them in 1 Sam. 30.23-24: 'You shall not do so, my brothers [*'eḥāy*], with what the Lord has given us… For the share of the one who goes down into the battle shall be the same as the share of the one who stays by the baggage; they shall share alike'. David still calls these men 'my brothers' and reaches out to them with an expression of *jeong* in order to hold on to a fragile bond between them. The narrative claims that because of David's action on that day (and also because David has made it a statute [*ḥōq*] and an ordinance [*mišpāṭ*] for Israel), this egalitarian practice 'continues to the present day' (30.25). This was a radical understanding of the distribution of goods and also of membership in David's kingdom, according to Brueggemann: 'David insists on equal shares for all, for now the basis of distribution is not risk or victory or machismo but simply membership in the community'.[72] We can add that David probably did not base his distribution on identity either, but on the *ḥesed* that maintained the solidarity of David's community.

In the episode that follows, David gives the spoil to his friends, to leaders of 'all the places where David and his men had roamed' (1 Sam. 30.30). He

72. Brueggemann, *First and Second Samuel*, p. 205.

shares his generosity equally among all his constituents. Of course, David was self-motivated, as Brueggemann observes: 'David is no doubt generous; his generosity, however, is never in conflict with his calculations'.[73] Was he buying loyalty? Yes, but he did care for all his constituents and did not limit his generosity to his own immediate circle or to a particular group with ethnic or other ties. His generosity was distributed equally among all his constituents regardless of their ethnic or regional identity. He knew that Israelites could be 'worthless men' as well as non-Israelites and that non-Israelites could be loyal to him as well as Israelites. He treated them equally and fairly; his practice of an ethos of egalitarianism contributed to establishing his hybrid kingdom on the *ḥesed* of his supporters.

David's radical inclusivism may have something to do with the fact that he may have had a hybrid identity. The book of Ruth may have been written as a polemic against David or an argument against the ethnic purification policy of Ezra during the Persian period, but it gives information about David that inspires postcolonial imagination. It claims that Ruth the Moabite was David's great-grandmother (Ruth 4.17), and the report in the David narrative about David leaving his parents with the king of Moab supports this claim (1 Sam. 22.3-5). McKenzie states, 'David's Canaanite heritage could well be historical, and his connection with the Moabites may be too. If so, Israel's greatest king was not of pure Israelite stock!'[74] Halpern summarizes the question of David's ethnic identity in this way:

> Altogether, David bears a name without a basis in Israelite nomenclature. His father is of indeterminate origin, and opponents invoke the father's name when heaping scorn on David. His genealogy is suspect. The status of his ancestral hometown is in some doubt. In fact, even the text of 1 Samuel maintains that he sought refuge for his family in Moab, a tradition that programs the peculiar tradition of Ruth that he had a distant connection to a Moabite ancestor... David's opponents may well have claimed he was a foreigner.[75]

The narrator of the David story may have been answering the charge that David was a foreigner, but the narrative is ambiguous about David's ethnic identity. It has both the people of Judah and the people of Israel owning as well as disowning David while he is embraced by the Philistines and other groups as their own. The elders of Judah are silent when David poses the following question: 'You are my kin [*'aḥay*, "my brothers"], you are my bone and my flesh; why then should you be the last to bring back the king?' (2 Sam. 19.12). The Israelites claim that David is their own, but the people of Judah reject this claim (19.42). David was neither an Israelite nor a

73. Brueggemann, *First and Second Samuel*, p. 205.
74. McKenzie, *King David*, p. 59.
75. Halpern, *David's Secret Demons*, p. 275.

Judahite, but he belonged to both at the same time, negotiating his identity accordingly. He was an ideal person to consolidate disparate peoples from the highlands and the lowlands. He did not favor one people over others. His connection to one group was not stronger than to others. His hybrid identity may have helped him to transgress different identity boundaries and to form a hybrid kingdom.

Ruth the Moabite followed her mother-in-law to Bethlehem and accepted Naomit's God as her own God (Ruth 1.16). Which God did David follow? Which tradition of Yahweh did David embrace? He utilized the Ark of the Covenant, which was associated with the northern tribes and functioned as the cultic object at Shiloh with Eli and his family as the priests during Saul's reign, as the state icon of his kingdom's religion in Jerusalem. In Jerusalem, he placed the Ark inside a special tent, set possibly with other cultic objects; David and his men brought the idols of the Philistines to Jerusalem (2 Sam. 5.21) and might have placed them with the Ark. Moreover, David appointed Abiathar from nearby Nob, whom the narrative claims is a member of the house of Eli, and Zadok from Jebus/Jerusalem as his chief priests. He also placed his sons as priests (2 Sam. 8.18). David wanted to show continuity with Saul's kingdom in terms of religion as well; he probably did not, however, give exclusive allegiance to Yahweh as Saul did. He embraced different traditions and was open to changes rather than adhering dogmatically to the past. He was unorthodox when it came to religion; he was an innovator of religious traditions who established Jerusalem as the center of his people's religions.[76]

David was no doubt a Machiavellian man of *ḥesed* who utilized *realpolitik* and the sword to achieve his goals and he had his share of faults and misdeeds. I am in no way trying to defend David, or to present him as more believable for modern skeptics, or more palpable to modern sensibilities. This is not a subtle attempt to enhance or amplify the narrator's image of David. I am trying to reconstruct David, based on a critical reading of the narrative and an interpretation of some archaeological evidence, which has inspired at least one person's postcolonial imagination. Even with all his faults, David practiced radical inclusivism in forming his army and his kingdom. His actions were influenced by an ethos of egalitarianism and simplicity, which may have been an important component to the worldview of the highlanders. He was an egalitarian who shared his generosity equally with his people regardless of their ethnic, regional, or religious identity. This

76. See R.S. Hess (*Israelite Religions: An Archaeological and Biblical Survey* [Grand Rapids: Baker Academic, 2007]), for a comprehensive survey of archaeological, inscriptional, and iconographical evidence that are related to understanding and reconstructing Israelite religions. Hess's survey shows the complex and diverse reality of religion in Palestine during the late Iron Age I; David's Jerusalem fits well in that reality.

principle later became a decree in his kingdom. Moreover, his hybrid identity helped him to connect with all groups without being attached to one group exclusively and to maintain a *ḥesed*-relationship with the disparate groups of people in his kingdom. He also was an innovator who not only tolerated different traditions but embraced them. All these elements contributed to the hybridization of his kingdom and inspired, at least this reader, to imagine David as postcolonial.

6

THE PURIFICATION OF THE DAVID STORY

David again was no doubt a Machiavellian man of *heṣed*, but he was also an inclusivist and an egalitarian who was open to forming a *heṣed*-relationship with all sorts of people regardless of their ethnic, tribal, or religious identity. In his time, David hybridized his kingdom and would have disdained the process of purification, which the narrator and the later editors implemented, a process that will be examined in this chapter.

The hybridization of David's kingdom at the historical level underwent the process of purification at the narrative level, in which the interstitial non/Israelites (like Gibeonites, Calebites, Kenites, Gittites, Hittites, *et al.*), who were also members of David's kingdom, were separated as 'foreigners' or 'outsiders' from the 'true' Israelites. The purification process separated 'Israelites' from 'others'. Those members of David's kingdom who were partitioned as 'outsiders' were like 'us' (from the perspective of 'true' Israelites) but 'not quite'; from time to time, especially in times of trouble, they were deemed to be not 'real' Israelites. In order to construct a coherent identity, the narrative tried to construct the identity of Israelites in opposition to non-Israelites, which included 'foreigners', 'natives', and other non-Israelites who played a vital role in constructing David's greater Israel and who were counted among its members. We have seen that it is often the 'real' Israelites who showed disloyalty to David and tried to undermine David's effort to build his kingdom. Yet, it is the *ḥesed* of the interstitial non/Israelites that is questioned, not the *ḥesed* of the 'real' Israelites. In the purification process, only the perceived identity of individuals matters; *ḥesed* is disregarded. As part of this purification process in the story, Saul, who was a fighter of Philistines, a nativist, and a faithful Yahwist, was vilified as unwilling to eliminate the others and unfaithful to Yahweh because he turned out to be the wrong man for God and Israel; in other words, he was defeated by the Philistines. David was the right man for God and Israel (because he established the kingdom of Israel and Judah) in the story for the wrong reasons (he is mis/portrayed as a Philistine fighter and a nativist contrary to his actual practices); perhaps he is the right person for our time, in which too many people become victims of the politics of identity and loyalty, because he would have challenged us to make connections across identity boundaries and would have encouraged us to form a community based on *ḥesed* rather than on 'differences'.

This chapter is divided into two sections. In the first section, *David and Goliath the Gittite: David as a Philistine Fighter and a Nativist*, I will examine how the narrator portrays David as a fighter of the Philistines, especially in the David and Goliath story at the beginning of his career. One reason for characterizing David as the archenemy of the Philistines is to construct David and Israel in opposition to the Philistines but also to show that David's loyalty to Saul and his house is not to be questioned.[1] This tendency to construct Israel's identity in contrast to others, especially the Philistines, who posed an external threat that galvanized highlanders into forming an ethnic group during the late Iron Age I, played a role in mis/portraying the historical David, who remarkably departed from Saul's policy and attitude toward others, as a Philistine fighter and a nativist. In the narrative, Saul was denigrated and rejected in favor of David, who was actually an inclusivist and formed solidarity with the Philistines. The narrative defends David's co-operation with the Philistines as a necessary result of Saul's irrational intent to harm David and maintains David's loyalty to Saul as genuine. In contrast to his practices influenced by the ethos of egalitarianism and simplicity, his hybrid identity, and an openness to different traditions, David is portrayed as a Philistine fighter and a nativist whose *ḥesed* to Yahweh is depicted as exclusivistic.

In the second section, *David and Uriah the Hittite: The Politics of Identity and* Ḥesed, I will examine the politics of identity and *ḥesed* in the narrative through an examination of the story of David and Uriah the Hittite (2 Sam. 11). While the process of hybridization was in effect, the process of purification was operative as well. The narrative insists on making a distinction between 'real' Israelites and non-Israelites. Although membership of David's kingdom was not limited to the people of Judah and Israel, the narrative moves in the direction of identifying the people of David's kingdom exclusively as the people of Judah and Israel. It disregards the loyalty these

1. It is important to note that just as it is evident that the 'Israelites' are an amalgamation of disparate groups whose identity is often fragmented and in a constant process of forming a coherent identity, the 'Philistines' too are presented as unified and constructed as a monolithic group in the narrative. But as Halpern (*David's Secret Demons*, p. 330) reminds us, 'it is almost a certainty that the Philistines presented a united front, if at all, only rarely... During the period of Assyrian domination, the Philistine city-state consistently revolted seriatim rather than in concert. This is a symptom that their politics were fragmented: competing over their borders, they fought one another far more often than they united'.

interstitial non/Israelites have shown to David; now their ethnic, cultural, or religious identity makes them 'outsiders'. The narrative's attitude is that they are not part of Israel anymore. The narrator, however, has a difficult time dealing with hybrid characters (interstitial non/Israelites), 'outsiders' living 'within us', like Uriah the Hittite. They become victims of identity politics in Israel in which their loyalty does not count; instead, only their identity counts, to their peril. Even though most of the betrayals to David came from within the house of David and the people of Judah and Israel, they are never in danger of being treated as 'outsiders', as non-Israelites. The narrative treats 'real' Israelites and non-Israelites differently based on their identity, regardless of their loyalty. Such a *realpolitik* of liminality, where hybrids are embraced for their *ḥesed* but victimized for the sake of constructing a coherent, homogenous identity of Israel, is part of the purification process in the narrative.

There is no question that some materials in the David narrative have been added later than the original narrative by the editors of the DH. Some parts or all of the story of David and Goliath and the story of Uriah the Hittite fall into this category. My interest here is not to investigate the compositional history of these two stories, which can be quite complicated and could lead us into a quagmire of minutiae that would discourage us from seeing larger issues.[2] Even if we can identify the purpose that may have motivated the later editors (Deuteronomists) and the historical contexts from which they worked, we cannot know for certain which text comes from which editor. This does not mean that we should ignore the fact that the DH reflects the historical contexts from which the editors worked and their theologies/ideologies. What is certain is that the DH reflects the ongoing process of identity formation of the people of Israel. Following T.C. Römer's suggestion, I think it is helpful in general to speak of three socio-historical contexts from which three successive editings of the DH took place.[3] During the Neo-Assyrian period, Josiah launched a purification of the cult, and, in the

2. See the following for works that deal with textual issues of the story of David and Goliath: Arie van der Kooij, 'The Story of David and Goliath: The Early History of Its Text', *ETL* 68 (1992), pp. 118-31; Simon J. de Vries, 'David's Victory over the Philistine as Saga and as Legend', *JBL* 92 (1973), pp. 23-37; Alexander Rofé, 'The Battle of David and Goliath: Folklore, Theology, Eschatology', in J. Neusner, B.A. Levine, and E.S. Frerichs (eds.), *Judaic Perspectives on Ancient Israel* (Philadelphia: Fortress Press, 1987), pp. 117-51; D. Barthélemy *et al.* (eds.), *The Story of David and Goliath: Textual and Literary Criticism—Papers of a Joint Research Venture* (Fribourg, Suisse: Éditions Universitaires; Göttingen: Vandenhoeck & Ruprecht, 1986).

3. Römer (*The So-called Deuteronomistic History*), proposes a compromise between the Cross school and the Smend school by presenting a three-stage development of the DH from three successive socio-historical contexts: the Neo-Assyrian period, the Neo-Babylonian period, and the Persian period.

process, the scribes inscribed in the narrative the formation of identity of the people as one people under one God, one cult, one monarchy in one land. Their work continued through the Babylonian exile, where they reshaped the previous work as a 'history' in order to deal with the crisis of the fall of Jerusalem and the temple; in the process they tried to inscribe the people's identity outside the land and without the cult. The purification of identity continues in the final stage of editing, during the Persian period, when the DH went through more redactions after the Deuteronomic scribes returned from the exile and argued that they were the legitimate people of God rather than 'the people of the land' who had remained in Judah. At whatever stage one puts the text in question, the purification process of identity will be evident.

David and Goliath the Gittite:
David as a Philistine Fighter and a Nativist

Was David loyal to the house of Saul and did he continue Saul's nativist policy?

First, we need briefly to examine the narrator's depiction of David as being loyal to Saul, that David was a faithful ally to the house of Saul, before we turn our attention to the notion that David was a Philistine fighter. David enters Saul's service through two different means. In one scenario, he is introduced to Saul by a servant in Saul's court as 'a son of Jesse the Bethelehemite who is skilled in playing, a man of valor, a warrior, prudent in speech, and a man of good presence; and the Lord is with him' (1 Sam. 16.18). He enters Saul's court as a musician and becomes Saul's armor-bearer (16.21). In the other scenario, after David kills Goliath, he becomes Jonathan's armor-bearer (18.4) and after more success on the battlefield, Saul sets him over 'men of war' (18.5).[4] According to both accounts, David, like his older brothers, is in Saul's service. He is clearly associated with Saul's court and is in good standing in it. The narrator reinforces this claim by having everyone in Saul's court love David. He is loved by Saul, Jonathan, and Saul's entire court. Moreover, Saul's daughter, Michal, loves him and is given to him as a wife. It is certain that David is portrayed as having some legitimacy to the succession of Saul's throne as well; even Jonathan and Saul recognize this claim (23.17; 24.20).

4. Saul sets David as either a commander over fifties/hundreds/thousands or as a general over a larger division; cf. to the way David appoints 'commanders of thousands' and 'commanders of hundreds' and divides his army into three divisions commanded by Joab, Abishai, and Ittai during Absalom's revolt (2 Sam. 18.1-2) and the warning from Samuel about how the king will take young men and set them over 'commanders of thousands' and 'commanders of fifties' (1 Sam. 8.12).

David dramatically demonstrates his *ḥesed* to Saul when he displays his sorrow upon hearing news of Saul's death and kills the Amalekite messenger who brings that news (2 Sam. 1.1-16). McCarter notes that this pericope devotes 'considerable space to fresh demonstration of a theme that runs throughout the story of David's rise, viz. that David looked upon Saul with loyalty and affection'.[5] Furthermore, the narrative defends David's loyalty to the house of Saul with one of the most heartfelt songs in the Hebrew Bible (1.19-27). He has this lament included in 'The Song of the Bow' and orders it to be taught to the people of Judah (2 Sam. 1.18a). McCarter again summarizes the message of David's action:

> In this way the details of v. 18a contribute to the general impression made by the inclusion of the elegy itself in the narrative that David's loyalty to Saul persisted to the last, that he remembered Saul with honor and affection, and that the news of Saul's death inspired in him a deep sense of public loss joined with no more selfish private emotion than grief.[6]

The song itself clearly amplifies David's *ḥesed* to Saul and supports the claim that he has always been faithful to him (he was just misunderstood by Saul).

The narrator exaggerates David's connections and his unswerving loyalty to Saul; such an overstress raises questions. The question is whether David was loyal to the house of Saul as the narrator claims he was. David's actions say otherwise. The narrative defends David's decision to exterminate the entire house of Saul but cannot deny it (2 Sam. 21.1-14). David twice asks, 'Is there still anyone left of the house of Saul to whom I may show kindness for Jonathan's sake?' (9.1, 3). This question haunts the narrative. Does extending *ḥesed* to the crippled son of Jonathan make up for the slaughtering of Saul's children? Shimei does not think so. He condemns outright David as a man of blood responsible for the bloodbath of Saul's house: 'Out! Out! Murderer! Scoundrel! The Lord has avenged on all of you the blood of the house of Saul, in whose place you have reigned; and the Lord has given the kingdom into the hand of your son Absalom. See, disaster has overtaken you; for you are a man of blood' (16.7-8). Moreover, Michal's attitude toward David may represent the feeling of the entire house of Saul: 'She despised (*bzz*) him in her heart' (6.16). The last words concerning Michal bespeak the fate of her father's house: 'And Michal the daughter of Saul had no child to the day of her death' (6.23).

The narrative acknowledges the fact that David was in the Philistine camp at the time of Saul's last battle and served Achish of Gath as his bodyguard but denies that these facts are indications of David's disloyalty to Saul. The

5. McCarter, *II Samuel*, p. 65.
6. McCarter, *II Samuel*, p. 77.

narrative defends David's decision to join the Philistines—David had no choice but to seek refuge among the Philistines because Saul's pursuit of David's life was relentless. Even though the narrative removes David from the camp prior to the battle, David's own rule—'For the share of the one who goes down into the battle shall be the same as the share of the one who stays by the baggage; they shall share alike' (1 Sam. 30.24)—implicates him in Saul's death and the defeat of the army of Israel. That is, even though he does not participate in the battle, he is still part of the Philistine army; therefore, he partakes in defeating the Israelites, including the deaths of Saul and Jonathan. We know that at least David took his share of the spoil of the battle; it is telling that he ends up with Saul's crown and armlet. Moreover, there is no denying that David had a close Philistine connection, as I have argued throughout this book. Achish completely trusted David and made him his bodyguard. The narrative claims that David's loyalty to him was a charade and that he remained faithful to Saul and Israel during the Ziklag period just as he remained loyal to Saul during the wilderness period when Saul was seeking his life. Nevertheless, the narrative's portrayal of David as being loyal to the house of Saul is no more than a thin veil behind which David's disloyalty to the house of Saul shows through.

David is not only portrayed as Saul's most faithful servant and ally but also as a Philistine fighter who continued Saul's policy of nativism against the Philistines. David's reputation as a killer of Philistines needs to be examined. The narrative gives a clear impression that David was a fighter of Philistines, which is in conflict with the historical reality, as I have argued in Chapter 5. There is a strong case to be made that David emerged as a formidable rival to Saul with the help of the Philistines and reversed Saul's policy of fighting against the Philistines. He remained most likely their ally throughout his career. As I mentioned above, the narrative can only justify David's service to Achish and his participation in the army of the Philistines but cannot deny the fact that he entered Achish's service. Therefore, his reputation as a Philistine fighter and a loyal servant of Saul had to be amplified and defended in the narrative. Halpern argues that there is nothing in the narrative to suggest that 'the Philistines ever regarded him as a mortal foe'.[7] In spite of what the text wants the reader to believe, David not only tolerated the Philistines but co-operated with them in order to establish his kingdom. David did not continue Saul's policy against the Philistines. However, there is a story in the beginning of David's career that has captured the imagination of countless numbers of people over the years and has ingrained so deeply in their hearts the image of David as a Philistine fighter, that it would be almost impossible to view David as a friend of the Philistines.

7. Halpern, *David's Secret Demons*, p. 283.

David the Israelite and Goliath the Philistine

We now turn to the story of David and Goliath the Gittite. The Philistines and Israel are divided into two camps on the opposite sides of a mountain with a valley between them. The text clearly divides them on a horizontal plane as if they are on a stage; the Philistines on one side of the stage and the Israelites on the other. The Philistines show up first and encamp at a site that belongs to Judah, suggesting that they are the aggressors. Moreover, their campsite in Socoh ('brushwood' or 'hedge'), actually between Socoh and Azekah ('enclosed'), becomes a liminal space, and it becomes ambiguous as to whom this land belongs: to the Philistines or to Judah. Saul and the Israelites respond to the Philistines and encamp in a valley designated by a prominent terebinth, thus shifting the contest to the vertical plane. The Israelites may have a tall tree in their campsite, but the Philistines have a tall soldier named Goliath from Gath.

Goliath from Gath comes out of the Philistine camp to occupy the space between two armies. He is called *'îš habbēnayim* ('man of the between-ness') who will serve as the champion of the Philistines. He not only represents the Philistines, but his description also reflects the historical reality of the Philistines in terms of their wealth, militancy, and technology (17.4b-7). He is as tall as a tree, perhaps symbolizing the Philistines' pride against the lowly Hebrews. He wears a sophisticated armor and is draped in metals, reflecting the Philistines' superior technology in relation to the simple highlanders (cf. David's outfit below). Overall, he is an awesome sight to behold. Out of brushwood (Socoh) emerges the tree that intends to humiliate and put the Israelites in their lowly place. We will see that what the narrative sets up is more than a contest between two 'champions' in a battle between two armies: it is a battle between two ways of living ('civilizations') and between gods.

Surprisingly, it is not Saul, who is the tall man of Israel, who 'stood head and shoulders above everyone else' (1 Sam. 9.2; 10.23), who comes out to battle Goliath the Philistine. It is a young man named David who will come out to the in-between space to face the man of between-ness. David not only represents Israel but also embodies the historical reality of the Israelites at that time; David reflects an ethos of egalitarianism and simplicity. The narrative describes David's family: Jesse his father was old, his eldest brothers were in Saul's service, and David the youngest was a 'go-between' for his brothers in Saul's service and his father's sheep at Bethlehem (17.13-15). The transition to monarchy meant Saul needed a standing army; David's three brothers either volunteered for service or were conscripted. David probably wanted to join Saul's service as well, but he had to take care of his father's sheep for now. He probably will not get a share of his father's land because there were seven brothers ahead of him; there will be no land left for the youngest. He did not know where his fortune was. Under such circumstances, David had nothing to lose; thus he asks what will be done for the man who kills the Philistine (17.26).

When David volunteers to take up the challenge, Saul discourages him. Saul compares David and Goliath in this way: 'You are not able to go against this Philistine to fight with him; for you are just a boy, and he has been a warrior from his youth' (v. 33). This could have been the description of the difference between the army of the Philistines and the army of the Israelites. The Philistines have a long history of fighting as a professional army; in contrast, the army of Israel has been formed only recently. This is a mismatch. David, however, describes his experience as a shepherd (vv. 34-36) and states with confidence, 'The Lord who saved me from the paw of the lion and the paw of the bear, will save me from the hand of the Philistine' (v. 37). The text seems to be saying that although the Philistines may have an advantage in terms of technology and experience, the Israelites have experienced God in their lives and trust God to be on their side. To confirm this point, David rejects Saul's armor, which symbolizes the way of the Philistines, and takes a shepherd's equipment—a sling, five smooth stones, a pouch, and a staff—to the battle (vv. 38-40), which reflects a worldview influenced by an ethos of egalitarianism and simplicity, a distinct trait of the highlanders, especially in contrast to the Philistines' hierarchical worldview.

Goliath takes a stand at early morning (*škm*) and evening for forty days (v. 16). In the meantime David gets up early in the morning (*škm*), leaves the sheep with a keeper, takes his provisions, and goes to the Israelite camp. When he arrives at the Israelite camp, the army of Israel and the army of the Philistines are drawing up for battle (v. 21). David leaves the provisions in charge of the keeper of the baggage and 'runs to the ranks' (*wayyārāṣ hamma'arākah*) of the Israelites (v. 22). The 'man in-between', the Philistine from Gath, Goliath, comes out of the ranks of the Philistines; the Philistine speaks the same words as before, and David hears them for the first time (v. 23). The stage is being prepared for David and Goliath to finally meet.

First we need to hear what these two men say before they face each other. Goliath proposes a wager to the Israelites with these words (vv. 8-9):

> Why have you come out to draw up for battle? *Am I not a Philistine*, and are you not *servants of Saul*? Choose *a man* for yourselves, and let him *come down* to me. If he is able to fight with me and kill me, then we will be *your servants*; but if I prevail against him and kill him, then you shall be *our servants* and serve us.[8]

Goliath wants to settle this conflict between Philistines and Israelites with a fight between two men standing for their respective armies and people. What

8. Italicized words are repeated in the story and link Goliath's statement with the following actions, especially with David's statements. The repeated vocabulary indicates that there is a dialogue going on between Goliath and David even before they face each other.

is at stake is clearly stated: to determine the pecking order in the region; to set the master–slave hierarchy in place. The Israelites do not respond, perhaps out of fear. They have no word or man to counter Goliath's action. Then Goliath taunts them, 'Today I *defy* [*ḥrp*] the *ranks* [*ma'arkôt*] of Israel! Give me a *man*, that we may fight together [*yḥd*]' (v. 10). It is appropriate to note at this point that Goliath is obviously expecting a hand-to-hand battle. Unfortunately for him he will not get such a fight. He will face a very unorthodox fighter.

We have already examined David's first words, but they are worth looking at again. He is obviously responding to Goliath's words (v. 26): 'What shall be done for *the man* who kills *this Philistine*, and takes away the *reproach* [*ḥrp*] from Israel? For who is *this uncircumcised Philistine* that he should *defy* [*ḥrp*] the *armies* [*ma'arkôt*] of the living God?' When Saul questions his ability to fight the Philistine, David assures him, 'Let no one's heart fail because of him; *your servant* [cf. 'servants of Saul' in v. 8] will go and fight with *this Philistine* [cf. 'Am I not a Philistine' in v. 8]' (v. 32). He is responding directly to Goliath's challenge. He is confident because he believes the living God of Israel will help him (and Israel). He says to Saul (and to the whole of Israel), 'The Lord, who saved me from the paw of the lion and from the paw of the bear, will save me from the hand of this Philistine' (v. 37).

Goliath is flabbergasted when he sees David. He obviously thinks David is not a worthy opponent; perhaps that is what the Philistines thought about the Israelites, the Hebrews who were beneath them. Goliath picks up the message implied in David's outfit and shouts at David, 'Am I a dog, that you *come to me* with sticks?' Then he curses (*qll*) David by his gods (v. 43). David remains silent; it is not because he is afraid; he is searching Goliath's huge body for the right spot to strike. Goliath breaks the silence and says to David, '*Come to me* [cf. vv. 8, 43], and I will give your flesh to the birds of the air and to the wild animals of the field' (v. 44). From the beginning of his wager, Goliath anticipates the man will come to him.

David uses the same words, but he sets the battle on a higher plane. He says to the Philistine, '*You come to me* with sword and spear and javelin; but *I come to you* in the name of the Lord of hosts, the God of the armies of Israel, whom you have defiled [*ḥrp*]' (v. 45). For Goliath, the battle becomes personal and a fight between two men, which is a shift from the earlier understanding that a competition is to settle the conflict between two peoples. Yet David never loses the sight of the real meaning and the ramifications of this battle and states plainly what this battle symbolizes for his people (vv. 46-47):

> This very day the Lord will deliver you into my hand, and I will strike you down and cut off your head, and I will give *the dead bodies of the Philistine army* [cf. v. 44] this very day to the birds of the air and to the wild animals of

> the earth, so that all the earth may know that there is a God in Israel, and that *all this assembly* [namely, Israelites] may know that the Lord does not save by sword and spear; for the battle is the Lord's and he will give you into *our hand*.

When David does not budge, Goliath decides to draw nearer to meet David (v. 48a); it is Goliath who first moves to draw closer to David and not the other way around. Goliath is anxious; he wants to finish David off as quickly and decisively as possible. It takes several verbs to move Goliath: *qām* (he got up), *wayyēlek* (and he walked), and *wayyiqrab* (and he drew near) but for David it takes only one swift motion; he quickly runs (*waymahēr wayyārāṣ*) to meet the Philistine (v. 48b). Then David slings a stone, strikes Goliath on his forehead, and takes Goliath's sword and cuts off his head (vv. 49-51). From Goliath's perspective, he is struck on his forehead, falls face down to the ground, and has his head cut off with his own sword by David (vv. 49-51). David emerges from this battle a fighter of Philistines, a hero who will always be remembered for slaying a giant with faith in one hand and a sling in the other; the ultimate underdog for the ages.

Later David will take the sword of Goliath from Nob during his escape from Saul (1 Sam. 21.8-9) and stop at Gath. The people there have no recollection of him killing Goliath who is from Gath (1 Sam. 21.10-15). There is some textual confusion as to who really killed Goliath: 'Then there was another battle with the Philistines at Gob; and Elhanan son of Jaare-oregim, the Bethlehemite, killed Goliath the Gittite, the shaft of whose spear was like a weaver's beam' (2 Sam. 21.19). Apparently Goliath was one of four renowned giants from Gath killed by David's servants (2 Sam. 21.22): 'These four were descended from the giants in Gath; they fell by the hands of David and his servants'. In spite of these notes, however, there is no question that the image of David as the fighter *par excellence* of the Philistines is sealed in the memory and the imagination of all who read the David story.

A Nativist Attitude Toward Others in the Narrative

David as a fighter of Philistines influences our understanding of David's attitude and therefore the narrative's feeling toward the others. A certain amount of ethnocentrism is expected in a writing like the David story (or the DH); it is, after all, a 'history' of a particular people. Still we need to acknowledge and attend to this ethnocentrism. There exists in the narrative a nativist attitude toward those who are identified as non-Israelites. For example, when Amnon tries to force Tamar to lie with him, she protests that such a folly (*nebālah*) is not done in Israel (2 Sam. 13.12; cf. Judg. 20.6). What does the text mean by this statement? It could mean that there is a certain standard by which all Israelites should live and, therefore, to do such a thing is to behave like a non-Israelite. The statement implies that such a thing is done outside of Israel and by non-Israelites, but not by 'real' Israelites. Tamar is accusing Amnon of behaving like a foreigner, an outsider. This attitude that an ethical behavior is a characteristic of being an Israelite and an unethical behavior like rape can be a characteristic of being a foreigner is plainly expressed by this statement.[9] Yet Amnon does rape her because Israelites too do such a folly. They are no different from others in spite of what the text suggests.

The narrative inscribes a nativist attitude that imposes a certain amount of disrespect for the life of others in the narrative. The narrative sometimes disregards the life of others, which is clearly expressed in the following episode. The narrator has David raiding towns not belonging to Judah and has him killing their inhabitants and making sure no survivor remains (1 Sam. 27.8-12). The text states as a matter of fact that David did not leave any survivor, 'neither man nor woman alive to be brought back to Gath', for he thought, 'They might tell about us, and say, "David has done so and so"' (27.11). The text claims that 'Such was his practice all the time he lived in the country of the Philistines' (27.11). The narrative clearly notes that David never attacked any town belonging to Judah. This claim, as discussed before, is highly unlikely to be true. He probably did not differentiate his targets on ethnic identity. He had no qualm about thinking of killing all males belonging to the town of Nabal (ch. 25). Yet the narrative prevents David, via Abigail, from shedding the blood of supposed Israelites. It even has David acknowledge that he would have incurred bloodguilt had he gone through with his plan (25.33-34):

> Blessed be your good sense, and blessed be you, who have kept me today from bloodguilt and from avenging myself by my own hand! For as surely as the Lord the God of Israel lives, who has restrained me from hurting you, unless you had hurried and come to meet me, truly by morning there would not have been left to Nabal so much as one male.

Although the reason given for bloodguilt if David had gone through with his intent in the above statement is that he would have taken revenge with his own hand rather than leaving vengeance to God, but the real reason is that he would have killed fellow Israelites. The narrative strongly denies what is plain in the text, that David would have killed Israelites.

David, however, takes revenge with his own hand against his (read, Israel's) 'enemies'; there is no hint, however, of concern for a possible bloodguilt (i.e. he is taking vengeance with his own hand), because he is

9. The Levite in the book of Judges clearly expresses this attitude when he bypasses Jebus/Jerusalem (a non-Israelite city at the time) for Gibeah (a Benjaminite city) because he imagines the worst from the non-Israelites (Judg. 19.12).

dealing with non-Israelites. Surprisingly, the text reveals that even the Amalekites do not practice such horrendous acts as David had practiced when he raided towns not belonging to Judah. When the Amalekites sacked Ziklag, the text says, they took captive 'the women and all who were in it, both small and great; they killed none of them, but carried them off, and went their way' (1 Sam. 30.2). The question is not whether the Amalekites were more humane in their dealing with their victims. That they probably also had little regard for the life of others is evidenced by the fact that an Amalekite belonging to the raiding group abandons his sick Egyptian slave to die of hunger and thirst (30.11-14). With the help of the Egyptian slave, David chases the Amalekites, tries to kill all of them, and would have done so were it not for the fact that somehow four hundred men escape (30.17). The point is that the narrative lacks the sense of uneasiness or anxiety when it comes to killing non-Israelites as it has with fellow Israelites.

Two incidents in which David kills messengers involve 'foreigners' or interstitial non/Israelites. After the messenger tells David of Saul's death, David asks, 'Where do you come from?' And the messenger answers, 'I am the son of a resident alien, an Amalekite' (2 Sam. 1.13). He is an Amalekite like the Amalekites who attacked Ziklag, but, at the same time, he is not one of them. He is one of the resident aliens, an 'outsider' living among the Israelites. How would the narrative treat this person who occupies an in-between space in David's kingdom? David has him killed immediately (1.15). There is no struggle, anxiety, or qualm here. He is viewed as a foreigner, as an enemy. But the narrator does justify this execution to the reader (it is not to the Amalekite that David speaks, since he is already dead), 'Your blood be on your head; for your own mouth has testified against you, saying, "I have killed the Lord's Anointed"' (1.16). The Amalekite does not deserve an explanation, but the reader does; it is his own fault, not David's. The Amalekite dies without knowing why he is being executed. It appears that Amalekites remain Amalekites even if they are resident aliens and the narrator uses the reader's prejudice against the Amalekites to put doubt in the reader's mind of the messenger's story and to have the ancient audience sympathize with David's execution.[10]

In the case of the Beerothite brothers, David at least has the courtesy of explaining to them why he will kill them. Yet he does more than execute them; he humiliates them by cutting off their hands and feet and then hanging their bodies for public view (2 Sam. 4.12). The narrator can get

10. McCarter (*II Samuel*, p. 64) observes this prejudice, 'As soon as the ancient audience learned the messenger's identity (v. 8), it would have begun to suspect him of treachery, for treachery was what it had come to expect of Amalekites...and its cynicism had just been reinforced by the story of the rape of Ziklag in I Sam 30.1-3'.

away with this spectacle perhaps because they are not perceived as 'real' Israelites; they are really Gibeonites, not Israelites, the text seems to be saying. David dishonors them by not giving them a decent burial, but he gives a proper burial to Israelites, even to those who were his enemies. He takes the head of Ishbaal and gives it a proper burial at Hebron (4.12), where Abner's body is also buried (3.32). He also gives Saul and Jonathan an honorable burial (21.14). David's negative attitude towards the others and his positive affection towards the Israelites are identical to the narrator's nativist attitude and act as the means to the purification process of the editors.

Even an enemy deserves some honor if he is a 'real' Israelite but not if he is considered a non-Israelite. When an interstitial non/Israelite is viewed as an other, then his/her life is allowed to be treated with disrespect. After Absalom is killed by Joab's men and the force of the rebellion is crushed by David's men, Ahimaaz son of Zadok wants to run to David with the news of the battle. Joab discourages Ahimaaz from being a messenger, showing a certain paternal concern for a fellow Israelite, and prefers to send a Cushite, a foreigner (18.21). The Cushite does not appear to know the risk of bringing bad news to David. He goes because his commander orders him to do so. Joab knows exactly into what kind of situation he is putting the Cushite. David has killed messengers who bring bad news in the past (see above). So he prefers to let a foreigner risk his life. Then, finally, David kills a faithful Yahwist who happens to be an interstitial non/Israelite, Uriah the Hittite. The narrator has Uriah killed because he too is not a 'real' Israelite. Halpern summarizes this view in this way:

> Resentment of these murders [Saul's grandchildren] represented a huge political deficit. Shimei's taunt...all this follows from that open wound. And this is why David's one admitted murder is of a foreigner, albeit in his service—especially in his service. It is not just that Uriah had no following, politically: he is identified, despite his Yahwistic name, a name indicating a family commitment to the Israelite state god, as a Hittite. Good for David: he killed that foreigner![11]

Once again, David's attitude and actions against the perceived others influence the reader's attitude toward them and become the means by which the editors partition 'real' Israelites from 'outsiders', even if they are members of David's kingdom and living 'inside' the land among the 'real' Israelites.

David and Uriah the Hittite: The Politics of Identity and Ḥesed

In the story in 2 Samuel 11, David is depicted as a typical sedentary monarch of the ancient Near East who orders his servants to do his bidding, rather than as a charismatic leader who leads and motivates his people more

11. Halpern, *David's Secret Demons*, p. 370.

by his actions than by his words.[12] From the story's first verse, David repeatedly sends people to carry out his orders: 'David sent [*šlḥ*] Joab with his officers and Israel with him' to besiege Rabbah. But David stays (*yšb*) in Jerusalem. Upon seeing a beautiful woman washing (*rḥṣ*) her body David sends (*šlḥ*) someone to inquire about the woman (v. 3). Upon learning who she is, he sends (*šlḥ*) messengers to take her, and she comes to him, and he lies with her (v. 4). Upon learning of her ensuing pregnancy David sends (*šlḥ*) someone to Joab with the following message: 'send [*šlḥ*] me Uriah the Hittite' (v. 6a). And Joab sends (*šlḥ*) Uriah to David (v. 6b). There is not any hesitation or pause or break between David's sending of a messenger and Joab's sending of Uriah.

David commands; his servants follow his orders. He does not move from his space; his messengers are his feet and his mouth. They bring Bathsheba; Joab sends Uriah. Bathsheba comes to him; Uriah comes to him (v. 7). David does not go to them. He does the sending again when Uriah comes to him in order to cover-up his liaison with Bathsheba; he commands Uriah to his house, 'Go down [*yrd*] to your house, and wash [*rḥṣ*] your feet' (v. 8). But Uriah does not follow David's command. He does not go down (*yrd*) to his house (v. 9). The servants tell David, 'Uriah did not go down [*yrd*] to his house' (v. 10a). David is surprised (v. 10b): 'Why did you not go down [*yrd*] to your house?' No one has disobeyed David in the story until now. Upon hearing Uriah's statement of loyalty to the ark (God) and his comrades in the battlefield (v. 11) David comes up with a different strategy: 'Remain [*yšb*] here today also, and tomorrow I will send [*šlḥ*] you back' (v. 12). Uriah stays (*yšb*) in Jerusalem and David hopes Uriah would do what he did when he stayed (*yšb*) in Jerusalem instead of going out into the battlefield. Uriah, however, does not do what David did; he does not lie with Bathsheba. Then finally David gets Uriah drunk, but again Uriah does not go down (*yrd*) to his house (vv. 12b-13). Uriah will not go down to his house to have sex with his wife and break the law that bans sexual relationships during war (cf. 1 Sam. 21.4-5) so that David can be free from his dilemma. Uriah is a faithful soldier, but his loyalty lies foremost with God. To eat, drink, or lie with his wife while his comrades and the ark (God) are in the battlefield is to betray his very identity as a man of uncompromising *ḥesed*.

Now David understands with what kind of man he is dealing and why he has failed to move Uriah to go down to cover up his misconduct. Uriah is 'the quintessence of fidelity. He is too disciplined for David or for his own

12. Czövek shows that David ceases to act as a charismata after he build his house in Jerusalem and acts more like a sedentary monarch who rules from one's palace with near absolute power. Czövek states that in his early career David was a charismatic military king who 'considers deliverance his call and relies on Yahweh's intervention' but now he is 'keen on controlling everything by centralizing power' (*Three Seasons*, p. 118).

good'.[13] Uriah does not go down (*yrd*) but he can be sent (*šlḥ*). Uriah cannot be maneuvered to disobey God, but he can be moved to obey his commander. He writes a letter to Joab and sends (*šlḥ*) it by the hand of Uriah so that 'he may be struck down and die' (v. 15). He is counting on the fact that Uriah, as a loyal soldier, will not open the letter. Joab improvises David's instructions, but for Uriah the consequence is the same: Uriah is killed (v. 17). Joab sends (*šlḥ*) a messenger to deliver the message to David: 'Your servant Uriah the Hittite is dead also' (v. 21). The messenger improvises Joab's message, but for David the message is the same: 'Your servant Uriah the Hittite is dead also' (v. 24). David and Joab have corroborated in betraying the one who has been most loyal.[14] Along with Uriah, many a loyal man also had to die because Joab had to revise David's orders. David consoles Joab by conceding that it was necessary, 'Do not let this matter trouble you, for the sword devours now one and now another; press your attack on the city and overthrow it' (v. 25). Joab and David have betrayed the loyalty of Uriah and other faithful soldiers. When Bathsheba's mourning for her husband is over, David 'sent [*šlḥ*] and brought her to his house, and she became his wife, and bore him a son' (v. 27). Bathsheba, like Abigail, does not wait long after her husband's death to become David's wife.[15]

David looks comfortable in following a script influenced more by an ethos of authoritarianism and hierarchy than by an ethos of egalitarianism and simplicity. He may have been a Machiavellian man of *ḥesed* who used *realpolitik* and the sword, but there is evidence to suggest that he was also an egalitarian and an inclusivist who embraced hybridity and multiple traditions of religion and treated all his constituents fairly. This remarkably unorthodox David may be closer to the historical reality than the David of the narrative who continues Saul's policy of nativism and exclusivism and who acts as a typical monarch of the ancient Near East. But the David of 2 Samuel 11 comes from the later editors who framed David's troubled

13. Brueggemann, *First and Second Samuel*, p. 274.

14. 4QSam[a] identifies Uriah the Hittite as 'Joab's armor-bearer' in v. 3 (McCarter, *II Samuel*, p. 279). Bodner (*David Observed*, p. 91) entertains the affect this vocational epithet has on the relationship between Joab and Uriah and what Joab did to him: 'On the one hand, it locates Uriah within the larger matrix of the "master/armor-bearer" motif, exemplified by Jonathan's armor-bearer in 1 Sam. 14, and also the David/Saul relationship as David is introduced to the royal court (see 1 Sam. 16.21)… On the other hand, the variant could grimly accentuate Joab's Machiavellian cunning, as he is willing to sacrifice his own armor-bearer to safeguard the king's cover-up operation, and, by extension, protect his own interests as commander of the national troops'.

15. Alter (*The David Story*, p. 256) remarks, 'Normally, the mourning period would be seven days. Bathsheba, then, is even more precipitous than Gertrude after the death of Hamlet the elder in hastening to the bed of a new husband. She does, of course, want to become David's wife before her big belly shows'.

years between two sins (this story and 2 Sam. 24) in order to indicate that his problems were consequences of his sins.[16]

What is of interest to us is that it also reflects the process of purification that tries to partition Israelites and others. In this process, Uriah the Hittite becomes a victim of the politics of identity and *ḥesed* in Israel. The story is not simply about David's sin that caused troubles during his reign; it is also about how Uriah becomes an 'outsider' in order to formulate a coherent identity for the Israelites. David's negative attitude toward the others like Uriah the Hittite is also a reflection of the narrator's nativist stance and a means by which the later editors' purification process operates. Uriah becomes a victim for the sake of Israel's purported singular and authentic identity.

Uriah the Hittite

The story of David and Uriah the Hittite in 2 Samuel 11 is one of the most well-known stories in the Bible and better known as the story of 'David and Bathsheba', 'David's Adultery with Bathsheba', 'the Bathsheba Affair', or simply 'David's Sin'. Although it is remembered in the DH as 'the matter of Uriah the Hittite' (1 Kgs 15.5) and God punishes David for taking the life and the wife of Uriah (2 Sam. 12.9), many do not identify it as the story concerning Uriah the Hittite. If the titles by which a story is remembered are any indication of what the reader thinks the story is about, then Uriah the Hittite does not have a prominent place in the imagination of readers. In order to see more clearly the process of purification that partitions interstitial non/Israelites as 'outsiders', who may be 'like us' but 'not quite', it is necessary to read 2 Samuel 11 from the perspective of Uriah the Hittite.[17]

16. For example, McKenzie (*King David*, pp. 155-56) argues that this episode is a later addition influenced by the desire to create a sin–punishment scheme: 'It was added in its present place in order to produce a scheme of "sin and punishment" or "cause and effect" with respect to Absalom's revolt. In the battle account in which the Bathsheba story is embedded (2 Sam. 10.1–11.1a + 12.26-31), David mentions the loyalty that had been shown him by the Ammonite king, Nahash (2 Sam. 10.2). This act of loyalty apparently consisted of sending provisions to David when he fled from Absalom (2 Sam. 17.27-29). There is no other interaction between Nahash and David in the Bible that would qualify as this act of loyalty. This means that David's affair with Bathsheba probably took place after Absalom's revolt rather than before it. As it now stands, however, the book of 2 Samuel describes Absalom's revolt as punishment for David's affair with Bathsheba and murder of her husband, Uriah'.

17. This story has been popular among church fathers and rabbis in the past and is still popular among scholars today, most of the attention going to David. The rabbis of the distant past made excuses for David and exonerated David by concluding that Bathsheba was given a bill of divorce and found Uriah to be a rebel deserving of death (McCarter, *II Samuel*, p. 288). The early Christian fathers formulated David into a theological paradigm, connecting the story of David's sin with his repentance and pardon by

Who was Uriah the Hittite anyway? He was, of course, the husband of Bathsheba and an unfortunate victim of David's attempted cover-up; but he was also an officer of Israel's army who was killed while fighting for Israel. He is named in the list of the Thirty (2 Sam. 23.24-39), which may have been David's elite corps of officers that was formed during his flight from Saul, especially during the Ziklag period when he served Achish. Mazar argues that the last seven names, which include Uriah, should be distinguished from the rest because they were either from a distant region or from the indigenous population.[18] Mazar assumes that the last seven officers were added on to the earlier list of officers who joined David at the outset of his career. (One can easily argue that it may have been the other way around, that is, officers from Israel and Judah may have joined David after the Ziklag period.) If this is the case, that is, that the list partitions the Israelites and the non-Israelites, then it probably was not the intent from the time of David (when Israel's ethnic identity was not yet clearly drawn) but a scheme imposed by later scribes (when they tried to define clearly Israel's identity). If the later scribes tried to arrange the list by separating the non-Israelites from the Israelites, then their effort was undermined by the interstitial non/Israelites in the list.[19] The division between Israelite officers and non-Israelite soldiers in the list is not neat or evident; the list is not based on

God (M. Petit, 'La rencontre de David et Bersabee [II Sam. 11,2-5, 26-27]: les interpretations des peres des premiers siecles', in G. Dorival and O. Munnich [eds.], *Selon les Septante* [Paris: Cerf, 1995], pp. 473-81). Then the historical-critical scholars in modern times analyzed the story as part of a historical document, the so-called Succession Narrative of Solomon or Court History of David, which was understood as a reliable source for reconstructing the history of ancient Israel; see, e.g., R.N. Whybray, *The Succession Narrative: A Study of II Samuel 9–20; 1 Kings 1 and 2* (Naperville, IL: SCM Press, 1968). In more recent years, some scholars read the story as literature and applied narrative techniques to interpret the story; see, e.g., M. Sternberg, *The Poetics of Biblical Narrative: Ideological Literature and the Drama of Reading* (Bloomington: Indiana University Press, 1985). There are others, especially feminist scholars, who have tried to rescue Bathsheba from the patriarchal text and its patriarchal interpreters; see, e.g., J.C. Exum, 'Bathsheba Plotted, Shot, and Painted', in her *Plotted, Shot, and Painted: Cultural Representations of Biblical Women* (Sheffield: Sheffield Academic Press, 1996), pp. 19-53. Uriah the Hittite, however, has received scant attention from scholars and average readers alike; see U.Y. Kim, 'Uriah the Hittite: A (Con)Text of Struggle for Identity', *Semeia* 90/91 (2002), pp. 69-85. I have significantly revised this article for this section.

18. B. Mazar, 'The Military Elite of King David', *VT* 13 (1963), pp. 310-20.

19. There are other schemes that may have organized the list. For example, Czövek (*Three Seasons*, pp. 159-60) notes that this list of warriors is 'headed by Asahel (v. 24), of whose death we read in ch. 2 and concludes with Uriah (v. 39), the only other mighty man reported killed in 2 Samuel' and concludes that 'the inclusion of the mighty men by the two killed, Asahel and Uriah, marks the end of an army based on bravery'.

identity at the time of David. There are interstitial non/Israelites in the list who transgress the border that was constructed later between the 'real' Israelites and the non-Israelites. For example, how do we know whether Hezro from Carmel, who appears in the Israelite group according to Mazar, was considered an Israelite and not a non-Israelite (Calebite) at the time of David? How do we know whether Ittai son of Ribai of Gibeah of the Benjaminites, who may have been the same person as Ittai the Gittite, was considered an Israelite or not when he served in David's army? Why is it that Uriah the Hittite is considered a non-Israelite?

Although Na'aman questions the existence of the institution of the Thirty, he nevertheless regards the list to reflect the organization of David's professional army.[20] Uriah was named in what appears to be an important official list of an elite group of officers in the Israelite army. He is marked as a Hittite but serves in David's army. This reflects David's attitude or policy towards non-Israelites: he embraced them based on their *ḥesed* rather than on their ethnic identity. From Uriah's perspective, his identity as an interstitial non/Israelite did not prevent him from being accepted as one of Israel's own, at least in Israel's army.

Where did Uriah come from? Uriah could have been a native of Jerusalem. The story indicates that his house was in Jerusalem and David therefore tried to get him to go down to his house: 'Uriah slept at the entrance of the king's house with all the servants of his lord, and did not go down to his house' (2 Sam. 11.9). The fact that David's servants stayed in the king's house and that Uriah had his house in Jerusalem may indicate that he was a native of Jerusalem. As a comparison, Joab would go to Bethlehem from time to time because his house was located there; David's servants stayed in his house/palace because their houses were not in Jerusalem. We can assume that these servants would have gone to their houses when they were not in service. The fact that Uriah has a house while the servants stayed at David's house may signify that Uriah had his house before David built one for himself in Jerusalem. The fact that Uriah's house was so near the king's house may also suggest that he was a prominent member of the royal-military circle, a member of the entrenched aristocracy that antedated David's conquest of Jerusalem.[21] If this was so, then Uriah was a member of the ruling elite that had been conquered by David. Yet David did not disfranchise them; instead he incorporated them into his army and administration.[22]

20. N. Na'aman, 'The List of David's Officers', *VT* 38 (1988), pp. 71-79.

21. J. Rosenberg, 'The Institutional Matrix of Treachery in 2 Samuel 11', *Semeia* 46 (1989), pp. 103-16. Or, Uriah may have been the king of Jebus/Jerusalem as Wyatt, '"Araunah the Jebusite" and the Throne of David', argues (see below).

22. Zadok the priest may have been another prominent member of Jebus/Jerusalem who was added to David's administration.

Uriah (*'ûrîyah*) is a good Yahwistic name, which means 'Yahweh is my light/fire'.[23] There are four other individuals by this name in the Hebrew Bible, and all of them are either a prophet or a priest of Yahweh (2 Kgs 16.10-16; Jer. 26.20-23; Neh. 3.21; 8.4). How did an 'outsider' (either a foreigner or a native) end up with a Yahwistic name? Although the name Yahweh is tied to Israel in general in the Hebrew Bible, in reality Yahweh was not exclusively associated with Israel. Did he change his original Hittite name to a Yahwistic name 'as a tactfully patriotic concession to the winds of change' after David conquered Jerusalem?[24] It may be that 'Uriah' is not an Israelite name, that is, it may not indicate Uriah's Israelite-ness. Still, as it is used in the Hebrew Bible, the term 'Uriah' alone indicates that he is an Israelite. It is the term 'Hittite' that will separate him from other Israelites.

Wyatt has a theory that explains why Uriah the Hittite has a house in Jerusalem and why he is called a Hittite. After noting the fact that he is consistently called Uriah the Hittite, which suggests that Uriah was, in fact, a Hittite or a Hurrian, Wyatt argues that 'the explanation of his name in terms of a typical Hebrew theophoric name is misguided' and that the form *'wryh*, which is related to the term *'wrnh* (Araunah or more likely 'lord or king', already discussed in Chapter 5), should be read as a Hurrian theophoric name, 'Yah is lord', rather than the Hebrew, 'Yah is my light'.[25] Moreover, Wyatt argues that 'the king' ('the Araunah') of the Jebusites was, in fact, Uriah the Hittite. He was the king of the Jebusites who negotiated the threshing floor with David (2 Sam. 24) and, rather than turning the power over to David immediately, he may have agreed to a co-regency. Uriah's death in battle might have been a fiction propagated primarily 'to retain loyalty and avoid any sense of betrayal' from the officials who defected to David.[26] The notion that Uriah the Hittite may have been the last king of the Jebusites will affect his wife's identity as well (more below).

Having a 'right' name probably would not have mattered during David's time when he tried to form a coalition of disparate groups, but names would have been a concern later in ancient Israel's history. How important was it to have a right name in Israel? There is a hint in the story that it was, in fact, important to have a right name. In the story Abimelech is mentioned as the son of *yĕrubbešet* (2 Sam. 11.21), but we know that Abimelech's father's

23. Alter (*The David Story*, p. 250) notes that 'Although Uriah's designation as Hittite has led some interpreters to think of him as a foreign mercenary, the fact that he has a pious Israelite name ("the Lord is my light") suggests that he is rather a native or at least a naturalized Israelite of Hittite extraction. In any case, there is obvious irony in the fact that the man of foreign origins is the perfect Good Soldier of Israel, whereas the Israelite king betrays and murders him'.

24. Rosenberg, 'The Institutional Matrix', p. 108.

25. Wyatt, '"Araunah the Jebusite" and the Throne of David', p. 3.

26. Wyatt, '"Araunah the Jebusite" and the Throne of David', p. 10.

name was *yĕrubba'al* (Judg. 9.1). There are several *ba'al*-names that have been put to 'shame' (*bōšet*) by later scribes. Why were the scribes compelled to change Jerubbaal's name? They were probably trying to establish Israel's group boundary; Israelites were not Baal worshipers. This distinction was used to draw Israel's identity in contrast to those who practiced Baalism. The faith in and loyalty to Yahweh was the basic group boundary of ancient Israelites. In that case, then, as we have it in the narrative, Uriah the Hittite is a faithful Yahwist.

In the narrative it is Uriah, in contrast to David, who is loyal to Yahweh. Uriah's response to David's question as to why he did not go down to his house reads like a confession of faith: 'The ark and Israel and Judah remain in booths; and my lord Joab and the servants of my lord are camping in the open field; shall I then go to my house, to eat and to drink, and to lie with my wife? As you live, and as your soul lives, I will not do such a thing' (2 Sam. 11.11). Brueggemann assumes that Uriah is a foreigner and makes this comment: 'Uriah the Hittite, a foreigner, is not even a child of the torah. But he is faithful. It is a stunning moment of disclosure and contrast'.[27] Whedbee expresses a similar sentiment, making an interesting parallel with David's hybridity, but still sees Uriah as a foreigner:

> Once again we find superb evidence of the narrative strategy of indirection and ironic contrast. Uriah is a Hittite, hence, like David's ancestress Ruth, a proselyte in the Israelite community, whereas David as Israelite king is, of course, to be the examplar [*sic*] of Hebrew tradition. Yet we have a reversal of roles—the one-time alien now instructs the native king in Israel's holy war traditions.[28]

Rosenberg also remarks that Uriah exemplifies a remarkable vitality of faith, calling him 'an orthodox Israelite', taking root in those who may be considered outside Israel.[29] Uriah's statement is made remarkable by the 'fact' that he is not a 'true' Israelite. If he were a 'true' Israelite, then the irony and the contrast between Uriah and David would be less prominent.

There are those, however, who question Uriah's motive in making his statement and do not consider his identity as important. Sternberg and others, for example, have pointed out that one of the ambiguities of the text lies in whether to understand Uriah's statement at face value or to hear it as a sarcastic indictment against David's action because he knows what David has done.[30] McKenzie notes that David brought Uriah from the battle for no

27. Brueggemann, *First and Second Samuel*, p. 273.

28. Whedbee, 'On Divine and Human Bonds', p. 154.

29. Rosenberg, 'The Institutional Matrix', p. 111.

30. Sternberg, *The Poetics of Biblical Narrative*, pp. 201-209. Sternberg has drawn attention to many ambiguities in this narrative and argued that they are intentional and therefore irresolvable. See also G.A. Yee, 'Fraught with Background: Literary Ambiguity

good reason, therefore, 'This made Uriah suspect that his loyalty was being tested. The result was that he became especially conscientious in displaying his faithfulness to David and the army (11.6-13). This in turn made him particularly observant of the vows of celibacy that he had taken in preparation for war'.[31] Alter summarizes two more viable understandings of Uriah's statement in this way:

> If Uriah does *not* know that David has cuckolded him, he is the instrument of dramatic irony—the perfect soldier vis-à-vis the treacherous king who is desperately trying to manipulate him so that the husband will unwittingly cover the traces of his wife's sexual betrayal. If Uriah *does* know of the adultery, he is a rather different character—not naïve but shrewdly aware, playing a dangerous game of hints in which he deliberately pricks the conscience of the king, cognizant, and perhaps not caring, that his own life may soon be forfeit.[32]

Yet willingness to observe ambiguity in Uriah's statement may have been influenced, in fact, by Uriah's identity as a foreigner. This is not surprising, since Uriah is, in fact, ambiguous. Uriah is an interstitial non/Israelite. Would they have questioned Uriah's sincerity if Uriah were a 'real' Israelite? The scribes did not remove the ambiguity of Uriah's identity by dropping the ethnic term 'Hittite' from Uriah's name. Why did the scribes not claim Uriah as their own, as an Israelite, who was indeed loyal to Yahweh? We would not have known that Uriah was a foreigner if not for the marker 'Hittite' that was attached to his name. They replaced the *ba'al*-particle from Israelites 'heroes', but not the 'Hittite' from Uriah's name. The way Uriah's hybridity is handled indicates the struggle for Israel's identity in the text. They want to identify Israelites as anti-Baalists, but they accept Jerubbaal as their own, albeit with some misgivings. On the other hand, Uriah is left outside of Israel's boundaries even though he is a loyal Yahwist. We will see that the scribes ultimately claim David as their own even though he is unfaithful to Yahweh and to his men in the story, but they will not embrace Uriah, who was faithful to Yahweh and to Israel, as their own.

The Politics of Identity and Ḥesed *in the Text*

We have seen that Uriah the Hittite was a loyal officer of David's (Israel's) army and a faithful follower of Yahweh; however, the way David (and the narrative) treats Uriah reflects a purification process in which Uriah is viewed as an 'outsider' in order to inscribe a coherent identity to Israel in

in 2 Samuel 11', *Int* 42 (1988), pp. 240-53; M. Garsiel, 'The Story of David and Bathsheba: A Different Approach', *CBQ* 55 (1993), pp. 244-62 (256-58).

31. McKenzie, *King David*, p. 158.
32. Alter, *The David Story*, p. 252.

contrast to others to the reader. What exactly does it mean that Uriah was a Hittite? Who were the Hittites, and from where did they come? The term is probably not referring to the Hittites whose capital was in central Anatolia and who established a considerable empire in the second millennium BCE that eventually collapsed at the end of the Late Bronze Age.[33] Hoffner asks, 'Was it the intention of the biblical writers to indicate that persons bearing the name *Hittite* or *sons of Heth* belonged to that foreign people from the north?'[34] Hoffner's opinion is that 'passages referring to Hittites during the Israelite monarchy almost certainly refer to the Syrian kingdoms earlier controlled by the Hittite Empire during the fourteenth and thirteenth centuries'.[35] F.F. Bruce says that the Hittites are presented clearly in the Bible in two ways: 'First, as one of the ingredients in the population of Canaan, and secondly, as inhabitants of a territory to the north of Palestine'.[36] John Van Seters thinks that the use of the term 'Hittite', like the term 'Amorite' in the Hebrew Bible, was rhetorical rather than historical;[37] that is, they were used to mark those people whom the later editors believed to be non-Israelites in order to differentiate them from the Israelites. Van Seters, referring specifically to Uriah and Ahimelech the Hittite (1 Sam. 26.6), says that by the term Hittite 'the author wishes merely to assert that they were non-Israelite'.[38] The later scribes did not care or know who the Hittites were and from where they came. In our story, the Hittite is used to refer neither to a person from a specific kingdom (which had long passed) nor a specific place, but to indicate 'somewhere' outside of Israel. Thus the people marked with this term were considered non-Israelites from the perspectives of the later editors even though they may have been living in Canaan longer than the Israelites (who also came from 'somewhere' outside Canaan according to the tradition). No doubt disparate groups of people living in Israel were labeled with ethnic terms not only to give information about where they came from but to mark them as 'outsiders' living 'within us'. Calling Uriah a Hittite is no more than 'othering' the interstitial non/Israelites according to an identity discourse that attempts to formulate a coherent identity.

33. H.A. Hoffner, 'Hittites', in A.J. Hoerth, G.L. Mattingly, and E.M. Yamauchi (eds.), *Peoples in the Old Testament World* (Cambridge: Baker, 1994), pp. 127-55.

34. Hoffner, 'Hittites', p. 152.

35. Hoffner, 'Hittites', p. 152. The Assyrians and the Babylonians continued to refer to the west of the Euphrates River as the land of Hatti during the Neo-Assyrian and the Neo-Babylonian periods.

36. F.F. Bruce, *The Hittites and the Old Testament* (London: Tyndale Press, 1947), p. 6.

37. J. Van Seters, 'The Terms "Amorite" and "Hittite" in the Old Testament', *VT* 22 (1972), pp. 64-81.

38. Seters, 'The Terms "Amorite" and "Hittite"', p. 80.

R. Schwartz sees the story as a site of struggle for Israel's identity as well.[39] After noting that the story is surrounded by accounts of war with the Ammonites (2 Sam. 10.1–11.1 + 12.26-31), she comments, 'This is no accident: Israel's war with the sons of Ammon is a war of definition, the sexual violations are tests of definition, for in both, Israel's borders—who constitutes Israel and who does not—are at stake'.[40] She continues that David is the one who acts as a *nabal* ('fool'), an outsider who violates sexual fidelity, which is analogous to being unfaithful to God; meanwhile, Uriah, a non-Israelite, an 'other', is the one who is faithful to God when he keeps sexual fidelity.[41] Therefore, Schwartz concludes:

> Both sexual fidelity and divine fidelity are preoccupations of a narrative that tends to construct identity as someone or some people *set apart*, with boundaries that could be mapped, ownership that could be titled. But if, as I have been arguing, the parameters of Israel's identity are very much at issue—which God is allowed and which is not, and which woman is allowed and which is not—then the identity of the nation and the people is not mapped, but in the process of being anxiously drawn and redrawn.[42]

The question I will consider as this discussion continues below is whether David's sexual infidelity threatens his Israelite identity in particular and the identity of Israel in general. We will see that his Israelite identity is protected because his infidelity is against a non-Israelite.[43]

In such a context, Uriah himself is a text of struggle for Israel's identity. The text struggles with Uriah's 'in-betweenness'. Uriah is marked as an 'other', yet he is serving in Israel's army. He may have been a member of a ruling family in Jerusalem when the Jebusites controlled the city, yet he managed to keep his position in the army. He is a faithful Yahwist with a Yahwistic name, yet he is not claimed by the Israelites. Instead, he is labeled a Hittite, a term to indicate that he is non-Israelite. When Uriah was 'wanted', the Israelites claimed him as their own by placing him in their army and by differentiating him from the Jebusites (no Jebusite shows up in the list of the Thirty). But when Uriah was 'unwanted', they abandoned him with other non-Israelites and branded him as an other. Who, then, was an Israelite? An Israelite was a Yahwist, yet David was unfaithful to Yahweh. An Israelite was an anti-Baalist, yet Jerubbaal (an Israelite hero) has a

39. R.M. Schwartz, 'Adultery in the House of David: The Metanarrative of Biblical Scholarship and the Narrative of the Bible', *Semeia* 54 (1991), pp. 35-55.

40. Schwartz, 'Adultery in the House of David', p. 45.

41. Schwartz, 'Adultery in the House of David', pp. 46-50.

42. Schwartz, 'Adultery in the House of David', p. 50.

43. We have also seen how Amnon violated sexual fidelity by raping Tamar. She accused him of behaving like a *nabal* (a fool or a foreigner). He paid with his life because his infidelity was against an Israelite, albeit a female Israelite.

Baalistic name. Uriah is a site where the politics of identity and *ḥesed* is played out. His *ḥesed* to David, Israel, and God makes him 'one of us' but his constructed (given) identity makes him 'not exactly one of us' and disrupts a formation of a coherent identity of Israel in which 'true' Israelites are faithful Yahwists.

Uriah ruptures the identity narrative also through his wife Bathsheba, whose double identity disrupts the identity discourse and reflects the politics of identity and *ḥesed*. She is disloyal to her husband in the story but her identity as an Israelite has to be maintained for the reasons to be discussed shortly. First, we need to examine how she is introduced in the story. She is identified in the story with two terms representing two different relationships, 'the daughter of Eliam, the wife of Uriah the Hittite' (1 Sam. 11.3b). She seems to have two loyalties and perhaps also two competing identities. She is the daughter of a well-known officer in the Israelite army (2 Sam. 23.35) and the wife of a Hittite. Where does her ultimate loyalty lie? Is it with her Israelite father or with her Hittite husband? It is unfair to ask these questions, but Bathsheba's identity (not her choice, but the scribes' construction) begs such questions.

Bailey notes that Bathsheba's double identity is almost universally ignored.[44] McCarter comments that 'it is unusual for a woman's patronym to be given, especially when she is identified by her husband's name... This suggests that the identity of Bathsheba's father was significant'.[45] Bailey agrees that the patronymic relationship, which comes first, is more significant than the marital relationship.[46] Alter notes that 'It is unusual to identify a woman by both father and husband. The reason may be...that both men are members of David's elite corps of warriors'.[47] These authors seem to be in agreement that if there is anything significant about her double identity, then it has to do with her patronymic.

Bailey, for example, thinks that there is a very good reason for Bathsheba's double identity. He suggests that the significance of her patronymic is that it links her to the important family of Ahithophel, who was David's trusted counsel but who defected to Absalom (2 Sam. 15).[48] This connection is important to Bailey's understanding of this story because he argues that the affair happened after Absalom's revolt. He thinks that David's affair with Bathsheba was a premeditated scheme conceived by both in order to

44. R.C. Bailey, *David in Love and War: The Pursuit of Power in 2 Samuel 10–12* (JSOTSup 75; Sheffield: JSOT Press, 1990), p. 171.

45. McCarter, *II Samuel*, p. 285.

46. Bailey, *David in Love and War*, p. 87.

47. Alter, *The David Story*, p. 250; Eliam the son of Ahithophel the Gilonite (2 Sam. 23.34) and Uriah the Hittite (2 Sam. 23.39) are listed under the Thirty.

48. Bailey, *David in Love and War*, pp. 85-90.

advance their interests through their marriage: Bathsheba wanted to improve her status after her grandfather dragged her family down by defecting to Absalom, and David wanted to reconcile his relationship with those who were associated with Ahithophel.[49]

Although I disagree with his hypothesis,[50] Bailey's work is important in that the unusual identification of Bathsheba is taken seriously into account in his reading of the story and suggests an episode of *realpolitik* in David's court at that time. I agree that this is indeed an episode of *realpolitik*, but not in David's court. It reflects a politics of identity of the later editors who wished to maintain Bathsheba's identity as an Israelite while separating her husband as a foreigner.

Bathsheba's patronymic was significant not because her father or grandfather was important but because her husband, Uriah, was marked as a non-Israelite. If the scribes had written his name without the term 'Hittite', then Bathsheba would likely have been identified simply as 'the wife of Uriah' without her patronymic, since her identity as an Israelite woman would have been unambiguous. But, as the wife of a 'foreigner', without her patronymic, her identity would have been ambiguous. Was she an Israelite or a foreigner like her husband? Wyatt argues that Bathsheba, like her husband, must have been of non-Israelite origin, citing the fact that there is no West Semitic parallel to her name ('daughter of the seven or the oath'), and suggesting that Bathsheba can be read as a Hurrian name.[51] Bathsheba's identity as an Israelite was suspect not only because she was married to a Hittite but also because her name was non-Israelite.[52] The scribes removed the ambiguity

49. Alter (*The David Story*, p. 251) seems to have a similar thought as Bailey's when he comments that the sentence 'she came to him' in v. 4 may hint at Bathsheba's active participation in this affair and reveal an opportunistic trait in her character: 'When the verb "come to" or "come into" has a masculine subject and "into" is followed by a feminine object, it designates a first act of sexual intercourse. One wonders whether the writer is boldly toying with this double meaning, intimating an element of active participation by Bathsheba in David's sexual summons. The text is otherwise entirely silent on her feelings, giving the impression that she is passive as others act on her. But her later behavior in the matter of her son's succession to the throne (1 Kings 1–2) suggests a woman who has her eye on the main chance, and it is possible that opportunism, not merely passive submission, explains her behavior here as well'.

50. One can easily argue that Ahithophel defected to Absalom because of what David did to his granddaughter and her husband. For example, Bodner (*David Observed*), argues that Ahithophel's strategy against David, advising Absalom to sleep with David's concubines and desiring to lead the army to kill David himself, can be explained by his enmity toward David because of David's affair with his granddaughter and subsequent treatment of Uriah.

51. Wyatt, '"Araunah the Jebusite" and the Throne of David', p. 4.

52. Wyatt ('"Araunah the Jebusite" and the Throne of David', p. 4) also comments on Ezekiel's view of Jerusalem's mother as a Hittite, which indicates this suspicion of

when they added 'the daughter of Eliam', who could have been a well-known Israelite without necessarily being a son of Ahithophel. Her double identity might have meant something like this: Bathsheba was an Israelite (see, her father was an Israelite) who happened to be married to a Hittite (a non-Israelite).

It was important to have Bathsheba identified unambiguously as an Israelite woman for the sake of Solomon and the subsequent kings. Bathsheba was the daughter of Eliam and the wife of Uriah, but, more importantly, she would become a wife of David and the mother of Solomon. Exum discusses the importance of having the 'right' wife and the 'right' mother for Israel's identity.[53] Exum suggests that although it was through the father that the male line of descent was supposedly determined, it was the mother who not only confirmed the child's Israelite identity but also competed with the father in determining the line of descent in Israel. She continues that mothers had an intrinsic advantage over fathers because motherhood was verifiable; therefore, it was just as important, if not more so, to have the right mother as the right father in determining Israel's identity. C. Carmichael, in his discussion of three proverbial-type laws in Deuteronomy, suggests that these laws reflect Judah's historical struggle to perpetuate his line.[54] Moreover, these laws are interested in the establishment of David's house and are concerned with the future of the house in Solomon's time. It was crucial for David, the founder of the dynasty, to have the right wife, an Israelite woman, in order to secure and perpetuate his dynasty. David's lineage was of great interest to and was closely monitored in the biblical texts. The book of Kings lists the names of the mothers of all Judean kings except for Jehoram and Ahaz, but only Jeroboam's is named among the northern kings (1 Kgs 11.26). There is a strong interest in David's lineage and also in having the right mothers for the kings of Judah.

Bathsheba's identity: 'We may also note the interesting observation of Ezekiel (Ezekiel 16.3, 45), addressing Jerusalem, that "your father was an Amorite and your mother a Hittite". The background to this expression is the mythical presentation of a city in terms of a goddess or queen, and while the identity of the Amorite father remains obscure, it is quite likely that Ezekiel looks upon Bathsheba as "Hittite" by virtue of her marriage to Uriah, if not in her own right, as the personification of the city, with perhaps more than a hint at her adultery'.

53. J.C. Exum, 'The (M)other's Place', in Exum, *Fragmented Women: Feminist (Sub)versions of Biblical Narratives* (Valley Forge, PA: Trinity Press International, 1993), pp. 94-147.

54. C.M. Carmichal, *Law and Narrative in the Bible* (Ithaca, NY: Cornell University Press, 1985), pp. 181-205. The three proverbial-type laws are prohibitions against sowing mixed seed in a vineyard (Deut. 22.9), plowing with an ox and an ass (22.10), and wearing wool and linen (22.11).

Among the mothers named in the book of Kings, only Rehoboam's mother, Naamah the Ammonite (1 Kgs 14.21), was not an Israelite. The negative attitude toward union with foreigners was clearly expressed in the law forbidding mixed seed and throughout the DH. Moreover, in 1 Kgs 11.1-13, Solomon's marriages to foreign women are the cause of his apostasy and for God's judgment to divide his kingdom. Carmichal, in speaking of Rehoboam, comments that 'it is a truly remarkable fact that this half-Israelite, half-Ammonite product is the only son attributed to Solomon'.[55] Thus, Solomon was accused of threatening David's house because he had planted a mixed seed on the throne. Rehoboam lost all but one tribe (Judah) because he was the product of the wrong mother. Bathsheba was the right wife to David and the right mother to Solomon who helped to legitimatize David's dynasty and Solomon's succession, but it was Naamah, the wrong wife to Solomon and the wrong mother to Rehoboam, who threatened the very foundation of David's dynasty.

Wyatt also supports the importance of Bathsheba in her role as mother by looking at the office of 'queen-mother' (*gĕbîrah*). He notes that the Deuteronomist gives the name of the king's mother, not that of the queen, and suggests, 'It appears to be by virtue of his sonship to her that he holds his royal title'. He continues 'the possibility must be considered that it is through the female line, not the male line, that the rightful occupation of the throne descends, so that a king reigns by virtue of his relationship to the chief Queen, who has, as it were, the keys of the kingdom'.[56] He adds that 'the second aspect of this matrilineal principle is the likely presence of the rite of *hieros gamos* ["holy wedding"] in ancient Israel and Judah, which would be intimately connected with the title to the throne'.[57] If we accept Wyatt's theory that Uriah the Hittite was the last king of the Jebusites, then Bathsheba was the *gĕbîrah* before the appearance of David. David takes Bathsheba because she holds the key to his becoming the legitimate king of Jebus/Jerusalem. Moreover, Solomon is the son of the rite of *hieros gamos* between David and Bathsheba, thereby securing Solomon's ascension. Wyatt notes that it is usually the case that king and *gĕbîrah* are enthroned together and together they represent the royal power, and he concludes that 'Bathsheba appears to fulfill precisely this role, and perhaps her receiving of Adonijah in audience in 1 Kgs 2.13-18 is also evidence of her political role'.[58]

It appears that Bathsheba, either as *gĕbîrah*, mother, or wife, is the one who holds the key to the legitimacy of her men. If the story left Bathsheba's

55. Carmichal, *Law and Narrative in the Bible*, p. 182.
56. Wyatt, '"Araunah the Jebusite" and the Throne of David', p. 4.
57. Wyatt, '"Araunah the Jebusite" and the Throne of David', p. 6.
58. Wyatt, '"Araunah the Jebusite" and the Throne of David', p. 8.

identity as 'the wife of Uriah the Hittite' without her patronymic, then her Israelite-ness would have been ambiguous and would have threatened the 'purity' of David's (Judah's) lineage, but by adding 'the daughter of Eliam', the editors assured the reader that she was, in fact, an Israelite woman. Therefore, Bathsheba's unusual double identity was a result of Uriah being labeled a non-Israelite.

Then why does the narrative even bother labeling Uriah as a Hittite? It is done to protect David while also explaining the troubles that will befall him in his later years and his allowing a purification process to take place. Schwartz argues that adultery and other sexual taboos are designed to maintain and protect the co-operation among men over the exchange of women.[59] When David steals Bathsheba from Uriah, he is not only disrupting this co-operation between men, thereby causing fear and hostility, but he is also threatening the identity of Israel. Schwartz points out that 'vigorous laws on adultery are invoked to police Israel's borders because adultery clearly threatens the identity of Israel'.[60] There are serious consequences to those who break this co-operation. In light of such an understanding of the co-operation among men over the exchange of women and the consequences to those who break the co-operation, it is striking that David does not hesitate at all to bring her to his house after finding out to whom Bathsheba belongs. Brueggemann thinks David behaves in this way because he is acting like a king: 'Now David knows who she is—and whose she is. David does not pause, however, because he is the king. The mention of Uriah might have given David pause, but it does not'.[61] Sternberg explains the lack of hesitation on the part of David as an example of biblical narrative techniques:

> The note or pose of 'there is nothing much to tell' mainly arises from the paratactic series of verbs, which make up the bulk of the passage and laconically unroll a rapid sequence of external actions in almost assembly-line fashion... The clash between matter and manner in the discourse greatly sharpens the irony... This again shows how the Bible exploits the fact that literature is a time-art, in which the temporal continuum is apprehended in a temporal continuum and things unfold sequentially rather than simultaneously.[62]

Bailey thinks that there is 'a lack of attention to sexual details and descriptions' precisely because David was not interested in sex, but in Bathsheba's

59. Schwartz, 'Adultery in the House of David', pp. 46-47.

60. Schwartz, 'Adultery in the House of David', p. 48.

61. Brueggemann, *First and Second Samuel*, p. 273. Brueggemann ('Abuse of Command: Exploiting Power of Sexual Gratification', *Sojourner* 26 [1997], pp. 22-25), blames David's prompt action on military culture, in which the abuse of command (high ranking officers are used to getting their way), is pervasive.

62. Sternberg, *The Poetics of Biblical Narrative*, pp. 197-98.

political connectedness.[63] Or we can attribute David's quick response to a sexual lust, blind love, mid-life crisis, or other factors that weaken David's usual self-control.[64]

The fact that Uriah was a non-Israelite needs to be considered in trying to understand David's behavior, which is tantamount to trying to understand the editors' attitude toward Uriah and other non-Israelites. The question is whether David would have paused if Uriah had been a 'real' Israelite. There was another king who killed a man in order to steal his property. King Ahab stole a property (vineyard) from a man named Naboth after having him killed (1 Kgs 21). There are many similarities between the story involving David (2 Sam. 11–12) and the story with Ahab (1 Kgs 21).[65] When Naboth refuses to sell his vineyard, Ahab returns home resentful and sullen (1 Kgs 21.3-4). But Ahab does not try to take Naboth's vineyard by force; it is only after Jezebel engineers Naboth's death that he takes possession of the vineyard (1 Kgs 21.5-16). Even Ahab, who is considered one of the most unfaithful kings in Israel's history, hesitated before taking Naboth's vineyard because he respected Naboth's property right. The co-operation between men in the protection of property is maintained before a woman (Jezebel in this case) disrupts this co-operation.

David was also faithful (or portrayed as so) in observing this co-operation between men in the protection of property (which included women) throughout his life. In 1 Samuel 25, David is saved from taking Nabal's property, including Abigail, unlawfully when Nabal, Abigail's husband, conveniently dies before David comes to take his life (and Abigail as his wife). David also takes back Michal from Paltiel because he owned her first and still had the property right over her: 'Give me *my wife* Michal, to whom I became engaged at the price of one hundred foreskins of the Philistines' (2 Sam. 3.14). The biblical texts are very careful to portray David as someone who does not take things unlawfully from the men who are considered Israelites; that is, David faithfully observes this co-operation with his fellow Israelites.

In the case with Bathsheba, however, this co-operation was not observed because her husband, Uriah, was not considered an Israelite. David did not hesitate because Uriah was marked as a foreigner who was outside the circle of co-operation. Moreover, David did not fear the consequences that can arise from breaking this co-operation because Uriah was viewed as an unattached individual, not as a member of a specific clan or community. This would have made a difference in the way Uriah would have been treated. In comparison, the woman of Tekoa told a story about how her clan

63. Bailey, *David in Love and War*, pp. 87-88.

64. Yee ('Fraught with Background'), makes these suggestions.

65. J. Chinitz, in 'Two Sinners', *JBQ* 25 (1997), pp. 108-13, lists nineteen elements that are similar between these two stories.

wanted to kill her son for the murder of her other son (2 Sam. 14). In Uriah's case there was no *gō'ēl* ('redeemer') to avenge his blood. There was no community that could have retaliated on his behalf. No breach of this co-operation goes unpunished unless a victim is outside the community. David had nothing to fear from killing Uriah.

Bathsheba's double identity and David's lack of hesitation can be explained by Uriah being partitioned as an outsider. Bathsheba's Israeliteness had to be unambiguous since she had to be the right wife of David and the right mother of Solomon. David did not hesitate in stealing Bathsheba because the co-operation among Israelite men did not extend to the outsiders. It is Uriah who ruptured Bathsheba's identity and suspended David's loyalty to the co-operation among men in the exchange of women (property).

God acts as Uriah's gō'ēl

Then God enters the story and acts as the *gō'ēl* for Uriah. The last sentence in 2 Samuel 11 comes from the narrator with the note that God is not pleased with what David had done: 'The thing that David did was evil in the eyes of Yahweh' (2 Sam. 11.27b; my translation). Now it is God who sends (*šlḥ*) Nathan to David. Nathan tells a parable about a rich man (*'îš*), who had many sheep (*ṣō'n*), but took the only ewe lamb (*kibśah*) of a poor man, who raised it like his own daughter (*bat*), and served it when a traveler came to his house (2 Sam. 12.2-4). Nathan's parable certainly is a commentary on the story in 2 Samuel 11, and the shared vocabulary between the parable and the story makes this obvious. The poor man (Uriah) acquired, nourished, and raised the only ewe lamb like his own daughter (*bat*). The 'daughter' (Bathsheba, *bat šeba'*) used to eat (*'kl*) from his mouth, drink (*šth*) from his cup, and lie (*škb*) in his bosom. In the story, it is David getting up from his couch (*miškābô*, 11.2) that leads to lying (*škb*, 11.4) with Bathsheba (*bat šeba'*). In the story Uriah does not lie with his wife; instead, he lies (*škb*) with the servants at the entrance of the king's house (11.9). Then Uriah says that he would never eat (*'kl*), drink (*šth*), and lie (*škb*) with his wife while the ark and his comrades are in the battlefield (11.11). David invites Uriah to eat (*'kl*) and drink (*šth*) in his presence and gets him drunk but Uriah goes out to lie (*škb*) on his couch (*miškābô*) with the servants (11.13).

The shared vocabulary continues in God's judgment against the house of David (12.7-12). Bodner makes a connection between Eliab's speech that questioned David's heart and the episodes in 2 Samuel 11–12 and shows that a number of terms that Eliab uses are intimately connected with 2 Samuel 11–12: 'few' (*mĕ'aṭ*, 12.8), 'flock' (*haṣṣō'n*, 12.2, 4), 'evil' (*rōa'*, 12.9, 11), 'see' (*r'h*, 11.2), and 'battle' (*milḥāmah*, e.g. 11.7, 25).[66] I will indicate these terms in Eliab's speech (1 Sam. 17.28):

66. Bodner, *David Observed.*

> His eldest brother Eliab heard him talking to the men; and Eliab's anger was kindled against David. He said, 'Why have you come down? With whom have you left those *few sheep* [*mĕ'aṭ haṣṣō'n*] in the wilderness? I know your presumption and the evil [*rōa'*] of your heart; for you have come down just to see [*r'h*] the battle [*milḥāmah*].

Moreover, Bodner notes an interesting parallel between Eliab's reaction to David and David's reaction to the rich man (who stands for David) in the parable: 'It is striking that just as Eliab's "wrath is kindled against David"... so David's "wrath is kindled against the man"...of Nathan's parable—and, of course, that "man" is David himself'.[67] Then he suggests that if Eliab's speech is heard in light of 2 Samuel 11–12, Eliab's words sound rather different:

> It may be that the Deuteronomist's literary strategy encourages the reader not simply to make a series of psychological pronouncements on Eliab as merely a jealous older sibling on the rampage. Rather, in light of the broader narrative, the reader is obliged to leave Eliab's disturbing words *unfinalized* (to use Bakhtin's terminology), and to keep them open-ended as a potential point of insight into David's complex personality.[68]

I would add the word 'to go down' (*yrd*) to Bodner's list of shared vocabulary in Eliab's speech and 2 Samuel 11–12. Eliab accuses David's coming down(mentioned twice in 1 Sam. 17.28) to the camp with ill intent; in 2 Samuel 11, David orders Uriah to go down to his house (vv. 8, 10) with ill will, but Uriah does not go down to his house (vv. 9, 10, 13). For Uriah's refusal to go down to his house, David orders him killed and then takes Bathsheba as his wife, but God will stand up for Uriah and punish David for stealing his life and wife. David has despised God by striking down Uriah the Hittite and taking 'his wife to be your wife' (12.9). According to David's formula for retribution, the rich man 'shall restore the lamb fourfold' (12.6), God will avenge the wrong done to the poor man (Uriah) fourfold. Alter states God's punishment in this way: 'the fourfold retribution for Uriah's death will be worked out in the death or violent fate of four of David's children, the unnamed infant son of Bathsheba, Tamar, Amnon, and Absalom'.[69] Yet God will spare David's life. Even though God acts as Uriah's *gō'ēl* and punishes David, God still loves David, forgives him, and promises to sustain his kingdom forever. This surprising turn of events may have been easier to accept because Uriah was a Hittite.

67. Bodner, *David Observed*, p. 23.

68. Bodner, *David Observed*, pp. 23-24. This connection between Eliab's speech and 2 Sam. 11 and 12 is another sign that 1 Sam. 17 and 2 Sam. 11–12 went through a process of purification by the same hands.

69. Alter, *The David Story*, p. 258.

Conclusion

The process of purification in the text divides the 'real' Israelites and 'outsiders'. The 'outsiders' were not actually non-Israelites; many were interstitial non/Israelites who gave their *ḥesed* to David and were instrumental in establishing his kingdom and sustaining his kingship. David, however, is portrayed as being loyal to the house of Saul and as a Philistine fighter who has continued Saul's policy of nativism, which are contrary to historical reality. The image of David as a Philistine fighter has been entrenched in the imagination and the heart of countless numbers of readers through the story of David and Goliath. Once the dichotomy between David (and the Israelites) and Goliath (and the Philistines) is set up, it becomes convenient and natural to have a negative attitude toward the others (the Philistines) regardless of their ethnic identity or the differences among them. Even though a coherent identity of the Israelites cannot be maintained, always only a step away from being fragmented and in the process of on-going reinscription, the Israelites are united in their view of the others as different from them. Who gets to be included in Israel as a 'real' Israelite and who gets left out as an 'outsider' has less to do with an individual's ethnic identity (who one is) or with Israel's ethnic identity (what Israel is) but more to do with the politics of identity in which some interstitial non/Israelites are perceived to be less authentic than others.

The negative attitude of the narrator (and therefore the editors) toward those who are constructed as the others affects the reader's view of Uriah the Hittite and those like him when reading the narrative. Moreover, even though Uriah clearly is a victim of the identity politics in Israel, in spite of his uncompromising loyalty to his king, country, and God, the interpreters of this story, following the narrator's cues, do not treat Uriah fairly or rally to defend him. In contrast, even though some 'real' Israelites (including David) have proven to be unfaithful to their king (in David's case, to Saul), country, and God, they do not become victims of identity politics; they are punished as Israelites but never as 'outsiders'. The treatment and view of Uriah and others like him as 'outsiders' is part of the process of purification that allows inscribing a coherent and singular identity of Israel possible.

Although Uriah is not depicted in the Bible as an evil person (in fact, he was a 'good/loyal' man), many readers rally around David and give Uriah bad press in order to save David's face and to ameliorate his crime. I already mentioned that the rabbis branded Uriah as a rebel deserving of his death. More recently, one reader characterizes Uriah in this way:

> [A] career soldier in David's armed forces then engaged in an ongoing war with Ammon… He lived close to the palace with his lovely wife, Bathsheba. Intensely loyal to David and to his comrades-in-arms, he put duty first and

> was insensitive to the needs of his wife who had to cope with the life of an army wife with an absentee husband.[70]

This is remarkably similar to the sketch of Uriah's character in the 1951 film, *David and Bathsheba* (starring Gregory Peck and Susan Hayward). Exum observes that Uriah is depicted in the film as 'a heartless follower of the letter of the law, and would invoke the law to have his wife stoned if he had reason to suspect her of adultery'.[71] In one telling scene, David becomes exasperated when he finds Uriah sleeping in the guards' room instead of sleeping with Bathsheba in his own house, and after hearing Uriah's speech on loyalty, spits these words at Uriah: 'You stupid, blind fool'. That is exactly how Uriah is portrayed in the film. In the 1985 film, *King David* (starring Richard Gere), Bathsheba describes him as a wife beater/abuser. One scholar calls him 'poor, dumb Uriah' and makes the following remark: 'In David's story, the king is the recipient of the greatest narrative interest, while little nobodies like Uriah are barely sketched'.[72]

This is a disturbing and dangerous reading practice, continuing the process of purification the editors started long ago. Once a reader identifies himself or herself with David, then Uriah is naturally seen as the other. There are many ramifications that come with such a practice. Our identity is formed not only by 'who we are' but also by 'who we are not'. This makes it easier to create negative stereotypes and to demonize those who are not exactly like us. Yet we have seen in the story that Uriah was the faithful one, not David. It was David who acted like a *nabal* (a fool or a foreigner). It was Uriah, not David, who behaved as a man of *ḥesed*. Uriah was a loyal soldier who served in Israel's army in the name of God and king, but he was called a Hittite and killed as an 'outsider'.

Uriah was a victim of identity politics in Israel, and in spite of his exemplary behavior he was not viewed as a 'real' Israelite. He was a hybrid Israelite, having more than one identity, who could be easily partitioned as an 'outsider'. There are many people today who are victims of identity politics because they do not fall neatly into one authentic identity; thereby, their identity is questioned even if they display outstanding loyalty to their country and its people. It is when we stand in the interstitial space that we can accept people with hybrid and multiple identities as authentic. God invites all of us to the in-between space where *ḥesed* can be experienced across various boundaries and where identity politics is a means to hybridization rather than purification.

70. H. Rand, 'David and Ahab: A Study of Crime and Punishment', *JBQ* 24 (1996), pp. 90-97 (91).

71. Exum, 'Bathsheba Plotted, Shot, and Painted', p. 48.

72. W.H. Willimon, 'A Peculiarly Christian Account of Sin: David and Bathsheba and Sin as Conflict of Narratives', *Theology Today* 50 (1993), pp. 220-28 (224).

EPILOGUE

THE POLITICS OF IDENTITY AND LOYALTY IN NORTH AMERICA

David certainly was a Machiavellian man of *ḥesed* who used *realpolitik* and the sword to establish his kingdom and to sustain his kingship. I have strived to 'recover' some features in the David of history that have been overwritten in the process of constructing the David of narrative and faith. I have argued that there are important features in David that appeal to the postcolonial imagination and ought to be envisioned and practiced in our time. He was radically inclusive and an egalitarian who was open to making connections with all sorts of people regardless of their ethnic, tribal, or religious identity, thereby demonstrating the transgressive nature of hybridity. He had hybridized his army and kingdom by forming a *ḥesed*-relationship with constituents across various boundaries and differences. He built his hybrid kingdom on *ḥesed* rather than on identity. We have seen how he was able to rise to power by riding God's *ḥesed* to kingship and by using the loyalty and *jeong* of his followers to establish his kingdom. During the latter part of his career, which was fraught with troubles, David continued to rely on God's *ḥesed* and to take advantage of the uncompromising loyalty and *jeong* of his allies, friends, and subjects to maintain control over his kingdom and sustain his kingship. However, it was the later scribes who turned him into a nativist and an exclusivist and divided those who showed *ḥesed* to David into the 'real' Israelites and the others (non-Israelites, including interstitial non/Israelites), thereby attesting to the politics of identity and *ḥesed* in ancient Israel. They purified or dehybridized his kingdom and reconstituted the kingdom of all people into a kingdom of 'real' Israelites under one god and one cult. David would have disdained such a process of purification.

I appreciate the narrator's David as a man after God's own heart who was loyal to his people and faithful to his God, and I understand that there are good reasons as to why this David has captured the heart and the imagination of countless numbers of people over the years. Yet I also hope the postcolonial David will appeal to the heart and the imagination of people around the world today. I would like to accentuate the David who exercised the transgressive power of hybridity to forge a *ḥesed*-relationship with all sorts of people in order to form a kingdom that was composed of people of different ethnic, tribal, and religious identity, including several groups of Philistines. It is this David we need to imagine and imitate in our world where too many people are victims of the politics of identity and loyalty, including North America. If David could speak to us today he would encourage us to welcome the process of hybridization and challenge us to treat one another equally and to form a *ḥesed*-relationship with one another regardless of our differences and across boundaries.

Once again, I have not tried to deconstruct the narrator's David or to portray the postcolonial David as all positive. David was neither an angel nor an innocent shepherd boy who rose to power on God's providence alone; he was an ambitious man who did not hesitate to use *realpolitik* and the sword to achieve his aspirations. Perhaps this was what one needed to do in order to succeed in those times just as it seems to be the case in the world today. I think David would have fit comfortably in our time. If he were to run for the president of the United States he would be a coalitionist and a unifier, forming ties across various identity groups, retaining his supporters through *ḥesed*, and actively searching for allies among all sorts of people in order to win the election.

Barack Obama and King/David

While I was writing this book, the campaign toward the election for the president of the United States had been going on for over a year (but it felt like it had been going on forever!) and the Democratic nomination had yet to be settled. During this campaign, I believe that one Democratic candidate, Barack Obama, has grabbed the heart and the imagination of millions of Americans, especially the young people who are usually known for their apathy in the political process. It is still unknown whether he will win the Democratic nomination, but he has already stirred uncommon excitement in the presidential campaign and lifted it from its usual doldrums.

I would like to reflect on Obama's identity and story because they attest to the politics of identity and loyalty in America. First of all, Obama reminds me of King David. He is no doubt a politician who also must have used some sort of '*realpolitik* and the sword' to be in his position. He has formed an eclectic coalition across various boundaries and has exhorted Americans to imagine a better America in which all identity groups can live in greater harmony. I think Obama will welcome the process of hybridization in America as David did in forming his own kingdom. Moreover, Obama, like David, has a hybrid identity. He is the son of a black man from Kenya and a white woman from Kansas who married at a time when miscegenation was still a felony in over half the states in America. He understands what it is to be in the space of 'in-betweenness' where identities are contested and negotiated and, at the same time, where 'new' identities emerge and are forged. I could see him using the transgressive power of hybridity to forge the diverse population into a hybrid America based on *ḥesed* rather than on identity.

In his memoir[1] Obama describes his childhood in Hawaii and Indonesia, marked by ambivalence toward his mixed racial identity, his time in Chicago as a community organizer, characterized by his commitment and the need to prove his loyalty to the African American community, and his emotional trip to Kenya where he discovers his lost heritage yet realizes that his future is tied to America. Throughout his life, his loyalty to either black or white America has been questioned and the burden of demonstrating his fidelity often fell on him because of his hybrid identity. While in college, for example, he criticized a multiracial person for avoiding black people while claiming her multicultural heritage, but he realized that he saw himself in her struggle and contradictions: 'I kept recognizing pieces of myself. And that's exactly what scared me. Their confusion made me question my own racial credentials all over again... I needed to put distance between them and myself, to convince myself that I wasn't compromised'.[2] He felt the need to prove his loyalty to the black community: 'it remained necessary to prove which side you were on, to show your loyalty to the black masses'.[3] He was afraid that his black identity and allegiance to the black community would be discovered to be a fraud, especially when compared to his friend whose black credentials were unquestionable: 'His lineage was pure, his loyalties clear, and for that reason he always made me feel a little off-balance, like a younger brother who, no matter what he does, will always be one step behind'.[4] He belonged to two worlds and yet, at the same time, he belonged to neither. He found himself in the in-between space where his loyalty was repeatedly tested from those who belonged comfortably in one world: 'The constant, crippling fear that I didn't belong somehow, that unless I dodged and hid and pretended to be something I wasn't I would forever remain an outsider, with the rest of the world, black and white, always standing in judgment'.[5]

Obama was deemed either 'too black' for some or 'not black enough' for others. The fact that his father was not an African American but an African and the fact that his early years were spent outside of the mainland and abroad seem to justify the notion to some Black Americans that he is not a 'real' African American. A popular radio host actually called him 'Halfrican

1. B. Obama, *Dreams from my Father: A Story of Race and Inheritance* (New York: Crown Publishers, 2004 [1st edn 1995]).
2. Obama, *Dreams from my Father*, p. 100.
3. Obama, *Dreams from my Father*, p. 101.
4. Obama, *Dreams from my Father*, p. 101.
5. Obama, *Dreams from my Father*, p. 111.

American'. The idea that Obama is not fully African American or that his identity can be quantified in this way is troubling. There are many (racial- and/or cultural-) hybrid Americans who are needlessly pressured to make a choice between their multiple heritages, which are inseparably encoded in their genetic or cultural makeup. Some people question their loyalty and authenticity to a particular racial/ethnic community/identity if they do not define themselves with a single identity or pledge allegiance to one community. Why can't Obama be accepted as fully black and fully white without requiring him to choose a single identity in order to demonstrate his loyalty to a particular community? Christians have little problem accepting Jesus Christ, a hybrid *par excellence*, as fully human and fully God, yet hybrid Americans are not allowed to identify fully with each of their multiple racial/ethnic/religious/national heritages. Some would argue that it is impossible to be fully attached to more than one national/racial/ethnic/religious identity group. Nevertheless, I believe we are at a juncture in American history when we cannot continue to be Americans in the same way as before when individuals are deemed to belong to one racial/ethnic/religious/national category and not another. Obama's identity symbolizes the globalization of American identities and his rise to prominence and power may represent the beginning of an open and honest process of hybridization in the United States.

Obama often describes himself as an unconventional presidential candidate with a 'funny' name, which has been a target of mockery and used by some to question his religious ties and patriotic intentions. In his memoir he writes that it was in Kenya, the land of his father, where his name and his identity represented by that name were liberated from misunderstanding and judgment:

> For the first time in my life, I felt the comfort, the firmness of identity that a name might provide, how it could carry an entire history in other people's memories, so that they might nod and say knowingly, 'Oh, you are so and so's son'. No one here in Kenya would ask how to spell my name, or mangle it with an unfamiliar tongue. My name belonged and so I belonged, drawn into a web of relationships, alliances, and grudges that I did not yet understand.[6]

Even though he realized that his destiny, just as his mother had foreseen and planned, was tied to America, he reconnected to his father's land and for a brief time experienced what it was like to be an insider who did not need to prove or qualify his authenticity: 'Here the world was black, and so you were just you; you could discover all those things that were unique to your life without living a lie or committing betrayal'.[7]

6. Obama, *Dreams from my Father*, p. 305.

7. Obama, *Dreams from my Father*, p. 311. I have no doubt that if he had stayed longer in Kenya he would have felt like an outsider again. The Kenyans would have treated him as an American (as a foreigner) rather than a Kenyan.

Obama's struggle with his hybrid identity and name resonate with the politics of identity and loyalty in ancient Israel, attested particularly in the Uriah the Hittite episode. He is an African American (or a black American) according to the identity politics in the United States, in which the rule of 'one drop of black blood makes one black' still applies. There are many notable hybrid Americans who are considered African Americans and claimed by African Americans as their own.[8] But for Obama to identify exclusively with the African American community would be political suicide; he is running, after all, for the president of the United States and the black community represents a significant yet only one of several minority voting blocks. He needs support from other communities besides the African American community, including whites and the Latino community, which has become the largest minority group and in many ways is in competition with the black community for political power. He cannot, however, appear too close to the whites or other racial/ethnic communities since that will bring suspicion from the black community; he will be accused of 'selling out' and will appear inauthentic to his 'true' color. Maintaining support from varied constituents, forging ties across various identity boundaries, while appearing authentic to and winning the loyalty of one particular community, is indeed a delicate dance Obama must perform. David somehow was able to pull it off; we will see whether Obama can succeed as well.

Obama reminds me of another 'king'. Forty years ago on 4 April 1968 one of the most influential and captivating dreamers of modern time was assassinated in front of his motel room in Memphis, Tennessee. Martin Luther King, Jr was only thirty-nine years old when his campaign to build the 'beloved community' based on economic justice and racial harmony came to an abrupt halt by a lone gunman's bullet, but as many have stated, 'The dreamer may be dead, but the dream lives on', and many can attest that his life and work continue to influence and inspire countless numbers of people to work toward advancing this vision. Most people acknowledge that even though the United States is still far from being the society that King dreamed of, it has made much progress toward becoming a nation that does not discriminate against a person by the color of his or her skin. Yet the march to a more perfect and harmonious union is slow and sometimes feels like it has stopped or is going backward. Once every few months an incident happens, sometimes as big as the Katrina disaster or as small as a popular radio show host using racial slurs to describe a women's college basketball team, which reminds all the people of the United States how deep racial wounds are, how wide the racial divide is, and how far America has to go to become the 'beloved community'.

8. Why don't whites or other racial/ethnic groups also claim them as their own?

A more recent controversy involves the inflammatory remarks made by Jeremiah Wright, a former pastor of Barack Obama. I will not comment on Wright's incendiary words except to say that the volatile reaction to Wright's statements, especially the God 'bless' America statement, was not surprising. For an American it is difficult to juxtapose the word 'damn' or 'curse' with the word 'America'; it is unthinkable.[9] The idea of God cursing or punishing the United States seems un-American and unpatriotic. The assumption behind the people's outrage seems to be that a 'real' American would never say or imagine God 'blessing' America. The fact that Obama is associated with someone who uttered these words seems to have placed his loyalty to America under suspicion.

Obama's speech on race in America, which he gave on 18 March 2008, in Philadelphia, was in response to the overwhelming criticism he received for not severing his relationship with the pastor and for not condemning Wright's sermons in the strongest terms.[10] He begins his speech with the opening line from the U.S. Constitution, 'We the people, in order to form a more perfect union', and frames the controversy as an opportunity to work through 'a part of our union that we have yet to perfect' (racism) and to move toward a better future for all Americans. It is undoubtedly a campaign speech, but I think it also expresses Obama's sincere reflection on race and identity in the United States. He points out that 'the profound mistake' of Wright's angry sermons is not that he spoke about racism but that he spoke as if America is static and has no hope for change. Obama corrects this distorted view of America with these words: 'But what we know—what we have seen—is that America can change. That is true genius of this nation'.[11] He, however, defends his unwillingness to break his relationship with his pastor: 'I can no more disown him than I can disown the black community. I can no more disown him than I can my white grandmother' who on

9. This may be comparable to juxtaposing the word 'bless' (a euphemism for curse in some cases in the Hebrew Bible, for example, Job 1.5, 11; 2.5, 9) with the word 'God'; it must have been difficult for ancient Jewish scribes to imagine anyone 'bless' God. The prophets of the Hebrew Bible, however, uttered words that were far more inflammatory than Wright's words. They prophesized to the Israelites that God would punish his own people for their acts of injustice and idolatry. They viewed the destruction of Samaria by the Assyrians and of Jerusalem by the Babylonians as God's punishment on Israel. In spite of their controversial statements, the prophets and their provocative words were included in the sacred scripture. From such a perspective, Jeremiah Wright may be viewed a prophetic voice and the inability or reluctance to allow God 'to bless' America is surprising.

10. Go to http://www.cbsnews.com/stories/2008/03/18/politics/main3947908.shtml (accessed 20 March 2008) for a transcript of this speech provided by Obama's campaign.

11. http://www.cbsnews.com/stories/2008/03/18/politics/main3947908.shtml (accessed 20 March 2008).

occasions uttered racial or ethnic stereotypes.[12] He acknowledges the imperfection in his pastor and his grandmother and explains that they are a part of America and a part of him. His wish to confront directly racial fractures in America rather than to ignore them is commendable. His speech expressed the need to examine the politics of identity (race) and loyalty in America and has stirred a sincere dialogue on race across the United States.

I am planning to visit South Korea this summer for the first time since I came to the United States in 1976. It might be puzzling to some people, and to me as well, as to why it took me so long to make a trip to my 'homeland'. Even though from time to time I feel 'unhomely' and am treated as a foreigner in my adopted country, I have embraced the United States as my home and have not seen the need or had the desire to connect with Korea. I always felt that my destiny was tied to the United States. In fact, I had encoded my belief in King's dream of the 'beloved community' in my daughter's name. Twelve years ago my daughter was born while I was writing the final paper for a course on the theology and life of Martin Luther King, Jr. I was so inspired by King's theological vision and commitment to justice and the fact that she was born on his birthday that I had to give her a name in his honor. My wife and I gave her Justice as her middle name, though I had no idea back then that her first name, Hope, would articulate Obama's 'audacity of hope' campaign. I am a believer in King's dream, and I believe that Obama is expanding that vision and inspiring more people to believe in it. Perhaps this notion is not so different from David's effort to build a hybrid kingdom in which disparate groups of people were included regardless of their ethnic, tribal, or religious identity. As long as there are believers, the dream will continue to live on.

A Father's Dream

I had to observe a remembrance of another tragic event that shattered many dreams while I was writing this book. It has been one year since the largest school massacre in U.S. history took place at Virginia Tech on 16 April 2007. When it happened, the tragedy unfolded before my eyes on the TV screen and I was horrified as the number of victims given by the news stations continued to rise. A lone gunman killed thirty-two students and faculty and wounded twenty five people before taking his own life. As I was praying for the victims, at the same time, I was also hoping for the perpetrator not to be a minority, especially not an Asian. This probably is a sentiment shared by many minorities in the United States whenever a high-profile incident like this happens. We fear the connection people often make

12. http://www.cbsnews.com/stories/2008/03/18/politics/main3947908.shtml (accessed 20 March 2008).

between criminals and their entire racial/ethnic community—except, of course, in the case of whites. I was being selfish but also pragmatic when I wished for the gunman to be non-Asian, but the lone gunman turned out to be Seung-Hui Cho, whose parents emigrated from Korea to the United States when he was eight years old. In the media Cho was identified as a South Korean national. He could have had his U.S. citizenship, which would have made it more complicated to identify him, but the fact that he was officially not a U.S. citizen but a permanent resident made it easy to disown him as America's own. The process of purification was at work. The South Korean government and some representatives of various Korean American communities in the United States apologized for Cho's unspeakable violence. At first I thought this was an odd gesture. Does the U.S. government offer apologies to the victims of a crime committed by an American in another country? And I cannot imagine any European nation apologizing to the people of the United States for an act of violence committed by its citizen. Why apologize for one troubled person's irrational rampage, amplified by the easy access to guns in America? Why did they feel that they had to ask for forgiveness on behalf of Cho who grew up and was educated in the United States? Perhaps they knew what could happen not only to Koreans living in the United States but to all who look like them if Americans linked Cho with his racial/ethnic community. They were trying to appease those who could put the process of purification in motion. It really would not have mattered even if Cho were an U.S. citizen; it would have been easy to brand him as a foreigner, an outsider, an other, and definitely not a 'real' American.

My son came home from school the other day and confided in me that two of his classmates have been chasing him during the recess, calling him 'Chinese' and mocking his slanted eyes. Kids make fun of each other constantly. No surprise there. Picking on a trait a kid has that seems funny, different, or simply out of place brings unwanted attention from other kids who do not have this trait. They tease and badger the kid for fun but also perhaps to affirm their identity as the norm. In extreme cases, some kids bully physically another who seems out of place or has a different trait from the 'norm'. But why did these kids pick on my son's ethnic appearance? They could have made fun of his big head; he does have a big head for his size. His family sometimes teases him about his head and I am guilty as charged. My feeling was ambivalent toward my son's tormentors. I could see, having grown up in America, why my son's ethnic trait is an easy target. I was saddened to acknowledge once again that to live in the United States is to participate in the politics of identity whether one likes it or not. Ironically, when my son told me about this he was attending a public school whose student body consists of ninety-five percent students of color, a term used to refer to non-white students, but only one percent Asian American. My son's harassers were not white but also students of color, from other minority groups. I was saying to myself that they should have known better than to make fun of his ethnic/racial trait since they and their families probably also experienced some kind of racial discrimination for their identity in America. Then again, they are only kids. What do they know about racial formation and identity politics in the United States? Do they know that they are also considered 'different' according to the politics of identity in which whites are considered 'real' Americans?

What do I say to my son? 'Hey, son, welcome to America and its identity politics. Better get used to it'. I told him that he is not Chinese technically—my son loves the word 'technically'—but that he is Korean. Yet what does that mean to him, that he is Korean? He knows next to nothing about Korea. He has never been to Korea and is not part of a Korean community in the United States. At least I was born in Korea and lived there for ten years. The other day one of my good friends scolded me for not teaching my kids Korean. I vehemently defended my kids' inability to speak Korean. I knew well that my children will always be considered Korean, 'not American enough', in the United States and occasionally they will be treated and perceived as foreigners, but I also know that no matter how much my kids try to be Korean, they will be 'not Korean enough' to those who feel that at least they must speak some Korean (or pass other litmus tests) to be considered 'real' Koreans.

I told my son that he is one hundred percent American, as much of an American as any other Americans. I did not mince words; I told him that white people from Europe came to this land and turned even the indigenous folks into strangers in their own land. Therefore, it is no surprise that sometimes the peoples of color are treated as outsiders, even among the peoples of color themselves.

Some will argue that racism is just another form of discrimination that affected not only Native Americans and people of Africa, Asia, and South America in the United States but was also suffered by Irish, Italian, Polish, or other European immigrants. Yet there is a significant difference in that descendants from Europeans are eventually incorporated into the American national discourse; they eventually enter into the normative racial category. Non-whites, however, are permanently pushed into the racial categories of the Other. There are ramifications that come with being separated in that way. Racism is a wide network of power and knowledge that perpetuates inequality between constructed opposite groups. The reality, however, is that the identity politics that define whites as 'real' Americans cannot be sustained. There are too many hybrid Americans in the United States, and the American discourse of identity needs to take this into account. I acknowledge that the United States as a society has made great strides in including peoples of color into the American national identity discourse since I was in grade school, but the process of purification or the *realpolitik* of liminality continues to operate and divide 'real' Americans from other hybrid Americans in order to maintain a coherent (even a single) national identity in the United States.

I also know that my son's experience of America will be different from mine. There is a difference between the experience of early generations of Asians, characterized by terms like 'marginality' and 'liminality', and of later generations, characterized by terms like 'hybridity' and 'heterogeneity'.[13] My characterization of hybridity in my first book, *Decolonizing Josiah*, may have been limited to a confrontation between two competing cultures, and this understanding may be due to my experience of being an early generation Asian American. Hybridity has the transgressive dimension that allows identity to be constantly renegotiated. I am guilty of essentializing the hybrid space in order to construct a space from which Asian Americans can stand without appealing to the national discourse. By making the space in which Asian Americans stand more static than it really is I have neglected the transgressive power of hybridity and may have enclosed Asian Americans within unintended concrete boundaries. We end up replacing one dichotomous relation with another if we neglect the transgressive power of hybridity. It is not an easy task to describe the hybrid space where it is safe and empowering for those with multiple or heterogeneous identity and which, at the same time, is a place of negotiations for power and identity. It is not easy to articulate simultaneously the coalition-building and the politics of difference among Asian Americans. There is a need to have a constructed space of one's own, but the reality of its instability and the exclusion of those who are different undermines this space and needs to be acknowledged.

In saying that, I am not ready to give up using terms like 'West and Rest' or other similar dyads. I want to do away with the master—slave dichotomy as much as anyone, and in my thinking I do try to avoid simple dualism, but there is a political benefit of using such dyads to redress the inequality between the West and the Rest at this point in global history just as racial categories are necessary at this moment in American history to address inequalities between different racial/ethnic groups.

I hope my son does not have to employ these ideological constructs to address different experiences and to redress inequalities among different groups in America, but I do not want my kids to be as naïve as I was when I was growing up. When I received my U.S. citizenship at eighteen years old, I was innocent enough to believe that I became a 'real' American. Too soon did I learn that I was still viewed and treated as a foreigner and an outsider. I realized that it takes more than a certificate to become a 'real' American; it takes more than a U.S. passport to cross the group boundaries formed by a long history of identity politics in the United States. At the same time I am

13. I would like to thank Frank Yamada for his comment on this matter.

reminded whenever I deal with Koreans that I am no longer accepted as 'authentic' Korean either.

From time to time I feel 'unhomely' in the United States and know that I cannot return to Korea. I feel that in some ways I can never have the sense of rootedness or belongingness in the United States; however, I also do not want to view America as unchangeable or to overdraw the borders that may separate me as an Asian American from other communities in America. Identity borders are not fixed and stable; they are more often fragile and porous. People belonging to an ethnic community often both recover links to their homeland and lose members to the dominant group. Even within the Asian American community, a strategy of disidentification is used to distinguish one group from another and a strategy of solidarity is used to form a coalition among distinctive groups within this community. Identities are drawn and redrawn constantly. Identity is not only given, it is also negotiated and contested. Lisa Lowe describes the constant negotiation of Asian American identity in this way:

> What is referred to as 'Asian American' is clearly a heterogeneous entity. From the perspective of the majority culture, Asian Americans may very well be constructed as different from, and other than, Euro-Americans. But from the perspective of Asian Americans, we are perhaps even more different, more diverse among ourselves... As with other diasporas in the United States, the Asian immigrant collectivity is unstable and changeable, with its cohesion complicated by inter-generationality, by various degrees of identification and relation to a 'homeland', and by different extents of assimilation to any distinction from 'majority culture' in the United States.[14]

Indeed the simultaneous process of hybridization and purification seems to be in operation among Asian Americans as well. I hope the transgressive power of hybridity makes Asian Americans more receptive and active in transforming the United States into a hybrid America.

As I mentioned above, I have finally decided to visit Korea this summer. I have not seen my father and the land of my origin for thirty-two years. I probably would not have planned this visit if not for the fact that I received a job offer from a prestigious university in Korea. For many 'real' Koreans they would have taken the job offer in a heartbeat. I declined it rather quickly because I have hardly imagined returning to Korea before and now, with a family, the move would be a logistical nightmare. But this incident got me thinking about why I have resisted or have not been proactive in visiting Korea. Perhaps I believed that I had to disconnect with Korea in order to be a 'real' American. Why can't I be fully Korean and fully American?

14. L. Lowe, 'Heterogeneity, Hybridity, Multiplicity: Marking Asian American Differences', *Diaspora* 1 (1991), pp. 24-44 (27).

I think it will be a good idea to show my kids that Korea is a real place and I want them to feel the freedom Obama felt when he visited Kenya: a sense of belongingness and comfort that comes with familiarity and being perceived as an insider ('one of us'). But soon enough I know that their 'American-ness' will be discovered by native Koreans and they will face uncomfortable situations where they have to explain or qualify themselves. I want them to know Korea and respect their Korean heritage, but I know that their future is tied to America. I always believed or wanted to believe that America is my home and the home of my kids even if my kids and I have to answer on occasions that dreaded question, 'Where are you from?' It is a question not only of location but also of identity and loyalty. It is something we need to deal with; I believe America is worth the trouble. But I hope someday soon when my kids answer 'Hartford, Connecticut', America would be satisfied with that and assume them as her own. This is just a father's dream.

Bibliography

Alter, R., *The David Story: A Translation with Commentary of 1 and 2 Samuel* (New York: Norton, 1999).

Bailey, R.C., *David in Love and War: The Pursuit of Power in 2 Samuel 10–12* (JSOTSup, 75; Sheffield: JSOT Press, 1990).

Barth, F. (ed.), *Ethnic Groups and Boundaries: The Social Organization of Culture Difference* (Long Grove, IL: Waveland Press, 1969).

Barthélemy, D., *et al.* (eds.), *The Story of David and Goliath: Textual and Literary Criticism—Papers of a Joint Research Venture* (Fribourg, Suisse: Éditions Universitaires; Göttingen: Vandenhoeck & Ruprecht, 1986).

Bhabha, H.K., 'DissemiNation: Time, Narrative, and the Margins of the Modern Nation', in H.M. Bhabha (ed.), *Nation and Narration* (London: Routledge, 1990), pp. 291-322.

Bodner, K., *David Observed: A King in the Eyes of his Court* (Hebrew Bible Monographs, 5; Sheffield: Sheffield Phoenix Press, 2005).

Bowen, B.M., 'A Study of ḥsd' (unpublished PhD dissertation, Yale University, 1938).

Britt, B., 'Unexpected Attachments: A Literary Approach to the Term חסד in the Hebrew Bible', *JSOT* 27.3 (2003), pp. 289-307.

Bruce, F.F., *The Hittites and the Old Testament* (London: Tyndale Press, 1947).

Brueggemann, W., 'Abuse of Command: Exploiting Power for Sexual Gratification', *Sojourner* 26 (1997), pp. 22-25.

—*First and Second Samuel* (Interpretation; Louisville, KY: John Knox Press, 1990).

Carmichal, C.M., *Law and Narrative in the Bible* (Ithaca, NY: Cornell University Press, 1985).

Chinitz, J., 'Two Sinners', *JBQ* 25 (1997), pp. 108-13.

Clark, G.R., *The Word* Ḥesed *in the Hebrew Bible* (JSOTSup, 157; Sheffield: Sheffield Academic Press, 1993).

Cross, F.M., *Canaanite Myth and Hebrew Epic* (Cambridge, MA: Harvard University Press, 1973).

—'The Structure of the Deuteronomic History', in *Perspectives in Jewish Learning* (Annual of the College of Jewish Studies, 3; Chicago: College of Jewish Studies, 1968), pp. 9-24.

—'The Theme of the Book of Kings and the Structure of the Deuteronomistic History', in *idem*, *Canaanite Myth and Hebrew Epic*, pp. 274-89.

Czövek, T., *Three Seasons of Charismatic Leadership: A Literary-Critical and Theological Interpretation of the Narrative of Saul, David and Solomon* (Regnum Studies in Mission; Milton Keynes: Paternoster Press, 2006).

De Vries, S.J., 'David's Victory over the Philistine as Saga and as Legend', *JBL* 92 (1973), pp. 23-37.

Donaldson, L.E. (ed.), *Postcolonialism and Scripture Reading* (Semeia 75; Atlanta: Society of Biblical Literature, 1996).

Exum, J.C., 'Bathsheba Plotted, Shot, and Painted', in Exum, *Plotted, Shot, and Painted: Cultural Representations of Biblical Women* (Sheffield: Sheffield Academic Press, 1996), pp. 19-53.

—'The (M)other's Place', in Exum, *Fragmented Women: Feminist (Sub)versions of Biblical Narratives* (Valley Forge, PA: Trinity Press International, 1993), pp. 94-147.

Fanon, F., *The Wretched of the Earth* (New York: Grove Press, 1966).

Faust, A., *Israel's Ethnogenesis: Settlement, Interaction, Expansion and Resistance* (London: Equinox, 2006).

Foskett, M.F., and J.K. Kuan (eds.), *Ways of Being, Ways of Reading: Asian American Biblical Interpretation* (St. Louis, MO: Chalice Press, 2006).

Garsiel, M., 'The Story of David and Bathsheba: A Different Approach', *CBQ* 55 (1993), pp. 244-62.

Gellner, E., *Nations and Nationalism* (Ithaca, NY: Cornell University Press, 1983).

Glueck, N., Ḥesed *in the Bible* (trans. A. Gottschalk; Cincinnati: Hebrew Union College Press, 1967).

Grabbe, L.L. (ed.), *Good Kings and Bad Kings: The Kingdom of Judah in the Seventh Century BCE* (London: T.&T. Clark, 2007).

Gunn, D.M., *The Story of King David* (JSOTSup, 6; Sheffield: JSOT Press, 1978).

Halpern, B., *David's Secret Demons: Messiah, Murderer, Traitor, King* (Grand Rapids: Eerdmans, 2001).

Hermann, S., '"Realunion" und "Charismatisches Königtum". Zu zwei offenen Fragen der Verfassungen in Juda und Israel', *Eretz-Israel* 24 (1993), pp. 97-103.

Heschel, A., *The Prophets* (New York: Harper & Row, 1962).

Hess, R.S., *Israelite Religions: An Archaeological and Biblical Survey* (Grand Rapids: Baker Academic, 2007).

Hoffner, H.A., 'Hittites', in A.J. Hoerth, G.L. Mattingly, and E.M. Yamauchi (eds.), *Peoples of the Old Testament World* (Cambridge: Baker, 1994), pp. 127-55.

Joh, W.A., *Heart of the Cross: A Postcolonial Christology* (Louisville, KY: Westminster/John Knox Press, 2006).

—'The Transgressive Power of Jeong: A Postcolonial Hybridization of Christology', in C. Keller, M. Nausner, and M. Rivera (eds.), *Postcolonial Theologies: Divinity and Empire* (St. Louis, MO: Chalice Press, 2004), pp. 149-63.

Kim, U.Y., 'Cherethites and Pelethites', in K.D. Sakenfeld (ed.), *New Interpreter's Dictionary of the Bible A–C*, I (Nashville: Abingdon Press, 2006), pp. 585-86.

—*Decolonizing Josiah: Toward a Postcolonial Reading of the Deuteronomistic History* (The Bible in the Modern World, 5; Sheffield: Sheffield Phoenix Press, 2005).

—'Postcolonial Criticism: Who Is the Other in the Book of Judges?', in G.A. Yee (ed.), *Judges and Method* (Minneapolis: Fortress Press, 2nd edn, 2007), pp. 161-82.

—'The *Realpolitik* of Liminality in Josiah's Kingdom and Asian America', in M.F. Foskett and J.K. Kuan (eds.), *Asian American Biblical Interpretation* (St. Louis, MO: Chalice Press, 2006), pp. 84-98.

—'Time to Walk the Postcolonial Talk', Review article on R.S. Sugirtharajah (ed.), *The Postcolonial Biblical Reader*, *RRT* 13.3 (2006), pp. 271-78.

—'Uriah the Hittite: A Con/Text of Struggle for Identity', *Semeia* 90/91 (2002), pp. 69-86.

Knauf, E.A., 'The Glorious Days of Manasseh', in Grabbe (ed.), *Good Kings and Bad Kings*, pp. 164-88.

Kooij, A.V.D., 'The Story of David and Goliath: The Early History of its Text', *ETL* 68 (1992), pp. 118-131.
Kwok, Pui-lan, *Discovering the Bible in the Non-Biblical World* (Maryknoll, NY: Orbis Books, 1995).
—*Postcolonial Imagination & Feminist Theology* (Louisville, KY: Westminster/John Knox Press, 2005).
Latour, B., *We Have Never Been Modern* (trans. C. Porter; Cambridge, MA: Harvard University Press, 1993).
Lemche, N.P., 'Kings and Clients: On Loyalty Between the Ruler and the Ruled in Ancient Israel', *Semeia* 66 (1994), pp. 119-32.
Levenson, J.D., '1 Samuel 25 as Literature and as History', *CBQ* 40 (1978), pp. 11-28.
Levenson, J.D., and B. Halpern, 'The Political Import of David's Marriages', *JBL* 99.4 (1980), pp. 507-18.
Long, V.P., *The Art of Biblical History* (Foundations of Contemporary Interpretation, 5; Grand Rapids: Zondervan, 1994).
Lowe, L., 'Heterogeneity, Hybridity, Multiplicity: Marking Asian American Differences', *Diaspora* 1 (1991), pp. 24-44.
Matthews, V.H., *Studying the Ancient Israelites: A Guide to Sources and Methods* (Grand Rapids: Baker Academic, 2007).
Mazar, B., 'The Military Elite of King David', *VT* 13 (1963), pp. 310-20.
McCarter, P.K., *I Samuel: A New Translation with Introduction, Notes, and Commentary* (Anchor Bible, 8; Garden City, NY: Doubleday, 1980).
—*II Samuel: A New Translation with Introduction, Notes, and Commentary* (Anchor Bible, 9; Garden City, NY: Doubleday, 1984).
—'The Apology of David', *JBL* 99.4 (1980), pp. 489-504.
McKenzie, S.L., *King David: A Biography* (Oxford and New York: Oxford University Press, 2002).
Memmi, A., *The Colonizer and the Colonized* (Boston: Beacon Press, 1965).
Miller, J.M., and J.H. Hayes, *A History of Ancient Israel and Judah* (Louisville, KY: Westminster/John Knox Press, 2nd edn, 2006).
Miscall, P.D., *1 Samuel: A Literary Reading* (Bloomington: Indiana University Press, 1986).
Moran, W.L., 'The Ancient Near Eastern Background of the Love of God in Deuteronomy', *CBQ* 25 (1963), pp. 78-79.
Na'aman, N., 'The List of David's Officers', *VT* 38 (1988), pp. 71-79.
Nicol, G.G., 'The Alleged Rape of Bathsheba: Some Observations on Ambiguity in Biblical Narrative', *JSOT* 73 (1997), pp. 43-54.
Obama, B., *Dreams from my Father: A Story of Race and Inheritance* (repr., New York: Crown Publishers, 2004 [1st edn 1995]).
Petit, M. 'La rencontre de David et Bersabee (II Sam. 11,2-5, 26-27): les interpretations des peres des premiers siecles', in G. Dorival and O. Munnich (eds.), *Selon les Septante* (Paris: Cerf, 1995), pp. 473-81.
Polzin, R., *David and the Deuteronomist: A Literary Study of the Deuteronomic History*. III. *2 Samuel* (Bloomington: Indiana University Press, 1993).
—*Samuel and the Deuteronomist: A Literary Study of the Deuteronomistic History*. Part 2. *1 Samuel* (Bloomington: Indiana University Press, 1989).
Rand, H., 'David and Ahab: A Study of Crime and Punishment', *JBQ* 24 (1996), pp. 90-97.

Rofé, A., 'The Battle of David and Goliath: Folklore, Theology, Eschatology', in J. Neusner, B.A. Levine, and E.S. Frerichs (eds.), *Judaic Perspectives on Ancient Israel* (Philadelphia: Fortress Press, 1987), pp. 117-51.

Römer, T.C., *The So-called Deuteronomistic History: A Sociological, Historical, and Literary Introduction* (London and New York: T.&T. Clark, 2007).

Rosenberg, J., 'The Institutional Matrix of Treachery in 2 Samuel 11', *Semeia* 46 (1989), pp. 103-16.

Rost, L., *Die Überlieferung von der Thronnachfolge Davids* (BWANT 3/6; Stuttgart: Kohlhammer, 1926).

Said, E., *Orientalism* (New York: Random House, 1978).

Sakenfeld, K.D., *Faithfulness in Action: Loyalty in Biblical Perspective* (Philadelphia: Fortress Press, 1985).

—*The Meaning of* Ḥesed *in the Hebrew Bible: A New Inquiry* (HSM, 17; Missoula, MT: Scholar Press, 1978).

Schwartz, R.M., 'Adultery in the House of David: The Metanarrative of Biblical Scholarship and the Narrative of the Bible', *Semeia* 54 (1991), pp. 35-55.

Segovia, F., and M.A. Tolbert (eds.), *Reading from This Place*, I (Minneapolis: Fortress Press, 1995).

Seow, C.L., 'Ark of the Covenant', in *ABD*, I, pp. 386-93.

—*Myth, Drama, and Politics of David's Dance* (HSM, 46; Atlanta: Scholars Press, 1989).

Shenhav, Y., *The Arab Jews: A Postcolonial Reading of Nationalism, Religion and Ethnicity* (Stanford: Stanford University Press, 2006).

Snaith, N., *Distinctive Ideas of the Old Testament* (London: The Epworth Press, 1944).

Spivak, G.C., 'Can the Subaltern Speak?', in P. Williams and L. Chrisman (eds.), *Colonial Discourse and Post-colonial Theory* (New York: Columbia University Press, 1994), pp. 66-111.

Stavrakopoulou, F., 'The Blackballing of Manasseh', in Grabbe (ed.), *Good Kings and Bad Kings*, pp. 248-63.

Sternberg, M., *The Poetics of Biblical Narrative: Ideological Literature and the Drama of Reading* (Bloomington: Indiana University Press, 1985).

Steussy M.J., *David: Biblical Portraits of Power* (Columbia: University of South Carolina Press, 1999).

Sugirtharajah, R.S. (ed.), *The Postcolonial Biblical Reader* (Malden, MA: Blackwell, 2006).

—*Voices from the Margin: Interpreting the Bible in the Third World* (Maryknoll, NY: Orbis Books, new edn, 1995).

Sweeney, M., 'King Manasseh of Judah and the Problem of Theodicy in the Deuteronomistic History', in Grabbe (ed.), *Good Kings and Bad Kings*, pp. 264-78.

Thompson, J.A., 'The Significance of the Verb *Love* in the David–Jonathan Narratives in I Samuel', *VT* 24 (1974), pp. 34-38.

Van Seters, J., 'The Terms "Amorite" and "Hittite" in the Old Testament', *VT* 22 (1972), pp. 64-81.

VanderKam, J.C., 'Davidic Complicity in the Deaths of Abner and Eshbaal: A Historical and Redactional Study', *JBL* 99.4 (1980), pp. 521-39.

Whedbee, J.W., 'On Divine and Human Bonds: The Tragedy of the House of David', in G.M. Tucker, D.L. Petersen, and R.R. Wilson (eds.), *Canon, Theology, and Old Testament Interpretation* (Philadelphia: Fortress Press, 1988), pp. 147-65.

Whitelam, K., *The Invention of Ancient Israel: The Silencing of Palestinian History* (London: Routledge, 1996).

Whybray, R.N., *The Succession Narrative: A Study of II Samuel 9–20; 1 Kings 1 and 2* (Naperville, IL: SCM Press, 1968).

Willimon, W.H., 'A Peculiarly Christian Account of Sin: David and Bathsheba and Sin as Conflict of Narrative', *Theology Today* 50 (1993), pp. 220-28.

Wyatt, N., '"Araunah the Jebusite" and the Throne of David', in *'There's Such Divinity Doth Hedge a King': Essays on Royal Ideology in Ugaritic and Old Testament Literature* (SOTSMS; London: Ashgate, 2005), pp. 1-14; first published in *ST* 39 (1985), pp. 39-53.

Yee, G.A., 'Fraught with Background: Literary Ambiguity in 2 Samuel 11', *Int* 42 (1988), pp. 240-53.

Young, R.J.C., *Postcolonialism: A Very Short Introduction* (Oxford: Oxford University Press, 2003).

Indexes

Index of References

INDEX OF AUTHORS

CPSIA information can be obtained at www.ICGtesting.com
Printed in the USA
BVOW010132281011

274613BV00006B/22/P

9 781906 055585